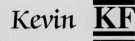

MILLER'S
Collectables
PRICE GUIDE

MILLER'S
Collectables
PRICE GUIDE

Consultant
Judith Miller

General Editor
Madeleine Marsh

1998–99
(Volume X)

MILLER'S COLLECTABLES PRICE GUIDE 1998–9

Compiled, edited and designed by
Miller's Publications Ltd
The Cellars, High Street
Tenterden, Kent TN30 6BN
Telephone: 01580 766411

Consultant: Judith Miller

General Editor: Madeleine Marsh
Editorial & Production Co-ordinator: Sue Boyd
Editorial Assistants: Christine Cooper, Shirley Reeves, Jo Wood
Production Assistants: Gillian Charles, Nancy Charles, Caroline Bugeja
Design: Kari Reeves, Matthew Leppard
Advert Design: Simon Cook
Photographic Co-ordinator & Advertising Executive: Elizabeth Smith
Advertising Assistants: Jill Jackson, Melinda Williams
Index compiled by: Hilary Bird, Goudhurst, Kent
Additional photography: Ian Booth, Robin Saker, Roy Farthing, Dennis O'Reilly

First published in Great Britain in 1998
by Miller's, an imprint of Mitchell Beazley,
both imprints of Reed Consumer Books Ltd
Michelin House, 81 Fulham Road
London SW3 6RB

A CIP catalogue record for this book is
available from the British Library

ISBN 1-84000-055-4

Film output: Perfect Image, Hurst Green, E. Sussex
Illustrations and bromide output: A S Group, Ashford, Kent
Colour origination: Pica Colour Separations, Singapore
Printed and bound in England by William Clowes Ltd,
Beccles and London

HOW TO USE THIS BOOK

I t is our aim to make this guide easy to use. In order to find a particular item, turn to the contents list on page 7 to find the main heading, for example, Ceramics. Having located your area of interest, you will see that larger sections have been sub-divided by subject or maker. If you are looking for a particular factory, maker, or object, consult the index which starts on page 488.

130 **CERAMICS** • Clarice Cliff

Clarice Cliff

A Clarice Cliff jardinière, decorated with Branch and Square design, c1929–30, 3½in (9cm) high.
£375–425 *MEG*

A Clarice Cliff Fantasque bowl, decorated with Comets pattern, brightly coloured in orange, yellow, green, blue and purple, printed mark to base, c1930, 6½in (16.5cm) diam.
£650–750 *WL*

A Clarice Cliff ashtray, decorated with Orange Roof Cottage pattern, early 1930s, 5in (13cm) diam.
£150–200 *RIC*

Clarice Cliff

Clarice Cliff (1899–1972) dominated ceramic design during the 1930s and is probably the most famous and collectable name in Art Deco pottery. She produced a vast number of shapes and patterns, and prices today depend on rarity. The Carpet pattern *(right)* was copied by Cliff from a magazine illustration of a carpet designed by Da Silva Bruhns (1881–1980), Brazilian painter, rug designer and weaver – Bruhns' work was much imitated and this vase reflects his cubist style. This sophisticated modernism was perhaps, however, a little too much for the British ceramics market. The Carpet pattern with its curved lines and dots was only produced in 1930, and its rarity is reflected in its price range.

A Clarice Cliff Bizarre vase, decorated with Carpet pattern in orange, grey and black, moulded 'No. 358', 1930, 7½in (19cm) high.
£3,400–3,800 *RBB*

A Clarice Cliff Conical jug, decorated with Umbrellas and Rain pattern, c1929, 7in (18cm) high.
£600–700 *RIC*

A Clarice Cliff Fantasque vase, decorated with Broth pattern, shape No. 355, 1929–30, 7in (18cm) high.
£550–650 *GH*

FURTHER READING
Leonard Griffin and Louis K. and Susan Pear Meisel, *Clarice Cliff The Bizarre Affair*, Thames & Hudson, 1989

A Clarice Cliff cigarette holder and ashtray, c1930, 3¼in (8cm) high.
£350–400 *CSA*

Cross Reference
Colour Review

l. A Clarice Cliff Conical bowl, decorated with Tennis pattern, c1931, 4½in (11.5cm) diam.
£400–500 *RIC*

A Clarice Cliff vase, decorated with Summerhouse pattern, shape No. 368, c1931, 3½in (9cm) high.
£420–450 *BKK*

Information Box
covers relevant collecting information on factories, makers, care, restoration, fakes and alterations.

Cross Reference
directs the reader to where other related items may be found.

Further Reading
directs the reader towards additional sources of information.

Price Guide
price ranges are worked out by a team of trade and auction house experts, and are based on actual prices realised. Remember that Miller's is a PRICE GUIDE not a PRICE LIST and prices are affected by many variables such as location, condition, desirability and so on. Don't forget that if you are selling it is quite likely you will be offered less than the price range. Price ranges for items sold at auction tend to include the buyer's premium and VAT if applicable.

Caption
provides a brief description of the item including the maker's name, medium, date, measurements and in some instances condition.

Source Code
refers to the 'Key to Illustrations' on page 9 that lists the details of where the item was photographed.

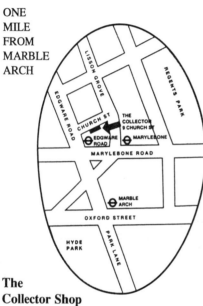

CONTENTS

ACKNOWLEDGEMENTS

We would like to acknowledge the great assistance given by our consultants who are listed below. We would also like to extend our thanks to all the auction houses, their press offices, dealers and collectors who have assisted us in the production of this book.

DAVID HUXTABLE
SO3/05 Alfies Antique Market,
13–25 Church Street, Marylebone,
London NW8 8DT
(Advertising Tins)

ALAN BLAKEMAN
BBR Elsecar Heritage Centre,
Wath Road, Elsecar, Barnsley, Yorks S74 8AF
(Advertising, Packaging, Bottles, Breweriana)

ROBERT LEVY
(The Unique One) 2802 Centre Street,
Pennsauken, NJ 08109, USA
(Amusement Machines)

RUSSELL SINGLER
Animation Art Gallery,
13–14 Great Castle Street, London W1N 7AD
(Animation Art)

DEBBIE WEISS
30 Bramham Gardens, London SW5 OHF and
400 East 58th Street, New York 10022
(Animation Art)

CHRIS BELTON
Ancient & Gothic
PO Box 356, Christchurch, Dorset
BH23 1XP
(Antiquities)

RALPH KIAER
Helios Gallery, 292 Westbourne Grove,
London W11 2RH
(Antiquities)

TONY O'DONNELL
Posh Tubs, Moriati's Workshop,
High Halden, Ashford, Kent TN26 3LZ
(Bathrooms)

ADAM LOVEJOY
When We Were Young, The Old Forge,
High Street, Harmondsworth Village,
Middlesex UB7 OAQ
(Nursery Ceramics)

ANDREW HILTON
Special Auction Services,
The Coach House, Midgham Park,
Reading RG7 5UG
(Fairings)

HELEN MARTIN
St Clere Antiques, PO Box 161
Sevenoaks Kent TN15 69A
(Carlton Ware)

MARK OLIVER
Phillips Auctioneers, 101 New Bond Street,
London W1Y OAS
(Royal Doulton, Beswick, Wade Whimsies)

PETER DIXON
Unit H3 & 4 Antiquarius, 135 King's Road,
London SW3 4PW
(Clocks)

ALAN SEDGWICK
E-mail: Alan.Sedgwick@BTInternet.com
(Carnival Glass)

DR D. DOWSON
Old Tackle Box, PO Box 55, Cranbrook, Kent
TN17 3ZU
(Fishing Tackle)

JEANNETTE HAYHURST
32a Kensington Church Street, London W8 4HA
(Glass)

JIM BULLOCK
Romsey Medal Centre, 5 Bell Street,
Romsey, Hants SO51 8GY
(Military Medals)

ANNE METCALFE
Sweetbriar Gallery, Robin Hood Lane, Helsby,
Cheshire WA6 9NH
(Paperweights)

SIMON MARSHALL
The Stone Gallery, 93 High Street, Burford,
Oxon OX18 4QA
(Paperweights)

KEN LAWSON
Specialised Postcard Auctions,
25 Gloucester Street, Cirencester GL7 2DJ
(Postcards)

PAUL WANE
Tracks, PO Box 117, Chorley,
Lancashire PR7 2QZ
(Rock & Pop)

GAVIN PAYNE
The Old Granary, Battlesbridge Antique
Centre, Nr Wickford, Essex SS11 7RF
(Telephones)

MARTIN BARNETT
Candlestick & Bakelite, PO Box 308,
Orpington, Kent BR5 1TB
(Telephones)

LESLIE WATKINS
Off World, Unit 20 Romford Shopping Halls,
Market Place, Romford, Essex RM1 3AT
(Sci-Fi Toys)

BRIAN LEE
c/o Romsey Auction Rooms,
86 The Hundred, Romsey, Hants SO51 8BX
(Toy Trains)

KEY TO ILLUSTRATIONS

Each illustration and descriptive caption is accompanied by a letter code. By referring to the following list of Auctioneers (denoted by *), Dealers (•) and Clubs (§), the source of any item may be immediately determined. Please note that the inclusion of a collectable in this book does not guarantee that the item, or any similar item, is available for sale from the contributor. Advertisers in this year's directory are denoted by (†).

If you require a valuation for an item, it is advisable to check whether the dealer or specialist will carry out this service and if there is a charge. Please mention Miller's when making an enquiry. Having found a specialist who will carry out your valuation it is best to send a photograph and description of the item to the specialist together with a stamped addressed envelope for the reply. A valuation by telephone is not possible.

Most dealers are only too happy to help you with your enquiry, however, they are very busy people and consideration of the above points would be welcomed.

AAC • Arundel Antiques Centre, 51 High Street, Arundel, Sussex BN18 9AJ
Tel: 01903 882749

AAG • The Animation Art Gallery, 13-14 Great Castle Street, London W1N 7AD
Tel: 0171 255 1456

AAV * Academy Auctioneers & Valuers, Northcote House, Northcote Avenue, Ealing, London W5 3UR Tel: 0181 579 7466

ABC • Academy Billiard Co, 5 Camp Hill Industrial Estate, West Byfleet, Surrey KT14 6EW
Tel: 01932 352067

ABr • Avril Brown, Bartlett Street Antique Centre, Bath, Somerset BA1 2QZ
Tel: 01225 310457/446322

ACA • Acorn Antiques, Sheep Street, Stow-on-the-Wold, Glos GL54 1AA
Tel: 01451 831519

ACC •† Albert's Cigarette Card Specialists, 113 London Road, Twickenham, Middlesex TW1 1EE Tel: 0181 891 3067

Ada • Dale Adams, Fountain Antiques Market, 6 Bladud Buildings, Bath, Somerset BA1 5LS Tel: 01225 339104

AEF • A & E Foster, Little Heysham, Naphill, Bucks HP14 4SU Tel: 01494 562024

AG * Anderson & Garland (Auctioneers), Marlborough House, Marlborough Crescent, Newcastle-upon-Tyne, Tyne & Wear NE1 4EE Tel: 0191 232 6278

AH * Andrew Hartley, Victoria Hall Salerooms, Little Lane, Ilkley, Yorkshire LS29 8EA
Tel: 01943 816363

AL • Ann Lingard, Ropewalk Antiques, Rye, Sussex TN31 7NA Tel: 01797 223486

ALB • Albany Antiques, 8-10 London Road, Hindhead, Surrey GU26 6AF
Tel: 01428 605528

ALI • Alien Enterprises, Stratford Model Centre, The Minories, Stratford-upon-Avon, Warwickshire CV37 6QW Tel: 01789 299701

AMH •† Amherst Antiques, 23 London Road, Riverhead, Sevenoaks, Kent TN13 2BU
Tel: 01732 455047

AND •† Joan & Bob Anderson, Middlesex
Tel: 0181 572 4328

ANG •† Ancient & Gothic, PO Box 356, Christchurch, Dorset BH23 1XQ
Tel: 01202 478592

ANO • Art Nouveau Originals, Stamford Antiques Centre, The Exchange Hall, Broad Street, Stamford, Lincolnshire PE9 1PX
Tel: 01780 762605

ANP •† Annette Power, The Collector, 9 Church Street, Marylebone, London NW8 8EE
Tel: 0171 706 4586

AnS •† The Antique Shop, 30 Henley Street, Stratford-upon-Avon, Warwickshire CV37 6QW
Tel: 01789 292485

ANT • Anthemion, Bridge Street, Cartmel, Grange-over-Sands, Cumbria LA11 7SH
Tel: 015395 36295

ANV • Anvil Antiques, Cavendish Street, Cartmel, Cumbria LA11 6PU
Tel: 01539 536362

ARE • Arenski, 185 Westbourne Grove, London W11 2SB
Tel: 0171 727 8599

ARP • Arundel Photographica, The Arundel Antiques Centre, 51 High Street, Arundel, Sussex BN18 9AJ Tel: 01903 882749

ASA • A. S. Antiques, 26 Broad Street, Pendleton, Salford, Greater Manchester M6 5BY
Tel: 0161 737 5938

ASe • Alan Sedgwick.
E-mail: Alan.Sedgwick@BTInternet.com

ASG • Asahi Gallery, 44A Kensington Church Street, London W8 4DB

ASH • Ashburton Marbles, Grate Hall, North Street, Ashburton, Devon TQ13 7QD
Tel: 01364 653189

ATH •† Apple Tree House, (Janet Beaumont).
Tel: 01752 600031

AWT • Antique Associates at West Townsend, 473 Main Street PO Box 129W, West Townsend, MA 01474 USA
Tel: 508-597-8084

AXT • Alexis F. J. Turner, The Workshop Gallery, 144a Bridge Road, East Moseley, Surrey KT8 9HW Tel: 0181 542 5926

BAD • Badgers Antiques (David Wainwright), Kent
Tel: 01233 758337

BAf • Books Afloat, 66 Park Street, Weymouth, Dorset DT4 7DE Tel: 01305 779774

BaH • Calamus, The Shambles, Sevenoaks, Kent TN13 1AL Tel: 01732 740603

BAL •† A. H. Baldwin & Sons Ltd, Numismatists, 11 Adelphi Terrace, London WC2N 6BJ
Tel: 0171 930 6879

BaN •† Barbara Ann Newman, London House Antiques, 4 Market Square, Westerham, Kent TN16 1AW
Tel: 01959 564479/Mobile: 0850 016729

BB •† Brian Bates, Staffordshire
Tel: 01782 680667

BBR *† BBR, Elsecar Heritage Centre, Wath Road, Elsecar, Barnsley, Yorkshire S74 8HJ
Tel: 01226 745156

BCO • British Collectables, 1st Floor, 9 Georgian Village, Camden Passage, Islington, London N1 8DU Tel: 0171 359 4560

Bea * Bearnes, Rainbow, Avenue Road, Torquay, Devon TQ2 5TG Tel: 01803 296277

Bea(E) * Bearnes, St Edmund's Court, Okehampton Street, Exeter, Devon EX4 1DU Tel: 01392 422800

Ber • Berry Antiques, Berry House, 11-13 Stone Street, Cranbrook, Kent TN17 3HF Tel: 01580 712345

BET • Beth, GO 43-44, Alfies Antique Market, 13-25 Church Street, Marylebone, London NW8 8DT Tel: 0171 723 5613

BEV •† Beverley, 30 Church Street, Marylebone, London NW8 8EP Tel: 0171 262 1576

BEX •† Daniel Bexfield Antiques, The Bond Street Antiques Centre, 124 New Bond Street, London W1Y 9AE Tel: 0171 491 1720

BIG * Bigwood Auctioneers Ltd, The Old School, Tiddington, Stratford-upon-Avon, Warwickshire CV37 7AW Tel: 01789 269415

BIL •† Box in the Lanes, Cabinet 112 (Basement), Bartlett Street Antiques Centre, Bath, Somerset BA1 2QZ Tel: 0468 720338

BKK •† Bona Arts Decorative Ltd, Bizarre House, 124 High Street, Marlborough, Wiltshire SN8 Tel: 01252 514100

BKS * Brooks Ltd, 81 Westside, London SW4 9AY Tel: 0171 228 8000

BOH • Bohemia, 11 Warner Street, Accrington, Lancashire Tel: 01254 231119

Bon * Bonhams, Montpelier Street, Knightsbridge, London SW7 1HH Tel: 0171 393 3900

Bon(C) * Bonhams, 65-69 Lots Road, Chelsea, London SW10 0RN Tel: 0171 393 3900

Bon(W) * Bonhams West Country, Devon Fine Art Auction House, Dowell Street, Honiton, Devon EX14 8LX Tel: 01404 41872

BRA • Billiard Room Antiques, The Old School, Church Lane, Chilcompton, Bath, Somerset BA3 4HP Tel: 01761 232839

BRT • Britannia, Grays Antique Market, Stand 101, 58 Davies Street, London W1Y 1AR Tel: 0171 629 6772

BRU • Brunel Antiques, Bartlett Street Antiques Centre, Bath, Somerset BA1 2QZ Tel: 01225 310457/446322

BrW • Brian Watson Antique Glass, The Grange, Norwich Road, Wroxham, Norwich, Norfolk NR12 8RX Tel: 01603 784177

BS • Below Stairs, 103 High Street, Hungerford, Berkshire RG17 0NB Tel: 01488 682317

BSA • Bartlett Street Antiques, 5/10 Bartlett Street, Bath, Somerset BA1 2QZ Tel: 01225 446322/310457

BTC •† Beatcity, PO Box 229, Chatham, Kent ME5 0PW Tel: 01634 305383/0370 650890

BWC §† British Watch & Clock Collectors Association, 5 Cathedral Lane, Truro, Cornwall TR1 2QS Tel: 01872 241953

CAB •† Candlestick & Bakelite, PO Box 308, Orpington, Kent BR5 1TB Tel: 0181 467 3743/3799

CAC • Cranbrook Antique Centre, High Street, Cranbrook, Kent TN17 3DN Tel: 01580 712173

CaC * Cato Crane & Co, Liverpool Auction Rooms, 6 Stanhope Street, Liverpool, Merseyside L8 5RF Tel: 0151 709 5559

CAG * The Canterbury Auction Galleries, 40 Station Road West, Canterbury, Kent CT2 8AN Tel: 01227 763337

CaH • The Camera House, Oakworth Hall, Colne Road (B6143), Oakworth, Keighley, Yorkshire BD22 7HZ Tel/Fax: 01535 642333

CAN • The Candle Shop, Covent Garden, London WC2 Tel: 0171 379 4220

CAT • Lennox Cato, 1 The Square, Edenbridge, Kent TN8 5BD Tel: 01732 865988/ Mobile 0836 233473

CBP *† Comic Book Postal Auctions Ltd, 40-42 Osnaburgh Street, London NW1 3ND Tel: 0171 424 0007

CCC •† Crested China Co, The Station House, Driffield, Yorkshire YO25 7PY Tel: 01377 257042

CCI § Carlton Ware Collectors International, PO Box 161, Sevenoaks, Kent TN15 6GA Tel: 01474 853630

CCO • Collectable Costume, Fountain Antique Centre, 3 Fountain Buildings, Lansdowne Road, Bath, Somerset BA1 5DU Tel: 01225 428731

CDC * Capes Dunn & Co, The Auction Galleries, 38 Charles Street, Off Princess Street, Greater Manchester M1 7DB Tel: 0161 273 6060/1911

CEX • Corn Exchange Antiques Centre, 64 The Pantiles, Tunbridge Wells, Kent TN2 5TN Tel: 01892 539652

CFA • Cambridge Fine Art, Priesthouse, 33 Church Street, Little Shelford, Nr Cambridge, Cambs CB2 5HG Tel: 01223 842866

CHA • Chislehurst Antiques, 7 Royal Parade, Chislehurst, Kent BR7 6NR Tel: 0181 467 1530

CHe •† Chelsea Clocks & Antiques, Antiquarius, Stand H3-4, 135 Kings Road, London SW3 4PW Tel: 0171 352 8646

ChS • The Chair Set, 84 Hill Rise, Richmond, Surrey TW10 6UB Tel: 0181 332 6454

CLW/ Collectors' World, Alfies Antique Market,
CWo 13-25 Church Street, Marylebone, London NW8 8DT Tel: 0171 723 6066

CMF •† Childhood Memories, The Farnham Antique Centre, 27 South Street, Farnham, Surrey GU9 7QU Tel: 01252 724475/793704

CMO • Brian Cargin & Chris Morley, Ginnell Antiques Gallery, 18-22 Lloyd Street, Gr. Manchester M2 5WA Tel: 0161 833 9037

CoA • Country Antiques (Wales), Castle Mill, Kidwelly, Carms, Wales SA17 4UU Tel: 01554 890534

COB •† Cobwebs, 78 Northam Road, Southampton, Hampshire SO14 0PB Tel: 01703 227458

COM • Combe Cottage Antiques, Castle Combe, Chippenham, Wiltshire SN14 7HU Tel: 01249 782250

CORO • Coromandel, PO Box 9772, London SW19 3ZG Tel: 0181 543 9115

COT • Cottage Antiques, Bakewell & Woburn Antiques Centres, Bucks Tel: 01283 562670

CP •† Cat Pottery, 1 Grammar School Road, North Walsham, Norfolk NR28 9JH Tel: 01692 402962

CPA • Cottage Pine Antiques, 19 Broad Street, Brinklow, Nr Rugby, Warwickshire CV23 0LS Tel: 01788 832673

CS •† Christopher Sykes, The Old Parsonage, Woburn, Milton Keynes, Bedfordshire MK17 9QL Tel: 01525 290259

CSA	•†	Church Street Antiques, 10 Church Street, Godalming, Surrey GU7 1EH Tel: 01483 860894
CSK	*†	Christie's South Kensington Ltd, 85 Old Brompton Road, London SW7 3LD Tel: 0171 581 7611
CT	•	Children's Treasures, 17 George Street, Hastings, Sussex TN34 3EG Tel: 01424 444117/422758
CtC	•	Clinton Cards, 8 High Street, Tenterden, Kent TN30 6AP Tel: 01580 762090
CTO	•†	Collectors' Corner, PO Box 8, Congleton, Cheshire CW12 4GD Tel: 01260 270429
DA	*	Dee, Atkinson & Harrison, The Exchange Saleroom, Driffield, Yorkshire YO25 7LD Tel: 01377 253151
DAN	•	Andrew Dando, 4 Wood Street, Queen Square, Bath, Somerset BA1 2JQ Tel: 01225 422702
DBr	•	David Brown, 23 Claude Street, Larkhall, Lanarkshire, Scotland ML9 2BU Tel: 01555 880333
DgC	•	Dragons Lee Collectables, Kent Tel: 01622 729502
DH	•	The Dog House, 309 Bloxwich Road, Walsall, West Midlands WS2 7BD Tel: 01922 30829
DIA	•	Mark Diamond Associates Tel: 0181 508 4479
DIC	•	D & B Dickinson, The Antique Shop, 22 & 22a New Bond St, Bath, Somerset BA1 1BA Tel: 01225 466502
DKH	•	David K. Hakeney, 400 Wincolmlee, Hull, Humberside HU2 0QL Tel: 01482 228190
DN	*	Dreweatt Neate, Donnington Priory, Donnington, Newbury, Berkshire RG13 2JE Tel: 01635 31234
DNW	*	Dix-Noonan-Webb, 1 Old Bond Street, London W1X 3TD Tel: 0171 499 5022
DOL	•†	Dollectable, 53 Lower Bridge Street, Chester, Cheshire CH1 1RS Tel: 01244 344888/679195
DOR	•	Dorset Reclamation, Cow Drove, Bere Regis, Wareham, Dorset BH20 7JZ Tel: 01929 472200
DRJ	•	The Motorhouse, DS & RG Johnson, Thorton Hall, Thorton, Bucks MK17 0HB Tel: 01280 812280
DRU	•	Drummonds of Bramley, Birtley Farm, Horsham Road, Bramley, Guildford, Surrey GU5 0LA Tel: 01483 898766
DSP	•	David & Sarah Pullen, PO Box 24, Bexhill-on-Sea, Sussex TN39 4ZN Tel: 01424 848035
DUD	•	Dudley Howe, SO55/56/57, Alfies Antique Market, 13-25 Church Street, London NW8 8DT Tel: 0171 723 6066
DW	*†	Dominic Winter Book Auctions, The Old School, Maxwell Street, Swindon, Wiltshire SN1 5DR Tel: 01793 611340
E	*	Ewbank, Burnt Common Auction Room London Road, Send, Woking, Surrey GU23 7LN Tel: 01483 223101
Ech	•†	Echoes, 650a Halifax Road, Eastwood, Todmorden, Yorkshire OL14 6DW Tel: 01706 817505
ED	•	Elite Designs, Sussex Tel: 01424 434856
EIM	•†	Christopher Eimer, PO Box 352, London NW11 7RF Tel: 0181 458 9933
ELG	•†	Enid Lawson Gallery, 36a Kensington Church Street, London W8 4DB Tel: 0171 937 8444
EW	•	Elaine Whobrey, Glos Tel: 01451 821670
FAM	•	Fountain Antiques Centre, 3 Fountain Buildings Lansdown Road, Bath, Somerset BA1 5DU Tel: 01225 428731/471133

FB	•	Francis Bowers Chess Suppliers, 34 Middle Road, Whaplode Spalding, Lincolnshire PE12 6TW Tel: 01406 370166
FD	•	Frank Dux Antiques, 33 Belvedere, Bath, Somerset BA1 5HR Tel: 01225 312367
FMN	•†	Forget Me Knot Antiques, Over the Moon, 27 High Street, St Albans, Herts AL3 4EH Tel: 01727 848907
FOX	•	Foxhole Antiques, Swan & Foxhole, Albert House, Stone Street, Cranbrook, Kent Tel: 01580 712720
G&CC	•†	Goss & Crested China Co, 62 Murray Road, Horndean, Hampshire PO8 9JL Tel: 01705 597440
GAK	*	G. A. Key, 8 Market Place, Aylsham, Norfolk NR11 6EH Tel: 01263 733195
Gar	•	Garry, Alfies Antique Market, 13-25 Church Street, Marylebone, London NW8 8DT Tel: 0171 723 6066
GAZE	*	Thomas Wm Gaze & Son, Diss Auction Rooms, Roydon Road, Diss, Norfolk IP22 3LN Tel: 01379 650306
GBr	•	Geoffrey Breeze Antiques, 6 George Street, Bath, Somerset BA1 2EH Tel: 01225 466499
GEM	•	Gem Antiques, 28 London Road, Sevenoaks, Kent TN13 1AP Tel: 01634 743540
GH	*	Gardiner Houlgate, The Old Malthouse, Comfortable Place, Upper Bristol Road, Bath, Somerset BA1 3AJ Tel: 01225 447933
GIN	•	The Ginnell Gallery Antique Centre, 18-22 Lloyd Street, Gt. Manchester M2 5WA Tel: 0161 833 9037
GKR	•†	GKR Bonds Ltd, PO Box 1, Kelvedon, Essex CO5 9EH Tel: 01376 571711
GL	•†	Gordon Litherland, 25 Stapenhill Road, Burton-on-Trent, Staffordshire DE15 9AE Tel: 01283 567213
GLA	•	Glasform Ltd, 123 Talbot Road, Blackpool, Lancashire FY1 3QY Tel: 01253 695849
Gle	*	Glendinings & Co, 101 New Bond Street, London W1Y 9LG Tel: 0171 493 2445
GLT	•	Glitterati, Assembly Antique Centre, 6-8 Saville Row, Bath, Somerset BA1 2QP Tel: 01225 333294
GM	•†	Philip Knighton, 11 North Street, Wellington, Somerset TA21 8LX Tel: 01823 661618
GN	•	Gillian Neale Antiques, PO Box 247, Aylesbury, Bucks HP20 1JZ Tel: 01296 423754
GSP	*	Graves, Son & Pilcher, Hove Auction Rooms Hove Street, Hove, Sussex BN3 2GL Tel: 01273 735266
GV	•	Garth Vincent, The Old Manor House, Allington, Nr Grantham, Lincolnshire NG32 2DH Tel: 01400 281358
GWA	•	Great Western Antiques, Torre Station, Newton Road, Torquay, Devon TQ5 2DD Tel: 01803 200551
HAK	•	Paul Haskell, Kent Tel: 01634 669362
Hal	*	Halls Fine Art Auctions, Welsh Bridge, Shrewsbury, Shropshire SY3 8LA Tel: 01743 231212
HALL	•	Hall's Nostalgia, 21 Mystic Street, Arlington, MA 02174 USA Tel: 001 617 646 7757
HAM	*	Hamptons Antique & Fine Art Auctioneers, 93 High Street, Godalming, Surrey GU7 1AL Tel: 01483 423567
Har	•	Patricia Harbottle, Geoffrey Vann Arcade, 107 Portobello Road, London W11 2QB Tel: 0171 731 1972 Saturdays only

HarC •† Hardy's Collectables/Hardy's Clobber, 862 & 874 Christchurch Road, Boscombe, Bournemouth, Dorset BH7 6DQ Tel: 01202 422407/303030

HAX * Halifax Property Services, Fine Art Department, 53 High Street, Tenterden, Kent TN30 6BG Tel: 01580 763200

HB •† Adrian Harrington, 64a Kensington Church St, London W8 Tel: 0171 937 1465 and Peter Harrington, 100 Fulham Road, London SW3 6HS Tel: 0171 591 0220/0330

HCC * H C Chapman & Son, The Auction Mart, North Street, Scarborough, Yorkshire YO11 1DL Tel: 01723 372424

HCH * Hobbs & Chambers, Market Place, Cirencester, Glos GL7 1QQ Tel: 01285 654736

HEA • Peter Hearnden, Kent Appointment only Tel: 01634 374132

HEG •† Stuart Heggie, 14 The Borough, Northgate, Canterbury, Kent CT1 2DR Tel: 01227 470422

HEI • Heirloom Antiques, 68 High Street, Tenterden, Kent TN30 6AU Tel: 01580 765535

HEL • Helios Gallery, 292 Westbourne Grove, London W11 2PS Tel: 01225 336097/Mobile: 0973 730843

HEM • Hemswell Antique Centre, Caenby Corner Estate, Hemswell Cliff, Gainsborough, Lincolnshire DN21 5TJ Tel: 01427 668389

HEY • Heytesbury Antiques, PO Box 222, Farnham, Surrey GU10 5HN Tel: 01252 850893 Mobile: 0836 675727 Open by appointment only

HOB •† Hobday Toys, 44 High Street, Northwood, Middlesex HA6 2XY Tel: 01923 820115

HOLL * Dreweatt Neate Holloways, 49 Parsons Street, Banbury, Oxfordshire OX16 8PF Tel: 01295 253197

HRQ • Harlequin Antiques, 79 Mansfield Road, Daybrook, Nottingham, Notts NG5 6BH Tel: 0115 967 4590

HUX •† David Huxtable, Alfies Antique Market, Stand S03/05 (Top Floor), 13-25 Church Street, Marylebone, London NW8 8DT Tel: 0171 724 2200

HYD * H Y Duke & Son, Dorchester Fine Art Salerooms, Dorchester, Dorset DT1 1QS Tel: 01305 265080

IW •† Islwyn Watkins, 1 High Street, Knighton, Powys, Wales LD7 1AT Tel: 01547 520145

JAL • J. A. Allen, 4 Lower Grosvenor Place, London SW1W 0EL Tel: 0171 834 0090

JAS • Jasmin Cameron, M16 Antiquarius, 131-141 King's Road, London SW3 5ST Tel/Fax: Shop 0171 351 4154 Mobile: 0374 871257 Home: 01494 774276

JBB • Jessie's Button Box, Fountain Antique Centre, 3 Lansdown Road, Bath, Somerset BA1 5DY Tel: 0117 929 9065

JFG • Jafar Gallery, London Tel: 0181 300 2727

JH * Jacobs & Hunt, 26 Lavant Street, Petersfield, Hampshire GU32 3EF Tel: 01730 262744

JHa • Jeanette Hayhurst Fine Glass, 32a Kensington Church Street, London W8 4HA Tel: 0171 938 1539

JIL • Jillings Antiques, 8 Halken Arcade, Motcomb Street, London SW1X 8JT Tel: 0171 235 8600

JMC • J & M Collectables, Kent Tel: 01580 891657

JO • Jacqueline Oosthuizen, 23 Cale Street, Chelsea, London SW3 3QR Tel: 0171 352 6071

JON • Jon Bird, Kent Tel: 01227 273952

JPr • Joanna Proops Antiques/Textiles, 34 Belvedere, Bath, Somerset BA1 5HR Tel: 01225 310795

JRe • John Read, 29 Lark Rise, Martlesham Heath, Ipswich, Suffolk IP5 7SA Tel: 01473 624897

JUN •† Junktion, The Old Railway Station, New Bolingbroke, Boston, Lincs PE22 7LB Tel: 01205 480068

JV • June Victor, S041-43, Alfies Antique Market, 13-25 Church Street, London NW8 8DT Tel: 0171 723 6066

KES •† Keystones, PO Box 387, Stafford, Staffordshire ST16 3FG Tel: 01785 256648

L * Lawrence Fine Art Auctioneers, South Street, Crewkerne, Somerset TA18 8AB Tel: 01460 73041

L&E * Locke & England, Black Horse Agencies, 18 Guy Street, Leamington Spa, Warwickshire CV32 4RT Tel: 01926 889100

LA • Lane Antiques, 40 Pittshanger Lane, Ealing, London W5 1QY Tel: 0181 810 8090

LAY * David Lay (ASVA), Auction House, Alverton, Penzance, Cornwall TR18 4RE Tel: 01736 361414

LB • Lace Basket, 116 High Street, Tenterden, Kent TN30 6HT Tel: 01580 763923/763664

LBe • Linda Bee, Art Deco Stand J20-21, Gray's Antique Market, 1-7 Davies Mews, London W1Y 1AR Tel: 0171 629 5921

LBr •† Lynda Brine, Assembly Antique Centre, 5-8 Saville Row, Bath, Somerset BA1 2QP Tel: 01225 448488

LCC • The London Cigarette Card Co Ltd, Sutton Road, Sutton Road, Somerton, Somerset TA11 6QP Tel: 01458 273452

LEG • Legend Lane, Albion Mill, London Road, Macclesfield, Cheshire SK11 7SQ Tel: 01625 424661

LF * Lambert & Foster, 77 Commercial Road, Paddock Wood, Kent TN12 6DR Tel: 01892 832325

LHB • Gallery Les Hommes Bleus, Bartlett Street Antique Centre, 5/10 Bartlett Street, Bath, Somerset BA1 2QZ Tel: 01225 316606

LIB • Libra Antiques, 81 London Road, Hurst Green, Etchingham, Sussex TN19 7PN Tel: 01580 860569

Lof • The Loftspace, Arundel Antiques Centre, 51 High Street, Arundel, Sussex BN18 9AJ Tel: 01903 882749/690285/884729

LUC • R.K. Lucas & Son, The Tithe Exchange, 9 Victoria Place, Haverfordwest, Wales SA16 2JX Tel: 01437 762538

MAC • The Mall Antique Centre, 400 Wincolmlee, Hull, Humberside HU2 0QL Tel: 01482 327858

MAP •† Marine Art Posters, 71 Harbour Way, Merchants Landing, Victoria Dock, Port of Hull, Yorkshire HU9 1PL Tel: 01482 321173

MAR * Frank R. Marshall & Co, Marshall House, Church Hill, Knutsford, Cheshire WA16 6DH Tel: 01565 653284

MAW * Thomas Mawer & Son, The Lincoln Saleroom, 63 Monks Road, Lincoln, Lincolnshire LN2 5HP Tel: 01522 524984

MB • Mostly Boxes, 93 High Street, Eton, Berkshire SL4 6AF Tel: 01753 858470

MEG • Megarry's and Forever Summer, Jericho Cottage, The Green, Blackmore, Essex CM4 0RR Tel: 01277 821031/822170

MER • Mere Antiques, 13 Fore Street, Topsham, Exeter, Devon EX3 0HF Tel: 01392 874224

MGC • Midlands Commemoratives, The Old Cornmarket Antique Centre, 70 Market Place, Warwick, Warwickshire CV34 4SO Tel: 01926 419119

Mit * Mitchells, Fairfield House, Station Road, Cockermouth, Cumbria CA13 9PY Tel: 01900 827800

MJW • Mark J. West, Cobb Antiques Ltd, 39a High Street, Wimbledon Village, London SW19 5YX Tel: 0181 946 2811

ML • Magic Lanterns at By George, 23 George Street, St Albans, Herts AL3 4ES Tel: 01727 865680/853032

MLa • Marion Langham, London Tel: 0171 730 1002

MLL • Millers Antiques Ltd, Netherbrook House, 86 Christchurch Road, Ringwood, Hampshire BH24 1DR Tel: 01425 472062

MON • Monty Lo, Stand 369, Grays Antique Market, 58 Davies Street, London W1Y 1AR Tel: 0171 493 9457

MRo • Mike Roberts, 4416 Foxfire Way, Fort Worth, Texas, 76133 USA Tel: 001 817 294 2133

MRT • Mark Rees Tools, Somerset Tel: 01225 837031

MRW •† Malcolm Russ-Welch, PO Box 1122, Rugby, Warwickshire CV23 9YD Tel: 01788 810 616

MSB • Marilynn and Sheila Brass, PO Box 380503, Cambridge, MA 02238-0503 USA Tel: 617 491 6064

MSh • Manfred Schotten, The Crypt Antiques, 109 High Street, Burford, Oxfordshire OX18 4RG Tel: 01993 822302

MSW * Marilyn Swain Auctions, The Old Barracks, Sandon Road, Grantham, Lincs NG31 9AS Tel: 01476 568861

MTa • Maggie Tallentire, The Anvil, Cavendish Street, Cartmel, Grange-over-Sands, Cumbria LA11 6QA Tel: 015395 36362

MUL •† Mullock & Madeley, The Old Shippon, Wall-under-Heywood, Church Stretton, Shropshire SY6 7DS Tel: 01694 771771

NAR • Colin Narbeth & Son Ltd, 20 Cecil Court, Leicester Square, London WC2N 4HE Tel: 0171 379 6975

NC • The Nautical Centre, Harbour Passage, Hope Square, Weymouth, Dorset DT4 8TR Tel: 01305 777838

NCA • New Century, 69 Kensington Church Street, London W8 4DB Tel: 0171 937 2410

ND * Nock Deighton, Livestock & Auction Centre, Tasley, Bridgnorth, Shropshire WV16 4DB Tel: 01746 762666

No7 • No 7 Antiques, 7 Nantwich Road, Woore, Shropshire CW3 9SA Tel: 01630 647118

NP • Neville Pundole, 8A & 9 The Friars, Canterbury, Kent CT1 2AS Tel: 01227 453471

NTM •† Nostalgia Toy Museum, High Street, Godshill, Isle of Wight PO38 3HZ Tel: 01938 526254

NW • Nigel Williams Rare Books, 22 & 25 Cecil Court, London WC2N 4HE Tel: 0171 836 7757

NWE • North Wiltshire Exporters, Farmhill House, Brinkworth, Wiltshire SN15 5AJ Tel: 01666 824133/510876

NWi • Neil Wilcox, 113 Strawberry Vale, Twickenham, Middlesex TW1 4SJ Tel: 0181 892 5858

OBS • Button Shop Antiques, Old Button Shop, Lytchett Minster, Poole, Dorset BH16 6JF Tel: 01202 622169

OD • Offa's Dyke Antique Centre, 4 High Street, Knighton, Powys, Wales LD7 1AT Tel: 01547 528635

OLM • The Old Mill, High Street, Lamberhurst, Kent TN3 8EQ Tel: 01892 891196

OPH • Old Pine House, 16 Warwick Street, Royal Leamington Spa, Warwickshire CV32 5LL Tel: 01926 470477

ORI •† Oriental Gallery, Glos Tel: 01451 830944

ORIG • The Originals, GO 87/88, Alfies Antique Market, 13-25 Church Street, London NW8 8DT Tel: 0171 723 6066

OT • Old Timers, Box 392, Camp Hill, PA 17001-0392 USA Tel: 001 717 761 1908

OTA •† On The Air, 42 Bridge Street Row, Chester, Cheshire CH1 1NN Tel: 01244 348468

OTB •† Old Tackle Box, PO Box 55, Cranbrook, Kent TN17 3ZU Tel/Fax: 01580 713979

OTC •† Old Telephone Company, The Old Granary, Battlesbridge Antiques Centre, Nr Wickford, Essex SS11 7RF Tel: 01245 400601

OTS •† The Old Toy Shop, 7 Monmouth Court, Southampton Road, Ringwood, Hampshire BH24 1HE Tel: 01425 476899

OW •† Off World, Unit 20, Romford Shopping Halls, Market Place, Romford, Essex RM1 3AT Tel: 01708 765633

P *† Phillips, Blenstock House, 101 New Bond Street, London W1Y 0AS Tel: 0171 629 6602

P(B) * Phillips, 1 Old King Street, Bath, Somerset BA1 2JT Tel: 01225 310609

P(Ba) * Phillips Bayswater, 10 Salem Road, Bayswater, London W2 4DL Tel: 0171 229 9090

P(C) * Phillips Cardiff, 9-10 Westgate Street, Cardiff, Wales CF1 1DA Tel: 01222 396453

P(EA) * Phillips, 32 Boss Hall Road, Ipswich, Suffolk IP1 59J Tel: 01473 740494

P(O) * Phillips, 39 Park End Street, Oxford, Oxfordshire OX1 1JD Tel: 01865 723524

PaM • Puppets & Masks, 3 Kensington Mall, London W8 4EB Tel: 0171 221 8629

PBr • Pamela Brooks, Leicestershire Tel: 0116 230 2625

PC • Private Collection

PCh * Peter Cheney, Western Road Auction Rooms, Western Road, Littlehampton, Sussex BN17 5NP Tel: 01903 722264/713418

PER • Persiflage, Stand F00 6-8, Alfies Antique Market, 13-25 Church Street, London NW8 8DT Tel: 0171 723 6066

PGH • Paris, 42A High Street, Tenterden, Kent TN30 6AR Tel: 01580 765328

PJa • P. Jacques, SO59/60, Alfies Antique Market, 13-25 Church Street, London NW8 8DT Tel: 0171 723 6066

PKT • Glitter & Dazzle, Pat & Ken Thompson, Hampshire Tel: 01329 288678

PLB • Planet Bazaar, 151 Drummond Street, London NW1 Tel: 0171 387 8326

POSH •† Posh Tubs, Moriati's Workshop, High Halden, Ashford, Kent TN26 3LZ Tel: 01233 850155

PPe • Past Perfect, 31 Catherine Hill, Frome, Somerset BA11 1BY Tel: 01373 453342

PPH • Period Picnic Hampers Tel: 0115 937 2934

PSA • Pantiles Spa Antiques, 4, 5, & 6 Union House, The Pantiles, Tunbridge Wells, Kent TN4 8HE Tel: 01892 541377

QSA • Quiet Street Antiques, 3 Quiet Street, Bath, Somerset BA1 2JG Tel: 01225 315727

RAC • Rochester Antiques Centre, 93 High Street, Rochester, Kent ME1 1LX Tel: 01634 846144

RAD • Radio Days, 87 Lower Marsh, Waterloo, London SE1 7AB Tel: 0171 928 0800

RAR * Romsey Auction Rooms, 86 The Hundred, Romsey, Hampshire SO51 8BX Tel: 01794 513331

RBA •† Roger Bradbury Antiques, Church Street, Coltishall, Norfolk NR12 7DJ Tel: 01603 737444

RBB * Russell, Baldwin & Bright, Fine Art Salerooms, Ryelands Road, Leominster, Hereford HR6 8NZ Tel: 01568 611122

RdeR • Rogers de Rin, 76 Royal Hospital Road, London SW3 4HN Tel: 0171 352 9007

RDG ▫ Richard Dennis Gallery, 144 Kensington Church Street, London W8 4BN Tel: 0171 727 2061

REN • Paul & Karen Rennie, 13 Rugby Street, London WC1N 3QT Tel: 0171 405 0220

RIC • Rich Designs, 1 Shakespeare Street, Stratford-upon-Avon, Warwickshire CV37 6RN Tel: 01789 261612

RIS • Risky Business, 44 Church Street, Marylebone, London NW8 Tel: 0171 724 2194

RMA • Right to the Moon Alice, Alice and Ron Lindholm, 240 Cooks Fall Road, Cooks Fall, NY 12776, USA Tel: 607 498 5750

RMC •† Romsey Medal Centre, 5 Bell Street, Romsey, Hampshire SO51 8GY Tel: 01794 512069

RTh •† The Reel Thing, 17 Royal Opera Arcade, Pall Mall, London SW1Y 4UY Tel: 0171 976 1830

RTw • Richard Twort, Somerset Tel: 01934 641900

RUM •† Rumours, 10 The Mall, Upper Street, Camden Passage, Islington, London N1 0PD Tel: 01582 873561

RUS • Trevor Russell, Staffordshire Tel: 01889 562009

RWB • Roy W Bunn Antiques, 34-36 Church Street, Barnoldswick, Colne, Lancashire BB8 5UT Tel: 01282 813703

RYA • Robert Young Antiques, 68 Battersea Bridge Road, London SW11 3AG Tel: 0171 228 7847

S * Sotheby's, 34-35 New Bond Street, London W1A 2AA Tel: 0171 493 8080

S(LA) * Sotheby's, 9665 Wilshire Boulevard, Beverly Hills, California, 90212 USA Tel: (310) 274 0340

S(NY) * Sotheby's, 1334 York Avenue, New York, NY 10021 USA Tel: 001 212 606 7000

SAF * Saffron Walden Auctions, 1 Market Street, Saffron Walden, Essex CB10 1JG Tel: 01799 513281

SAM • Samarkand Galleries, 8 Brewery Yard, Sheep Street, Stow-on-the-Wold, Glos GL54 1AA Tel: 01451 832322

SAS *† Special Auction Services, The Coach House, Midgham Park, Reading, Berkshire RG7 5UG Tel: 0118 971 2949

SCA • Susie Cooper Ceramics (Art Deco), GO70-4 Alfies Antique Market, 13-25 Church Street, London NW8 8DT Tel: 0171 723 0449

SCO • Peter Scott, Stand 39, Bartlett Street Antiques Centre, Bath, Somerset BA1 2QZ Tel: 01225 310457 or 0117 986 8468 Mobile: 0850 639770

SCR •† Herzog, Hollender Phillips & Company, The Scripophily Shop, PO Box 14376, London NW6 1ZD Tel/Fax: 0171 433 3577

SER •† Serendipity, 168 High Street, Deal, Kent CT14 6BQ Tel: 01304 369165

SFL • The Silver Fund, 139A New Bond Street, London W1Y 9FB Tel: 0171 499 8501

SHa • Shapiro & Co, Stand 380, Gray's Antique Market, 58 Davies Street, London W1Y 1LB Tel: 0171 491 2710

SLN * Sloan's, C G Sloan & Company Inc, 4920 Wyaconda Road, North Bethesda, MD 20852 USA Tel: 0101 301 468 4911/669 5066

SMAM • Santa Monica Antique Market, 1607 Lincoln Boulevard, Santa Monica, California 90404 USA Tel: 310 314 4899

SMI •† Janie Smithson Antiques, Lincolnshire Tel: 01754 810265 Mobile: 0831 399180

SnA • Snape Maltings Antique & Collectors Centre, Saxmundham, Suffolk IP17 1SR Tel: 01728 688038

SOL •† Solent Railwayana Auctions, 31 Newtown Road, Warsash, Hampshire SO31 9FY Tel: 01489 578093/584633

Som • Somervale Antiques, 6 Radstock Road, Midsomer Norton, Bath, Somerset BA3 2AJ Tel: 01761 412686

SPa • Sparks Antiques, 4 Manor Row, High Street, Tenterden, Kent TN30 6HP Tel: 01580 766696

SPE • Sylvie Spectrum, Stand 372, Gray's Antique Market, 58 Davies Street, London W1Y 1LB Tel: 0171 629 3501

SpP *† Specialised Postcard Auctions, 25 Gloucester Street, Cirencester, Glos GL7 2DJ Tel: 01285 659057

SPS • Sparkle at the Stables, Long Stables, Stables Market, Chalk Farm Road, Camden, London NW1 8AH Tel: 0181 809 3923 (Photograph courtesy Reed Books, photographer Tim Ridley)

SPU • Spurrier-Smith Antiques, 28, 39, 41 Church Street, Ashbourne, Derbyshire DE6 1AJ Tel: 01335 343669/342198

SRA *† Sheffield Railwayana Auctions, 43 Little Norton Lane, Sheffield, Yorkshire S8 8GA Tel: 0114 274 5085

SRC • Soviet Russia Collectables, PO Box 6, Virginia Water, Surrey GU25 4YU Tel: 01344 843091

SSW • Spencer Swaffer, 30 High Street, Arundel, Sussex BN18 9AB Tel: 01903 882132

StC • St Clere Antiques, PO Box 161 , Sevenoaks, Kent TN15 6GA Tel: 01474 853630

STE •† Stevenson Brothers, The Workshop, Ashford Road, Bethersden, Ashford, Kent TN26 3AP Tel: 01233 820363

STG • Stone Gallery, 93 The High Street, Burford, Oxfordshire OX18 4QA Tel/Fax: 01993 823302

STH • Steppes Hill Farm Antiques, Steppes Hill Farm, Stockbury, Nr Sittingbourne, Kent ME9 7RB Tel: 01795 842205

SUC • Succession, 18 Richmond Hill, Richmond, Surrey TW10 6QX Tel: 0181 940 6774

SUF * Suffolk Sales, Half Moon House, High Street, Clare, Suffolk CO10 8NY Tel: 01787 277993

SUS • Susannah, 142/144 Walcot Street, Bath, Somerset BA1 5BL Tel: 01225 445069

SVB • Steve Vee Bransgrove, 6 Catherine Hill, Frome, Somerset BA11 1BY Tel: 01373 453225

SWB •† Sweetbriar Gallery, Robin Hood Lane, Helsby, Cheshire WA6 9NH Tel: 01928 723851

SWO * G. E. Sworder & Sons, 14 Cambridge Road, Stansted Mountfitchet, Essex CM24 8BZ Tel: 01279 817778

TAC • Tenterden Antiques Centre, 66-66A High Street, Tenterden, Kent TN30 6AU Tel: 01580 765655/765885

TBoy • Toy Boy, Alfies Antique Market, 13-25 Church Street, Marylebone, London NW8 8DT Tel: 0171 723 6066

TC • Timothy Coward, Devon Tel: 01271 890466

TCF • 20th Century Frocks, 65 Steep Hill, Lincoln, Lincolnshire N1 1YN (opposite Jews House) Tel: 01522 545916

TED •† Teddy Bears, 99 High Street, Witney, Oxfordshire OX8 6LY Tel: 01993 702616

TH •† Tony Horsley, Sussex Tel: 01273 550770

THA • Town Hall Antiques, Market Place, Woburn, Bedfordshire MK17 9PZ Tel: 01525 290950

Thom/ S. & A. Thompson, Stand V12 Antiquarius
THOM 131/141 Kings Rd, London SW3 5ST Tel: 0171 352 8680

TIH • Time In Our Hands, The Platt, Wadebridge, Cornwall PL27 7AD Tel: 01208 815210

TMA * Brown & Merry, Tring Market Auctions, Brook Street, Tring, Herts HP23 5EF Tel: 01442 826446

TMi • Tim Millard Antiques, Stand 31-32 Bartlett Street Antique Centre, Bartlett Street, Bath, Somerset BA1 2QZ Tel: 01225 469785

TOT •† Totem, 168 Stoke Newington Church Street, London N16 0JL Tel: 0171 275 0234

TOY • The Toy Store, 7 Thomas Street, Manchester City Centre, Greater Manchester M4 IEU Tel: 0161 839 6882

TP •† The Collector, Tom Power, 9 Church Street, Marylebone, London NW8 8EE Tel: 0171 706 4586

TPA • Times Past Antiques, 59 High Street, Eton, Windsor, Berkshire SL4 6BL Tel: 01753 857018

TRE • The Treasury, 61a Downing Street, Farnham, Surrey Tel: 01252 722 199

TT •† Treasures in Textiles, 53 Russian Drive, Liverpool, Merseyside L13 7BS Tel: 0151 281 6025

TUO • The Unique One, 2802 Centre Street, Pennsauken, NJ 08109 USA Tel: 001 (609) 663 2554

TVA • Teme Valley Antiques, 1 The Bull Ring, Ludlow, Shropshire SY8 1AD Tel: 01584 874686

TVM • Teresa Vanneck-Murray, Vanneck House, 22 Richmond Hill, Richmond-upon-Thames, Surrey TW10 6QX Tel: 0181 940 2035

VCL •† Vintage Cameras Ltd, 256 Kirkdale, Sydenham, London SE26 4NL Tel: 0181 778 5416

VH • Valerie Howard, 2 Campden Street, Off Kensington Church Street, London W8 7EP Tel: 0171 792 9702

VS *† T. Vennett-Smith, 11 Nottingham Road, Gotham, Notts NG11 0HE Tel: 0115 983 0541

VSt • Vera Strange Antiques, 811 Christchurch Road, Boscombe, Bournemouth, Dorset BH7 6HP Tel: 01202 429111

W&S • Pat Woodward and Alma Shaw, Unit G43, Ground Floor, Gloucester Antiques Centre, In The Historic Docks, Severn Road, Gloucester, Glos GL1 2LE

WAB •† Warboys Antiques, Old Church School, High Street, Warboys, Cambs PE17 2SX Tel: 01487 823686

WAC • Worcester Antiques Centre, Reindeer Court, Mealcheapen Street, Worcester, Worcs WR1 4DF Tel: 01905 610680

Wai • Peter Wain, 7 Nantwich Road, Woore, Shropshire CW3 9SA Tel: 01630 647118

WAL *† Wallis & Wallis, West Street Auction Galleries, Lewes, Sussex BN7 2NJ Tel: 01273 480208

WaR • Wot a Racket, 250 Shepherds Lane, Dartford, Kent DA1 2PN Tel: 01322 220619

WCA • Wooden Chair Antiques Centre, Waterloo Road, Cranbrook, Kent TN12 0QG Tel: 01580 713671

WEE • Weedon Bec Antiques, 66 High Street, Weedon, Northants NN7 4QD Tel: 01327 349910

WeH • Westerham House Antiques, The Green, Westerham, Kent TN16 1AY Tel: 01959 561622/562200

WEL • Wells Reclamation & Co, The Old Cider Farm, Coxley, Nr Wells, Somerset BA5 1RQ Tel: 01749 677087/677484

WIM • Wimpole Antiques, Stand 349, Gray's Antique Market, 58 Davies Street, London W1Y 1AR Tel: 0171 499 2889/0171 624 7628

WL * Wintertons Ltd, Lichfield Auction Centre, Wood End Lane, Fradley, Lichfield, Staffordshire WS13 8NF Tel: 01543 263256 (Photographs courtesy of Crown Photos 01283 762813)

WP •† West Promotions, PO Box 257, Sutton, Surrey SM3 9WW Tel: 0181 641 3224

WRe • Walcot Reclamations, 108 Walcot Street, Bath, Somerset BA1 5BG Tel: 01225 444404

WSA • West Street Antiques, 63 West Street, Dorking, Surrey RH4 1BS Tel: 01306 883487

WTA •† Witney and Airault 20th Century Decorative Arts, The Lanes Gallery, 32 Meeting House Lane, Brighton, Sussex BN1 1HB Tel: 01273 735479

WW * Woolley & Wallis, 51-61 Castle Street, Salisbury, Wiltshire SP1 3SU Tel: 01722 424500

WWA • Wonderful World of Animation, 30 Bramham Gardens, London SW5 0HF Tel: 0171 370 4859/001 212 888 3718 USA

WWY •† When We were Young, The Old Forge, High Street, Harmondsworth Village, Middlesex UB7 0AQ Tel: 0181 897 3583

YAG • The York Antiques Gallery, Route 1, PO Box 303, York, ME 03909 USA Tel: 207-363-5002

YC •† Yesterday Child, Angel Arcade, 118 Islington High Street, London N1 8EG Tel: 0171 354 1601

ZEI • Zeitgeist, 58 Kensington Church Street, London W8 4DB Tel/Fax: 0171 938 4817

INTRODUCTION

This year *Miller's Collectables Price Guide* celebrates its tenth anniversary. The first edition, now a collector's piece itself, came out in 1989, and sold less than 15,000 copies. Today the guide has annual sales of 120,000 and is acknowledged around the world as the bible for all those who love collecting. This success reflects the massive expansion in the collectables market.

As traditional antiques have grown harder to find at affordable prices, and with younger collectors entering and regenerating the market, so interest in collectables has grown. Today there are enthusiasts for every conceivable subject, and the concept of the date line has shrunk. Once upon a time, an object had to be over a century old to qualify as an antique, today we include objects in this guide that had not even been created when the first issue came out – for example *Star Wars* and science fiction toys which can fetch tens or even hundred of pounds.

Many of the items in this book, from dolls to Wade Whimsies, were originally created for children. This year we devote a new section to Baby Collectables: looking at nursery china, and charting the history of infant feeding from the blue and white pap boat, to the infamous glass 'killer bottle', to modern day, hygienic plastics.

Given the passage of time, even the most utilitarian items can become collectable, a fact that would no doubt astonish and perhaps sometimes embarrass their original owners. Under Bathrooms, you can find everything from 18th century portable urinals, to Victorian baths to 'collectable' lavatory paper. Delving still further into the private lives of our ancestors, we also for the first time include a feature devoted to Underwear, uncovering bras, suspenders, stockings, and unashamedly looking at knickers from 19th century bloomers to the 1950s 'bum enhancer', one of the most curious items ever to be included in a Miller's guide.

The majority of collectors tend to concentrate on more traditional areas. Ceramics are a mainstay of the collectables market and subjects covered this year include Doulton, Poole, Fairings and Carlton Ware. In our glass section, we provide a comprehensive survey of Carnival glass, which like Victorian fairings, provides a good example of how cheap and cheerful objects, created for the masses and sold for pennies can be transformed within a few generations into valuable antiques. As previously mentioned, this process has speeded up with the explosion of the collectables market. This year we include a special focus on 1960s and 1970s collectables – from lava lamps, to bean bags to mini dresses – currently very sought after by collectors, and guaranteed to provoke waves of nostalgia in anyone who remembers wearing platform shoes the first time around.

Which of today's objects will become the collectables of the future? Possible contenders ranging from Teletubbies and tazos to Vivienne Westwood jewellery can be found on page 432. Every year we ask readers to send in their suggestions and this year's winner is Mr John Somerville from Edinburgh who nominated Eggberts. Thanks to everybody who wrote in and please send us your tips for next year's hottest collectable. The winning entrant will receive a free copy of next year's *Miller's Collectables Price Guide*. If there are any other areas that you would like to see covered in this guide, please let us know.

The great excitement of compiling *Miller's Collectables Price Guide* is discovering the huge range of subjects that are collected. Even after ten years, the guide is still packed full of surprises. In what other book could you find a Neanderthal bone point, a 4in (10cm) lotus boot created for the tiny bound foot of a Chinese lady, suffragette memorabilia, and a selection of collectable vacuum cleaners? Such variety is the spice of life and what makes collecting so endlessly fascinating.

We hope that you have enjoyed reading *Miller's Collectables Price Guide* over the past decade and that it will continue to be the essential handbook for collectors in the next millennium. Thank you for your support and for sharing your collecting passions with us. As ever, happy hunting!

ADVERTISING & PACKAGING

l. An Isola The Bishop's Balm ointment pot, with base, c1880, 3½in (9cm) diam.
£800–1,000 *BBR*

The price range of this ointment pot reflects its good condition, the quality of design and above all the extreme rarity of this particular image. The 19thC saw a growth in popularity of patent salves and medicines and a decorative or informative pot was an important sales tool. Many pot lids on the market have only come to light in the last 20–30 years, rescued from Victorian rubbish dumps by collectors.

A brass advertising letter clip, c1860, 7in (17.5cm) high.
£80–100 *CHe*

A pine advertising sign, stencilled 'Howe', c1900, 45½in (115.5cm) long.
£325–375 *MSB*

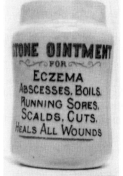

A Stone ointment pot, inscribed 'Stone ointment for eczema, abscesses, boils, running sores, scalds, cuts, heals all wounds', body staining but good condition, c1880, 3½in (9cm) high.
£130–150 *BBR*

A pottery figure, advertising Chairman's tobacco, c1900, 10in (25.5cm) high.
£145–180 *DBr*

A silver box, engraved 'Bryant & May's Wax Vestas', London 1901, 2 x 1½in (50 x 40mm).
£110–125 *GH*

Two tin and brass letter clips, inscribed 'M. Myers & Son and Perry & Co, London', c1901, 2½ x 3¼in (64mm x 83mm).
£22–28 each *WAB*

A Cadbury's chocolates box, c1902, 4¾ x 2½in (12 x 6.5cm).
£30–50 *MRW*

A Bird's Custard shop display carton, c1910, 14½in (37cm) long.
£60–70 *BBR*

A mahogany-framed barometer, with integral thermometer, advertising Taddy & Co Tobacco, c1912, 9 x 10in (23 x 25.5cm).
£180–200 *RTw*

A glass advertising sign, from a Naval tailors, with brass rim, c1910, 20 x 18in (51 x 45.5cm).
£250–300 *COB*

r. A Minter's Candies lithographed tin display case, c1920, 12½in (32cm) wide.
£125–150 *MSB*

> **Miller's is a price GUIDE not a price LIST**

A papier mâché shop display figure, 1920s, 27in (68.5cm) high.
£200–250 *JUN*

A papier mâché shop display figure, 1920s, 31in (78.5cm) high.
£300–350 *JUN*

A SylvaC model of a Scottie dog, advertising North British Rubber Company, c1920, 12in (30.5cm) high.
£300–350 *MUL*

A Rowntree's chocolates wooden box, 1920s, 12in (30.5cm) long.
£15–20 *OPH*

A Planters Peanuts cast iron figure money box, in the form of 'Mr Peanut', c1920–30, 11in (28cm) high.
£15–20 *BBR*

A Harrington's Bread paper bag, c1935, 12 x 8½in (30.5 x 21.5cm).
80p–£1 *RAD*

A Chicos Spanish Peanuts lithographed tin and glass jar, c1929, 11¼in (28.5cm) high.
£235–265 *MSB*

A Quaker Oats wooden box end panel, c1930s, 18in (45.5cm) long.
£8–10 *COB*

A Valentine's Meat Juice bottle, with contents and original box, 1930s, 3in (7.5cm) high.
£5–10 *SVB*

A Necco Bars lithographed tin display case, American, c1920, 15in (38cm) high.
£120–140 *MSB*

An Elizabeth Arden Blue Grass papier mâché model, 1930s, 13in (33cm) high.
£100–130 *DBr*

Born in Canada in 1878, Florence Nightingale Graham moved to New York where she changed her name and opened the first Elizabeth Arden beauty salon in 1909. Like her rival, Helena Rubenstein, Arden became one of the great cosmetic names of the century. Invariably dressed in pink, she owned 100 salons worldwide and manufactured countless products. Blue Grass, launched in 1934, was her best selling scent. The blue horse motif was inspired by the state of Kentucky, where Arden bred racehorses and according to legend, treated them with her own beauty preparations rather than horse liniment. Elizabeth Arden died in 1966.

l. A collection of labels, advertising various wines and soft drinks, framed and glazed, 1930s, 12¼ x 17¼in (31 x 44cm).
£20–30 *GL*

A McDougall's Self-Raising
Flour cotton bag, with contents
1930s, 11 x 5in (28 x 12.5cm).
£18–20 *SVB*

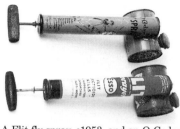

A Flit fly spray, c1953, and an O-Cedar
fly spray, 1940s, both 4in (10cm) long.
£12–15 each *SVB*

A Smith's Potato Crisps
waxed paper bag, 1940–50s,
8½ x 5½in (21.5 x 14cm).
£1–1.50 *RAD*

*Pre-packaged crisps first took
off in Britain in 1920 when
Frank Smith began selling
potato snacks to London pubs.
In these early years crisps were
sold in waxed paper bags that
were not airtight – the vendor
stored the crisps in their large
delivery tins, which kept them
fresh. Salt was contained
separately in the packets,
in a little twist of blue paper.
It was not until 1960 that
Golden Wonder introduced the
revolutionary concept of ready
salted crisps, paving the way
for the development of
flavoured varieties.*

A Milton antiseptic fluid bottle,
with original box, 1950s,
4in (10cm) high.
£8–10 *SVB*

A Falcon headwear shop display
bust, 1950s, 15in (38cm) high.
£80–100 *JUN*

l. A bottle of Bay Face Oil, by Biba,
unused, 1970s, 3¼in (8.5cm) high.
£14–16 *HUX*

*Black and gold, with Art Deco
influence, Biba packaging was
amongst the most distinctive of
its period. Barbara Hulanicky
launched her mail order fashion
business in 1964, naming it after
her sister, Biba. A small boutique
was followed in 1973 by a
massive and luxurious emporium
in London's Kensington High
Street, which sold everything
from clothes to cosmetics to food,
all stamped with Biba's
glamorous and feminine style.
The department store closed
down in the 1970s and today
Biba Products are becoming
increasingly desirable,
especially with young and
fashion-conscious collectors.*

l. A Biba Coffee
paper bag,
1970s, 8¼in
(21cm) high.
£3–4 *HUX*

Display Cards, Posters & Postcards

A Byrrh Tonique Hygienique postcard, by Victor Leydet, depicting a moustachioed wine worker, unused, 1908–10, 3½ x 6in (9 x 15cm).
£45–55 *SpP*

An advertising card for Man haircream, 'The Perfect Haircream', 1950, 9 x 11in (23 x 28cm).
£15–25 *JUN*

A K Shoes cardboard sign, 1930s, 16 x 11in (40.5 x 28cm).
£15–20 *RAD*

A Pedigree Shoes cardboard shop counter display, depicting King George V, 1930s, 18 x 12in (46 x 30.5cm).
£15–25 *COB*

A National Savings poster, 1940, 31½ x 19½in (80 x 50cm).
£60–80 *WP*

An educational poster, inscribed 'Mrs MacQueen's Sweet Shop', designed for schools, published by Macmillan & Co, 1950s, 17 x 21in (43 x 53.5cm).
£4–6 *HUX*

Enamel & Metal Signs

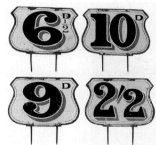

A brass nameplate, with enamelled lettering, c1900, 5 x 10in (12.5 x 25.5cm).
£15–25 *COB*

Four Victorian tin shop price tags, 4½ x 7in (11.5 x 18cm).
£20–25 each *SMI*

Two Maypole butter tin shop display signs, c1880, 5 x 12in (12.5 x 30.5cm).
£30–40 each *SMI*

r. A French Sun Assurance brass sign, c1910, 20 x 25in (51 x 63.5cm).
£70–100 *COB*

A Pullars Cleaners enamel
shop sign, with wooden
frame, 1910–20,
24 x 18in (61 x 45.5cm).
£80–100 *JUN*

A Santovin metal sign,
c1910, 27 x 20in
(68.5 x 51cm).
£125–150 *JUN*

A Player's metal sign, for use on a golf
course, 1930s, 7 x 12in (17 x 30.5cm).
£20–30 *COB*

l. A Wills's Star cigarettes
enamel sign, c1920,
34 x 52in (86.5 x 132cm).
£50–80 *JUN*

A Melox Dog Food
enamel sign, c1930,
26 x 17in (66 x 43cm).
£150–180 *JUN*

An Esso Elephant
Kerosene enamel sign,
with white and red
lettering on a red
background with blue
elephant, 1920–30s,
24 x 12in (61 x 30.5cm).
£160–180 *BBR*

A His Master's Voice enamel sign, featuring a
gramophone and Nipper, in white, yellow and
brown on black background, slight damage,
1920–30s, 18¾ x 26in (47.5 x 66cm).
£260–280 *BBR*

Tins

A biscuit tin, in the form of a mock-Tudor mansion, c1910, 6¼ x 9in (16 x 23cm).
£90–100 *HUX*

A Huntley & Palmers biscuit tin, in the form of a collection of books, c1910–20, 8 x 6in (20 x 25cm).
£250–300 *SUF*

A George Bassett & Co Ltd confectionery tin, designed as a calendar, 1920s, 6in (15cm) high.
£30–40 *Ber*

A Bisto gravy tin, c1925, 10in (25.5cm) high.
£70–80 *HUX*

In the 1900s, the wives of 2 members of the Cerebos Company (manufacturers of table salt and other condiments) suggested a new line to their husbands, a product that would make perfect and lump-free gravy. Cerebos' chemists set to work and created a powder that could be mixed with water and roasting juices. Next came a catchy slogan, 'Browns, Seasons, Thickens-in-One', the combined initials of which gave the gravy powder its name, Bisto. Launched in 1910, Bisto was a huge success. The famous sniffing Bisto Kids, first appeared in 1919 on a poster designed by illustrator Will Owen and an advertising legend was born. Objects featuring the Bisto Kids are popular with collectors today.

A Huntley & Palmers biscuit tin, in the form of a windmill, with lithographed detail, 1920s, 13¼in (34cm) high.
£550–650 *Bea(E)*

Cross Reference
Colour Review

A Hall's State Toffee confectionery tin, designed as an inkstand, c1930, 9¼in (23.5cm) wide.
£90–100 *GIN*

r. A biscuit tin in the form of a travelling trunk, 1920s, 7in (18cm) wide.
£60–80 *CHe*

A Huntley & Palmers biscuit tin, in the form of a suitcase, 1920s, 6 x 8in (15 x 20.5cm).
£110–120 *CHe*

An Eagle Sugar Cone tin, American, 1930s, 14¾in (37.5cm) high.
£160–190 *MSB*

A biscuit tin, depicting a farrier with children and donkeys, c1930, 8in (20.5cm) wide.
£8–10 *AL*

A Zam-Buk Herbal Balm tin, 1930s, 2½in (6.5cm) diam.
£3–5 *FAM*

A Barker & Dobson Barley Sugar confectionery tin, 1930s, 7in (18cm) long.
£10–15 *PPe*

A paper and tin confectionery container, in the form of a radio, German, c1930, 3½ x 3in (9 x 7.5cm).
£150–170 *AWT*

A Horlicks Tablets tin, 1940–50s, 4in (10cm) long.
£15–20 *SVB*

A Huntley & Palmers biscuits tin, known as 'The Rude Tin', depicting a garden tea party, c1980, 8in (20.5cm) diam.
£30–40 *DH*

This innocent looking container is known as 'The Rude Tin'. Legend has it that the designer was sacked by the biscuit company and before leaving wreaked a dire and subtle revenge. Almost but not quite imperceptibly concealed in this festive scene are a number of distinctly cheeky additions. The jam pot on the table is inscribed with a 4 letter word, dogs are mating in the herbaceous border and the pixies in the background are engaged in very adult pursuits. Only after the tin had been released were these miniature misdemeanours noticed and today it is a very sought after item.

A biscuit tin, depicting a Christmas scene, 1950s, 9in (23cm) square.
£15–20 *JUN*

l. A Blue Bird Assorted Toffees tin, entitled 'In Nelson's Days', from Harry Vincent Ltd, 1960s, 9 x 6in (23 x 15cm).
£15–20 *PPe*

AERONAUTICA

A pottery tobacco jar, in the form of an early bi-plane with pilot, coloured and glazed, inscribed 'Rougier 5', c1900, 6in (15cm) high.
£260–300 *CSK*

A Royal Flying Corps 9ct gold and enamel brooch, c1915, 1¼in (3cm) wide.
£80–100 *TVA*

A WWI poster from Ipswich advising of the dangers of bombing, 1915, 30in (76cm) long.
£60–70 *COB*

r. Two bronze commemorative plaques *above* by J. Dupon, inscribed 'Aero Club Royal De Belgique VIe Ralle Aerien International Knocke-Zoute 1933', 2⅝in (6.5cm) wide, *below* C. Mascaux, with relief artwork inscribed 'Syndicale Des Industries Aeronautiques Chambre 1908–1933 M. Charles Avenet', 2¾in (7cm) diam.
£200–250 *CSK*

A timepiece, thermometer and barometer, mounted in a globe on a marble plinth, surmounted by a model of an early single-engined twin propellered bi-plane with forward skids and pitch control, the chapter ring inscribed 'D. R. Pundole & Sons, Bombay, Made in France', some old damage, c1905, 17in (43cm) high.
£6,500–7,000 *CSK*

This timepiece more than tripled its auction estimate of £1,500–2,000 when sold at Christie's Transport Memorabilia sale. Its decorative appeal is also enhanced by a mechanical drive to the aeroplane, operated by a key. This was Christie's final specialist auction in this field, and transport memorabilia is now incorporated within other sales.

A bronze statuette of an early airman, possibly Austrian, holding a staff aloft, probably originally with a flag, mounted on a pink marble base, some wear and slight damage, signed 'NAM GREB', c1900, 13in (33cm) high.
£350–400 *CSK*

A spelter cigarette lighter, c1920, 11in (28cm) high.
£200–250 *JUN*

An RAF embroidered emblem, probably made by an airman's wife or mother, c1930, 20in (50.5cm) square.
£20–30 *COB*

A collection of RAF escape, evasion and survival items, including a BC-778-D portable emergency transmitter, cranking handle, wire aerial and aerial kite, a pair of black leather flying boots, and a WWII pattern 'Mae West', together with silk map, 1940s.
£300–350 *CSK*

A Glider Pilot Regiment white metal badge, 1945, 1½in (4cm) diam.
£10–12 *PC*

A collection of RAF flying helmets, goggles and oxygen masks, c1940.
£800–950 *CSK*

A Farnborough air show brochure, 1957, 8in (20cm) wide.
£5–10 *COB*

A collection of Richard Branson's Virgin Atlantic memorabilia, including a pilot's hat, flying helmet, goggles and photographs, c1980.
£175–225 *CSK*

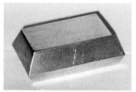

A metal aircraft nameplate, c1980, 10in (25.5cm) wide.
£10–15 *COB*

An oil on canvas, by Frank Wootton, *Airspeed Ambassador over Sydney Harbour*, signed, unframed, 1940s, 30in (76cm) high.
£1,500–2,000 *CSK*

Between 1939–45 Frank Wootton was the Official War artist to the RAF. He went on to become President of the Guild of Aviation Artists. His other specialities include sporting painting; including motor racing, horse racing and rowing.

Zeppelin Collectables

l. A Graf Zeppelin commemorative beer stein, with pewter cover, inscribed 'Deutsche Luftschiffer Ausstellung in Frankfurt', impressed 'Alt-Grenzal 1894', 9¾in (24.5cm) high.
£500–600 *CSK*

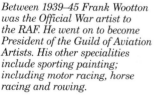

An aluminium paperweight made from airship Schuttlzlanz II, with documentation, early 20thC, 3in (7.5cm) wide.
£180–220 *PCh*

Fascination with airships is such that even the least decorative looking material can have considerable market value.

AMUSEMENT & SLOT MACHINES

As well as British and European amusement machines, this year's section includes a number of American slot machines. 'A slot is a three-wheel machine with a coin slot and a handle to pull,' explains New Jersey-based collector and dealer Bob Levy. 'The name comes from the late 1880s when they first made devices that operated when you put a coin in the slot.'

Slot machines really took off in the USA in the early 1900s. In 1910 The Mills Novelty company, copyrighted the classic fruit symbols on the wheels that are still in use today, and 1927 saw the introduction of the Jackpot feature.

Many of these machines are also referred to as 'coin-operated trade stimulators' since they were not just intended for casinos but designed to be placed on the counters of stores and saloons to amuse and entice customers. Games were affected when prohibition laws came into play and the gambling element had to be disguised. 'Machines paid out in gum, mints or tokens at varying times in the 1920s and 30s when cash pay-offs were illegal,' says Levy, although, as he admits, storeholders would often pay out in cash on the sly. Machines from the 1930s to 1940s are very popular with collectors because of their sophisticated mechanisms and handsome, often highly decorative cases. Enthusiasts prefer machines to be in full working order and value is affected by condition. Strict gaming laws still prevail in the USA and affect collecting. Some states permit the private ownership of machines over 25 years old, provided that they are not used for gambling, whilst in other states only machines manufactured prior to 1941 are allowed.

A penny-operated Kalloscop, by Polyphon Musikwerke, c1895, 12in (30.5cm) wide.
£1,800–2,000 *HAK*

A wooden game of skill, 'Get Tee Zee', by Price & Castell, 1899, 15½in (34.5cm) wide.
£1,700–1,800 *HAK*

A Tivoli penny-operated machine, by Hadon and Hurry, issues ticket on winning, 1897, 34¼in (87cm) high.
£900–1,200 *BB*

l. A Mother Shipton amusement machine, by John Dennison, Leeds, 1897, 21½in (52cm) wide.
£6,000–7,000 *HAK*

This is a particularly rare model, hence its high price.

A game of skill, by
Price & Castell, 1899,
14in (35.5cm) wide.
£1,600–1,800 *HAK*

A penny-operated Game
of the Barrels, penny
return style, 19thC,
17½in (44cm) wide.
£1,000–1,200 *BB*

A Heureka penny in
the slot machine, by
Polyphon Supply Co,
1900, 16in (40.5cm) wide.
£1,000–1,200 *HAK*

A Mills Novelty
'Little Perfection'
oak trade stimulator,
American, 1901,
12in (30.5cm) high.
£500–600 *TUO*

A Mother Shipton
Fortune Teller, with
blue information plate,
by Argyle Automatic
Co, London, 1901,
13½in (34cm) wide.
£1,800–2,200 *HAK*

A Coronet Game of
Skill, half-penny
operation with token
dispenser, 1901,
31in (79cm) high.
£800–1,000 *BB*

A penny-operated
amusement machine
with token dispenser,
by Pickwick H. Klein
& Co, London, 1900,
36in (91cm) high.
£1,200–1,500 *BB*

A game of skill machine,
by Pavilion Automatic
Skill Machine Co,
London, 1901,
16in (40.5cm) wide.
£1,700–2,000 *HAK*

r. An Electricity is
Life's Renovator, by
The Rose Automatic
Machine Co,
London, 1905,
15½in (39.5cm) wide.
£2,000–2,500 *HAK*

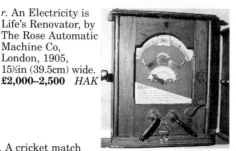

l. A cricket match
game machine, by
Automatic Sports Co,
London, 1903,
22in (56cm) wide.
£8,000–10,000 *HAK*

r. A billiard game
machine, by The Imperial
Automatic Novelty Co,
1903, 43in (110cm) high.
£1,200–1,500 *BB*

A Sports ball game, with token dispenser, 1908, 23in (58cm) high.
£550–650 *BB*

An Electricity is Life No. 2 machine, by United Automatic Machine Co, London, 1908, 24in (61cm) high.
£2,200–2,600 *HAK*

A Show Your Strength machine, by Mills Novelty Co, Chicago, 1904, 67in (170cm) high.
£5,500–6,500 *HAK*

A Lilliput half-penny-operated machine, with win, lost and reserved mechanism, German, 1908, 26in (66cm) high.
£1,200–1,500 *BB*

A *Le Magic* slot machine, with *mystère*, *magie* and *physique* options, by P. Beraud Paris, 1910, 19in (48cm) high.
£8,000–9,500 *HAK*

A penny-operated ball catching game, 'The Trapper', with token dispenser, by Ell & Co, 1912, 30½in (77cm) high.
£1,200–1,500 *BB*

An French all-win style amusement game, by Tourneza Fong et Lanchez, 1912, 18in (45cm) high.
£800–950 *BB*

r. A penny-operated ball catching game machine, with token dispenser by Handan-Ni Ltd London, 1913, Lilliput, 36in (90cm) high.
£1,000–1,200 *BB*

Did You Know?

When collecting and using vintage amusement machines, it is always important to ensure that you have coins of the appropriate size, period and nationality. Many collectors will concentrate on machines from their own country simply because the coins themselves are easier to obtain. In the USA particularly, there are also collectors of the different tokens dispensed by amusement machines and trade stimulators.

An 'All-Win' style ball game, with 4 ball reserve and pay tokens, 1914, 18½in (47cm) high.
£750–850 *BB*

An aluminium cigarette vending machine, for Woodbines, by Chas W. Biecknell Ltd, Birmingham, 1920s, 25in (63.5cm) high.
£140–150 *JUN*

A 'Penny in the Slot' amusement machine, by Caley, 1920, 25in (63.5cm) high.
£350–400 *JUN*

A 'Roll Out the Barrel' wall machine, Samson Novelty Co, 1920–30s, 24¾in (63cm) high.
£450–550 *SAF*

A Daval 'Chicago Club House' ball gum vender, aluminium 5 reel, American, 1933, 14in (35.5cm) high.
£300–400 *TUO*

A Pontoon 21 trade stimulator, c1930, 11in (30cm) wide.
£200–250 *SAF*

A Caille Brothers 'Superior' 5c jackpot slot machine, American, 1929, 25in (63.5cm) high.
£900–1,000 *TUO*

l. An All-Win De Luxe wall slot machine, c1930, 29in (74cm) high.
£700–800 *SAF*

A Mills novelty 'Bursting Cherry' slot machine, American, 1938, 27in (68.5cm) high.
£800–1,200 *TUO*

A Saxay chicken gift vending machine, with stand, c1940, 55in (138cm) high.
£350–400 *SAF*

r. A Nelson's Fruitlets machine, 1940s, 33in (84cm) high.
£180–210 *SPU*

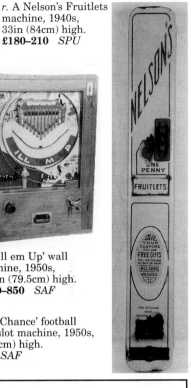

A 'Fill em Up' wall machine, 1950s, 31¼in (79.5cm) high.
£700–850 *SAF*

l. A 'Treble Chance' football game wall slot machine, 1950s, 31¾in (80.5cm) high.
£500–600 *SAF*

An 'Each Way' horse racing theme wall slot machine, 1950s, 31½in (80cm) high.
£550–650 *SAF*

A Mentos confectionery dispenser, with attached side vendor, original cards and keys, 1960s, 19½in (49.5cm) high.
£150–180 *SAF*

An American bubble gum dispenser, with chrome base, 1960s, 16in (40.5cm) high.
£90–120 *SAF*

ANIMATION ART

Created for children's films, today animation art is collected by adults across the world and at the top of the market can command extremely grown up prices. Among the most collectable items are period drawings (the preparatory work for the cartoon) and original production cels.

A cel is a painting on a sheet of clear acetate which is then laid over a background and filmed in sequence to create the impression of movement. An original production cel is a piece that was actually used in the making of the film: 'You should be able to pause your video and see the image freeze framed,' explains American dealer Debbie Weiss.

Such material is rare because it is only comparatively recently that animation art has become collectable. 'Studios used simply to throw things away once a film was finished, or perhaps reuse the celluloid for another film,' says British dealer Russell Singler. 'Many of the cels and drawings that have come down to us have only survived by chance because a cartoonist happened to take some pictures home, or a cleaner rescued an attractive image from the bin.'

Demand outstrips supply for original production material and this has led to the creation of reproduction cels, taken from the original cartoon artwork, not used in or created for the film itself, but designed for sale. The types illustrated here include 'sericels' (short for serigraph cels) in which the image is reproduced by silk-screen process, and hand-painted limited edition cels, in which the image is painted on the celluloid in traditional style. 'In actual film production this is a craft that is dying out,' says Singler. 'With Disney, for example, ever since the *Little Mermaid* (1989) drawings have been coloured in on computer rather than by hand, so techniques have changed.' Sericels are often produced in thousands, but hand-painted limited edition cels tend to be restricted to a few hundred.

Disney is the most famous name in the field but there is also huge demand for cartoon heroes created by other studios such as Warner Bros, Hanna Barbera, 20th Century Fox etc. The market is also profoundly influenced by fashions in television and video, for example, currently there is particular interest in *Simpsons* material.

'Everyone has their favourite film, and classic scenes will always command a premium,' says Debbie Weiss. Both she and Singler recommend collecting original production material and drawings where possible. 'Prices can be surprisingly reasonable when compared to reproduction pieces,' she concludes, 'and the best thing is you really feel that you have got hold of a little piece of the film and that your artwork is one of a kind.'

Walt Disney Studio

A gouache on celluloid production cel, *The Aristocats*, multi-cel set-up applied to a printed background, 1970, 11 x 14in (28 x 36.5cm).
£2,000–2,500   *S(NY)*

Items in this section have been arranged alphabetically by film or character.

A gouache on trimmed celluloid, *Bambi*, applied to an air brushed Courvoisier background, stamped 'original WDP', 1942, 7 x 7½in (18 x 19cm).
£2,500–3,000   *S(NY)*

r. A reproduction cel produced by silk-screen, *Bambi*, signed by Marc Davis, stamped 'Walt Disney Company Limited Edition Serigraph', 1980s, 10 x 12in (25 x 30.5cm).
£100–120   *WWA*

A graphite on paper concept artwork, *Bambi*, signed by artist Marc Davis, 1942, 5½ x 7½in (14 x 19cm).
£1,600–1,800   *S(NY)*

A gouache on celluloid original production cel, *Ben and Me,* featuring Amos Mouse, 1953, 6½ x 5½in (16.5 x 14cm).
£500–600 *S(NY)*

A drawing for *'Mickey's Service Station',* Donald Duck 'Long bill', 1935, 9 x 12in (23 x 30.5cm).
£275–325 *WWA*

Early drawings show Donald with a much longer beak than later designs.

A hand-painted limited edition production cel, Donald Duck in *Hockey Champ,* 1992, 12 x 16in (30.5 x 40.5cm).
£900–1,100 *AAG*

An original production cel, *Dumbo,* 1941, 6in (15cm) diam.
£2,800–3,200 *WWA*

A gouache on celluloid, *Dumbo* with airbrushed Courvoisier background, 1941, 8½ x 10in (21.5 x 25.5cm).
£2,700–3,300 *S(NY)*

A gouache on trimmed celluloid, *Fantasia,* Mickey in red on grey with air-brushed Courvoisier background, 1940, 7½in (19cm) diam.
£5,000–6,000 *S(NY)*

An original production cel, *Jungle Book,* with Shere Khan, 1967, 10 x 12in (25.5 x 30.5cm).
£1,450–1,650 *AAG*

A pair of graphite with coloured pencil on paper drawings, *Fantasia,* with sequence graphite of Brudus and Melinda, 1940, 9½ x 13in (24 x 33cm).
£800–950 *S(NY)*

r. An original production cel, *The Lion King* with The Hyenas, 1996, 14 x 12in (35.5 x 30.5cm).
£350–400 *AAG*

l. An original production cel, *Jungle Book,* with Baloo, 1967, 10 x 12in (25.5 x 30.5cm)
£1,000–1,200 *AAG*

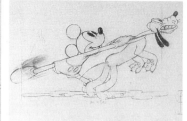

An original pencil drawing,
Mickey's Kangaroo, 1935,
9 x 12in (23 x 30.5cm).
£800–1,000 *WWA*

A graphite red and green
pencil on paper drawing,
Society Dog Show, 1939,
8½ x 11in (21.5 x 28cm).
£700–850 *S(NY)*

An original drawing, *Lucky
Rabbit*, pencil on paper,
late 1920s, 10 x 12in
(25.5 x 30.5cm).
£475–525 *WWA*

*This character was the precursor
to Walt Disney's most famous
creation – Mickey Mouse.*

An animation cel, *Peter Pan*, pencil
on paper, signed 'Marc Davis', 1980s,
12 x 15in (30.5 x 38cm).
£450–550 *WWA*

An original production cel,
Pinocchio, with coach and horses,
1940, 8in (20.5cm) wide.
£3,500–4,200 *AAG*

An original production
drawing, *Peter Pan*,
featuring Captain Hook,
pencil on paper, signed
'Marc Davis', 1953,
15 x 12in (38 x 30.5cm).
£875–1,000 *WWA*

A drawing from *The Chain Gang*,
the first Pluto cartoon, 1930s,
9 x 12in (23 x 30.5cm).
£450–550 *WWA*

An original pencil on paper
production drawing *Hawaiian
Holiday*, featuring Pluto, 1941,
9 x 12in (23 x 30.5cm).
£250–300 *WWA*

A gouache on celluloid, *Bone
Bandit*, applied to a watercolour
production background with
'used in ink 4-8-47 Margaret',
1948, 10 x 12in (25.5 x 30.5cm).
£1,000–1,200 *S(NY)*

Two thumbnail drawings,
Pinocchio, both graphite
on paper, matted and
framed together, 1940,
each 2½ x 3in (6.5 x 7.5cm).
£500–600 *S(NY)*

A production cel, *The Rescuers*, featuring Bernard, 1977, 14 x 10in (35.5 x 25.5cm). **£450–550** *AAG*

An original production cel, *Robin Hood*, featuring Skippy & Ma, 1973, 16 x 12in (40.5 x 30.5cm). **£550–650** *AAG*

An original production cel, *Snow White and the Seven Dwarfs*, Grumpy and the mirror, with Courvoisier set up, 1940s, 7 x 10in (18 x 25.5cm). **£2,800–3,300** *WWA*

This cel has been trimmed and glued to its background, probably in the 1940s–50s.

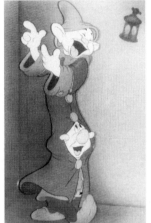

A storyboard, *Snow White and the Seven Dwarfs,* depicting Grumpy, graphite and coloured pencil on paper, 1937, 7 x 7½in (17.5 x 19cm). **£600–700** *S(NY)*

A drawing *Snow White and the Seven Dwarfs,* graphite and red and blue pencil on paper with full margins, 1937, 10 x 12in (25.5 x 30.5cm). **£800–950** *S(NY)*

A gouache, *Snow White and the Seven Dwarfs,* on trimmed celluloid applied to an airbrushed Courvoisier background, 1937, 9½ x 6in (24 x 15cm). **£4,700–5,500** *S(NY)*

r. A gouache, *Snow White and the Seven Dwarfs*, on trimmed celluloid applied to a wood veneer with Courvoisier background, 1937, 10½ x 13in (26.5 x 33cm). **£9,500–10,500** *S(NY)*

A drawing, *Snow White and the Seven Dwarfs*, depicting the Evil Hag, graphite and red pencil on paper with blue and green pencil around her eyes, 1937, 10½ x 9½in (26.5 x 24cm). **£1,100–1,300** *S(NY)*

Courvoisier Set Ups

In the late 1930s and '40s, the Courvoisier Gallery in San Francisco sold some cels from Walt Disney films. They were marketed as decorative pictures rather than historical film memorabilia. Cels would be cut to size and stuck down on backgrounds, often not the right background for the specific scene shown, but simply something that looked suitably attractive. Sometimes 2 separate cels would be pasted together to form one picture. In the trade these are known as Courvoisier set ups. Though no one today would treat animation art in such a cavalier fashion, Courvoisier pictures are very collectable, often providing the only cels available of certain scenes.

Other Studios

An original production cel,
Batman, depicting Catwoman,
1994, 10 x 12in (25.5 x 30.5cm).
£380–440 *AAG*

An original production cel,
Dangermouse, 1980s,
16 x 12in (40.5 x 30.5cm).
£100–120 *AAG*

An original production cel,
Roadrunner, 1960s,
10 x 8in (25.5 x 20.5cm).
£1,500–1,700 *AAG*

An original production cel,
The Jetsons, 1970s–80s,
10 x 12in (25.5 x 30.5cm).
£100–125 *WWA*

An original production cel,
Budgie – The Little Helicopter,
1994, 12 x 10in (30.5 x 25.5cm).
£100–120 *AAG*

An original pencil on paper
storyboard illustration, *The
Flintstones,* from The Swimming
Pool, signed by Joe Barbera,
1960, 11½in (29cm) wide.
£3,000–3,500 *WWA*

An original production cel,
The Flintstones, Fred Flintstone
and Boss, 1960s, 10 x 12in
(25.5 x 30.5cm).
£400–450 *AAG*

An original production cel,
Scooby Doo, 1980s,
10 x 12in (25.5 x 30.5cm).
£500–600 *AAG*

A gouache, Warner Bros,
Bugs Bunny, on trimmed
celluloid applied to a
watercolour production,
c1950s, 8½ x 11in (21.5 x 30cm).
£1,200–1,450 *S(NY)*

A publicity drawing,
The Flintstones, 1960s,
9 x 12in (23 x 30.5cm).
£150–175 *WWA*

An original production cel,
Garfield, 1990s, 10 x 12in
(25.5 x 30.5cm).
£300–340 *AAG*

An original production cel,
The Simpsons, depicting
Homer and the Zombies, 1990s,
14 x 16in (35.5 x 40.5cm).
£500–550 *AAG*

An original production cel, *The Simpsons,* featuring Itchy and Scratchy, 1990s, 10 x 12in (25.5 x 30.5cm).
£300–350 *WWA*

A hand-painted limited edition, Snoopy, Losing Altitude, signed by Bill Melendez, 1990s, 10 x 12in (25.5 x 30.5cm).
£500–550 *AAG*

An original production cel, Snoopy, 1970s, 9 x 12in (23 x 30.5cm).
£150–200 *WWA*

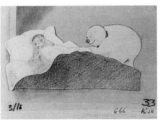

An original production cel, *The Snowman,* 1982, 10 x 12in (25.5 x 30.5cm).
£800–950 *AAG*

An original production cel, *Spiderman,* 1990s, 10 x 12in (30.5 x 25.5cm).
£300–350 *AAG*

An original production cel, Sylvester and Tweety, 1990s, 10 x 12in (25.5 x 30.5cm).
£370–420 *AAG*

An original production cel, Taz, from a National Football League Commercial, USA, c1980s, 10 x 12in (25.5 x 30.5cm).
£325–375 *WWA*

r. An original drawing and matching production cel, *Wacky Races,* featuring Dick Dastardly and Mutley, 1970s, 12 x 10in (30.5 x 25.5cm).
£50–75 *WWA*

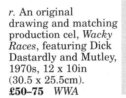

An original pencil on paper production drawing, Tom and Jerry, *Zoot Cat,* 1944, 10 x 12in (25.5 x 30.5cm).
£250–300 *WWA*

l. A pencil on paper storyboard animation, Top Cat, 1960s, 12 x 10in (25.5 x 30.5cm).
£100–125 *WWA*

An original production cel, Yogi and Boo Boo, signed by Bill Hanna and Joe Barbera and stamped, 1989, 10 x 12in (25.5 x 30.5cm).
£300–350 *WWA*

r. A sericel, *X men,* depicting Wolverine, 1990s, 10 x 12in (25.5 x 30.5cm).
£100–120 *AAG*

ANTIQUITIES

This section opens with a Neanderthal bone point circa 100,000–50,000BC, surely one of the oldest objects ever featured in *Miller's Collectables Price Guide*, and covers objects from Roman, Egyptian, Middle Eastern and Anglo-Saxon cultures, concluding with Medieval and Tudor remains. Old does not necessarily mean expensive. Though fine antiquities at the top end of the range fetch thousands of pounds, many of the historical fragments featured here are priced at under £100. 'People are often surprised by how affordable things are,' admits dealer Ralph Kiaer, 'there is a lot of the smaller material around, the collecting base is comparatively limited, and prices have not become inflated.'

The attraction of these rescued objects is that they can put you quite literally in touch with the ancient past, showing how people lived and died. 'Many items come from tombs and survived because, unlike domestic pieces, they were not used,' explains Kiaer. 'People would be buried with glass and pottery jars containing oils and food, as well as amulets and religious sculptures. Many of the objects that have come down to us have a ritual significance. Terracotta votive heads, for example, were buried in religious sites and were also scattered over fields to promote fertility.'

Kiaer buys mostly at auction and much of his stock comes from early collections. 'In the 18th and 19th centuries it was very fashionable and the mark of a classical education for a gentleman was to have a collection of small antiquities,' he says. 'A good provenance can increase the value and interest of a piece.'

Provenance is also very important given today's concerns about illegal importation and the pillaging of archaeological sites. 'With expensive pieces in particular you should always check where things come from,' advises dealer Chris Belton. 'New Treasure Acts are also coming into force in Britain to restrict finders, diggers and metal detectors.'

As Belton explains it is both provenance and experience that enables dating and identi-fication of ancient material. 'You recognise shapes, condition and patina,' he says. 'All these objects were hand-tooled, and at the lower end of the market there isn't really a problem with fakes because objects would simply be too costly to reproduce accurately.'

One of the best ways of finding out about small antiquities is to visit museums, not just major institutions such as the British Museum, but university collections and county archaeological and local museums. There you can see the small everyday objects used by our forbears hundreds and thousands of years ago. Many of these were not expensive objects to begin with, and even centuries later, collecting small antiquities can still be an affordable passion.

Bone & Stone

A middle Palaeolithic/Mousterian culture (Neanderthal man), sharp pointed bone implement, found in Ipswich, circa 100,000–50,000BC, 4in (10.5cm) long.
£35–40 *ANG*

A Bronze Age lozenge-shaped flint spear head, from Antrium, good condition, circa 2000BC, 2in (50mm) long.
£20–25 *ANG*

This spear head was found before 1912 and is from the collection of the late Rev Buick of Antrium.

An Egyptian Palaeolithic/Mousterian culture (Neanderthal man) stone sickle-type tool, from Abu Simbel, finely worked and marked 'Egypt 25' (1925), excellent condition, circa 80,000–40,000BC, 24½in (62cm) long.
£20–25 *ANG*

An Egyptian Neolithic semi-precious jasper brown lance head, of laurel leaf shape, very good condition, circa 4000BC, 3in (8cm) long.
£35–40 *ANG*

Ceramics

An Ancient Palestine and trans Jordan bronze age twin vessel, with two jars and intercommunicating channel, circa 3000BC, 5in (12.5cm) long.
£100–115 *BSA*

An Ancient Persian black-ware jar, on flared base, circa 1000BC, 10in (25.5cm) high.
£200–245 *BSA*

An Iron Age red-ware pottery oinochoe jug, with trefoil lip and flared foot, Ancient Ammonite, circa 8th–6th century BC, 6¼in (16cm) high.
£80–90 *BSA*

This was a container for wine.

An Hellenistic pottery alabaston, used for oils and scents, circa 3rd–2nd century BC, 6½in (16.5cm) high.
£110–130 *BSA*

An Ancient north African white-ware jug, from the El Djen area of Tunisia, circa 600BC, 8in (20.5cm) high.
£120–140 *BSA*

A Roman terracotta single-handled pot, from Cyprus, circa 1st–2nd century BC, 6in (15cm) high.
£75–85 *BSA*

An Ancient Israel pottery oil lamp, with star of David motif, circa 5th century AD, 4in (10cm) wide.
£20–25 *BSA*

An ancient Roman pottery vessel, for oils or perfumes, from Holy Land, circa 1st–3rd century AD, 2in (5cm) diam.
£20–25 *BSA*

r. An Ancient Roman red-ware terracotta flagon, with screw neck, from colonies of north Africa, circa 4th century AD, 9in (23cm) high.
£100–125 *BSA*

r. A Maya terracotta leg from a cult vessel, modelled as an ape/monkey warrior, complete, circa 6th–9th century AD, 5½in (14cm) high.
£75–85 *ANG*

Glass

A Roman Empire glass
tessera, with head
of Apollo, from Gaul,
1in (23mm) diam.
£45–50 *ANG*

*A tessera is a
gaming piece.*

A collection of Roman glass
tear bottles, very good
condition, circa 2nd–3rd
century AD, 2½–5in
(6.5–12.5cm) long.
£40–70 each *HEL*

An Ancient Roman
iridescent blue glass
vessel, used for
holding ointment, from
the Holy Land, circa
2nd–3rd century AD,
5in (12.5cm) high.
£80–100 *BSA*

An Ancient Roman
glass unguentarium,
from the Holy Land
used for oils and
perfumes, circa
1st–3rd century AD,
6¼in (16cm) high.
£60–80 *BSA*

A pair of Etruscan silver brooches, (fibulae), repaired,
circa 6th century BC, 3in (7.5cm) long.
£400–500 *HEL*

Jewellery & Metalware

A Bronze Age socketed axe head,
blade ragged, from Essex,
circa 900–600BC, 2¾in (7cm) long.
£85–95 *ANG*

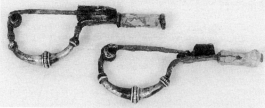

A Romano-British bronze 'Langton Down' type
brooch, found in Gloucestershire, larger than usual,
circa 1st century AD, 2½in (63mm) long.
£35–40 *ANG*

A Roman bronze amulet, depicting a
flying phallus with attachment chain,
good condition, circa 1st century AD,
2½in (65mm) long.
£300–400 *HEL*

*The phallus was an image venerated
by many cultures. A symbol of fertility
and the regenerative power of nature,
it appears throughout the decorative
arts in every media.*

A Romano-British bronze
face mask, from a vessel,
circa 1st–2nd century AD,
1in (25mm) high.
£30–35 *ANG*

An enamelled belt fitting, of
disc form with rear loop, from
Cambridgeshire, excellent
condition with much enamelling
remaining, circa 1st century
BC/AD, 1in (25mm) diam.
£30–40 *ANG*

A Roman bronze handle and boar figure for an iron knife, in the Celtic style, complete, with very fine definition and detail, 1½in (37mm) long.
£65–75 *ANG*

A Roman bronze 'knee' brooch from the Balkans, circa 2nd century AD, 1¼in (33mm) long.
£20–25 *ANG*

An enamelled brooch, the centre disc enamelled in blue with a red star in a hexagonal sunburst pattern, pin missing, circa 2nd century AD, ¾in (20mm) diam.
£30–40 *ANG*

A bronze finger ring, with carnelian gemstone engraved with a male portrait head, excellent condition, circa 2nd century AD, ¾in (20mm) diam.
£75–85 *ANG*

A Roman gold ring with inscribed carnelian bezel, perfect condition, circa 2nd–3rd century AD, 1in (25mm) diam.
£300–350 *HEL*

A Romano-British bronze 'sawfish' brooch, some red enamelling, found Midlands, pin and chain missing, circa 2nd–3rd century AD, 1in (30mm) long.
£20–25 *ANG*

A Roman Empire bronze stud, with silver bust of Minerva in fancy work border within beaded frame, ¼in (10mm) diam.
£65–75 *ANG*

A Romano-British bronze pendant/brooch, found Warwickshire, 1in (25mm) diam.
£20–25 *ANG*

A Romano-British bronze brooch, with glass 'gem', found Avon, circa 3rd century AD, 1in (25mm) diam.
£45–50 *ANG*

A Romano-British bronze crossbow brooch, circa 4th century AD, 2½in (65mm) long.
£25–30 *ANG*

A late Roman/Early Saxon gold pendant, circa 4th–5th century AD, 1in (25mm) diam.
£90–100 *ANG*

A Romano-British silver crossbow brooch, minus pin, circa 4th century AD, 1½in (40mm) long.
£25–30 *ANG*

A cruciform brooch, with small head-plate without wings, pin missing, circa 5th century AD, 3in (7.5cm) long.
£90–100 *ANG*

An Anglo-Saxon cruciform brooch, pin missing, circa 5th–6th century AD, 2½in (60mm) long.
£50–60 *ANG*

An Anglo-Saxon bronze saucer brooch, with facing stylised male face and full gilding, pin missing, circa 5th–6th century AD, ¾in (20mm) diam.
£55–65 *ANG*

A silver finger ring, with square bezel decorated with 2 large annulets, found in Cambridgeshire, circa 6th century AD, ¾in (20mm) diam.
£75–85 *ANG*

A lead steelyard weight, with bronze casing, wear and holed to base, with green patina, circa 13thC, 2½in (65mm) high.
£550–650 *TMA*

A zoomorphic bronze sword belt hook, in the form of a serpent, circa 13th–15thC, 2in (50mm) long.
£45–50 *ANG*

A bronze annular brooch, with talismanic inscription, pin missing, circa 13th–14thC, ½in (15mm) diam.
£25–35 *ANG*

A sword or dagger pommel, scent stopper type, decorated with flutes, found Dorset, late 15thC, ¾in (20mm) diam.
£30–35 *ANG*

A silver annular brooch, with styled pin, c1450, ½in (12mm) diam.
£45–50 *ANG*

A silver ring, with bezel in the form of a large gothic 'R' and cable hoop, from medieval Southampton, c1375–1425, ¾in (22mm) diam.
£150–180 *ANG*

A Tudor bronze crotal animal bell, c1550, 2in (50mm) diam.
£6-8 *BSA*

Sculptures & Figures

A Mycenaean pottery idol, with West Asian influences, small chips to base, otherwise excellent condition, circa 1400–1200BC, 4½in (11.5cm) high.
£400–500 *HEL*

An Egyptian polychrome wooden mummy mask, with details in black, circa 11th–8th century BC, 9½in (24cm) high.
£600–700 *BSA*

An ancient Egyptian wood sarcophagus mask, with headdress and much of the original gesso-painted decoration, circa 500–400BC, 10in (25.5cm) high.
£525–575 *BSA*

l. A Romano-Egyptian terracotta figure with exaggerated phallus, 1st century BC–2nd century AD, 3½in (9cm) high.
£180–200 *HEL*

An ancient Egyptian faïence ushabti from the Ptolemaic period, circa 3rd–1st century BC, 4in (10cm) high.
£40–45 *BSA*

Three Syrian pottery votive animal head fragments, 1st century BC, 2in (5cm) high.
£20–25 each *HEL*

Four Egyptian faïence ushabti fragments, 1st century BC, 3–5in (7.5–12.5cm)
£60–70 each *HEL*

Ushabti are small statuettes of figures which were deposited in the tombs of mummies.

ART DECO
Ceramics

A Beswick green shaded pottery vase, 1930s, 7½in (19cm) high.
£10–12 *MEG*

A Wedgwood teapot, decorated with bands of yellow and ochre and gold rims, c1930, 6in (15cm) high.
£20–30 *CSA*

Cross Reference
Ceramics Section
---

r. A Shelley Regency shape tea service, painted with bands in tones of green, printed marks, pattern No. 12168, c1930.
£180–220 *WL*

A Burleigh jug, outlined in black, with green leaf design, 1930s, 6¼in (16cm) wide.
£12–15 *WAC*

A Myott candlestick, with blue base, c1930, 3½in (9cm) high.
£10–15 *CSA*

A Carlton bathing belle dish, 1920s, 4¼in (11cm) long.
£80–100 *G&CC*

A Royal Lancastrian ceramic plaque, c1928–38, 11in (28cm) diam.
£200–230 *RAC*

Clocks & Barometers

An Art Deco brass-cased 8-day timepiece, with separate ink pot, on marble base, c1920, 24in (61cm) wide.
£180–200 *TPA*

An Art Deco burr-oak wall clock, by Gubelin, with 18-day movement, c1930, 14½in (37cm) high.
£300–350 *P*

An Art Deco alabaster and chrome barometer, 1930s, 6in (15cm) high.
£20–25 *GIN*

Glass

An Art Deco iridescent gold glass vase, with 'cracked' finish, American, c1920, 7in (18cm) high.
£300–400 *ANO*

An Art Deco cocktail set, comprising decanter and 6 glasses, with anchor motifs, silver overlay rims and top, 1930s, decanter 7in (18cm) high.
£150–170 *BEV*

An Art Deco blue pressed glass vase, c1930, 6in (15cm) high.
£20–25 *PC*

An Art Deco glass cocktail set, comprising decanter and 6 glasses, enamelled with black with geometric design, 1930s, decanter 10in (25.5cm) high.
£500–600 *ASA*

An Art Deco glass sweet jar, c1930, 9in (23cm) high.
£30–40 *JUN*

Lighting

l. A pair of Art Deco chrome lamps, with original parchment shades, 1930s 14in (35.5cm) wide.
£220–250 *HarC*

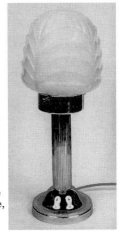

FURTHER READING

*Miller's Art Nouveau
& Art Deco Buyers Guide,*
Miller's Publications, 1995

---

r. A pair of Art Deco chrome lamps, with milk glass globe, 1930s, 15in (38cm) high.
£180–220 *ML*

Metalware

An Art Deco gold, silver and eggshell finish cigarette case, 1930s, 4½in (11.5cm) long.
£500–550 SUC

An Art Deco silver cigarette box, initialled and with reeded and machine-turned decoration, stamped 'Harrods', Birmingham 1936, 7in (18cm) long.
£275–325 Bea(E)

An Art Deco enamelled metal cigarette box, 1930s, 3in (7.5cm) wide.
£55–65 RAC

An Art Deco pull-out silvertone and enamel Princess compact, with lid and tassel, inner lid sprung to flip up on opening, Japanese, 1930s, 2¾ x 2¼in (7 x 5.5cm).
£50–60 PC

An Art Deco gilt lorgnette, with a spring clip, 1930s, 3½in (9cm) long.
£250–275 WIM

Statuettes & Decorative Figures

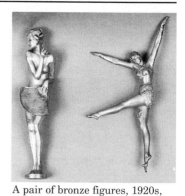

A pair of French spelter bookends, c1920, 7in (18cm) long.
£320–360 SSW

An Art Deco style spelter bas-relief of a runner, on marble base, signed 'R. Delandre', c1930, 12in (30.5cm) high.
£80–100 SSW

A pair of bronze figures, 1920s, 10in (25.5cm) high:
l. Lorenzl fan dancer.
£900–1,100
r. Chiparus 'Dancer of Olynthus'.
£2,200–2,500 SWO

l. An Art Deco bronze elephant, on a marble dish, Austrian, c1920, 10in (25.5cm) diam.
£400–450 ANO

r. An Art Deco bronze marble and gilt-metal inkwell, c1920, 10in (25.5cm) wide.
£300–350 WeH

ART NOUVEAU
Ceramics

A Brannam green bowl,
c1890, 6¼in (16cm) diam.
£60–80 *ANO*

A Minton pottery
vase, with peacock
design, c1890,
12in (30.5cm) high.
£180–250 *ANO*

An Art Nouveau
Continental porcelain
vase, with silver
overlay, c1900,
7in (18cm) high.
£130–150 *ANO*

An Amphora porcelain
ewer, Austrian, c1900,
8¾in (22cm) high.
£200–250 *ANO*

r. A Moorcroft
Macintyre biscuit
barrel, decorated with
irises in tones of yellow
and blue on a cobalt
blue background, EPNS
mounts and cover,
printed Macintyre
mark and signed in
green 'W.M.', c1900,
5¾in (14.5cm) high.
£700–850 *WL*

An Amphora vase,
Austrian, c1910,
10¼in (26cm) high.
£200–250 *ANO*

Clocks

An Art Nouveau
porcelain clock,
Austrian, c1900,
8in (20cm) high.
£200–250 *ANO*

An Art Nouveau
fruitwood and mother-
of-pearl inlaid clock,
with Arabic numerals,
early 20thC,
9½in (24cm) high.
£200–250 *P(Ba)*

An Art Nouveau oak
striking mantel clock,
of tulip baluster form,
inlaid with brass
stylised foliage,
12in (30.5cm) high.
£150–200 *GAK*

An Art Nouveau silver
miniature clock, with
enamel face, Birmingham
1905, 3¼in (8cm) high,
with leather case.
£170–230 *P(EA)*

Cross Reference
Clocks

Glass

An Almaric Walter *pâte de verre* figural bowl, in pale lemon and amber streaked with blue, with twin-handles fashioned as a cat and a dog, c1900, 5in (13cm) high.
£1,200–1,400 *P*

A Tiffany Studios bronze-mounted glass inkstand, c1900, 3½in (9cm) diam.
£100–150 *ZEI*

A pair of Art Nouveau blue glass spill vases, with WMF metal mounts, c1900–10, 3in (7.5cm) high.
£180–200 *RAC*

An Art Nouveau silvered-copper tobacco jar, designed by Edward Spencer for the Artificers' Guild, c1900, 7in (18cm) high.
£180–200 *ZEI*

Metalware

An Art Nouveau brass cigarette box, with locks at each end, c1900, 10in (25.5cm) wide.
£130–150 *CHe*

The locks at each end were to prevent servants stealing the cigarettes.

A WMF metal-mounted green glass decanter, with metal stopper, the metal mounts with female figures bathing in a river at the base, c1900, 15½in (39.5cm) high.
£700–800 *Mit*

An Arts and Crafts brass box, with lining, monogrammed 'C.D.E.', Dutch, c1900, 5½in (14cm) wide.
£250–300 *ANO*

An Art Nouveau wood and brass tobacco box, decorated with trees in a forest setting, Bavarian, c1900, 4in (10.5cm) high.
£150–180 *P*

An Alvin & Co silver overlaid green glass vase, dated Oct 30 1904, American, 14in (35.5cm) high.
£2,000–2,500 *SFL*

An Art Nouveau style pewter box, c1900, 8in (20cm) diam.
£250–280 *SUC*

An Orivit pewter biscuit tin, German, c1900, 7½in (19cm) wide.
£250–280 *SUC*

Select Glossary of Terms & Makers

Artificers' Guild: London based metalworking firm (1901–42) founded by painter and silversmith Nelson Dawson.

Kayserzinn: Pewter manufactured by the German company Kayser Söhne (1885–c1904).

Liberty Tudric Ware: Range of pewter manufactured for Liberty from 1903 to c1930. Archibald Knox was the most prominent designer of Tudric ware and also designed for Liberty's Cymric range of silver and metalware.

Orivit: Orivit pewter was produced by Rheinische Bronzegeisserei from the early 1900s. The company was bought by WMF.

WMF: Württembergische Metallwarenfabrik, German metal foundry, established in 1880, leading producers of Art Nouveau-style Continental pewter, works were electroplated and predominantly decorative.

An Art Nouveau style copper coal bin, with applied foliate brass decoration, on 3 brass paw feet, late 19thC, 14in (35.5cm) diam.
£130–160 *DA*

A WMF pewter sweetmeat dish, c1900, 8in (21cm) wide.
£85–95 *WAC*

An Art Nouveau Continental cake tray, depicting a Maiden on a shell, c1900, 7in (18cm) wide.
£175–200 *ZEI*

An Art Nouveau style copper wall light, with original Holophane shade, c1910, 13in (33cm) wide.
£120–140 *ML*

Named after its inventor, Holophane was a prismatic pressed glass used for lampshades to reflect and maximise the light without producing glare. The name can sometimes be found impressed on the neck of the shade.

An Orivit pewter dish, c1900, 11in (28cm) wide.
£65–75 *WAC*

r. An Edwardian silver liqueur tray, with single handle and six glasses, by Walker & Hall, Sheffield 1907, 12in (30.5cm) wide.
£275–325 *WL*

A WMF liqueur set, c1900, 12¼in (18cm) wide.
£175–195 *WAC*

A Kayserzinn pewter liqueur set, c1905, 14in (35.5cm) wide.
£250–280 *SUC*

An Art Nouveau silver-plated on copper double inkwell, German, c1900, 10in (25.5cm) wide.
£450–550 *ANO*

An Art Nouveau pewter inkstand, with 2 glass inkwells, c1900, 8in (20cm) wide.
£110–130 *PCh*

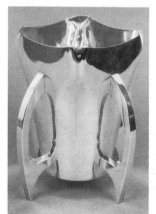

An Art Nouveau silver four-handled cup, with square rim and angular handles, Sheffield 1907, 6in (15cm) high.
£350–400 *WeH*

A Tudric pewter dish, c1900, 13½in (34cm) diam.
£35–40 *WAC*

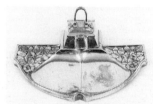

A Kayserzinn pewter inkstand, c1900, 8in (20cm) wide.
£100–150 *ASA*

An Art Nouveau pewter buckle, set with amethyst cabochons, c1900, 4in (10cm) wide.
£120–150 *ASA*

r. An Art Nouveau silver inkstand, with an enamelled portrait head, c1900, 2⅜in (7cm) high.
£350–400 *ASA*

Statuettes

An Art Nouveau silver photograph frame, depicting a lady picking apples, c1900, 11in (28cm) high.
£230–270 *GAZE*

l. An Egyptianesque group, by Gaston Leroux, depicting a musician on a stone statue of a Pharoah, c1890, 13½in (34cm) high.
£400–450 *P*

Gaston Veuvenot Leroux was born in Paris in 1854, and studied under Jouffroy and C. Deloye before becoming a member of the Société des Artistes Français in 1883. He won a travelling scholarship and several bronze medals from the Paris Expositions of 1885, 1889 and 1900, specialising in busts and statuettes of artistic comtemporaries.

An Art Nouveau electrotype bronze figure, c1900, 13½in (34cm) high.
£200–250 *WAC*

AUTOMOBILIA

A Peugeot dealers' double-sided enamel sign, 1920s, 19 x 39in (48 x 99cm).
£250–300 *JUN*

A car vanity mirror with clock, 1930s, 3½ x 5in (9 x 12.5cm).
£20–25 *GIN*

A Triumph Herald 1200 advertising brochure, 1959, 8¼ x 11¾in (21 x 30cm).
£8–10 *GIN*

A Shell glass petrol pump globe, with red lettering, 1930s, 22in (56cm) high.
£200–300 *JUN*

A Pink Paraffin pump globe, c1960, 14in (35.5cm) diam.
£60–80 *JUN*

FURTHER READING
Miller's Collectors Cars Price Guide, Miller's Publications October 1997

A *Motor Industry* magazine, August 1954, 9 x 6in (30 x 15cm).
£3–4 *SVB*

A Renault dealers' enamel sign, c1935, 45in (114cm) high.
£100–125 *JUN*

A collection of car key rings, 1960s–1970s, 1¼ x 2½in (3 x 6.5cm).
£2–3 each *COB*

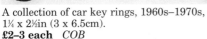

BABY COLLECTABLES
Bottles & Infant Feeding

This year Miller's devotes a special section to objects created for babies from the 19th to the 20th century, beginning with infant feeding. The earliest items shown are blue and white earthenware pap boats and bottles, much sought after by collectors today.

Many Georgian and Victorian mothers would not or could not breast feed and the alternatives were wet nurses or hand-feeding. Pap was a mixture of bread or rice flour and milk – usually asses, since cow's milk was considered too indigestible. It was served from a ceramic vessel with either a pinched lip or a spout; a sponge inside controlled the flow of milk but also acted as a magnet for germs. Poor hygiene and inappropriate feeding were major causes of high infant mortality in the 19th century. The mass-produced flat, circular glass bottles, that gradually replaced ceramic containers even gained the nickname 'killer bottles' since milk was conducted to the teat through a rubber tube that was almost impossible to clean effectively.

Round flasks were supplanted by boat-shaped bottles with a teat at one end and a valve at the other. Water could run straight through and they could be cleaned far more easily. The examples illustrated date from the 1920s, by which time infant feeding and childcare had become a major commercial concern. Firms such as Allenbury's provided ready-made foods and other products for every stage of infant development, and the baby industry expanded still further after 1945.

In the post-war baby boom there was a growing emphasis on child welfare. The new National Health Service provided help and advice for expectant and nursing mothers and the under fives, and thanks to improved health care and nutrition the new generation of post-war children was bigger and stronger than ever before.

In the late 19th century in poor areas such as London's East End, over 50 per cent of children died before the age of five. By the 1960s, the national infant mortality rate had plummeted to 21.7 for every 1,000 live births.

A Ridgway's Humphreys Clock series pap boat, depicting Little Nell with her grand-father, c1840, 3½in (9cm) long.
£100–120 *GN*

A Deakin & Bailey infant feeding bottle, decorated with Villa Scenery pattern, c1840, 7in (18cm) long.
£350–400 *GN*

This type of bottle was filled through the hole in the top and the flow of milk was regulated by covering this hole with the thumb.

A Norfolk Food of Strength tin, c1905, 3in (7.5cm) wide.
£15–20 *HUX*

A Norfolk Food of Strength cardboard shop display sign, inscribed 'My sole support, age 8 months, weight 29lbs – Expectation – Realization – Satisfaction', c1905, 18 x 26½in (45.5 x 67cm).
£40–50 *HUX*

l. A 'The Alexandra' glass feeding bottle, inscribed Maw Son & Sons, London, 1920s, 5½in (14cm) high.
£15–20 *HUX*

These bottles were named after Queen Alexandra.

A 'The Swan' glass feeding bottle, with screw top, 1920s, 5¾in (14.5cm) high.
£12–15 *DOL*

An Allen & Hanburys *Infant Feeding and Management* booklet for new mothers, 1925, 8 x 5½in (20.5 x 14cm).
£6–8 *HUX*

This booklet contains feeding and health-care advice along with advertisements for Allenburys' infant products.

An Allenburys food measuring jug, enamelled in green, 1920s, 5in (12.5cm) high.
£10–12 *SVB*

r. A Hygienic glass feeding bottle, c1920–30, 7½in (19cm) long.
£10–15 *DOL*

An Allenburys glass feeding bottle, with original box, 1920s, 7in (18cm) long.
£35–40 *DOL*

An Allenburys Rusks tin, inscribed 'An Ideal Food for Young Children', 1920s, 7½in (19cm) high.
£18–20 *HUX*

A Miniature Guildford glass feeding bottle, with spare teat, 1930s, 6½in (16.5cm) long.
£10–12 *GIN*

Rubber teats first appeared in the mid-19thC supplanting those made of cloth, leather and also preserved cows teats.

Cross Reference
Colour Review

An Ostermilk No. 2 full-cream milk food tin, 16oz, 1959, 5½in (12.5cm) high.
£7–10 *HUX*

Many post-WWII food products can be precisely dated by their 'use-by date', found here on the base of the tin.

A Hodders glass caster oil bottle, with cork stopper, 1930s, 5in (12.5cm) high.
£4–6 *FAM*

A Griptight heat-resisting glass feeder with narrow neck, 1950s, 7in (18cm) high.
£10–12 *HUX*

A child's plastic beaker, depicting Goofy, 1950s, 6¼in (16cm) high.
£15–20 *Orig*

Clothing

An Ayrshire hand-embroidered boy's christening robe, c1840.
£100–120 *CCO*

This robe is complete with triangular tab indicating that it was made for a boy. A girl's dress would not have a tab.

A Victorian christening dress, with lace inserts and tie belt, 38in (96.5cm) long.
£50–60 *MAC*

An Edwardian cream linen and silk baby's embroidered cape, 13in (33cm) long.
£24–28 *MAC*

l. An Edwardian nightdress, with appliqué and pin tucks, 28½in (72.5cm) long.
£28–32 *MAC*

A baby's cotton voile overall with appliqué and lace trim, 19thC.
£10–12 *Ech*

A pair of embroidered cotton robes, suitable for twins, c1900, 36in (91.5cm) long.
£90–100 *CCO*

A baby's embroidered voile nightdress, with lace trim, 1920s.
£20–25 *Ech*

A child's romper suit, with white cotton top and blue shorts, c1940–50, 22in (56cm) long.
£10–15 *HarC*

A blue lawn dress with white embroidery, 1940s, 16in (40.5cm) long.
£12–15 *JV*

r. An Edwardian cream net infant's jacket, with silk lining, 13in (33cm) long.
£24–28 *MAC*

Bonnets

A baby's embroidered bonnet, with lace trim, 1870s, 10in (25.5cm) long.
£15–18 *Ech*

A Victorian child's handmade cotton bonnet, to fit 1–2 years old.
£20–24 *CCO*

A Victorian baby's hand crocheted bonnet, c1900, to fit 3–6 months.
£14–18 *CCO*

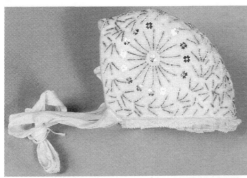

l. A baby's velvet bonnet, with silver sequins, Continental, 1930s, 6in (15cm) wide.
£20–25 *JV*

A box of child's socks by E. Torras, Calella, with original box, Spanish, 1940s, 5½ x 3in (14 x 7.5cm).
£18–20 *Ech*

Shoes & Socks

A pair of Victorian child's leather clogs, with laces, in worn condition, 5½in (14cm) long.
£60–75 *ANV*

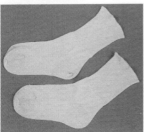

A pair of child's silk socks, c1920, foot 4¼in (11.5cm) long.
£8–10 *LB*

Baby's Gas Mask

A baby's gas mask, 1939–45, 18in (45.5cm) high.
£125–150 *GIN*

At the beginning of WWII all children were issued with gas masks that they had to carry with them at all times. Masks were fitted by the ARP wardens and for very young babies the masks enclosed the whole body

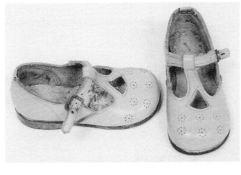

l. A pair of Globe Trotter baby's shoes, 1950s, size 4.
£12–15 *Ech*

Nursery Ceramics

Over the past five to ten years, collectors have been showing increasing interest in nursery ceramics. 'Some focus on a major artist such as Mabel Lucie Attwell or Beatrix Potter, while others concentrate on a favourite character such as Winnie-the-Pooh or Rupert Bear,' says dealer and collector Adam Lovejoy. Because these ceramics were created for children, finding wares in good condition and complete sets can be difficult, although there are some exceptions. 'Mabel Lucie Attwell pieces are often surprisingly well-preserved,' notes Lovejoy. 'They were expensive at the time – the kind of thing given for christening presents. Many parents thought they were really far too good for the children so kept them well out of reach.' In contrast the nursery rhyme ceramics devised by William Savage Cooper for Doulton tended to be bought by the same upper- and middle-class families but for daily use in the nursery. 'Condition can be more of a problem but William Savage Cooper is well worth looking out for,' advises Lovejoy. 'He hasn't had the exposure of some of the more famous names in the field and I think he is still undervalued.'

In the 19th century children's ceramics were often miniature versions of adult ware and also came with religious and educational designs as well as infant-oriented pictures. The 20th century saw the increased use of characters from children's literature and films and the introduction of famous ranges of nursery ware, such as Royal Doulton's Bunnykins, created by Barbara Vernon Bailey in 1934 and popular with generations of children.

'Nostalgia is the major spur for many collectors and the quality of image is all important when it comes to value,' says Lovejoy. 'Obviously perfect pieces attract the best prices but a fine picture on a chipped plate tends to be more desirable than an undamaged vessel with a scratched or badly worn image.'

Television and video have had a huge effect on the market for nursery ware, particularly when it comes to focusing on favourite characters. Lovejoy's tips for collectables of the future include ceramics celebrating Rupert Bear, Thomas the Tank Engine, Noddy and Paddington, the bear from darkest Peru, who celebrates his 40th anniversary in 1998. 'You want to pick classics,' concludes Lovejoy, 'characters who have been enjoyed by children in the past and will continue to be loved into the next millennium.'

19th Century

A child's plate inscribed 'Quarrelsome Children', an illustration from *The Cowslip*, by Elizabeth Turner, published in 1811, c1820–40, 6½in (16.5cm) diam.
£25–35 *OD*

An early Victorian child's plate, black and white transfer printed with moral message 'Good Thoughts should always be encouraged to prevent Bad Actions', 5¼in (13.5cm) diam.
£60–70 *ANT*

A Victorian child's cup, decorated with a picture of children racing penny farthing bicycles, handle restored, 3in (7.5cm) high.
£20–25 *LF*

r. A child's mug, with transfer print depicting the history of 'The House that Jack Built', c1840, 2½in (6.5cm) high.
£60–80 *IW*

A Staffordshire child's blue and white transfer printed part dinner service, comprising 37 pieces, 19thC.
£700–800 *TMA*

A Victorian child's plate, with black and white transfer print depicting a kite flying scene, 5½in (14cm) diam.
£55–65 *ANT*

A child's mug, with black transfer printed 'K', c1850, 2¾in (7cm) high.
£40–60 *IW*

K: Kiosk, meaning summer house.

A child's mug, with green transfer printed verse, 19thC, 3in (7.5cm) high.
£20–30 *OD*

l. A child's plate, with coloured transfer print, depicting Sir Robert Peel, c1850, 6¼in (16cm) diam.
£140–160 *IW*

r. A child's plate, with red transfer print 'Sacred History of Joseph and his Brethren', c1850, 6½in (16.5cm) diam.
£40–60 *IW*

A Victorian transfer printed nursery plate, 3¾in (9.5cm) diam.
£40–45 *ANV*

A child's plate, with transfer printed country scene, sponged design on borders, c1860, 7½in (19cm) diam.
£40–60 *IW*

A child's alphabet mug, 'C for Chit Chat', c1880, 2¼in (5.5cm) high.
£40–60 *IW*

A child's plate, with black transfer print 'England', c1870, 7¼in (18.5cm) diam.
£60–80 *IW*

A child's mug, with blue transfer print of a child feeding rabbits, c1890, 2¾in (7cm) high.
£40–60 *IW*

A Copeland Spode child's blue and white teaset, transfer printed with zoological subjects, comprising teapot and cover, milk jug, sugar basin and cover, slop bowl, 6 cups, 6 saucers and 6 plates, teapot handle repaired, late 19thC.
£450–500 *TMA*

A child's mug, with blue transfer 'T was a Tinker and mended a pot', c1890, 3in (7.5cm) high.
£40–60 *IW*

20th Century

An Ashstead Potteries Winnie the Pooh series teapot, c1930, 7in (18cm) wide.
£150–180 *WWY*

An Ashstead Potteries Winnie the Pooh series jug, c1930, 4in (10cm) high.
£50–70 *WWY*

l. A Royal Doulton mug, Peter Piper, designed by William Savage Cooper, 1906–39, 2¾in (7cm) high.
£60–80 *WWY*

A Royal Doulton nursery rhyme plate, 'Where are you going to my pretty maid?', designed by William Savage Cooper, 1906–39, 7in (18cm) diam.
£40–60 *WWY*

> **Miller's is a price GUIDE not a price LIST**

An Ashstead Potteries Winnie the Pooh series cup and saucer, c1930, saucer 6in (15cm) diam.
£60–80 *WWY*

A Corona Ware child's dinner service, 'Poor Bunny Bobtail', consisting of 6 dinner plates, 5 plates, 3 meat dishes, 2 tureens and gravy boat, 1935–37.
£55–65 *CMF*

A pair of porcelain circus plates, H & Co, Bavaria, c1920, 6in (15cm) diam.
£20 *AnS*

A Royal Doulton child's plate, Alice in Wonderland, 1906–39, 8in (20.5cm) diam.
£50–60 *WWY*

A Grimwades Beatrix Potter jug, depicting Peter's friends, c1926, 4in (10cm) high.
£80–100 *WWY*

This series was made in various sizes, miniature, small, medium and large. This jug is from the larger size set.

> **Cross Reference**
> Colour Review

A Royal Doulton Bunnykins bread and butter plate, designed by Barbara Vernon Bailey, c1937–52, 10in (25.5cm) diam.
£90–100 *WWY*

l. A Midwinter bread and butter plate, with faces around border, c1925, 10½in (26.5cm) diam.
£80–100 *WWY*

A Grimwades Beatrix Potter cup and saucer, depicting Tom Kitten, medium size, c1926, plate 4¾in (12cm) diam.
£80–100 *WWY*

A Grimwades Beatrix Potter trio, depicting Peter Rabbit, miniature size, c1926, plate 4in (10cm) diam.
£100–150 *WWY*

A Shelley Mabel Lucie Attwell
teapot, c1926–45, 9in (23cm) wide.
£250–300 *WWY*

A Shelley Mabel Lucie
Attwell stemmed egg cup,
c1926–45, 2½in (6.5cm) high.
£50–60 *WWY*

A Shelley Mabel Lucie
Attwell egg cup, c1926–45,
1¾in (4.5cm) high.
£70–90 *WWY*

A Shelley Mabel Lucie Attwell egg cup
and stand, depicting fairies playing,
c1926–45, stand 4in (10cm) diam.
£70–90 *WWY*

A Shelley Mabel Lucie Attwell Boo Boo set,
c1926–45, jug 6in (15cm) high.
£450–500 *WWY*

A Shelley Mabel Lucie Attwell cup
and saucer, 'Quacky the Sailor',
c1926–45, saucer 6in (15cm) diam.
£80–100 *WWY*

Locate the Source
*The source of each
illustration in Miller's
can be found by checking
the code letters below
each caption with the
Key to Illustrations.*

A Shelley Mabel Lucie
Attwell napkin ring
depicting 5 different scenes,
c1929, 2in (5cm) diam.
£75–85 *PC*

A Shelley Mabel Lucie
Attwell nursery plate,
c1930, 7in (18cm) diam.
£65–75 *PC*

A Shelley Mabel Lucie Attwell
nursery bowl, 1927–30,
8in (20.5cm) diam.
£55–65 *PC*

A Wedgwood Rupert bowl, 1980s,
6in (15cm) diam.
£15–20 *RAC*

Nursery Furniture & Accessories

A beechwood baby walker, early 19thC, 18in (45cm) high.
£250–275 *SPa*

A French ash high chair, with rush seat, c1830, 33in (84cm) high.
£175–225 *CPA*

A Victorian child's mahogany high chair, with cane seat and back, c1850, 35in (90cm) high.
£650–700 *ChS*

A bergère cradle and stand, late 19thC, 35in (90cm) long.
£100–120 *CaC*

l. A child's cot, with canework canopy and sides, raised on turned mahogany supports with splayed legs and bun feet, 19thC, 41in (104cm) long.
£450–550 *AG*

r. A child's high chair, converts into a low chair, c1910, 40in (101.5cm) high.
£180–210 *WCa*

Prams

A Victorian pram, 36in (95cm) long.
£450–500 *JUN*

A wicker work pram, with leather hood, c1890, 60in (152.5cm) long.
£450–500 *JUN*

> **Warning!**
> Items illustrated may not comply with EC safety regulations and must not be used for their original purpose!

r. A wicker pram, probably Dutch, 1930s, 40in (104cm) long.
£180–220 *JUN*

A Leveson wooden pram, with leather hood, c1915, 41in (104cm) long.
£150–200 *JUN*

Rattles

A George III silver rattle/whistle, with bright-cut engraved latticework and foliate decoration, with 2 rows of 3 dependent bells and coral teething bar, repaired, by Joseph Taylor, Birmingham, c1800, 4½in (11.5cm) long.
£225–275 *P(O)*

A George III silver rattle/whistle, the frill with 6 dependent bells, integral loop fitting and coral teething bar, by Theodosia Ann Atkins, 1816, 4¾in (12cm) long.
£400–500 *P(O)*

A Victorian silver and coral baby's rattle, by George Unite, Birmingham 1843, 4in (10cm) long.
£500–600 *BEX*

A silver and mother-of-pearl Father Christmas rattle, by Crissford & Norris, Birmingham 1929, 5in (12.5cm) long.
£500–550 *THOM*

Rattles and Coral

From ancient times coral has been considered a powerful charm for children. The Romans hung coral charms around babies necks to ward off sickness. Writing in 1594, Sir Hugh Platt claimed that the coral was a reliable indicator of health, turning pale when the infant was ill and regaining its colour on the child's recovery. Even as late as the 19thC, powdered coral was recommended as a cure for whooping cough. Coral was often used for teething sticks, since it was believed to sooth sore gums and protect against the evil eye. Similarly the bells often found on rattles were not just decorative or designed to entertain the baby, but their noise was thought to frighten off malignant spirits.

A gilt baby's rattle, with whistle and bone sucker, by Alphonse Lepicier, 33 Rue Rambuteau, Paris 1850, 6in (15cm) long.
£600–650 *TC*

l. A silver rattle, with ivory teething ring, Chester 1892, 3in (7.5cm) long.
£75–85 *PC*

A Victorian silver rattle/whistle, of knopped form, with embossed floral roundel decoration, 2 rows of dependent bells, integral loop fitting, coral teething bar, mouthpiece damaged, Birmingham 1860, 4½in (11.5cm) long.
£180–220 *P(O)*

r. A silver and ivory baby's rattle, by George Unite & Sons, Birmingham 1920, 5in (12.5cm) long.
£325–365 *BEX*

Silver & Metalware

A George IV child's silver mug, by William Sharp, London 1826, 3in (7.5cm) high.
£325–350 *BEX*

A Victorian silver christening mug, by G. Richards & E. Brown, London 1864, 3¼in (8.5cm) high.
£250–300 *BEX*

A Victorian silver christening mug, by Walter & John Barnard, London 1890, 3½in (9cm) high.
£200–225 *BEX*

A Victorian silver pincushion in the form of a rocking cradle, registered No. 291605, M & W, Sheffield 1896, 2¼in (5.5cm) long.
£180–200 *GH*

A Victorian baby's silver-backed brush, by C. Saunders & F. Shepherd, Birmingham 1900, 3½in (9cm) wide
£50–60 *BEX*

A child's silver-plated tray, with engraved pictures, by Reeds & Barton, c1920, 16½in (42cm) wide.
£250–275 *SFL*

A silver spoon and pusher, in original box, by E.V., Sheffield 1940, both 4in (10cm) long.
£60–70 *BEX*

A silver 'Old Mother Hubbard' christening spoon and pusher, with original box, Glasgow 1930, spoon 4in (10cm) long.
£200–225 *BEX*

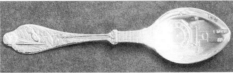

A silver christening spoon, depicting a stork holding a baby in its wings, the bowl engraved with a pendulum clock, by Docker & Burn Ltd, 1928, 6in (15cm) long.
£75–85 *BEX*

The child's date of birth can be engraved on the clock face.

An Art Deco style christening mug, by Walker & Hall, Sheffield 1944, 3½in (9cm) high.
£150–200 *BEX*

A child's silver plate, depicting characters from *Snow White and the Seven Dwarfs*, hallmarked 1945, 7¼in (18.5cm) diam.
£250–275 *SFL*

A child's chrome feeding dish, c1950–60, 8in (21cm) diam.
£5–10 *HEI*

Washing & Changing

A Staffordshire blue and white ceramic baby bath, on an iron stand, c1890, 16in (40.5cm) long.
£275–300 *GN*

An advertising insert for Pears soap, c1900, 8¾ x 5⅝in (22 x 14.5cm).
£5–7 *HUX*

A German bisque group of children sitting on a potty, c1900–10, 4in (10cm) high.
£65–75 *AnS*

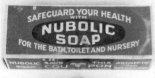

A Nubolic soap, for the bath, toilet and nursery, 1930s, 7in (18cm) wide.
£12–14 *HUX*

Even half a century on, this nursery soap still retains its powerful antiseptic smell.

r. A Cussons White Cross baby powder metal shop sign, mint condition, early 1950s, 15in (38cm) wide.
£8–10 *HUX*

A tin of Sanoid Zinc and Starch dusting powder, 1920s, 3¾in (9.5cm) high.
£10–12 *HUX*

r. A Shelley Mabel Lucie Attwell chamber pot, c1926–1945, 7½in (19cm) diam.
£250–300 *WWY*

A box of 'My Baby Lamb' brass safety pins, with original box, German, c1900, 4¾in (12cm) wide.
£6–8 *HUX*

An Alexandra inhaler, with multi-coloured foliate transfer, late 19thC, 5in (12.5cm) high.
£300–350 *BBR*

A Nut Brown enamel advertising sign, c1910, 30in (76cm) wide.
£40–50 *JUN*

A Black Cat cigarettes vesta case, c1910, 2½in (6.5cm) wide.
£80–100 *GH*

A Greensmith's card advertising sign, c1910, 24in (61cm) wide.
£100–120 *JUN*

A Jossot postcard, for Lejeune Tailleur, signed, c1903, 6in (15cm) high.
£20–30 *SpP*

A Byrrh Tonique Hygienique postcard, c1910, 6in (15cm) high.
£45–55 *SpP*

A Hovis baker's cart, restored, c1920, 70in (178cm) high.
£1,000–1,200 *JUN*

A *Sunlight Household Hints,* c1920, 6in (15cm) high.
£6–8 *COB*

A Dubarry talcum powder tin, 1920s, 4½in (11.5cm) high.
£28–35 *HUX*

A Morning Cheer coffee bag, American, 9½in (24cm) high.
£2–3 *RAD*

l. A McVitie's Digestive Biscuits metal-backed advertising shop display card, c1930, 19in (48.5cm) wide.
£130–150 *RAR*

r. A Susie Cooper hand-painted advertising jug, c1929, 5in (12.5cm) high.
£165–200 *SCA*

An Oxo promotional barometer, inlaid with coloured hardwood, porcelain dial, c1935, 12in (30.5cm) high.
£140–160 *RTw*

A Crawford's biscuit and money box, depicting Lucie Attwell's Fairy House, 8in (20.5cm) high.
£225–250 *HUX*

A Jacob's gypsy caravan biscuit tin, c1937, 7in (18cm) wide.
£220–250 *HUX*

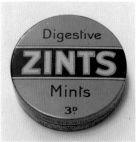

A Zints digestive mints tin, 1940s, 2½in (6.5cm) diam.
£4–5 *FAM*

A packet of Goodall's egg substitute powder, with contents, 1930s, 3in (7.5cm) wide.
£3–5 *SVB*

A Cornish Ware catalogue and price list, 1936–37, 8in (20.5cm) high.
£15–20 *PC*

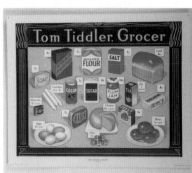

A Tom Tiddler Grocer educational poster, designed for schools, 1950s, 21in (53.5cm) wide.
£4–6 *HUX*

A Federation Self-Raising Flour tin advertising sign, 1940s, 9½in (24cm) high.
£15–20 *SVB*

A C.W.S. biscuit tin, inscribed East West Home's Best, c1950s, 9in (23cm) wide.
£3–5 *GIN*

A Sharps toffee tin, Edward Sharp & Sons Ltd, Maidstone, Kent, c1950s, 9in (23cm) wide.
£12–15 *PPe*

A Bournvita plastic mug,
c1950, 4in (10cm) high.
£25–30 *SVB*

A set of 6 Babycham glasses,
1960s, 11in (28cm) high.
£18–22 *RAD*

A Snoopy tin, marked
'United Feature Syndicate
Inc', 1965, 3½in (9cm) wide.
£4–6 *PPe*

A Farrah's original
Harrogate toffee tin,
1960s, 3in (7.5cm) wide.
£12–18 *DKH*

A Mobiloil bottle carrier, 1950s,
19in (48.5cm) high.
£40–50 *JUN*

A cardboard hat box,
by Moores of England,
c1959, 11in (28cm) high.
£20–30 *JUN*

A Cadbury's Smash Martian
bendy toy, c1967,
6¾in (17cm) high.
£25–30 *HUX*

The Autocar magazine,
advertising Morris Oxford cars,
May 1958, 11½in (29cm) high.
£3–4 *SVB*

A Hornby Dublo cardboard shop
display card, 1960s, 15¾in (40cm) long.
£375–425 *RAR*

A Man from U.N.C.L.E.
bubble gum wrapper, 1960s,
6½in (16.5cm) wide.
£6–8 *CTO*

A coin-operated glass automaton steamship and lighthouse, with musical movement, 19thC, 22½in (57cm) high.
£1,500–1,700 *SAF*

A black dancer amusement machine, by Walter Hart, Kent, c1910, 18in (45.5cm) high.
£1,500–2,000 *HAK*

An electric shock amusement machine, 1920s, 15¾in (40cm) high.
£600–700 *SAF*

An All-Win halfpenny machine, c1920, 26in (66cm) high.
£350–400 *JUN*

A penny-operated cigarette dispenser game of skill, c1930, 29¼in (74cm) high.
£550–650 *BB*

A chrome sample cigarette machine, 1930s, 14in (35.5cm) high.
£150–200 *JUN*

A Lucky Twelve wall machine, 1950s, 31½in (80cm) high.
£450–550 *SAF*

A Mills one-armed bandit, 1950s, 25in (63.5cm) high.
£300–400 *JUN*

A German Beromat wall machine, 1960–70s, 25⅛in (63.5cm) high.
£300–400 *SAF*

A gouache on trimmed
celluloid production set-up,
Alice in Wonderland, signed
by Bob Moore, c1951,
12½in (32cm) wide.
£10,000–12,000 *S(NY)*

An original production cel from
Dumbo, depicting Timothy Mouse,
c1941, 12in (30.5cm) wide.
£1,800–2,000 *AAG*

A full figure
animation maquette,
Quasimodo,
10in (25.5cm) high.
£2,000–2,500 *S(NY)*

An original production cel,
Hiawatha, Little Hiawatha,
1937, 14in (35.5cm) wide.
£1,100–1,200 *AAG*

A quarter scale model peach
with handle, *James and the
Giant Peach,* with portion
of miniature fence and
miniature prop car, 1990s,
peach 19in (48.5cm) high.
£1,100–1,300 *S(NY)*

A gouache on trimmed celluloid
Snow White and the Seven Dwarfs,
c1937, 7½in (19cm) high.
£8,750–9,500 *S(NY)*

An original production cel,
Lady and the Tramp, c1955,
15in (38cm) wide.
£6,000–6,200 *WWA*

An original production cel
101 Dalmations, Cruella DeVil,
c1961, 15in (38cm) wide.
£1,800–2,000 *WWA*

An original production cel
The Jungle Book, c1967,
12in (30.5cm) wide.
£400–500 *WWA*

An original production cel, *Batman
and Robin,* with colour xerox
background, 1970s, 12in (30.5cm) wide.
£100–125 *WWA*

An original production cel,
The Smurfs, 1980s, 12in
(30.5cm) wide.
£40–60 *WWA*

An original production cel,
Winnie the Pooh, late 1980s,
17in (43cm) wide.
£150–175 *WWA*

An Art Deco Pierette print,
by C. E. Shand, 1930s,
5½in (14cm) high.
£6–7 *JMC*

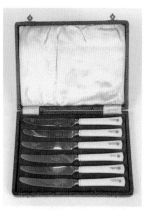

A set of 6 Art Deco Sheffield-plate
tea knives, in original case,
1930s, 8¼in (21cm) wide.
£40–45 *BEV*

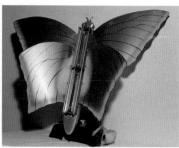

An Art Deco aluminium electric
butterfly fire, c1930, 32in (81.5cm) high.
£200–220 *BKK*

An Art Nouveau hand-painted
trinket pot, Austrian, c1900,
4in (10cm) wide.
£200–250 *ANO*

An Art Nouveau pottery centre-
piece, German, restored, late
19thC, 11in (28cm) high.
£150–200 *MEG*

A Nancy School biscuit
barrel, with gilt pewter lid
and mount, early 20thC,
12in (30.5cm) high.
£300–350 *L&E*

An Art Nouveau cranberry glass
bowl, with EPNS holder and
stand, c1900, 5in (12.5cm) high.
£150–180 *RAC*

A Fielding's Devon ware
vase, c1917, 8in (20cm) high.
£55–65 *WAC*

A Gallé cameo glass vase,
acid-etched with pine
cones, signed, c1900,
11¼in (28.5cm) high.
£2,000–2,200 *P*

An Art Nouveau style copper chamber
stick, c1900, 5in (12.5cm) diam.
£90–100 *WAC*

A Staffordshire child in cradle,
c1810–20, 4in (10cm) long.
£175–225 *TVM*

A Staffordshire figure group,
of a sleeping baby with guardian
angel, 19thC 7¼in (18.5cm) high.
£175–225 *ANT*

A child's painted oak chair,
c1850, 18in (45.5cm) high.
£35–40 *WCa*

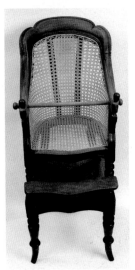

A Victorian child's mahogany
high chair, with cane seat and
back, 37in (94cm) high.
£250–300 *CaC*

A child's silver spoon and fork set,
by Richard Marlin and Ebenezer Hall,
registration mark, London 1870,
6in (15cm) long, with original box.
£125–145 *BEX*

Three Bakelite animal napkin rings,
1930s, 3in (7.5cm) high.
£20–25 each *Orig*

A child's silver and
coral rattle, c1860,
6in (15cm) long.
£350–400 *DIC*

A musical rattle, 1950s,
6½in (16.5cm) high.
£4–6 *DUD*

A Blédine French baby milk
tin, 1940s, 6in (15cm) high.
£12–14 *HUX*

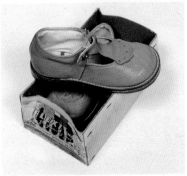

A pair of child's shoes, in original
box, unworn, 1950s, size 7.
£15–18 *Ech*

A ceramic pap feeder, with
The Seated Shepherd pattern,
c1820, 3½in (9cm) long.
£100–120 *GN*

A Bovey Tracey pottery
nursery mug, decorated with
an ice skating scene, c1840,
3in (7.5cm) high.
£225–250 *GN*

A Swansea child's plate,
transfer-printed with
Crucifixion, c1820,
6in (15cm) diam.
£80–100 *IW*

An Ashstead Potteries
Winnie The Pooh series plate,
c1930, 6in (15cm) diam.
£40–50 *WWY*

A Shelley Mabel Lucie
Attwell cup, 1926–45,
4in (10cm) high.
£120–140 *WWY*

A Doulton Bunnykins teapot,
c1937–52, 8½in (21.5cm) wide.
£150–200 *WWY*

A Doulton Bunnykins plate,
c1937–52, 8½in (21.5cm) diam.
£70–90 *WWY*

An *Express Newspapers*
Rupert egg cup, c1986,
2in (5cm) high.
£3–5 *DUD*

A Grimwades Beatrix Potter teapot,
depicting Peter Rabbit, c1926,
6in (15cm) wide.
£200–250 *WWY*

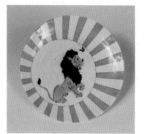

A Mason's Circus plate,
c1960s, 8in (20.5cm) diam.
£85–100 *RAC*

A Midwinter nursery rhyme plate,
c1925, 7in (18cm) diam.
£50–60 *WWY*

A Noddy bowl, 1940s,
6½in (16.5cm) diam.
£18–22 *CMF*

A pair of Shelley Mabel Lucie
Attwell jugs, 1926–45,
largest 6½in (16.5cm) high.
l. **£300–400**
r. **£200–300**   *WWY*

A Shelley Mabel Lucie
Attwell mug, 1926–45,
3in (7.5cm) high.
£75–95   *PC*

A Shelley Mabel Lucie
Attwell nightlight,
1926–45, 8in (20.5cm) high.
£500–600   *WWY*

A Shelley Mabel Lucie Attwell animal
set, including teapot and cream jug,
1926–45, teapot 7in (18cm) high.
l. **£250–300**
r. **£150–200**   *WWY*

A Mabel Lucie Attwell
wooden cut out, 1930s,
7½in (19cm) high.
£10–15   *DOL*

A *Welcome Weekly*
magazine, January 1934,
signs of wear,
8½in (21.5cm) high.
£3–4   *SVB*

l. An Ambassador
Mabel Lucie Attwell
cup and saucer, with
nursery rhyme, c1950s,
plate 6in (15cm) diam.
£40–50   *WWY*

A pair of prints, by Lilian Rowles,
c1930s, 14¾in (37.5cm) high.
£20–30 each   *TAC*

An advertisement for Lux,
c1900, 7in (18cm) high.
£4.50–5.50   *HUX*

A Prince Charles booklet, 1948,
9in (23cm) high.
£3–4   *HUX*

A Minton bourdalou, decorated with floral sheet pattern, c1825, 10in (25.5cm) long.
£400–500 *GN*

A ceramic Willow pattern bidet, c1820, 17in (43cm) wide, in mahogany stand.
£650–750 *GN*

A George III mahogany commode, with dummy drawers, 29½in (75cm) high.
£875–975 *ANT*

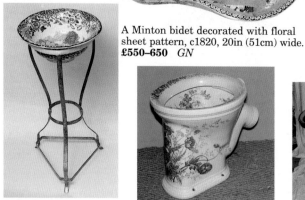

A Minton bidet decorated with floral sheet pattern, c1820, 20in (51cm) wide.
£550–650 *GN*

A ceramic foot bath and jug, decorated with a biblical scene, c1830, bath 20in (51cm) wide.
£3,000–3,300 *GN*

A Staffordshire wash bowl and iron stand, c1840, bowl 14in (35.5cm) diam.
£150–200 *GN*

A Progress wash down lavatory pan, c1890, 16in (40.5cm) high.
£650–750 *POSH*

A copper bath, restored, c1885, 68in (172.5cm) long.
£4,500–5,500 *DRU*

A Mintons slop pail with matching soap dish, late 19thC, pail 11½in (29cm) high.
£30–35 *CaC*

A Staffordshire Milford ware toilet set, late 19thC, bowl 15in (38cm) diam.
£30–40 *CaC*

A French bath, with lily feet,
early 20thC, 65in (165cm) long.
£800–1,000 *POSH*

A Wemyss chamber pot,
decorated with yellow irises,
c1910, 8¾in (22cm) diam.
£150–200 *RdeR*

A tin of Dhaussy bath
powder, c1930,
5in (12.5cm) diam.
£30–35 *HUX*

A Rosenthal soap dish, depicting a risqué
scene, c1950, 5½in (14cm) wide.
£50–65 *GIN*

A bottle of
Dubarry talcum
powder, with
original
box, 1930s, 5½in
(14cm) high.
£18–20 *HUX*

A brass bath and shower mixer,
1930s–50s, 15in (38cm) high.
£180–200 *PJa*

A pair of Goslett & Co brass
taps, 1930s–50s, 7in (18cm) high.
£30–40 *PJa*

A box of Bibby Araby
soap, with original box,
1930s, 4in (10cm) high.
£8–10 *HUX*

A roll of Populex
toilet paper, 1930s,
5in (12.5cm) high.
£6–8 *HUX*

A box of Radox Swan Lake
bath cubes, 1950s,
4½in (11.5cm) wide.
£4–5 *HUX*

A bar of Lifebuoy
soap, 1950s,
3¾in (9.5cm) long.
£5–8 *HUX*

A tin of Harpic lavatory
cleaner, 1950s,
6¾in (17cm) high.
£10–13 *HUX*

Kate Greenaway,
Almanack for 1889,
published by George
Routledge & Sons,
4in (10cm) high.
£70–80 *BAf*

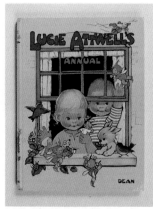

Mabel Lucie Attwell Annual,
published by Dean, 1960s,
10in (25.5cm) high.
£25–35 *WWY*

R Goulburn-Lovell, *Home Interiors,*
5 volumes, 5th edition, Caxton
Publishing Co., c1920–30,
21in (53.5cm) wide.
£850–950 *HB*

Beatrix Potter *A Fierce Bad Rabbit,* a
panoramic books, published by Frederick
Warne & Co, c1906, 4½in (11.5cm) wide.
£200–300 *WWY*

Dante Gabriel *Blessed
Damozel,* c1912,
6in (15cm) high.
£4–5 *TRE*

A Fierce Bad Rabbit, by
Beatrix potter, published by
Frederick Warne & Co,
1916, 5in (12.5cm) high.
£80–100 *WWY*

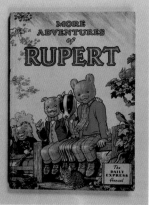

*Nursery Rhyme Picture
Book,* 1940–50,
8in (20.5cm) high.
£10–15 *MRW*

More Adventures of Rupert,
The Daily Express Annual,
1950, 12in (30.5cm) high.
£40–60 *WWY*

The Victor Book for Boys,
1971, 12in (30.5cm) high.
£5–6 *PPe*

Geoffrey Gambado, *Annals of Horsemanship*, c1795, 13½ x 9½in (34.5 x 24cm).
£200–250 *HB*

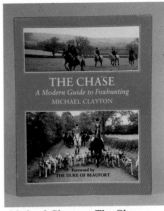

Michael Clayton, *The Chase*, published by Stanley Paul & Co Ltd, 1987, 10½in (26.5cm) high.
£15–20 *JAL*

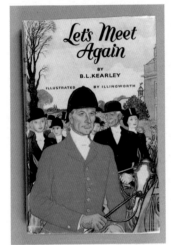

B.L. Kearley, *Let's Meet Again*, published by Ernest Benn Ltd, 1952, 8¾in (22cm) high.
£12–14 *JAL*

Anna Sewell, *Black Beauty*, published by Heirloom Library, 1951, 8in (20.5cm) high.
£6–8 *JAL*

Surtees, *Handley Cross or Mr Jorrock's Hunt*, set of 6, c1895, 6in (15cm) high.
£400–450 *HB*

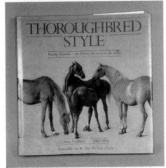

Anne Lambton and John Offen, *Thoroughbred Style*, published by Stanley Paul & Co., Ltd, 1987, 10¾in (27.5cm) high.
£15–20 *JAL*

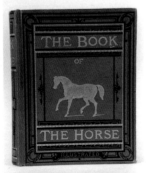

S. Sidney, *The Book of the Horse*, published by Cassell & Co Ltd, c1870,
£550–600 *HB*

Thelwell Goes West, published by Eyre Methuen, 1975, 8½in (21.5cm) high.
£12–15 *JAL*

A magic lantern, c1900,
18in (45.5cm) high.
£200–300 *JUN*

A Sanderson Camera
half plate camera, c1910,
6¼in (16cm) wide.
£200–300 *CaH*

A Sanderson Junior camera,
1920s, 4⅜in (11cm) long.
£200–250 *ARP*

A French bellows camera,
1900–10, 8in (20.5cm) wide.
£80–120 *HEG*

A Kodak Hawkette camera,
1930s, 7in (17.5cm) high.
£40–60 *ARP*

An Ensign Ful-Vue camera and
flash unit, c1955, 4in (10cm) wide.
£40–50 *HEG*

Three Ensign cameras,
1950s, 4in (10cm) wide.
£15–40 each *HEG*

A Finetta-Werk Finetta 88
camera, c1954, 5in (12.5cm) wide.
£40–50 *CaH*

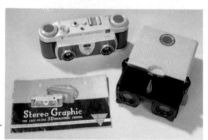

A Wray sterographic camera, viewer
and case, c1950, 7in (18cm) wide.
£150–200 *HEG*

A Rolleiflex SLX camera,
special demonstration model,
1980, 6in (15cm) wide.
£1,000–1,200 *ARP*

A Polaroid Autofocus 660 clear plastic
camera, late 1960s, 6in (15cm) high.
£65–75 *GIN*

A Canon 110ED automatic exposure
camera, 1980s, 5½in (14cm) wide.
£30–40 *ARP*

A Martell Brandy figure,
1940s, 6in (15cm) high.
£100–125 *BEV*

A Double Diamond figure,
1940s, 5½in (14cm) high.
£175–195 *BEV*

A Georges Beers water jug,
1940s, 4in (10cm) high.
£200–250 *SVB*

A Guinness toucan
figure, 1940s,
8in (20.5cm) high.
£325–350 *BEV*

A Canadian Club Whisky plastic
figure, 1960s, 12in (30.5cm) high.
£45–55 *COB*

A Gilbey's Gin water jug,
1960s, 7in (18cm) high.
£20–25 *COL*

A Wm. Younger Scotch Ale advertising
sign, c1930, 6in (15cm) wide.
£12–14 *SpP*

An Ainslie's King's Legend
Scotch Whisky tray, 1950s,
16½in (42cm) wide.
£30–35 *BBR*

An American beer mat,
1990s, 4in (10cm) square.
15–20p *PC*

A Dewar's Scotch Whisky
advertising poster,
published by Tuck, unused,
c1902, 6in (15cm) high.
£18–20 *SpP*

A bar set, 1950s,
7½in (19cm) high.
£10–12 *MAC*

A Wheatley & Sons
bottle, c1915,
10in (25.5cm) high.
£3–5 *MAC*

A disenfectant
bottle, c1920–30,
7¼in (18.5cm) high.
£2–3 *MAC*

BASKETS

A wicker bread basket, early 19thC, 18in (45.5cm) wide.
£55–65 *CPA*

A Chinese miniature rush basket, early 20thC, 1¾in (45mm) high.
£70–80 *MSB*

A Victorian wicker basket, c1880, 14in (35.5cm) wide.
£15–20 *CPA*

A wire basket, 1920s, 7in (18cm) high.
£10–15 *SUS*

A basketwork waste paper basket, mounted with Barbola ceramic flowers, 1920s, 15in (38cm) high.
£30–40 *SUS*

A wicker basket, with green woven handle and ends, c1930, 14½in (37cm) wide.
£15–20 *CPA*

An American miniature wicker basket, c1930, 4in (10cm) high.
£85–95 *MSB*

A raffia sewing basket, in the form of a house, with pink satin interior, 1950s, 10in (25.5cm) wide.
£10–12 *DUD*

l. A Huntley & Palmers biscuit tin, in the form of a basket, c1897, 7⅛in (18.5cm) wide.
£50–60 *HUX*

An American miniature wicker basket, c1930, 3½in (9cm) high.
£90–100 *MSB*

An Apache fibre bowl-shaped basket, c1900, 13in (33cm) diam.
£1,000–1,200 *YAG*

BATHROOM & WASHING COLLECTABLES

Expanding interest in interior decoration has led to a growing period style demand for architectural and reclamation items including bathrooms. Until recently Victorian and Edwardian baths were simply thrown away, but today they can have a very high value and buyers are attracted to house sales not just by the antiques on offer but by the fixtures and fittings. Good sources include schools, hotels, and other buildings whose function entailed a considerable number of bathrooms. As specialists in this field note, since these objects are being purchased as working antiques, careful renovation is all important to adapt vintage equipment for modern-day use. 'Most people only do up their bathroom once, so it has got to be right,' stresses dealer Posh Tubs.

Although today having a bathroom is taken for granted, a survey carried out as late as 1950 showed that nearly half of all British homes had no bathroom, and for many families washing meant either a trip to the public baths or a zinc tub in the kitchen. Today these tubs are purchased as decorative curiosities, often ending their working lives filled with flowers or coal.

A zinc roll-top slipper bath, c1880, 63in (160cm) long.
£550–600 *DOR*

A German galvanised rocking herbal bath, c1890, 53½in (136cm) long.
£250–300 *NWE*

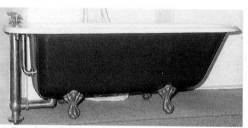

A Royal Doulton plunge bath, early 20thC, 75in (190.5cm) long.
£1,800–2,000 *POSH*

A French zinc bath, with wood-burning stove, c1920, 72in (183cm) long.
£800–1,000 *POSH*

A brass and copper heated towel rail, with twin top tube, 1920s, 37in (94cm) high.
£225–275 *WRe*

A pair of Bolding nickel-plated hot and cold taps, 1930–50s, 7½in (19cm) high.
£45–55 *PJa*

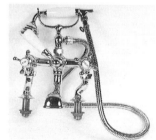

A nickel-plated bath and shower mixer set, 1950s, 14in (35.5cm) high.
£180–200 *PJa*

Ceramics: Bidets, Footbaths & Toilet Sets

A Nankin blue and white bidet, of waisted form, the interior painted with a river landscape incorporating pagodas, pavilions and other buildings, the exterior decorated with trailing flowers, 19thC, 23½in (60cm) long, in a mahogany stand.
£900–1,100 *P(O)*

A Spode blue and white bidet, decorated with Tower pattern, c1820, 18in (45.5cm) long, in mahogany stand.
£750–850 *GN*

A Davenport blue and white water jug, decorated with Geneva pattern, c1830, 10in (25.5cm) high.
£225–275 *GN*

Did You Know?

The bidet, a small shallow bath for female use, was first introduced in France in the 18thC.

A Losol jug and bowl set, with soap dish, c1915–25, jug 13in (33cm) high.
£150–165 *MAC*

A blue and white washbowl, decorated with Woodman pattern, in iron stand, c1825, 15in (38cm) diam.
£300–350 *GN*

A Copeland & Garrett blue and white footbath and jug, decorated with Portland vase pattern, 1833–47, footbath 19in (48.5cm) long.
£1,400–1,600 *GN*

A William Smith blue and white jug and bowl, decorated with Armorial pattern, c1840, bowl 14in (35.5cm) diam.
£350–400 *GN*

A Royal Doulton Art Deco toilet set, the borders painted in green, decorated with panels of coloured tulips on an off-white ground, comprising jug and bowl, tooth vase, soap dish and chamber pot, printed marks and registration number for c1910–20.
£200–230 *GAK*

Chamber Pots

Although houses began to have lavatories in the 19th century, chamber pots were still in regular use. They were kept in the bedroom either in a pot cupboard or under the bed, hence the popular nickname 'guzzunder'. They were also concealed inside commodes which, since they looked like ordinary pieces of furniture, could be placed in other areas of the house such as the smoking or dining room, where men would retire with their port after dinner.

Bourdalous – oblong-shaped chamber pots – were designed for female use. They were named after Father Louis Bourdalou (1632–1734), a Jesuit preacher at the court of Louis XIV, whose sermons were so long that ladies were reputedly forced to take along a receptacle which they could slip under their skirts in times of need. In Britain bourdalous were also known as slipper pots and coach pots, because they were used on long coach journeys, sometimes coming complete with carrying case. Bourdalous which were often finely decorated with blue and white transfer prints are sought after by collectors today. With chamber pots, value is largely dependent on decoration. In addition to the floral and other patterns illustrated here, they also came with comic mottoes and pictures on the inside of reviled public enemies ranging from Napoleon right up to Adolf Hitler in the 1940s, upon whom users were encouraged to relieve themselves.

A Ridgway's blue and white bourdalou, decorated with Fairy Queen pattern, 1840, 10in (25.5cm) long.
£250–300 *GN*

A Minton blue and white bourdalou, decorated with Swiss Chalet pattern, c1840, 9in (23cm) long.
£425–475 *GN*

A blue and white urinal, printed with figures in a landscape, within foliate scroll bandings, unmarked, 1840–50, 11in (28cm) long.
£220–250 *P(B)*

The oval-shaped mouth of this urinal suggests that it was intended for female use. Men's urinal pots came with a circular opening.

A Victorian chamber pot, hand-decorated with pink roses, 9in (23cm) diam.
£40–50 *TAC*

l. An Art Nouveau chamber pot, decorated with blue and white pattern, c1900, 5in (13cm) high.
£30–40 *GIN*

An Art Nouveau chamber pot, decorated with blue and white pansies, c1900, 9½in (24cm) diam.
£85–95 *PC*

An Art Deco style Bisto ware child's chamber pot, 1930s, 7½in (19cm) wide.
£25–30 *HEI*

A Victorian miniature slipware potty, inscribed 'Hand it over to me my dear', 2½in (6.5cm) high.
£40–50 *ANV*

Lavatories

The first water closet was invented by Sir John Harrington in 1596. Elizabeth I, his godmother, had one installed at Richmond Palace the following year, but it was not until the Victorian period that water closets became commonplace. In 1775 Alexander Cumming patented a water closet design, and three years later Joseph Bramah, a Yorkshire cabinet maker, produced an improved model in which the sluice valve was connected to a flush handle.

At the turn of the century came the invention of the Hopper closet, which included an S-bend in the soil pipe allowing a pool of water to remain in the basin, replaced after every flush. The most famous name in the field, however, was Thomas Crapper. In 1886 he devised the first standard flush-down WC, improving sanitation and, through his surname, brought a new word into the English language.

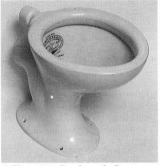

A Shanks Citizen lavatory pan, with embossed pattern, c1900, 17in (43cm) high.
£350–400 *POSH*

An Excelsior lavatory pan, with embossed border, c1895, 16in (40.5cm) high.
£400–500 *POSH*

A Victorian Doulton & Co white Simplicitas lavatory pan, 18in (45.5cm) high.
£300–400 *WRe*

A Gibbons brass penny in slot lock, c1940–50, 16½in (42cm) high.
£70–80 *POSH*

A waterfall toilet and church seat, with flushing cistern, toilet c1890, seat c1920, 36in (91.5cm) wide.
£1,800–2,000 *POSH*

l. A French child's lavatory pan, c1910–20, 9in (23cm) high.
£80–120 *WRe*

Cisterns

A Burlington cast iron high-level lavatory cistern, 1920s, 18in (45.5cm) wide.
£80–100 *WRe*

A Rowanco lavatory cistern, unrestored, 19thC, 19in (48.5cm) wide.
£35–40 *WEL*

Toilet Tissue

A roll of Bronco No. 3 toilet tissue, 1940s, 5in (13cm) high.
£6–8 *HUX*

A roll of Hillcrest medicated toilet tissue, 1930–40s, 5in (13cm) high.
£6–8 *HUX*

Soaps & Soap Dishes

A William Smith blue and white soap dish, decorated with Basket of Flowers pattern, c1840, 3in (7.5cm) diam.
£85–95 *GN*

A bar of Wright's Coal Tar soap, with original wrapper and box, 1930s, 3¼in (8.5cm) wide.
£5–8 *HUX*

r. A bar of Camay soap, in original wrapper, 1950s, 4in (10cm) wide.
£4–5 *HUX*

Pulls

A ceramic lavatory pull, with brass chain and plumber's name detail, 1920s, 5in (13cm) long.
£60–70 *BS*

A ceramic lavatory pull, with brass chain and fittings, 1920s, 4½in (11.5cm) long.
£50–60 *MAC*

A brass bath rack with soap holders, c1920s, 32in (81.5cm) extended.
£55–65 *PJa*

A twin pack of Fortress soap, with original box, 1930s, 6¼in (16cm) wide.
£8–10 *HUX*

A twin pack of Fairy soap, 1960s, 7in (18cm) wide.
£6–8 *HUX*

Toothpaste

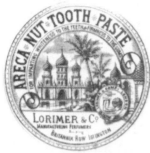

A Lorimer Areca Nut Toothpaste pot lid, with transfer print of mosque and palm trees, slight chip, c1900, 2½in (6.5cm) diam.
£45–55 BBR

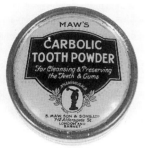

A tin of Maw's Carbolic Tooth Powder, transfer printed 'For cleansing and preserving the teeth and gums', 1920s, 2¾in (7cm) diam.
£10–12 HUX

A tin of Wilson's Cor-re-ga denture adhesive, with original box, 1950s, 2½in (6.5cm) high.
£5–7 HUX

A May Roberts Cherry Toothpaste lid, with transfer depicting young bonneted girl, arms folded, leaning on a wall draped with cherries, c1900, 2½in (6.5cm) diam.
£110–130 BBR

r. A Cherry Toothpaste lid, transfer printed 'Prepared by C. L. Metcalfe of Hull', depicting a shield with cherries and leaves, outer base chip, c1900, 3in (7.5cm) diam.
£35–45 BBR

A tube of Camberwick Green fruity flavour toothpaste, in original box, c1970, 5½in (14cm) high.
£6–7 HUX

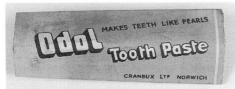

A tube of Odol toothpaste, in original box, 1940s, 4½in (11.5cm) wide.
£3–5 HUX

Toothpaste

Up until the 19thC it was usual to make one's own toothpowder, using products ranging from salt, to chalk to soot. The Victorian period saw the development of manufactured powders, sold in small ceramic pots through chemists, many containing areca nut, imported from Malaya. Tooth powder was gradually supplanted by toothpaste, supplied in tubes and pioneered by firms such as Colgate.

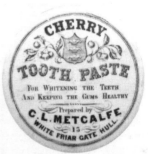

BICYCLES

A road racing tricycle, with twin front-steering, fixed rear wheel and racing pedals, restored, c1930.
£220–250 BKS

A tradesman's delivery tricycle, with cool box to front, handbrake to rear wheel and fitted with Brooks leather saddle, unrestored condition, with overpainted frame, c1930.
£350–450 BKS

An Ordinary bicycle, fitted with hollow forks and patent Aeolus Hub, the saddle, spokes, rear wheel and braking system replaced, the spine repaired, fitted with hand-decorated advertising pannier, c1880, leading wheel 52in (132cm) diam.
£1,500–1,800 S

This bicycle was ridden from England to Australia as a publicity stunt for Belleview Health Products in the late 1960s, and has remained unused since its return to the UK. The front wheel has its original hub but was re-spoked in Singapore during the long journey.

A Raleigh lady's three-speed roadster bicycle, the loop frame in original black livery, 1930s.
£175–225 RBB

> **Miller's is a price GUIDE not a price LIST**

A Gundle tradesman's bicycle, with carrying frame to front, unwritten sign, rod brakes, repainted, original condition, c1940s.
£140–180 BKS

A BSA enamel advertising sign, c1910, 44in (112cm) wide.
£250–300 JUN

A pedal bicycle, by J. C. Higgins for Sears Roebuck & Co, the tubular steel frame with pressed steel panels attached, painted in 2 shades of blue, with aerodynamic front and rear lighting, electronic horn located in crossbar housing and reverse-pedal brakes, marked with manufacturer, retailer and patent labels, early 1950s.
£500–600 CSK

A Halford Cycle Company French chalk tin, 1930s, 4½in (11.5cm) high.
£10–12 WAB

r. A Mandaw cycle bell advertising poster, c1910, 17½in (44.5cm) high.
£120–150 CSK

BOOKS

John Buchan, *The Thirty-Nine Steps*, recent full calf exhibition binding by the Cottage Bindery, Bath, first edition, 1915, 8vo.
£300–350 *DW*

Arthur J. Gaskin, *Good King Wenceslas*, a carol written by Dr Neale, with an introduction by William Morris, slightly frayed, Birmingham, 1895, 4to.
£80–100 *DW*

Gladys T. Clarke, *The Handwritten Manuscripts of Gladys T. Clarke*, a collection of 10 manuscripts, with a further volume written in Pitman's shorthand, c1900.
£1,800–2,000 *HAM*

This collection of 10 manuscript books dating from the early 1900s until the middle of the century, attracted considerable interest when it came up for auction. The volumes included pictures, stories and anecdotes produced by Gladys T. Clarke and speculation was rife that this could prove to be a successor to A Diary of an Edwardian Lady.

Sergeant Major Richard Elton, *The Art of Military*, printed by Robert Leybourn, with fold-out plans, re-bound into old covers, London, 1650, 11 x 7in (28 x 18cm).
£350–400 *BAf*

Constable's Miscellany XXXI, a history of the rebellions in Scotland from 1638–60, odd volume published in Edinburgh, some wear, 1828, 6 x 4in (15 x 10cm).
£4–8 *BAf*

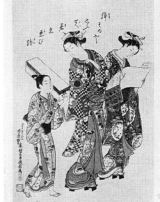

Marcus B. Huish, *Japan and its Art*, third edition, revised and enlarged, published by B.T. Batsford, 6 colour plates, 225 black and white illustrations, publisher's pictorial red cloth, gilt, London, 1912, 8¾ x 6¼in (22 x 16cm).
£65–75 *HB*

Nico and Beatrix Jungman, *Holland*, published by Adam & Charles Black, London, 75 colour plates, first edition, 1904, 9 x 6½in (23 x 16.5cm).
£65–75 *HB*

Book Sizes

The size or format of a book is expressed by the number of times a single sheet of paper is folded into the sections which, when gathered and sewn, make up the finished volume. Shown below are some of the usual descriptions of sizes:

Folio	1 fold	2 leaves	Fo or 2°
Quarto	2 folds	4 leaves	4to or 4°
Octavo	3 folds	8 leaves	8vo or 8°
Duodecimo	4 folds	12 leaves	12mo or 12°
Sextodecimo	5 folds	16 leaves	16mo or 16°
Vicesimo-quarto	6 folds	24 leaves	24mo or 24°
Tricesimo-secundo	7 folds	32 leaves	32mo or 32°

r. Jessie M. King (illustrator), *The High History of the Holy Graal*, translated by Sebastian Evans, printed black and red, light blue cloth blocked in black and gilt, 1903, 8vo.
£375–425 *DW*

Omar Khayyam, *Rubáiyát ...*, small pocket book, Fitzgerald's translation, 1910, 6½ x 3⅛in (16.5 x 9cm).
£6–7 *TRE*

John Cowper Powys, *Porius*, published by Macdonald, first UK edition, 1951, 8 x 5in (20.5 x 13cm).
£50–60 *BAf*

Charles Texier and R. Popplewell Pullan, *Byzantine Architecture*, published by Day & Son, original gilt decorated cloth, recent reback with original spine laid down to new front endpaper, 1864, folio.
£650–750 *DW*

John B. Papworth, *Rural Residences*, consisting of a series of designs for cottages, decorated cottages, small villas and other ornamental buildings, published by R. Ackermann, London, 1832, 11 x 7½in (28 x 19cm).
£600–700 *HB*

Olivia M. Stone, *Tenerife and its six Satellites*, or *The Canary Islands Past and Present*, 2 vols, original cloth, slightly soiled, first edition, 1887, 8vo.
£120–150 *DW*

John Ogilby, *Road Maps of England and Wales*, published by Osprey, 1971, 15¾ x 10⅜in (40 x 27.5cm).
£40–50 *JAL*
This is a modern reprint of the original 1675 first edition.

Southey, *The Life of Nelson*, published by Gibbings, illustrated by Frank Brangwyn, limited edition of 100 copies signed by the artist, c1912, 10¼ x 7¼in (26 x 18.5cm).
£200–250 *HB*

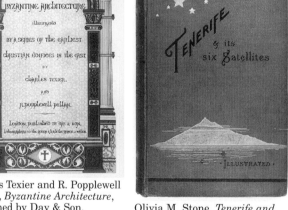

H. W. Wilson, *With The Flag to Pretoria,* published by Harmsworth Brothers Ltd, volumes 1 and 2, 1901, folio.
£30–40 *BAf*

Children's Books

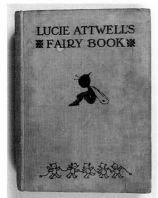

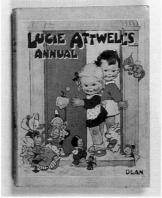

Mabel Lucie Attwell, *Lucie Attwell's Fairy Book*, 1932, 9½in (24cm) high.
£40–60 *WWY*

Mabel Lucie Attwell, *Lucie Attwell's Annual*, published by Dean, 1950s, 10in (25.5cm) high.
£40–50 *WWY*

C. Collodi, *Le Avventure di Pinocchio*, published by Bemporad & Figlio, original cloth, c1900, folio.
£275–325 *DW*

l. Beatrix Potter, *The Tale of Tom Kitten*, published by F. Warne & Co, first edition, 1907, 8vo.
£550–650 *DW*

Kathleen Hale, *Orlando (The Marmalade Cat) Keeps a Dog*, published by Country Life, original picture boards with linen backstrip, first edition, 1949, slim folio.
£110–130 *DW*

Beatrix Potter, *The Tale of Peter Rabbit*, with grey leaf end papers, published by F. Warne & Co, 1903, 5½in (14cm) high.
£20–25 *WWY*

Beatrix Potter, *The Tale of Squirrel Nutkin*, published by F. Warne & Co, 1912, 5½in (14cm) high.
£20–25 *WWY*

Arthur Rackham, *Arthur Rackham's Book of Pictures*, published by Heinemann, special publication in leather finish, first published 1913, third edition 1923, folio.
£275–300 *NW*

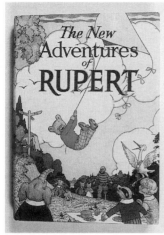

The New Adventures of Rupert, hardback, 1936, 10in (25.5cm) high.
£550–650 *WWY*

More Rupert Adventures, paperback Rupert annual, 1943, 10in (25.5cm) high.
£100–150 *WWY*

Rupert, hardback *Daily Express* annual, 1962, 10in (25.5cm) high.
£25–35 *WWY*

Equestrian Books

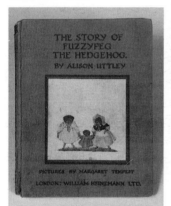

Alison Uttley, *The Story of Fuzzypeg the Hedgehog*, pictures by Margaret Tempest, published by William Heinemann, first edition, 1932.
£40–50 *RAC*

The Arab Horse Society, published by Langhams of Farnham, printed by The Herald Press, 13 volumes, 1953–65, 9¾in x 6¼in (26 x 16cm).
£4–5 each *JAL*

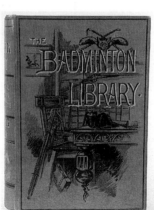

Robert Weir, Moray Brown and others, *The Badminton Library – Riding Polo*, published by Longmans Brown & Co, first edition, 1891, 8 x 6in (20.5 x 15cm).
£35–40 *HB*

The Duke of Beaufort, *The Badminton Library – Hunting*, third edition, 1886, 8 x 6in (20.5 x 15cm).
£50–60 *HB*

Edited by the Duke of Beaufort, the Badminton Library of Sports and Pastimes *was the most comprehensive sporting survey of its day. First published between 1885–96, the full set included 29 volumes and covered all the major sports of the period. Today collectors tend to focus on their own specialist area, rather than going for the complete run, and the examples shown are devoted to equestrian sports.*

The Duke of Beaufort, *The Badminton Library – Driving*, published by Longmans, third edition, 1890, 8 x 6in (20.5 x 15cm).
£35–40 *HB*

The Badminton Library – Racing, published by Longmans, fifth edition, 1900, 8 x 6in (20.5 x 15cm).
£30–35 *HB*

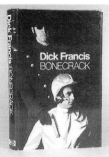

Dick Francis, *Bonecrack*, published by Book Club Associates, 1972, 8 x 5¼in (20.5 x 13.5cm). **£2–3** *JAL*

First edition published in 1971.

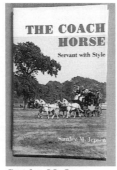

Stanley M. Jepsen, *The Coach Horse*, published by A. S. Barnes & Co, South Brunswick & New York, 1977, 10 x 6¾in (25.5 x 17cm). **£8–10** *JAL*

Maj Gen Geoffrey Brooke, *Horsemanship, Dressage & Show-jumping*, The Londsdale Library, published by Seeley Service & Co Ltd, London, 1959, 8 x 6in (20.5 x 15cm). **£12–15** *JAL*

First published in 1929.

r. Stephen Michael Brie, *Diamond Days*, published by Hodder & Stoughton, 1990, 9½ x 6½in (24 x 16.5cm). **£12–15** *JAL*

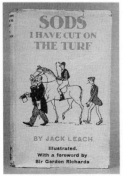

Elinore Havers, *The Surprise Riding Club*, 1966, 7½ x 5in (19 x 12.5cm). **£1–1.50** *TRE*

Rowland Hilder, *Horse Play*, published by Golden Gallery Press Ltd, illustrations by Rowland Hilder, 1973, 8¼ x 5¼in (21 x 13.5cm). **£2–3** *JAL*

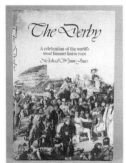

Michael Wynn Jones, *The Derby*, published by Croom Helm, London, 1979, 9½ x 6½in (24 x 16.5cm). **£12–15** *JAL*

Jack Leach, *Sods I Have Cut On The Turf*, illustrated by Osbert Lancaster, published by Victor Gollancz Ltd, 1961, 9 x 5¼in (23 x 13.5cm). **£12–15** *JAL*

M. F. McTaggart, *Stable & Saddle*, illustrated by Ludwig Koch, published by Methuen & Co Ltd, London, 1929, 10 x 7½in (25.5 x 19cm). **£12–15** *JAL*

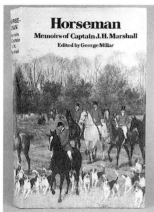

George Millar (editor), *Horseman – Memoirs of Captain J. H. Marshall*, published by The Bodley Head Press, 1970, 9 x 6in (23 x 15cm).
£10–12 *JAL*

E. S. Montgomery, *The Thoroughbred*, published by Arco Publishing Co, New York, third print, 1978, 9½ x 6½in (24 x 16.5cm).
£25–30 *JAL*

Peter Pryor, *The Classic Connection*, published by Courtney Publications, 1979, 8½ x 10in (21.5 x 25.5cm).
£40–50 *JAL*

W. J. Miles MRCVSL, *Modern Practical Farriery*, published by William Mackenzie, first edition, 1868, 12 x 10in (30.5 x 25.5cm).
£70–80 *JAL*

Nimrod, *Memoirs of the Life of John Mytton*, published by Kegan Paul, Trench, Trubner & Co Ltd, illustrations by H. Alken & T. J. Rawlins, with notices of his hunting, shooting, driving, racing, eccentric and extravagant exploits, late 19thC, 11 x 7½in (28 x 19cm).
£120–140 *HB*

Walter D. Osborne, *The Thoroughbred World*, published by Leon Amiel, Israel, 1970s, 11 x 9in (28 x 23cm).
£25–30 *JAL*

Captain E. D. Miller, *Modern Polo*, published by Hurst & Blackett Ltd, 1911, 9 x 6in (23 x 15cm).
£45–50 *HB*

Antoine de Pluvinel, *Maneige Royal Ou L'on Peur Remarquer Le Defaut Et la Perfection Du Chevalier*, published by Gottfried Muller, text in French and German, 1626, 13½ x 10in (34.5 x 25.5cm).
£3,000–3,500 *HB*

This is the first bilingual edition of one of the most famous and popular early works of equestrian instruction, composed by the French riding master Antoine de Pluvinel for Louis XIII. This is the first appearance of the German text. The handsome plates, after Crispin de Passe (Van de Pass), are copied from those contained in the first edition, printed in Paris in 1623. Most have engraved architectural borders and depict Louis XIII, the author, and other identified characters involved in performing various equestrian manoeuvres and exercises. Others show jousting, tournament riding, proper riding attire, armour, saddles and bridles.

FURTHER READING
Catherine Porter, *Miller's Collecting Books* Miller's Publications, 1995

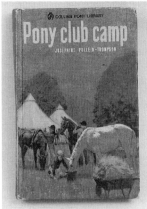

Josephine Pullein-Thompson, *Pony Club Camp*, published by Collins Pony Library, 1972, 7½ x 5in (19 x 13cm). **50p–£1** *TRE*

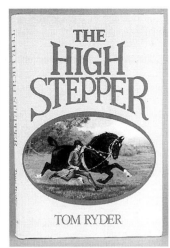

Tom Ryder, *The High Stepper*, published by J. A. Allen, London and New York, 1979, 10 x 7in (25.5 x 18cm). **£8–10** *JAL*

Charles Richardson, *British Flat Racing and Breeding*, published by The London & Counties Press Association Ltd, 3 volumes in one, limited edition of 600, 1923, 4to. **£300–350** *HB*

Solleysell, *The Complete Horseman*, 2 volumes in one, London 1717, 13 x 9in (33 x 23cm). **£250–300** *HB*

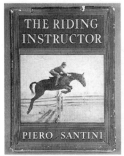

Piero Santini, *The Riding Instructor*, published by Country Life Ltd, London, 1952, 10 x 7⅜in (25.5 x 19.5cm). **£12–15** *JAL*

Pat Smythe, *Three Jays Against the Clock*, published by Cassell & Co Ltd, London, 1958, 8 x 5½in (20.5 x 14cm). **£4–5** *JAL*

Willie Shoemaker, *The Shoe*, published by Rand McNally & Co, USA, 1977, 11¼ x 9in (28.5 x 23cm). **£12–15** *JAL*

The first edition of this book was published in 1976.

W. S. Sparrow, *British Sporting Artists*, published by John Lane, The Bodley Head Ltd, first edition 1922, 11½ x 9½in (29 x 24cm). **£90–110** *HB*

Sporting Chronicle, *Form Book*, printed by Withy Grove Press Ltd, 1966, 6½ x 4¼in (16.5 x 11cm).
£10–12 *JAL*

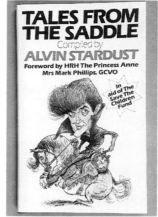

Alvin Stardust, *Tales from the Saddle*, foreword by HRH The Princess Anne, published by Stanley Paul, 1984, 9 x 6in (23 x 15cm).
£4–5 *JAL*

George Stubbs, *The Anatomy of the Horse*, published by G. Heywood Hill Ltd, London, 1938, 18 x 11in (46 x 28cm).
£95–115 *JAL*

This book was originally printed in 1766, by J. Purser for the author.

John Tickner, *Tickner's Show Piece*, published by Putnam, London, signed, 1958, 8¼ x 5½in (21 x 14cm).
£6–7 *JAL*

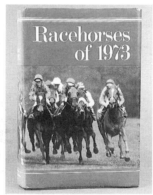

Racehorses of 1973, Timeform Publications, 1973, 7 x 4½in (18 x 11.5cm).
£20–25 *JAL*

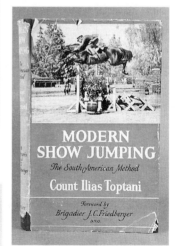

Count Ilias Toptani, *Modern Show Jumping*, published by Stanley Paul, 1959, 8½ x 5½in (21.5 x 14cm).
£12–15 *JAL*

This book was first published in 1954.

Wildrake (editor), *Cracks of the Day*, published by Rudolph Ackermann, first edition, c1840, 10 x 6¼in (25.5 x 16cm).
£250–350 *HB*

l. Dorian Williams, *Show Jumping*, published by Faber & Faber, 1968, 8¼ x 5¼in (21 x 13.5cm).
£2–3 *JAL*

BOTTLES
Glass

An onion-shaped
bottle, with seal
initialled 'CB', c1710,
6½in (16.5cm) high.
£600–650 *NWi*

r. A Riley's Dairies
Ltd milk bottle,
'Cream Line Milk
Bridlington,' 1940–50s,
8½in (21.5cm) high.
£4–5 *MAC*

A green glass bottle,
embossed J. Hindle
& Co, Chapel Lane,
Hull, 1930s,
10in (25.5cm) high.
£4–5 *MAC*

A whisky bottle,
embossed 'C. Pratt &
Sons, Lincoln', 1930s,
11¾in (30cm) high.
£2–3 *MAC*

l. A Codd bottle, c1875, 9½in (24cm) high.
£40–50 *JAS*

*In 1870 Hiram Codd invented a revolutionary design
for sealing fizzy drink bottles with a marble. The
bottle was filled and the gas pressure from the
carbon dioxide in the drink forced the marble up
against a rubber washer fitted in the neck, forming
an airtight seal. To open the bottle, you pressed down
on the marble, which was then trapped between two
indentations on the neck, thus preventing the drinker
from swallowing it and the bottle from re-sealing.
Codd's invention won medals at both the London
and Vienna Exhibitions of 1873 and also gained him
a place in the English language with the familiar
expression, 'a load of old codswallop', (wallop being
a slang term for the fizzy drink).*

r. A blue glass fire grenade
bottle, with original label
around neck plus original
wire, label reads 'Harpens
Hand Grenade Fire
Extinguisher', very
good condition, c1880,
5½in (14cm) high.
£45–55 *BBR*

*This bottle was designed to
be smashed in case of fire,
the contents were supposed
to put out the flames.*

l. A black glass bottle, embossed with vine leaves and 'L. Rose & Co', c1880, 12in (30.5cm) high.
£40–45
r. An olive green bladder-shaped bottle, embossed with vine leaves, good condition, c1880, 9½in (24cm) high.
£25–30 *BBR*

A root beer bottle, printed 'Ted's Creamy Root Beer', full and capped, very good condition, 1950s, 8½in (21.5cm) high.
£70–80 *HALL*

r. A whisky bottle, with cork and foil seal intact, paper label reads 'The Ultimate, Single Malt, Scotch Whisky Selection, matured in oak casks for 19 years, Distilled at the Macallan Distillery, on 1.5.75, bottled 6.94, cask No. 8347, No. 10 of 340, 11½in (29cm) high.
£100–120 *BBR*

The cork and foil should be intact on a filled bottle and the value is lessened if contents have evaporated—levels should remain well above the shoulder.

Did You Know?
In the 19thC chemists had to deal with a largely illiterate public. Bottles containing dangerous medicines or poison were not only inscribed with written warnings, but were also coloured (generally blue) to distinguish them from other products. They were also ridged, dimpled and unusually shaped so that they could be identified in poor lighting conditions and at night time.

Medicine

l. A brown glass drug round, with white and red paper label, 1930s, 8½in (22cm) high.
£15–20 *AXT*

r. A cobalt blue glass submarine poison bottle, slight dullness, registered No. 336907 to base, 3in (7.5cm) long.
£200–240 *BBR*

An emerald green glass triangular-shaped bottle, '12oz' size embossed to base, 'Not to be taken' and 'Caution' to top of panels, 'Patent' to bottom, Wilson's Patent March 17, 1899, good condition, 7½in (19cm) high.
£230–260 *BBR*

A pair of cobalt blue glass shop rounds, with recessed labels under glass in gold, red, black and white, c1880, 9in (23cm) high.
£160–180 *BBR*

l. A deep cobalt blue coffin-shaped poison bottle, with embossed initials in a circle at neck end, and within a shield beneath 'Patent/5658/Poison', late 19thC, 6in (15cm) long.
£6,800–8,000 *BBR*

In 1871 G. F. Langford was granted provisional patent protection for 'a bottle in the shape of a coffin, and may be externally ornamented with a death's head or other device'. Similar American patents were issued in 1876 and 1890. This bottle is historically interesting, extremely rare and in mint condition, hence its high price.

Stone & Earthenware

A green/grey glazed earthenware slab sealed flask, with ribbed sloping shoulders, seal reads 'T. S. Parkin, Worksop', Thomas Sissons Parkin, Market Place, base chip, 1848–52, 7in (18cm) high.
£380–460 *BBR*

A green/grey glazed earthenware flask, with impression to front 'S. Harrison, Spirit Merchant, Lincoln', small repair, c1860, 5½in (14cm) high.
£50–60 *BBR*

A stoneware ale bottle, with blue lip, black transfer printed 'Cascade Brewery Co Ltd, Dandelion Ale, Hobart Tasmania', c1900, 8½in (21.5cm) high.
£60–70 *BBR*

A stoneware root beer bottle, transfer printed 'C. Leary & Co, Old Fashioned Rootbeer', Newburyport, Mass, c1890, 8in (20.5cm) high.
£25–30 *AWT*

A stoneware ginger beer bottle, with green top, transfer printed 'Sketch's, Green, Ginger Beer, Johnston and Pembroke Dock', slight damage, c1900, 6¾in (17cm) high.
£15–20 *BBR*

A stoneware bottle, with stopper, transfer printed 'Morris & Son, Swinton', early 1900s, 7½in (19cm) high.
£5–10 *MAC*

r. A stoneware footwarmer, transfer printed 'Little Folks Footwarmer', with ornate wooden stopper and rings in carrying holes, some crazing, 1920s, 6in (15cm) high.
£100–120 *BBR*

BOXES

A carved cocquilla nut basket, c1750, 5in (14cm) wide.
£1,000–1,250 *MB*

A wooden fan box, with brass tack decoration, traces of green paint, c1800, 18in (45.5cm) long.
£60–80 *AWT*

An Oriental ivory workbox, the fitted interior including numerous carved ivory accessories including clamps, needle cases and thimbles, late 19thC, 10½in (26.5cm) wide.
£3,000–3,500 *RBB*

A rosewood miniature cabinet, with trailed vine inlaid bone decoration, supported on turned bun feet, 19thC, 10½in (26.5cm) wide.
£250–300 *TMA*

A Georgian flame-mahogany knife box, with herringbone stringing, fitted interior, 13¾in (35cm) high.
£500–600 *SPU*

A late Georgian parquetry box, with hinged top, with bone escutcheon, 7½in (19cm) wide.
£250–300 *TMA*

A wagoner's pine tool box, with metal hinges, 19thC, 17in (43cm) wide.
£50–60 *No7*

r. An Indian cut steel and bone inlaid box, Vizagapatam, c1840, 10¾in (27.5cm) wide.
£80–100 *SSW*

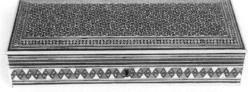

A Sheraton mahogany knife box, with central inlaid medallion, fitted interior, late 18thC, 14in (35.5cm) high.
£300–350 *SPU*

A blacksmith's wooden nail box, early 19thC, 13¼in (34cm) wide.
£70–80 *No7*

A saddler's elm work box, with a leather work tool, early 19thC, 17in (43cm) wide.
£180–220 *GAK*

An Indian lacquered box, Kashmir, c1860, 14in (35.5cm) long.
£90–100 *SSW*

An Indian brass-bound money box, Rajastan, 19thC, 10in (25.5cm) wide.
£200–250 *CORO*

A French ebonised work box, the top inset with a Longwy tile, lined in blue silk, c1890, 14¼in (36cm) wide.
£350–420 *ANO*

An enamelled gilt-metal framed jewel casket, with neo-classical decoration and pelleted rosette design, on scrolled gilt-metal paw feet, late 19thC, 8in (20.5cm) wide.
£180–220 *GAK*

Four Tunbridge Ware boxes, for pens, matches, needles and stamps, c1870, 2¼in (6cm) long.
£120–150 each *AMH*

A lady's tortoiseshell writing slope and manicure box, c1880, 12in (30.5cm) wide.
£8,000–9,500 *SHa*

l. A Mauchline ware cotton reel box, with Anchor sewing cottons label inside, late 19thC, 3in (7.5cm) long.
£35–45 *BIL*

r. A Mauchline ware trinket box, depicting Stirling Castle, made of wood from the field of Bannockburn, late 19thC, 3in (7.5cm) long.
£25–30 *BIL*

l. A reptile skin box, 1920s, 7in (18cm) wide.
£10–15 *WEE*

Snuff

A coquilla nut snuff box, with glass eyes, early 18thC, 3in (7.5cm) wide.
£140–160 *BIL*

A Sheraton design oval inlaid snuff box, c1790, 4¼in (11cm) wide.
£250–300 *AEF*

r. A carved horn snuff box, 19thC, 2in (5cm) wide.
£50–60 *BIL*

A coconut and macassar ebony snuff box, 18thC, 7½in (19cm) diam.
£320–350 *MB*

A horn snuff box, early 19thC, 3in (7.5cm) wide.
£60–70 *BIL*

A Vernis Martin tortoiseshell table snuff box, the top hand-painted with cherubs, with gold and silver inlay, French, 18thC, 3in (8cm) diam.
£400–450 *MB*

Vernis Martin was the French name given to japanning, the process of imitating Oriental lacquer in Europe. The name derives from the Martin Brothers, who specialised in lacquer work in 18thC France. The varnish that they developed (which included garlic juice) was extremely fine in texture and their work ranged from large commissions, such as panelling the Dauphin's apartments at Versailles, to producing small items such as fans and snuff boxes. Vernis Martin became the generic name for all French lacquer work.

A burr birch snuff box, with tortoiseshell lining, c1820, 8½in (21.5cm) wide.
£50–60 *MB*

Why not join the Miller's Club?
Tel: 0171 225 9244

A mahogany coffin-shaped snuff box, 19thC, 4in (10cm) long.
£45–50 *BIL*

A shop's papier mâché snuff box, with pewter inlay, inscribed 'John James', c1850, 5in (13cm) wide.
£70–80 *MB*

A hand-painted papier mâché snuff box, c1825, 3½in (9cm) wide.
£120–140 *MB*

A French horn snuff box, with silver piqué, 19thC, 2½in (6.5cm) wide.
£50–60 *BIL*

Tea Caddies

Tea was an expensive commodity when it first became fashionable on the Continent in the 17th century. In the late 1600s it could cost as much as 50 shillings a pound while in 1728 a London tea merchant was advertising black tea at prices ranging from 13 shillings to 20 shillings, and green tea from 12 shillings to 30 shillings. Costly boxes fitted with locks were made to hold these precious leaves.

The word caddy derives from 'catty', a Chinese measurement of weight. Caddies were often divided into two compartments, one for black and one for green tea, which could then be blended to taste. Some chests came complete with a mixing glass. By the second half of the 18th century, the East India Company was importing on a large scale, prices began to fall and gradually tea became Britain's national drink. By 1800 annual consumption was around 1½lbs per head, by 1900 it had gone up to 6lbs and in 1930 it reached a record high of 10lbs a head, the equivalent of five cups a day for every adult and child in Britain. The growing popularity of coffee, particularly after WWII, affected tea consumption, which has never again reached such a level.

A harewood inlaid tea caddy, 18thC, 7in (18cm) wide.
£1,000–1,200 *CAT*

A mahogany tea caddy, inlaid with a picture of a cannon, c1790, 9in (23cm) wide.
£300–350 *TMi*

A Georgian satinwood and mahogany inlaid tea caddy, with compartmented interior, 9in (23cm) wide.
£300–350 *AAV*

A late Georgian tortoiseshell tea caddy, on ivory compressed ball feet, 4¼in (11cm) wide.
£500–600 *TMA*

A tortoiseshell tea caddy, with serpentine front and ivory fittings, c1810, 5¾in (14.5cm) wide.
£1,500–1,800 *SSW*

A Regency rosewood and brass inlaid tea caddy, with compartmented interior, some damage, 8in (20.5cm) wide.
£110–130 *AAV*

This piece has some damage and requires restoration, hence its low price range.

l. A tortoiseshell tea caddy, with hinged lid enclosing twin-lidded compartments, on bun feet, early 19thC, 8in (20cm) long.
£900–1,000 *P(B)*

r. A burr walnut tea caddy, with ebonised rim, the interior fitted with two-domed compartments, brass escutcheon, 19thC, 9½in (24cm) long.
£200–250 *GAK*

A walnut pentagonal tea caddy, early 19thC, 9½in (24cm) high.
£400–450 *E*

An early Victorian figured mahogany sarcophagus-shaped tea caddy, with 2 compartments and blending bowl, 11¾in (30cm) wide.
£140–160 *CaC*

A mahogany tea caddy, 19thC, 14in (35.5cm) wide.
£120–150 *GAZE*

An oak spherical tea caddy, 1920–30s, 6in (15cm) high.
£25–35 *WEE*

A walnut boxwood-strung tea caddy, the interior fitted with recess for 2 compartments and central bowl, bowl now missing, 19thC, 11½in (29cm) wide.
£170–200 *GAK*

A mahogany tea caddy, with original liner and spade, brass fittings, c1880, 6½in (16.5cm) wide.
£180–200 *CHe*

Writing & Letter Boxes

A mahogany letter box, with 2 compartments, each inset with brass plaques inscribed 'Answer'd', 'Unanswer'd', 18thC, 8½in (21.5cm) long.
£375–425 *GAK*

An Anglo-Indian quill box, constructed with porcupine quills and wood, inlaid with ivory, c1800, 5½in (14cm) wide.
£150–175 *SSW*

l. A Victorian walnut writing and stationery box, with burr walnut veneer, ogee lid top adjusts to a calendar, the pair of doors reveal stepped stationery slots above a hinged writing flap, with a sunken brass handle, 13in (33cm) wide.
£375–425 *WW*

A Victorian oak fitted letter box, 9in (23cm) wide.
£100–125 *SPU*

A Swiss carved pearwood stamp box, inscribed 'From Niagara Falls', c1900, 2¼in (5.5cm) square.
£30–35 *BIL*

BREWERIANA

A Buchanan's menu holder, with black and white Scottie dogs, on square metal base, 1920s, 3½in (9cm) high.
£120–140 *BBR*

A Bass Worthington mug, by T. G. Green, 1950s, 7in (18cm) high.
£15–20 *RAC*

A Famous Grouse Scotch whisky mat, 1991, 5½in (14cm) long.
15–20p *PC*

A ceramic beer pull, decorated with hunting scenes, 1930s, 9in (30cm) high.
£15–20 *RAC*

A Fremlins beer mat, 1960s, 4in (10cm) wide.
40–50p *PC*

A Mackeson promotional barometer, modelled as a bottle opener, c1970, 18in (45.5cm) long.
£35–40 *RTw*

A Lamberhurst Brewery stone beer jar, c1905, 13in (33cm) high.
£25–35 *OLM*

A Lacons beer mat, with blue background, 1950s, 3½in (9cm) square.
50p–£1 *PC*

An Oakwell Brewery wooden barrel clock, with 8-day movement, in working order, c1910, 8¾in (22cm) high.
£320–350 *BBR*

The clock is accompanied by a letter from Barnsley Brewery Company dated 1970, confirming that these clocks were distributed to the company's public houses shortly before the outbreak of WWI.

A Teacher's whisky wooden box, c1920, 17in (43cm) wide.
£35–40 *AL*

l. A Scots Greys Whisky wooden framed pub mirror, blue with pink and gold lettering with central picture of soldiers charging, early 1960s, 48in (122cm) wide.
£250–280 *BBR*

A Truswell's Brewery beer mat, 1940–50s, 3½in (9cm) square.
£7–8 *ED*

Advertising Figures

A Beefeater Gin
composition advertising
figure, 1960s,
17in (43cm) high.
£125–150 *DBr*

An Abbot's Choice Scotch
Whisky composition
advertising figure,
1950s, 7in (18cm) high.
£80–100 *DBr*

A Boxer Ales
composition advertising
figure, 1950s,
6in (15cm) high.
£80–100 *DBr*

A Flowers Brewmaster
advertising figure, by
Carlton Ware 1960s,
10in (25.5cm) high.
£60–70 *RAC*

A Claymore ceramic
advertising figure,
depicting a newsboy
holding a newsheet,
on a square
plinth, 1880s,
16½in (42cm) high.
£950–1,200 *BBR*

A Courvoisier
composition advertising
figure, depicting
Napoleon, 1950s,
9in (23cm) high.
£70–80 *DBr*

A Currie's No. 10
Whisky composition
advertising figure, 1950s,
14in (35.5cm) high.
£100–120 *DBr*

A De Kuyper Black Hen
Advocaat composition
advertising egg, 1960s,
8in (20.5cm) high.
£40–50 *DBr*

A Highland Queen
Scotch Whisky
composition advertising
figure, 1950s,
14in (35.5cm) high.
£125–150 *DBr*

A Lemon Hart Rum
composition advertising
figure, 1950s,
9in (23cm) high.
£70–80 *DBr*

A Whyte & Mackay
whisky advertising
model, depicting an
osprey, by Royal
Doulton, 1977,
9in (23cm) high.
£45–50 *RAC*

Advertising Signs

A Bentley & Shaw's Town Ales glazed advertising sign, c1923, 36in (91.5cm) high.
£150–170 *MUL*

A King George IV Whisky multi-coloured advertising sign, signed Lawson Wood, c1910, 23in (58.5cm) high.
£110–130 *BBR*

A BOS Scotch Whisky advertising sign, with gold-coloured frame and black and red lettering, c1930s, 67½in (170cm) high.
£55–65 *BBR*

A John Haig's multi-coloured pressed tin sign, showing a maid holding a tray with a whisky bottle, soda water bottle and glass, slight surface marks and scratches, c1920s, 23½in (60cm) high.
£200–250 *BBR*

Guinness

A Guinness tinplate crate in the form of a bus, fitted with 8 bottles, finished in red livery, 1930s, 18½in (47cm) long.
£360–400 *WL*

A Guinness Stout beer mat, 1950s, 3½in (9cm) diam.
£1–2 *PC*

Cross Reference
Fakes

r. A plastic-covered tin multi-coloured stand-up advertising stand, 1950s, 8in (20cm) wide.
£180–200 *BBR*

l. A Carlton Ware 'Guinness is Good For You' lamp, with blue metal revolving ball, 1930s, 15in (38cm) high.
£330–360 *WL*

Two Guinness advertising barometers:
l. oak framed, c1970,
r. mahogany framed, c1955,
8in (20cm) diam.
£50–70 *RTw*

A Carlton Ware advertising ornament, modelled as a tankard, inscribed 'My Goodness My Guinness', printed mark, 1930s, 7in (18cm) high.
£280–340 *GAK*

A Guinness jug, by James & Co, Staffordshire, c1960, 8in (20cm) high.
£15–20 *RAC*

Pub Jugs

An Ainslie's Whisky jug, with
blue and yellow lustre effect,
inscribed 'Ainslie's, Whisky' on
2 sides, and 'Causton' on base,
c1880, 5in (12.5cm) high.
£380–420 *BBR*

A Cadenhead stoneware jug,
with pale green top and
tan lower, 1930–40s,
5in (12.5cm) high.
£55–65 *BBR*

Cross Reference
Colour Review

A Cowan's No. 4 water jug,
with bulbous body, minor
inside rim chip, by Campbell
& Son, Belfast, 1880s,
5½in (14cm) high.
£320–360 *BBR*

An Albion Brewery stoneware
jug, with brown top, lower
body grey, black transfer
body printed 'Albion Brewery
Gold Medal Ales', c1920–30,
5in (12.5cm) high.
£25–35 *BBR*

A Brakspear's water jug, by Wade,
with red body and black transfer
printed 'The Founder Robert
Brakspear 1740-1812', 1930–40s,
4¾in (12cm) high.
£65–75 *BBR*

A Dewar's limited edition bottle
and jug, depicting Mr Micawber,
1983, 5½in (14cm) high.
Bottle **£65–75**
Jug   **£150–180** *GL*

r. A Highland Fusilier water jug,
the mustard brown body with
black and gold print, unusual
large size, by Euroceramics,
1960s, 9½in (24cm) high.
£25–30 *BBR*

A Bell's Scotch Whisky water
jug, by Wade, c1970–89,
7in (18cm) high.
£12–18 *RAC*

A Black & White Scotch Whisky
water jug, possibly by Shelley,
1940s, 5in (12.5cm) high.
£100–150 *SVB*

A Grant's water jug, with blue
and white floral design
pattern inscribed 'Grant's
Stand Fast Special', chip and
hairline crack to rim, c1880,
3½in (9cm) high.
£100–120 *BBR*

A Phoenix Special Scotch water jug, with mottled green body, repairs to top and bottom edges, 1920s, 4in (10cm) high.
£110–130 *BBR*

A Saccone & Speed, water jug, by Wade, 1955–70, 7in (18cm) high.
£20–30 *RAC*

A Scottish coopered ale jug, c1780, 7in (18cm) high.
£250–300 *RYA*

l. A Jamie Stuart Scotch Liqueur water jug, with blue and white Willow pattern, chip to rim and hairline crack, c1900, 5½in (14cm) high.
£60–70 *BBR*

r. A White Horse water jug, by Wade, c1960s, 5½in (14cm) high.
£15–18 *RAC*

A Teacher's water jug, transfer printed 'Bury the Corkscrew', by James Green & Nephew, some wear to silver rim and handle, 1920s, 6½in (16.5cm) high.
£240–270 *BBR*

A Teacher's water jug, with unusual bottle-like man depicted below spout and bottle necks, by James Green & Nephew, 1920s, 6½in (16.5cm) high.
£400–450 *BBR*

l. A Wright & Greig's coloured water jug, with chocolate brown top, peach coloured base with blue and black lettering 'Wright & Greig's, Old Scotch Whisky', by Wm Brownlie, Glasgow, 1920s, 6in (15cm) high.
£260–300 *BBR*

BUCKLES & BUTTONS

A glass paperweight button, c1900, ¼in (6mm) diam.
£20–22 *MRW*

A set of 4 Victorian jet glass buttons, French, late 19thC, 1¼in (32mm) diam.
£15–30 *MRW*

A Victorian gilt and glass button, hand decorated in gold, 1¼in (32mm) diam.
£4–5 *OBS*

A set of 6 buttons, early 20thC, in original box, ¼in (6mm) diam.
£20–30 *Ech*

A set of 4 hand-painted tricoloured plastic buttons, c1920, 1¼in (32mm) wide.
£12–15 *JV*

An Art Nouveau embossed glass button, c1925, ¾in (19mm) diam.
£8–10 *MRW*

A glass button, by the London Glass Co, 1930s, ¾in (19mm) diam.
£3–4 *OBS*

A set of 5 coconut bark buttons and a matching buckle, 1930s, buckle 3in (75mm) wide.
£35–40 *JV*

A set of 6 Art Deco mother-of-pearl buttons, c1920, 1in (25mm) square.
£10–15 *JV*

r. A set of plastic horse buttons, 1950s, ½in (12mm) diam.
£7–9 *JV*

A set of 6 hexagonal wooden buttons, late 1930s, 2in (50mm) wide.
£12–15 *JV*

A set of porcelain buttons, depicting the first 6 Presidents of America, c1950, 1in (25mm) diam.
£25–30 *JBB*

CAMERAS

An Agfa Karat 35mm camera, 1938–41, 4½in (11.5cm) wide.
£25–35 *HEG*

An Argus Model A 35mm camera, with Bakelite body, Michigan, Chicago, USA, c1940, 5in (12.5cm) wide.
£15–20 *ARP*

An Ansco automatic 1A-roll film camera, c1924, 9in (23cm) wide.
£150–180 *CaH*

A Butcher camera with fixed Beck symmetrical lens, cameo and 8 plate backs, c1910, 5½in (14cm) high.
£60–80 *CaH*

l. A Chas Beseler Optiscope, New York, c1950, 16in (40.5cm) long.
£170–220 *CaH*

A Canon FP 35mm single lens reflex camera, Japan, c1964, 5½in (14cm) wide.
£70–100 *ARP*

A Coronet portrait box camera, brown-coloured, Birmingham, c1935, 5½in (14cm) long.
£20–30 *ARP*

A Certoruhm camera, with fixed lens, c1925, 6½in (16.5cm) high.
£65–85 *CaH*

An Eltan 2.5 35mm projector, by Elite Optics Ltd, c1950, 9in (23cm) wide.
£40–50 *CaH*

A Crystar 15 Camera, by Crystar Optical Co, Japan, c1955, 5½in (14cm) wide.
£45–65 *ARP*

An Ensign Commando Rangefinder camera, c1945, 6in (15cm) wide.
£80–100 *HEG*

An Epidiascope Ross lens type camera, with stand and 3 lenses, c1952, 13in (33cm) wide.
£300–350 *CaH*

A Falloroll red bellows roll film camera, by Alliance Roll Film Camera Co Ltd, c1902, 8in (20.5cm) long.
£65–75 *HEG*

A Franka Solida Record camera, 1950s, 5½in (14cm) wide.
£5–10 *RAC*

A Gic 16mm cine camera, with Dallmeyer interchangeable lens, c1950, 3½in (9cm) wide.
£70–80 *CaH*

An Ihagee Exakta VXIIA 35mm camera, Version 7, Dresden, Germany, 1961, 6in (15cm) wide.
£80–100 *ARP*

A Kodak No. 4 cartridge camera, with red bellows, in case, c1904, 9in (23cm) wide.
£100–150 *HEG*

A Kodak Retinette camera, 1960s, 5½in (14cm) wide.
£5–10 *RAC*

A Leitz enlarger, with Focomat 11c colour drawer and 2 lenses, mask and timer, c1970, enlarger 35½in (90cm) high.
£1,500–1,800 *CaH*

A Kodak Disc 6000 camera, USA, 1970s, 5in (13cm) wide.
£10–15 *ARP*

l. A Leica R-E camera, c1970, 5in (13cm) wide.
£350–400 *VCL*

A Minolta SR7 35mm single lens reflex camera, Osaka, Japan, c1962, 6in (15cm) wide.
£70–80 *ARP*

This was the first camera with a built-in cds exposure meter.

A Minox 35mm compact camera, c1990,
£50–60 *VCL*

A Microcord twin lens reflex camera, a Rolleicord copy with Ross Xpress lens in Epsilon or Pronter shutter, c1952, 5in (13cm) high.
£80–100 *HEG*

A Paillard Bolex camera, with interchangeable lens, H-16 deluxe and octameter finder, c1950, 9in (23cm) wide.
£250–300 *CaH*

l. An Olympus OM-2n camera, c1979, 5in (13cm) wide.
£80–100 *VCL*

A Hermagis Pathescope 9.5 cine camera, with fixed lens, c1926, 4½in (11.5cm) wide.
£40–50 *CaH*

A Nikon Nikkor H Auto camera, with interchangeable lens, F2 photomic and MD3 motor drive, c1971, 7in (18cm) high.
£750–900 *CaH*

A Pentacon Six camera, with interchangeable lens, Pentaprism finder and Orestegor F4-300mm lens, c1957–62, 6½in (16.5cm) long.
£450–500 *CaH*

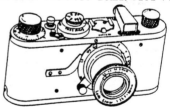

A Petri FT EE camera,
with automatic reflex lens,
c1969, 6in (15cm) wide.
£60–75 *HEG*

A Piccolette vest pocket
camera, 1919–26,
5in (12.5cm) high.
£60–75 *HEG*

A Rolleicord camera, c1967,
5in (12.5cm) high.
£50–60 *VCL*

A Sanderson Regular camera,
with Tessar interchangeable
lens, c1910, 4¼in (11cm) wide.
£140–180 *CaH*

A Voigtländer Vito camera,
Braunschweig, Germany,
c1948, 5in (12.5cm) wide.
£50–60 *ARP*

A Wallace Heaton Zodel camera,
with fixed Zodellar Anastigmat
lens, c1926, 5in (12.5cm) wide.
£50–75 *CaH*

A Wray Stereo Graphic camera,
c1955, 7in (17.5cm) wide.
£80–120 *HEG*

An QRS Kamra, by De Vry Corp,
Chicago-brown Bakelite, with Graf
fixed lens, c1928, 7¼in (18.5cm) wide.
£80–120 *CaH*

A James Sinclair and Co 35mm
cine camera, with leather case,
London, 1920s, 16in (40.5cm) high.
£320–350 *GIN*

A Welta Welti (1) camera,
c1935–50s, 5in (12.5cm) high.
£30–45 *HEG*

A Zorki-4K 35mm camera,
c1976, 5in (12.5cm) wide.
£15–20 *VCL*

l. A Zeiss Ikon Contax 11a
35mm camera, with exposure
meter and turret view finder,
c1950, 6in (15cm) wide.
£250–300 *DN*

CERAMICS
Animals

A Delft model of a wild boar, his back elaborately decorated in faïence colours with scrolls and foliage, with pale mauve body markings, on a similarly decorated oval base, ear restored and minor chips, 19thC, 7½in (19cm) high.
£400–450 *GAK*

A Royal Dux glazed model of a tiger, Czechoslovakian, c1930s, 20½in (52cm) long.
£375–425 *WeH*

A Meissen model of a lion cub, decorated in coloured enamels, on an oval base, painted mark in blue and incised 'B274', mid-20thC, 4in (10cm) high.
£160–180 *HOLL*

A Herman Auguste Kahler Plan green pottery bowl, in the form of 2 monkeys clasping hands, late 19thC, 11in (30cm) wide.
£270–300 *SUC*

A pair of Capodimonte models of a cock and hen, dressed as courtiers, c1960, 15½in (39.5cm) high.
£180–210 *CaC*

A Cat Pottery model of a sitting cat, No. 6, 1990s, 7½in (19cm) high.
£45–55 *CP*

A Goebel model of a bullfinch, c1962, 3¾in (9.5cm) high.
£20–30 *AAC*

A salt-glazed green and orange stoneware crocodile, by Jim Gladwin, designed by Roger Law & Pablo Bach, 1996, 8in (20cm) high.
£350–400 *RDG*

A Cat Pottery model of a brown corgi, 1990s, 24in (61cm) long.
£80–100 *CP*

Beswick

A Beswick 21 piece tea set, depicting a ballet scene, 1950s, plate 6¼in (16cm) diam.
£55–65 *RAD*

l. A Beswick black and white vase, with burnt orange interior, 1950s, 6in (15cm) high.
£18–22 *GIN*

Beswick Pottery

The Beswick factory was founded in 1894 to make decorative and domestic ware. In 1948 the factory launched a collection of 10 Beatrix Potter characters, designed by Arthur Gredington, who was already established as a fine modeller of animals and horses. The Beatrix Potter figures proved so popular that they inspired several other ranges of animal characters and figures from children's films and books.

David Hand's Animaland figures were released in 1949, created by Gredington from a series of British cartoons made by David Hand (former animator at Walt Disney) for the Rank Film organisation.

Beswick produced a number of Disney models, and in 1968 chief modeller Albert Hallam launched a new series to coincide with Winnie the Pooh and the Blustery Day.

Children's books continued to inspire the factory in the 1970s and 1980s. As well as creating new Beatrix Potter figures, graphic artist and design manager Harry Sales introduced collections inspired by characters ranging from Alice in Wonderland to Thelwell's ponies to Rupert Bear.

Look out for discontinued figures, rare variations in colour, modelling and marks and the Beswick backstamp, since in 1989 this trademark was changed to Royal Albert. The most desirable Beswick marks are the gold ones, which pre-date 1972. Value is also enhanced by the presence of an original box and period stickers. The Beatrix Potter figures have long been collectable but other cartoon and storybook characters (especially when in complete sets) are beginning to command some very high prices.

Two Beswick models of Hereford calves, No. 901A with mouth open, 901B with mouth closed, 1941–67, 4in (10cm) high.
£300–350 *P*

Three Beswick models of brown and black Persian cats, with grey 'swiss roll' colourway, 1964–66, largest 5½in (14cm) high.
l. No. 1898 **£150–200**
c. No. 1880 **£300–325**
r. No. 1886 **£200–225** *P*

Alice in Wonderland

A Beswick *Alice in Wonderland* model of the Cheshire Cat, 1973–82, 3½in (9cm) high.
£650–700 *P*

Five Beswick *Alice in Wonderland* figures, comprising Mock Turtle, Dodo, Gryphon, King and Queen of Hearts, 1973–83, largest 4¼in (11cm) high.
£500–550 *P*

A pair of Beswick *Alice in Wonderland* figures, Frog Footman and Fish Footman, 1975–83, 4¾in (12cm) high.
£450–500 *P*

David Hand Animated Figures

Two Beswick Animaland figures, designed by
David Hand, Ginger Nut and Zimmy Lion,
1949–55, largest 4¼in (11cm) high,
Ginger Nut **£350–400**
Zimmy Lion **£425–450** *P*

A pair of Beswick David Hand Animaland
models, Felia and Loopy Hare, 1949–55,
4¼in (11cm) high.
£350–400 each *P*

Horses

r. A Beswick model
of a grey Shire horse,
1940–present, 7in
(18cm) high.
£60–80 *MEG*

l. A Beswick model of
a bay pony, 1945–89,
4in (10cm) high.
£25–30 *MAC*

A Beswick model of a
colt, first version, 1939–71,
5in (12.5cm) high.
£45–50 *MAC*

A Beswick model of a
Black Beauty foal,
1976–89, 6in (15cm) high.
£20–30 *MAC*

l. A Beswick model
of a Shire horse,
1940–present,
8½in (21.5cm) high.
£40–50 *MAC*

Beatrix Potter

A Beswick model of
Babbity Bumble, 1989–93,
3in (7.5cm) high.
£60–80 *WWY*

A Beswick model
of Benjamin
Bunny, with gold
backstamp, 1952–72,
4¼in (11cm) high.
£250–300 *TP*

A Beswick model of
Mrs Rabbit, in a pink
skirt, 1951–74,
4in (10cm) high.
£180–220 *WWY*

A Beswick model of
Pickles, gold
backstamp, 1952–72,
4½in (11.5cm) high.
£350–375 *TP*

A Beswick model of
Timmy Willie, from
Johnny Town Mouse,
1949–93, 2¾in (7cm) high.
£70–80 *WWY*

A Beswick model of
Mr Jackson, in a pink coat,
1980–89, 3in (7.5cm) high.
£50–55 *TP*

A Beswick model of
Simpkin, with a green
coat, 1975–83,
4in (10cm) high.
£350–400 *TP*

A Beswick model of
Tommy Brock, gold
backstamp, 1955–74,
3½in (8.9cm) high.
£180–200 *TP*

Rupert Bear

A set of 5 Beswick Rupert
Bear figures, 1980–86,
largest 4¼in (11cm) high.
£1,000–1,200 *P*

Norman Thelwell

A Beswick Thelwell Pony
Express model, pony coloured
grey, 1983, 6in (15cm) high.
£80–100 *WWY*

A Beswick Thelwell Angel on
Horseback model, pony coloured
grey, 1983, 5¼in (13.5cm) high.
£80–100 *WWY*

Winnie the Pooh

A set of Beswick *Winnie the Pooh* characters, all with gold backstamp apart from Christopher Robin, 1971–90, largest 5in (12.5cm) high.
£700–800 *P*

Blue & White

A Dr Wall Worcester blue and white bowl, c1760, 8in (20.5cm) diam.
£400–450 *ALB*

A Dutch Delft blue and white inkwell, decorated with trailing flowers and leaves, rim chips, 18thC, 4½in (11.5cm) wide.
£340–360 *DN*

A Dutch Delft blue and white plate, decorated with a spray of wild flowers, c1760, 9¼in (23.5cm) diam.
£80–100 *BRU*

A blue and white meat dish, decorated with Long Bridge pattern, slight restoration, c1800–10, 21in (53cm) wide.
£60–80 *P(B)*

A blue and white transfer-printed mug, very damaged, c1800, 4¾in (12cm) high.
£25–30 *MEG*

r. A Spode pearlware blue and white two-handled tureen, cover and liner, with scroll handle, painted with the Forest landscape First pattern, damaged and restored, c1810, 10¼in (26cm) wide.
£150–175 *HOLL*

A blue and white oval meat dish, printed with an Indian sporting scene, unmarked, c1809–10, 15½in (39cm) diam.
£275–325 *P(B)*

> **Cross Reference**
> Colour Review

A Wedgwood blue and white plate, with floral border, c1810, 10in (25.5cm) diam.
£100–125 *SCO*

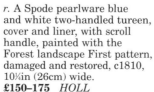

A pair of Spode blue and white plates, transfer-printed with the Sarcophagi & Sepulchres at the Head of the Harbour at Cacamo from the Caramanian series, mid-19thC, 10in (25.5cm) diam.
£280–320 *TMA*

A Davenport blue and white drainer dish, printed with Oxburgh Hall, impressed mark, c1810–15, 16½in (42cm) wide.
£220–260 *P(B)*

A Spode blue and white egg cup holder, decorated with daisy pattern, 1820, 7½in (19cm) diam.
£220–250 *SCO*

A blue and white plate, printed with the Durham Ox pattern within a floral border, c1820, 9¾in (25cm) diam.
£300–340 *P(B)*

A Spode blue and white comport, with moulded shell and scroll handles, gadrooned wavy border, mid-19thC, 14in (35.5cm) wide.
£320–360 *TMA*

A John Meir blue and white meat dish, printed with the River Fishing pattern, c1810–20, 21in (53cm) wide.
£300–350 *P(B)*

A Spode miniature blue and white teapot, decorated with Daisy and Bead pattern, c1815, 3in (7.5cm) high.
£220–250 *SCO*

A blue and white meat dish, printed with sheep and fishermen beside a bridge with church beyond, c1820s, 17in (43cm) wide.
£420–470 *P(B)*

r. A Ridgway plate, depicting Christchurch, Oxford, c1820, 10in (25.5cm) diam.
£120–140 *SCO*

A Herculaneum Pottery blue and white jug, printed with the Willow Pattern, impressed mark, spout chipped, c1810, 8¾in (22cm) high.
£90–110 *P(B)*

A Rogers blue and white meat dish, printed with the Monopteris pattern, c1814–36, 21¼in (54cm) wide.
£350–400 *P(B)*

A Wedgwood 58 piece blue and white dinner service, decorated with Ferrara pattern, early 19thC.
£900–1,100 *JH*

A blue and white plate, printed with the Piping Shepherd pattern, c1820, 9½in (24cm) diam.
£110–130 *P(B)*

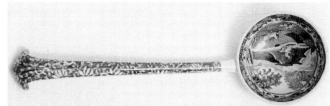

A blue and white pattern ladle, decorated with 'Spode's' Italian pattern, maker unknown, c1820, 13in (33cm) long.
£100–120 *SCO*

A Spode blue and white Eton College armorial dessert dish, c1820, 8in (20.5cm) wide.
£160–200 *SCO*

A Rogers blue and white meat plate, printed with the Camel pattern within canted geometric borders, some cracks, impressed mark 'Rogers 16', c1825, 17in (43cm) wide.
£330–360 *Hal*

A Davenport blue and white toilet bowl, with transfer printed floral border, damaged and repaired, 19thC, 13in (33cm) diam.
£80–100 *MEG*

A Staffordshire blue and white vomit pot, c1840, 5in (12.5cm) diam.
£180–220 *GN*

A blue and white Arcadian Chariots bowl, with glaze repair, unmarked, mid-19thC, 8in (20.5cm) diam.
£70–80 *MEG*

A blue and white pap boat, printed with a gentleman seated in his garden, probably Ridgway, 1840–50, 4¾in (12cm) long.
£60–80 *P(B)*

A blue and white teapot, decorated with transfer print of a child and dog, lid damaged, mid-19thC, 4in (10cm) high.
£30–40 *MEG*

A Staffordshire stoneware blue and white fish-shaped pickle dish, decorated with willow pattern, mid-19thC, 6in (15cm) wide.
£40–50 *MEG*

A blue and white two-handled basket, decorated with floral and scroll pattern border and pierced trelliswork body, mid-19thC, 8in (20.5cm) diam.
£300–350 *TMA*

Candle Extinguishers

Candle extinguishers became popular in the 19th century. The small figures are hollow and when placed over a candle put out the flame. Though they are functional items, they were also designed as ornaments. The Victorian period witnessed great developments in lighting, including in 1840 the introduction of the 'snuffless candle'. Made from a composite material including coconut oil, these came with plaited wicks which burnt themselves out and did not need trimming, unlike the bulky wicks on tallow candles. These new candles could also be blown out very easily, so an extinguisher was a decorative luxury rather than a necessity.

Candle extinguishers were made on the Continent, in France and Germany, with some of the finest examples coming from Meissen. In Britain major manufacturers included Minton and, above all, Royal Worcester. Extinguishers often came in pairs. Popular subjects include monks, priests, women, children and Oriental figures. Unsurprisingly, given their function, many characters are portrayed in nightcaps. Some extinguishers caricatured real people such as the great opera singer Jenny Lind, 'the Swedish Nightingale', while others focused on literary creations such as Sairey Gamp, the disreputable nurse from *Martin Chuzzlewit,* by Charles Dickens. W. H. Goss and the crested china companies also produced extinguishers in the form of conical hats. Figural examples from the 19th century are extremely collectable today, but buyer beware! In 1976 Royal Worcester rediscovered the original moulds for their Victorian extinguishers and many were re-issued. Though these reproductions are dated, there have been instances when the mark has been removed, so it is important to examine all pieces with extreme care.

A Meissen black candle extinguisher, depicting a priest, c1860, 3in (7.5cm) high.
£800–900 *TH*

A Staffordshire candle extinguisher, depicting a nun, c1870, 3in (7.5cm) high.
£50–60 *TH*

A pair of Royal Worcester candle extinguishers, entitled 'Girl with Muff' and 'Boy with Boater', by Kate Greenaway, c1880, 4in (10cm) high.
£1,400–1,500 *TH*

A Royal Worcester candle extinguisher, depicting a monk, c1880, 6½in (15cm) high.
£300–350 *TH*

This character was also made as a freestanding figure.

A Royal Worcester candle extinguisher, entitled 'Feathered Hat', c1880, 3¼in (8.5cm) high.
£800–900 *TH*

A Continental candle extinguisher, entitled 'Sairey Gamp' on base, c1890, 3½in (9cm) high.
£150–180 *TH*

A Goss candle holder and extinguisher, decorated with forget-me-nots, c1890–1925, 2½in (6.5cm) high.
£75–100 *G&CC*

A Royal Worcester candle extinguisher, entitled 'French Cook', c1898, 2½in (6.5cm) high.
£160–180 *TH*

A set of 3 Royal Worcester candle extinguishers, entitled 'Mr Caudles', 3¼in (8.5cm) high.
l. 1955. **£140–160**
c. 1908. **£200–220**
r. 1880. **£220–250** *TH*

Mr Caudle is a character from Mrs Caudle's Curtain Lectures *by Douglas Jerrold, first published in* Punch *magazine in 1846. Job Caudle was lectured by his nagging wife in bed, after the curtains were drawn, hence the figures' dress.*

Three Royal Worcester candle extinguishers, depicting Tyrolean hats, c1905, 2½in (6.5cm) high.
£120–140 each *TH*

A Goss candle extinguisher, with Brugge crest on cone, c1890–1920, 2½in (6.5cm) high.
£15–20 *G&CC*

l. A pair of Continental candle extinguishers, entitled 'Hansel and Gretel', c1890, largest 3in (7.5cm) high.
£175–200 *TH*

r. A Royal Worcester candle extinguisher, depicting a monk, c1919, 4⅜in (12cm) high.
£120–135 *HEI*

A collection of Royal Worcester candle extinguishers, entitled 'Mob Cap', 'Feathered Hat', 'Japanese' and 'Hush', all reproduced from old factory moulds, c1976–86, largest 3½in (9cm) high.
£70–110 each *TH*

Carlton Ware

In 1890 J. Wiltshaw and J. & H. Robinson founded a china factory at the Carlton Works, Stoke-on-Trent. From 1894 their trade name became Carlton Ware, and the company remained in production until 1989. Carlton Ware's great strength lay in its variety. The firm covered every aspect of the market from expensive lustre ware to low cost crockery, from advertising ceramics created for firms such as Guinness to crested china trinkets produced for a burgeoning tourist industry. Carlton Ware was renowned for having an exceptionally well-trained workforce and kept well abreast of new technology and contemporary fashions. 'Buy Carlton – first with the latest and the best' ran the company slogan.

Lustre ware was among the most distinctive work produced by the factory in the inter-war years and is increasingly sought after today. Vases, bowls, ginger jars and other classic shapes were decorated with an iridescent high-gloss glaze in colours ranging from dark red to deep blue to lime green to black. Works were painted with fantasy Oriental landscapes, exotic naturalistic imagery (spiders' webs, water lilies, birds of paradise) and vibrant Art Deco motifs. Rich gilding not only added to the air of luxury but also hid small imperfections in the pots.

While lustre pieces were aimed at the luxury end of the market, Carlton also catered for popular taste. Today the firm is probably best known for its brightly coloured tea sets, toast racks, jam pots etc, modelled in the form of flowers and fruits that were produced in vast numbers from the mid-1920s onwards, capturing perfectly the period fascination for novelty shapes and fanciful designs. Wares were embossed with plants and trees and even shaped in the form of the flowers, as in the case of Pink Buttercup, one of the most collectable of all the floral ranges. These fun and decorative products were extremely successful. Salad ware, introduced in 1929, remained in production until 1976, when new health regulations prohibited the use of the lead paint used to colour the vivid red tomatoes and lobster claws on their lettuce leaf background.

After WWII the factory reflected changes in fashion and the new contemporary style. Colours became less spring-like and shapes more abstracted and streamlined. Compared to many 1920s and 1930s pieces, post-war designs are still inexpensive and could be a good starting point for new collectors. In 1967 the firm was taken over by Arthur Wood & Sons. Under this new management Carlton Ware was to have one of its greatest successes with the Walking Ware range (cups and tea-ware on feet) designed by Roger Mitchell and Danka Napiorkowska and produced from 1975. Another interesting and now collectable line was the series of novelty designs produced with Fluck and Law, creators of the *Spitting Image* television series, whose wickedly accurate caricatures of royalty and other public figures summoned up the spirit of the 1980s.

A Carlton Ware plate, brown transfer-printed and hand-enamelled with carnations, pattern No. 621, blue crown mark, c1890–94, 8½in (21.5cm) diam.
£80–100 *StC*

A Carlton Ware two-handled vase, hand-painted with daisies, ribbon mark, c1890–94, 8¼in (21cm) high.
£60–80 *StC*

A Carlton Ware tinted faïence milk and sugar set, on silver-plated stand, pattern No. 605, c1890–94, 5in (12.5cm) high.
£50–60 *StC*

> **Cross Reference**
> Colour Review

A Carlton Ware bacon dish, white with moulding, ribbon mark, c1890–94, 11in (28cm) wide.
£40–50 *StC*

A Carlton Ware mug, with blue transfer-printed bird pattern, some damage, ribbon mark, c1890–94, 3½in (9cm) high.
£30–40 *StC*

A Carlton Ware tea kettle, white with gilt highlights, pattern No. 850, ribbon mark and 'Rd 149800', c1890–94, 6½in (16.5cm) high.
£60–80 *StC*

A Carlton Ware souvenir cup and saucer, with brown transfer print depicting Tadcaster Church, ribbon mark, c1890–94, saucer 5¼in (13.5cm) diam.
£70–80 *StC*

A Carlton Ware match striker, marked, c1894–1900, 2½in (6.5cm) high.
£25–30 *MAC*

A Carlton Ware beaker, commemorating Queen Victoria's jubilee, brown transfer-printed and hand-enamelled, pattern No. 856, blue crown mark, 1897, 3½in (9cm) high.
£80–90 *StC*

A Carlton Ware box and cover, with lithographic printed floral chintz pattern, blue crown mark, early 20thC, 3½in (9cm) wide.
£20–30 *StC*

A Carlton Ware tinted faïence tobacco jar, blue transfer-printed, chipped, crown mark, 'Rd No. 330913', late 19thC, 4in (10cm) high.
£40–50 *StC*

A Carlton Ware vase, decorated with Marguerite pattern in red, blue and gilt Imari colours, restored, blue crown mark, late 19thC, 9in (23cm) high.
£150–200 *StC*

A pair of Carlton Ware vases, decorated with blue transfer Petunia pattern, restored, blue crown mark, late 19thC, 9in (23cm) high.
£200–300 *StC*

A Carlton Ware cream and sugar set, on silver-plated stand, decorated with Petunia pattern, brown transfer-printed blushware and hand-enamelled, pattern No. 945½, brown crown mark, 'Rd 258145', late 19thC, 7in (18cm) high.
£100–150 *StC*

A Carlton Ware vase, the matt black ground hand-enamelled with Parrots pattern, slight damage, black crown mark, early 20thC, 6½in (16.5cm) high.
£20–30 *StC*

A Carlton Ware vase, decorated with Old Wisteria transfer pattern, hand-enamelled with chequered banding, pattern No. 2238, blue crown mark, early 20thC, 9¼in (23.5cm) high.
£80–100 *StC*

A Carlton Ware biscuit barrel, with silver-plated lid, decorated with lithographic transfer of peonies on a blush ground, black crown mark, early 20thC, 5¼in (13.5cm) diam.
£40–60 *StC*

A Carlton Ware mug and cover, decorated with blue and white transfer-printed classical scene with figures, black crown mark, early 20thC, 4½in (11.5cm) high.
£100–120 *StC*

A Carlton Ware fluted egg cup and stand, with separate egg-shaped cruets, in purple lustre with mother-of-pearl lustre interior, 1920s, 2½in (6.5cm) high.
£70–90 *StC*

A Carlton Ware biscuit barrel, with silver-plated mounts and stand, decorated in blue with white classical figures, blue crown mark, early 20thC, 9¾in (25cm) high.
£100–150 *StC*

A Carlton Ware preserve pot and lid, with green lustre body, on silver-plated stand, slight damage, black crown mark, 1920s, 2½in (6.5cm) high.
£20–25 *StC*

A Carlton Ware bitters dispenser, with orange base, silver top and black transfer-printed figures, shape No. 304, black crown mark, 1920s, 7in (17.5cm) high.
£100–125 *StC*

A Carlton Ware yellow lustre bowl, c1925, 9¼in (23.5cm) diam.
£90–110 *AAC*

A Carlton Ware pen holder, with brightly coloured bird, c1925, 18in (45.5cm) wide.
£65–75 *BSA*

A Carlton Ware vase and cover, decorated with black and tan chinoiserie pattern, c1930, 12in (30.5cm) high.
£250–300 *CSA*

A pair of Carlton Ware ashtrays, depicting a bride and groom, black script mark, 1930s, 2½in (6.5cm) wide.
£150–200 *StC*

A collection of Carlton Ware items, decorated with Anemone pattern, 1930s, 4½in (11.5cm) high.
£30–60 each *CSA*

A Carlton Ware cheese dish and cover, with embossed Blackberry design, registered Australian design mark, 1930s, 3in (7.5cm) high.
£60–70 *StC*

A Carlton Ware pale green mug and cover, with embossed Foxglove design, c1940, 5in (12.5cm) high.
£60–80 *StC*

Due to war time restrictions imposed by the Board of Trade, hand-painted ceramics were produced only for export.

A Carlton Ware Art Deco coffee pot, with figurehead handle, pattern No. 3684, restored, black script mark, 1930s, 5½in (14cm) high.
£200–300 *StC*

A Carlton Ware blue table bell, and yellow napkin ring, in the form of crinoline ladies, c1930, largest 4in (10cm) high.
£30–40 each *StC*

A collection of Carlton Ware jugs, c1935, largest 3¼in (8cm) high.
£20–30 each *CSA*

A Carlton Ware black and gilt jug, c1935, 7in (18cm) high.
£150–200 *CSA*

A Carlton Ware musical tankard, entitled 'Last Drop', c1935, 5¼in (13.5cm) high.
£250–300 *CSA*

A Carlton Ware dish, decorated with New Poppy design, c1935, 8in (20.5cm) wide.
£40–50 *CSA*

A Carlton Ware Rouge Royale handpainted leaf dish, 1950s, 13½in (34.5cm) long.
£8–10 *MAC*

l. A Carlton Ware cup and saucer, with embossed Foxglove design, registered Australian design mark, early 1940s, saucer 5¾in (14.5cm) diam.
£40–50 *StC*

A Carlton Ware cheese dish and cover, the cover with embossed fruit, c1950, 8¾in (22cm) long.
£55–65 *LUC*

A pair of Carlton Ware black vases, with label on base, 1950s, 3¼in (8.5cm) high.
£12–15 *MAC*

A Carlton Ware cup and saucer, decorated with Orbit pattern, lithographic scriptz mark, 1950s, saucer 6in (15cm) diam.
£20–30 *StC*

A Carlton Ware lustre sauce tureen, with duck handle, slight damage, rubber stamp mark, late 1970s, 6½in (16.5cm) diam.
£25–35 *StC*

A Carlton Ware milk jug, hand-decorated with Linen pattern, shape No. 2443, script mark, c1960, 6½in (16.5cm) high.
£20–30 *StC*

A Carlton Ware lustre cup on feet, with transfer mark, 1970s, 3¼in (8.5cm) high.
£10–12 *MAC*

A Carlton Ware curling stone trophy, advertising Beneagles Scotch Whisky, c1980, 4¾in (12cm) diam.
£40–50 *StC*

A Carlton Ware cup on feet, commemorating the Silver Jubilee, c1977, 4¼in (11cm) high.
£15–17 *MAC*

Two Carlton Ware egg cups, depicting 'Spitting Images' of HM The Queen and Fergie, designed by Fluck & Law, c1980, 4in (10cm) high.
£30–35 each *PC*

Clarice Cliff

A Clarice Cliff Conical jug, decorated with Umbrellas and Rain pattern, c1929, 7in (18cm) high.
£600–700 RIC

Clarice Cliff

Clarice Cliff (1899–1972) dominated ceramic design during the 1930s and is probably the most famous and collectable name in Art Deco pottery. She produced a vast number of shapes and patterns, and prices today depend on rarity. The Carpet pattern *(right)* was copied by Cliff from a magazine illustration of a carpet designed by Da Silva Bruhns (1881–1980), Brazilian painter, rug designer and weaver – Bruhns' work was much imitated and this vase reflects his cubist style. This sophisticated modernism was perhaps, however, a little too much for the British ceramics market. The Carpet pattern with its curved lines and dots was only produced in 1930, and its rarity is reflected in its price range.

A Clarice Cliff Bizarre vase, decorated with Carpet pattern in orange, grey and black, moulded 'No. 358', 1930, 7½in (19cm) high.
£3,400–3,800 RBB

A Clarice Cliff Fantasque bowl, decorated with Comets pattern, brightly coloured in orange, yellow, green, blue and purple, printed mark to base, c1930, 6½in (16.5cm) diam.
£650–750 WL

A Clarice Cliff Fantasque vase, decorated with Broth pattern, shape No. 355, with Lawley's gold backstamp, 1929–30, 7in (18cm) high.
£550–650 GH

A Clarice Cliff jardinière, decorated with Branch and Square design, c1929–30, 3½in (9cm) high.
£375–425 MEG

FURTHER READING
Leonard Griffin and Louis K. and Susan Pear Meisel, *Clarice Cliff The Bizarre Affair,* Thames & Hudson, 1989

A Clarice Cliff ashtray, decorated with Orange Roof Cottage pattern, early 1930s, 5in (13cm) diam.
£150–200 RIC

A Clarice Cliff cigarette holder and ashtray, decorated with Orange House pattern, c1930, 3¼in (8cm) high.
£350–400 CSA

l. A Clarice Cliff Conical bowl, decorated with Tennis pattern, c1931, 4½in (11.5cm) diam.
£400–500 RIC

A Clarice Cliff vase, decorated with Summerhouse pattern, shape No. 368, c1931, 3½in (9cm) high.
£420–450 BKK

A Clarice Cliff vase, decorated with Apples pattern, shape No. 366, c1931–32, 6in (15cm) high.
£1,200–1,500 *RIC*

A Clarice Cliff Bizarre beer pitcher, decorated with Idyll pattern, c1932, 11in (28cm) high.
£950–1,000 *GH*

A Clarice Cliff octagonal cake plate, decorated with Applique Idyll pattern, c1932, 7½in (19cm) diam.
£250–300 *CSA*

A Clarice Cliff vase, decorated with Limberlost pattern, c1932, 3¾in (9.5cm) high.
£250–300 *RIC*

A Clarice Cliff Bizarre oval tapered vase, decorated with Patina Country pattern, internally decorated with Delecia running glazes, shape No. 212, printed 'Patina Bizarre by Clarice Cliff', c1932, 5½in (14cm) high.
£250–300 *AG*

A Clarice Cliff vase, decorated with Orange Chintz pattern, shape No. 362, c1932, 8in (20.5cm) high.
£700–800 *RIC*

A Clarice Cliff bowl, decorated with Patina Country pattern, c1932, 9in (23cm) diam.
£250–300 *WTA*

A Clarice Cliff reeded trumpet vase, decorated with a butterfly, the base moulded with flowers in shades of orange, yellow and green, c1930, 10in (25.5cm) high.
£160–180 *GH*

A Clarice Cliff Fantasque Bizarre biscuit barrel and cover, with swing handle, decorated with Blue Chintz pattern, minor chips to rim, c1932, 6½in (16.5cm) high.
£230–260 *GH*

A Clarice Cliff Havre bowl, decorated in Pastel Autumn pattern, c1932, 9in (23cm) diam.
£260–280 *WTA*

A Clarice Cliff Bon Jour shape tea set, decorated with Field Flowers pattern, designed by Eva Crofts, black printed marks, 1930s, teapot 5½in (14cm) high.
£550–650 *Hal*

A Clarice Cliff Bon Jour shape teapot, painted with pink roses, damaged, 1930s, 5in (12.5cm) high.
£140–160 *GH*

A Clarice Cliff sugar bowl, decorated with Coral Firs pattern, c1933, 3¼in (8.5cm) high.
£150–250 *RIC*

A Clarice Cliff preserve pot and cover, painted with stylised flowers and foliage, 1930s, 4in (10cm) diam.
£70–90 *GH*

A Clarice Cliff plate, decorated with brown and green lined pattern, c1933, 7in (18cm) diam.
£50–60 *RAC*

Two Clarice Cliff Bizarre Conical shape sugar sifters, one decorated with Rhodanthe pattern, one with Crocus, 1930s, 5½in (14cm) high.
£330–400 each *GH*

l. A Clarice Cliff Elegant flower basket, decorated with Canterbury Bells design, c1932, 12½in (32cm) high.
£500–600 *CSA*

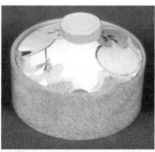

A Clarice Cliff Bizarre preserve pot and cover, decorated with Viscaria pattern, 1930s, 4in (10cm) diam.
£160–190 *GH*

A Clarice Cliff bowl, decorated with Canterbury Bells pattern, c1932, 8in (20.5cm) diam.
£220–250 *MEG*

A Clarice Cliff Athens shape jug, decorated with Honolulu pattern, c1933, 8in (20.5cm) high.
£600–700 *RIC*

r. A Clarice Cliff Conical shape sugar sifter, c1935, 5½in (14cm) high.
£500–600 *CSA*

A Clarice Cliff posy trough, decorated with My Garden pattern, c1935, 7¼in (18.5cm) diam.
£150–180 *CSA*

A Clarice Cliff Bizarre bowl, decorated with Kelverne pattern, shape No. 632, mid-1930s, 8in (20.5cm) diam.
£220–260 *GH*

A Clarice Cliff Bizarre Fantasque square shaped bowl, with electro-plated rim, decorated with Blue Autumn pattern, Newport Pottery, c1935, 8in (20.5cm) square.
£450–500 *AG*

A Clarice Cliff Bizarre bowl, decorated with Aurea pattern, c1935, 8¼in (21cm) diam.
£250–300 *GSP*

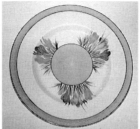

A Clarice Cliff cake plate, decorated with Spring Crocus pattern, c1938, 10in (25.5cm) diam.
£40–50 *CSA*

A Clarice Cliff teapot and jug, decorated with embossed wheat and flowers, Newport Pottery, c1935, jug 7½in (19cm) high.
£250–300 *MAR*

A Clarice Cliff Bizarre Fantasque tapered biscuit barrel, with electroplated rim, cover and swing handle, decorated with Blue Autumn pattern, Newport Pottery, c1935, 5in (12.5cm) diam.
£450–500 *AG*

A Clarice Cliff Lotus shape jug, decorated with Anemone pattern, late 1930s, 11½in (29cm) high.
£380–420 *GH*

A pair of Clarice Cliff lobed oval vases, decorated with My Garden pattern, shape No. 178, printed marks, Wilkinson Ltd, c1940, 7½in (19cm) wide.
£60–80 *GAK*

Coalport

A Coalport coffee can and saucer, painted in puce monochrome, with a river landscape, within gilt line borders, c1800–05, coffee can 2½in (6.5cm) high.
£120–160 *DN*

A Coalport inkstand, with 2 lift-out wells, decorated with flowers and insects, the oval scroll-moulded tray with pierced pink borders and details, c1830–35, 9¾in (25cm) wide.
£350–450 *WW*

A Coalport figure, in a blue dress, entitled 'Collette', damaged, c1946, 7½in (19cm) high.
£40–50 *TAC*

r. A Coalport figure, in a pink dress, entitled 'Rosemary', from Ladies of Fashion series, 1975–84, 8in (20.5cm) high.
£125–145 *TP*

A Coalport figure, entitled 'Wig Maker', No. 44 of 1,000, 1970s, 8½in (21.5cm) high.
£125–145 *TP*

A Coalport figure, in a red coat, entitled 'Margaret', from Ladies of Fashion series, 1978–89, 8½in (21.5cm) high.
£145–165 *TP*

A Coalport figure, in a yellow dress, entitled 'Serenade', from Ladies of Fashion series, 1984–86, 7¾in (19.5cm) high.
£125–145 *TP*

A Coalport figure, in a yellow coat, entitled 'Linda', from Ladies of Fashion series, 1978–88, 8in (20.5cm) high.
£125–145 *TP*

Commemorative
Military & Naval

A pearlware bowl, printed in blue with portrait of Nelson and sailing ships in background, within a circular border inscribed with Nelson's signal and name, flanked by verse and naval trophies, the rim with a repeated design including flowers and butterflies, lined in brown, minor damage, early 19thC, 8in (20.5cm) diam.
£600–700 *SAS*

A pottery plate, printed in *rouge de fer* with an allegorical scene depicting Neptune, the border with female figures, naval trophies and 4 classical heads in profile of Nelson, the reverse inscribed 'No. 2', early 19thC, 9¾in (25cm) diam.
£400–500 *SAS*

r. A plate, printed in black with 4 oval portrait medallions depicting the President of France, King George V, The Tsar and King of the Belgians, surmounted by coloured enamel flags, beneath a cartouche, inscribed, dated '1914', 9in (23cm) diam.
£50–60 *SAS*

A Herculaneun plate, painted with a portrait of Nelson, c1815, 10in (25.5cm) diam.
£650–750 *TVM*

A bone china mug, commemorating the Boer War, with a portrait of Lord Roberts, c1900, 3½in (9cm) high.
£100–125 *W&S*

A ceramic Toby jug, commemorating the Gulf War, in the form of Norman Schwarzkopf, by Kevin Francis, c1991, 8¼in (21cm) high.
£100–150 *BRT*

l. A Staffordshire mug, commemorating the Boer War, in the form of Lord Kitchener, c1900, 6¼in (16cm) high.
£55–65 *OD*

Political

A pottery mug, printed in pink with named portraits of Earl Grey and Lord John Russell, centred by a spray of union flowers, crown and inscription 'Champions of Reform', 1832, 3¼in (8.5cm) high.
£150–200 *SAS*

A porcelain mug, with scroll handle, printed in black with a named portrait of Sir Robert Peel, flanked by wheat ears, gilt rims, slight damage, 1850, 3in (7.5cm) high.
£180–200 *SAS*

Sir Robert Peel died following a fall from his horse whilst riding in Hyde Park on 29th June 1850.

A porcelain mug, painted with 2 head-and-shoulder portraits inscribed 'Grey 2912' and 'Ridley 2912', the base inscribed 'H. J. Gow April 18th 1878', hairline crack, 3½in (9cm) high.
£300–400 *SAS*

The South Northumberland by-election of 18th April 1878 produced a tie between Grey the Liberal and Ridley the Conservative (hence reversed tie and cravat colours, Grey with blue cravat and Ridley with red tie) of 2,912 votes each. Following a re-count Ridley was declared elected with 2,909 against Grey's 2,903. In the 1880 election Grey was elected with 3,896 votes.

A Burleigh Ware character jug, in the form of Sir Winston Churchill smoking a cigar, 1940s, 5½in (14cm) high.
£125–150 *W&S*

An octagonal plate, printed in black with a portrait of the Hon Edward Blake, MA QC, within twin branches of maple leaves around the border, gilt rim, small chip, late 19thC, 9½in (24cm) diam.
£300–350 *SAS*

Blake was born in Ontario in 1833. He was Prime Minister of Ontario from 1871–72 and leader of the Canadian Liberal party 1880–87. He died in Toronto in 1912. It is thought this portrait may have been inspired by a photograph taken by W. J. Topley of Ottawa.

A character jug, in the form of a 'Spitting Image' caricature of Neil Kinnock, by Kevin Francis, No. 45 of 650 limited edition, 1985, 5in (13cm) high.
£85–95 *ANP*

A Price's Gurgling Jug, modelled as Edward Heath, 1970s, 19in (48.5cm) high.
£55–65 *MGC*

l. An Astoria shape china mug, commemorating 'The Champions of Democracy', with printed colour portraits of Winston Churchill and Franklin D. Roosevelt, by Alfred Meakin, 1940s, 3½in (9cm) high.
£55–65 *MSB*

Royalty
Queen Victoria

A pottery nursery plate, commemorating the marriage of Queen Victoria and Prince Albert of Saxe Coburg, printed in brown, the rim lined in black, 1840, 7in (18cm) diam.
£180–220 *SAS*

A Foley porcelain teapot and cover, commemorating Queen Victoria's Diamond Jubilee, the lobed body set with a gilded handle and spout, enamelled with royal coat-of-arms and inscription, by Wileman, 6¼in (16cm) high.
£130–150 *SAS*

A Coalport plate, commemorating the Golden Jubilee, printed in blue with a portrait of Queen Victoria, 1897, 10½in (27cm) diam.
£120–150 *W&S*

r. A Doulton Lambeth vase, commemorating the Golden Jubilee of Queen Victoria, 1887, 7½in (19cm) high.
£150–180 *W&S*

r. A Foley shell-moulded dish, in memory of Queen Victoria, with sepia portrait draped with a purple curtain surmounted by flags and a crown, inscribed, by Wileman, 1901, 4in (10.5cm) diam.
£100–120 *SAS*

Edward VII

A Scottish pottery jug, commemorating the marriage of the Prince of Wales, later Edward VII, and named portrait of Princess Alexandra on reverse, by Bell & Co, 1863, 8¾in (22cm) high.
£140–160 *SAS*

A porcelain plate, commemorating the Coronation of Edward VII, printed all over in blue with central oval medallion, with gilded gadrooned border, by S. Kepple, 1902, 10in (25.5cm) diam.
£130–145 *SAS*

l. A pottery plate, commemorating the proclamation of Edward VII, with 3 named portraits including Queen Victoria, inscribed and dated, by William Lowe, dated '1901', 9½in (24cm) diam.
£120–140 *SAS*

George V

A Coalport plate, commemorating the Coronation of George V, printed in blue with a border of naval vessels, inscribed and dated, the rim printed with the arms of the Dominions, 1911, 10¼in (26cm) diam.
£80–100 *SAS*

A MacIntyre mug, commemorating the Coronation of George V and Queen Mary, 1911, 3½in (9cm) high.
£75–95 *W&S*

A Paragon plate, commemorating the Silver Jubilee of George V and Queen Mary, with silver rim, 1935, 10½in (27cm) diam.
£140–160 *W&S*

Edward VIII
(Duke of Windsor)

A Wedgwood plate, commemorating the Coronation of George V, printed all over in blue with central portrait, 1911, 10¼in (26cm) diam.
£80–100 *SAS*

A bone china mug, with gold handle, for the proposed Coronation of Edward VIII, designed by Dame Laura Knight, 1936, 3½in (9cm) high.
£250–300 *W&S*

Two Mercian mugs, one in memory of the Duke of Windsor 1972, the other in memory of the Duchess of Windsor, printed in black, 1986, 4¼in (11cm) high.
£70–80 *SAS*

Significant Royal Dates

Victoria (1819–1901)
Coronation 1838
Marriage to Prince Albert 1840
Death of Prince Albert 1861
Golden Jubilee 1887
Diamond Jubilee 1897
Death of Queen Victoria 1901
Edward VII (1841–1910)
Marriage to Princess Alexandra 1863
Coronation 1901
Death of Edward VII 1910
George V (1865–1936)
Marriage to Princess Mary 1893
Coronation 1910
Silver Jubilee 1935
Death of George V 1936
Edward VIII, later Duke of Windsor (1894–1972)
Accession and Abdication 1936

Marriage to Wallace Simpson 1937
Death of Duke of Windsor 1972
Death of Duchess of Windsor 1986
George VI (1895–1952)
Marriage to Elizabeth Bowes-Lyon 1923
Coronation 1937
Death of George VI 1952
Elizabeth II (b. 1926)
Marriage to Prince Phillip 1947
Coronation 1952
Investiture of Prince of Wales 1969
Marriage of Princess Anne and Captain Mark Phillips 1973 (divorced 1992)
Silver Jubilee 1977
Marriage of Prince Charles and Lady Diana Spencer 1981
40th Anniversary 1992
Golden Wedding 1997
Death of Diana, Princess of Wales 1997

George VI

A Wedgwood white pottery beaker, commemorating the Coronation of George VI, printed in grey on a blue ground with portraits including the Princesses, 1937, 4½in (11.5cm) high.
£35–45 *SAS*

A Paragon plate, commemorating the Coronation of George VI and Queen Elizabeth, 1937, 8½in (21.5cm) diam.
£85–95 *W&S*

r. A Shelley two-handled loving cup, commemorating the Coronation of George VI and Queen Elizabeth, highly enamelled in colour and gold, interior rim inscribed, 1937, 3¼in (8.5cm) high.
£225–250 *W&S*

A Burleigh Ware mug, commemorating the Coronation of George VI and Queen Elizabeth, designed by Dame Laura Knight, printed marks, 1937, 3¼in (8.5cm) high.
£45–55 *MAC*

Elizabeth II
(& the Royal Family)

A Wedgwood mug, commemorating the Coronation of Queen Elizabeth II, printed in black with a lion and unicorn supporting a crown, gilt rims, by Guyatt, 1953, 4in (10cm) high.
£40–50 *SAS*

An Aynsley bone china mug, commemorating the wedding of Princess Anne and Mark Phillips, 1973, 3½in (9cm) high.
£20–25 *W&S*

r. A Wedgwood tankard, with EPNS lid, commemorating the wedding of Prince Charles and Lady Diana Spencer, limited edition, 1981, 6in (15cm) high.
£75–95 *W&S*

Contemporary Studio Ceramics

A John Calver footed dish, decorated in yellow on an orange ground, with cut rim, 1990s, 6in (15cm) wide.
£40–50 *ELG*

A Mick Arnup buff-coloured stoneware vase, decorated with pale green patterns, 1990s, 17¾in (45cm) high.
£220–260 *ELG*

A Norah Braden stoneware jar and lid, with matt speckled beige exterior and brown banded decoration, inscribed 'Made by Norah Braden for Bendicks, Kensington', c1932, 5¼in (13.5cm) high.
£350–400 *Bon*

This piece was one of a set of 12 commissioned by Bendicks, circa 1932, one of which is in the Victoria and Albert Museum.

Locate the Source

The source of each illustration in Miller's can be found by checking the code letters below each caption with the Key to Illustrations.

A Michael Cardew yellow and brown earthenware vessel, with 3 double looped scrolled handles, slight damage, impressed 'MC', with Winchcombe Pottery seals, c1930, 6¼in (17cm) high.
£800–1,000 *Bon*

A Russell Coates porcelain dish, with green and orange enamelled Celtic design, 1990s, 11¾in (30cm) wide.
£150–200 *ELG*

A Ladi Kwali stoneware water pot, with rust red, green and black decorated panels of crocodiles and abstract forms, c1960, 11½in (29.5cm) high.
£6,500–7,500 *Bon*

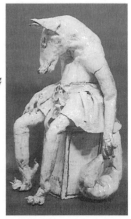

r. A Gareth Nash 'CJ' ceramic sculpture, 1990s, 26in (66cm) high.
£975–1,250 *ELG*

A Shoji Hamada stoneware tea cup, decorated with red rust and olive green foliate on grey glaze, 1950s, 3⅓in (8.5cm) high.
£550–650 *Bon*

l. A Bernard Leach stoneware vase, depicting 12 leaping fish on speckled buff ground, impressed 'BL' and with St Ives seals, c1965, 15½in (39.5cm) high.
£5,000–6,000 *Bon*

An Emily Myers lidded pot, decorated in terracotta and blue, 1990s, 6in (15cm) diam.
£65–80 *ELG*

A Philip Webb tazza, the interior designed with a black hare on a buff ground, from a William Morris tile, Dennis China Works, c1996, 4in (10cm) high.
£100–120 *NP*

A Dame Lucie Rie stoneware vase, with speckled off-white glaze, impressed 'LR' seal, c1957, 5in (12.5cm) high.
£400–500 *Bon*

A David Rousseau raku vase, coloured in mustard and orange, 1990s, 8in (20.5cm) high.
£70–80 *ELG*

r. A Sally Tuffin bowl, decorated with an orange and a black fish, Dennis China Works, c1995, 9in (23cm) wide.
£120–140 *NP*

A Christine Smith slipware rugby plate, decorated in brown and cream, 1990s, 11½in (30cm) diam.
£100–150 *ELG*

A Winchcombe pottery cruet set, probably by Sidney Tustin, 1950s, 6½in (16.5cm) diam.
£30–40 *IW*

A George Wilson glazed porcelain bowl, with petrol blue and platinum design, 1990s, 5¼in (13cm) diam.
£50–65 *ELG*

A Juliet Thorne paper and clay sculpture, entitled 'Human Form', 1990s, 9¾in (25cm) high.
£60–75 *ELG*

l. A Tessa Wolfe Murray earthenware vase, with glazed and smoked window design, 1990s, 6¼in (16cm) high.
£40–50 *ELG*

Susie Cooper

A Susie Cooper jug, decorated with orange, yellow and black bands, Gray's Pottery, c1928, 5½in (14cm) high.
£30–40   *CSA*

A Susie Cooper graffito jug, c1938, 9½in (23.5cm) high.
£70–80   *CSA*

A Susie Cooper Rex shape teapot, decorated with Dresden Spray design, c1939, 5½in (14cm) high.
£100–120   *CSA*

A Susie Cooper coffee can and saucer, decorated with Venetia design, c1965, can 2½in (6.5cm) high.
£10–12   *CSA*

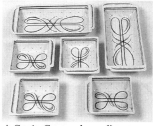

A Susie Cooper hors d'oeuvre set, painted with scroll motif on a cream ground, painted mark '2226', c1930s, largest 6in (15cm) wide.
£80–100   *HYD*

A Susie Cooper vase, with matt blue glaze, impressed decoration and incised signature, c1935, 7½in (19cm) high.
£80–90   *CSA*

A Susie Cooper jug, decorated with Parrot Tulip design, c1950, 5in (12.5cm) high.
£50–60   *CSA*

A Susie Cooper Quail shape jug, decorated with Glen Mist design, c1960, 4½in (11.5cm) high.
£15–20   *CSA*

A Susie Cooper tea-for-two, painted with bands in shades of orange, yellow, grey and black, Gray's Pottery, c1928, teapot 6in (15cm) high.
£130–160   *GH*

A Susie Cooper coffee set, pattern No. 1169, 1930s, coffee pot 8in (20.5cm) high.
£250–300   *GH*

A Susie Cooper Quail shape teapot, decorated with Whispering Grass design, c1955, 5½in (14cm) high.
£40–50   *CSA*

A Susie Cooper plate, decorated with Wild Strawberry design, c1953, 8¼in (21cm) diam, and a butter dish, c1970, 4in (10cm) diam.
£10–15 each   *CSA*

Cottages
Legend Lane

A Legend Lane model, La Chaumine, French series, 1992–93, 3¼in (8.5cm) high.
£40–45 *LEG*

A Legend Lane model, Vine Lodge, 1991–92, 3in (7.5cm) high.
£45–50 *LEG*

A Legend Lane model, Navigation Mews, 1992–93, 3in (7.5cm) high.
£45–50 *LEG*

A Legend Lane model, Dovedale Cottage, 1992–93, 3in (7.5cm) high.
£45–50 *LEG*

Lilliput Lane

A Lilliput Lane dealer sign, Pack Horse Bridge, North America, 1985, 4½in (11.5cm) wide.
£400–500 *ANP*

A Lilliput Lane 'paint your own' model, 1992, 2½in (6.5cm) high.
£100–120 *ANP*

A Lilliput Lane dealer sign, Bridge House, 1982–83, 4¼in (11.5cm) high.
£400–450 *ANP*

A Lilliput Lane model, Little Lost Dog, 1987–88, 2½in (6.5cm) high.
£250–275 *ANP*

This item was presented as a joining gift to Lilliput Lane Collectors Club members.

l. A Lilliput Lane model, Cornflower Cottage, special edition, Summer Fair 1996, code No. 12028, 1996, 4in (10cm) high.
£100–120 *ANP*

A Lilliput Lane model, Arbury Lodge, special edition, Collectors Fair 1997, code No. 12106, 1997, 3⅓in (8.5cm) high.
£90–100 *ANP*

A Lilliput Lane model, Honeysuckle Cottage III, limited edition, first versions, code No. 12096, 1997, 3in (7.5cm) high.
£450–500 *ANP*

A Lilliput Lane model, Rose Cottage, Scirsgill, 2nd edition, 1991–97, 4⅓in (11.5cm) wide.
£80–110 *ANP*

r. A Lilliput Lane model, Fire Station, limited edition, 1995–96, 5½in (14cm) wide.
£550–600 *ANP*

l. A Lilliput Lane model, Porlock Down, Collectors Club special, 1996–1997, 3½in (9cm) high.
£65–75 *ANP*

Wade

Three Wade cottages, first issued 1980, largest 1½in (4cm) high.
£8–10 each *AAC*

A Wade church, first issued 1980, 2⅓in (6.5cm) high.
£10–12 *AAC*

David Winter

A David Winter model, Scrooge's Counting House, 1987, 6⅓in (16.5cm) high.
£230–250 *Lof*

A David Winter model, The Parsonage, 1984, 9in (23cm) high.
£260–280 *Lof*

A David Winter model, Crofter's Cottage, 1986, 5in (12.5cm) high, with original box.
£60–70 *Lof*

A Gallé faïence model of a smiling cat, signed 'E. Gallé à Nancy', c1890, 13in (33cm) high.
£5,750–6,500 *P*

l. A money box, Jemma, Dutch, c1950, 12in (30.5cm) high.
r. A lion, c1950, 6in (15cm) high.
£20–25 each *AND*

A Cat Pottery model of a tiger, 1990s, 7½in (19cm) long.
£40–45 *CP*

A Beswick teapot, depicting Sairey Gamp, 1939–73, 5in (13cm) high.
£40–50 *SnA*

A Beswick model of a fox, 1945–present, 5¼in (13cm) high.
£15–20 *MAC*

A Beswick Tom Kitten and Butterfly, 1985–88, 3½in (9cm) high.
£120–150 *SAS*

A Beswick model of Benjamin Bunny, 1972–c1980, 4in (10cm) high.
£180–220 *WWY*

A Beswick Squirrel Nutkin, 1980–90s, 3½in (9cm) high.
£70–90 *WWY*

A Beswick figure of seated Jester, No. 1087, 1947–65, 5in (12.5cm) high.
£600–625 *P*

A Beswick figure of Cecily Parsley, 1964–86, 4in (10cm) high.
£90–100 *SnA*

A Beswick figure of Anna Maria, marked, 1955–72, 3in (7.5cm) high.
£275–300 *TP*

A Beswick model of Timmy Willie Sleeping, c1986, 3¾in (9.5cm) wide.
£90–110 *SnA*

A delft blue and white bowl, with iron-red rim, c1770, 10in (25.5cm) diam.
£260–300 *ALB*

A delft blue and white bowl, with Oriental decoration, c1800, 15½in (40cm) diam.
£90–100 *CaC*

A blue and white meat dish, transfer printed with Durham Ox pattern, surface scratched, c1802, 20in (50cm) wide.
£500–600 *P(B)*

A blue and white meat dish, transfer printed with figures beside a ruined temple, restored, c1812–47, 19in (48cm) wide.
£160–200 *P(B)*

A Stubbs blue and white tureen stand, made for the American market, c1820, 14in (35.5cm) wide.
£320–350 *SCO*

A blue and white jug, transfer printed with Pulteney Bridge, damaged, c1814, 6in (15cm) high.
£110–140 *P(B)*

A blue and white Shipping Series soup plate, c1820, 10in (25.5cm) diam.
£240–280 *SCO*

A Wedgwood blue and white Ferrera pattern cheese dish, c1910, 9¾in (24.5cm) wide.
£40–50 *MEG*

A Staffordshire blue and white vomit pot, maker unkown, c1840, 4in (10cm) diam.
£180–220 *GN*

A blue and white Willow pattern teapot, body cracked, 19thC, 9½in (24cm) wide.
£50–70 *MEG*

A blue and white Boy on a Buffalo pattern mug, c1880, 6in (15cm) high.
£80–100 *P(B)*

A Swansea blue and white Willow pattern meat dish, late 19thC, 22in (56cm) wide.
£100–120 *P(B)*

A Clarice Cliff Inspiration Rose pattern ginger vase, c1930, 12½in (32cm) high.
£4,200–4,800   BKK

A Clarice Cliff egg cup stand, cups missing, c1930, 5½in (14cm) high.
£320–350   GH

A Clarice Cliff Bizarre Canterbury Bells pattern tea-for-two set, c1932.
£1,200–1,500   GH

A Clarice Cliff Bizarre bowl, decorated in Nasturtium pattern in red, orange, yellow and green, c1932, 9in (23cm) diam.
£230–260   GSP

A Clarice Cliff Bizarre Gayday vase, 1930s, 5¾in (14.5cm) high.
£110–130   GH

A Clarice Cliff Tree and House pattern jug, 1930s, 11½in (30cm) high.
£1,200–1,500   RIC

A Carlton Ware vase,
marked, c1880,
11¼in (28.5cm) high.
£300–350 *StC*

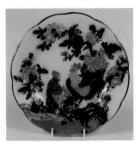

A Carlton Ware plate,
marked, early 20thC,
8¾in (22cm) diam.
£120–150 *StC*

A Carlton Ware Art Deco pedestal
dish, decorated with Scimitar pattern,
marked, 1920s, 12in (30.5cm) wide.
£1,500–2,000 *StC*

A Carlton Ware bowl, c1930,
5in (12.5cm) high.
£40–50 *YY*

A Carlton Ware Rouge Royale dish,
1920–30, 8½in (21.5cm) wide.
£60–70 *MAC*

A Carlton Walking Ware
cup, RSJ range, 1980,
4in (10cm) high.
£25–30 *PC*

A Carlton Ware cheese dish, black
script mark, c1930, 7in (18cm) long.
£80–90 *StC*

A Carlton Ware
vase, chipped,
early 20thC,
5¾in (14.5cm) high.
£20–30 *StC*

A Carlton Ware lustre bowl, decorated with
Hollyhocks pattern, c1930, 10in (25.5cm) diam.
£100–120 *CSA*

A Carlton Ware Foxglove pattern salad
bowl and servers, c1939, 11in (28cm) long.
£80–90 *CSA*

A Carlton Ware vase,
blue script mark, 1930s,
12½in (32cm) high.
£150–200 *StC*

A Carlton Ware Denim
pattern teapot, marked,
1970s, 10¼in high.
£30–40 *StC*

A blue and white transfer printed jug, commemorating Nelson, c1811, 6in (15cm) high.
£400–480 *BRT*

A Royal Doulton stoneware tyg, commemorating Nelson, with original silver rim, hallmarked London 1905, 7¼in (18.5cm) high.
£400–450 *SAS*

A French bisque figure group, commemorating the Franco–Prussian Alliance, 1896, 8in (20.5cm) high.
£400–450 *BRT*

A Royal Doulton porcelain beaker, commemorating the coronation of Edward VII, with gilt rim, 1902, 4in (10cm) high.
£110–130 *SAS*

A Paragon mug, commemorating the coronation of King George VI, with gilt lion handle and coat-of arms, 1937, 3¼in (8.5cm) high.
£20–30 *SAS*

A pottery jug, commemorating the coronation of King George VI, restored, 1937, 7¼in (18.5cm) high.
£130–150 *SAS*

A Kevin Francis pottery figure of the Queen Mother, c1985, 9in (23cm) high.
£100–120 *SAS*

A Naples porcelain figure of Prince Charles, 1969, 14¾in (37.5cm) high.
£300–350 *SAS*

A Kevin Francis Toby jug, depicting Mikhail Gorbachov, 1996, 9in (23cm) high.
£100–150 *BRT*

A Doulton jug, by
L. Rawlings, 1885–1939,
8in (20.5cm) high.
£100–120 *MAC*

A Royal Doulton cup
and saucer, c1908,
saucer 6in (15cm) diam.
£28–32 *HEI*

Two Royal Doulton character jugs, The Poacher,
1955, and Robinson Crusoe, 1960–82,
7½in (19cm) high. **£50–60 each** *HYD*

A Doulton flambé model
of a monkey, The Dunce,
1929, 6in (15cm) high.
£1,000–1,200 *P*

A Royal Doulton plate, painted
with a Dutch scene, c1930,
10½in (26.5cm) diam.
£10–12 *CaC*

A Royal Doulton jug, embossed
with figures, The White Hart Inn,
c1950, 6in (15cm) high.
£30–35 *CaC*

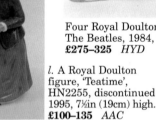

Four Royal Doulton character jugs, depicting
The Beatles, 1984, 5½in (14cm) high.
£275–325 *HYD*

l. A Royal Doulton
figure, 'Teatime',
HN2255, discontinued
1995, 7½in (19cm) high.
£100–135 *AAC*

A Charles Vyse model of a
woman and child, 'Barnet
Fair', c1933, 11in (28cm) high.
£5,000–5,500 *Hal*

Two Royal Doulton Bunnykins Oompah
Band series figures, 'Drummer' and
'Trumpeter', 1990, 3¾in (9.5cm) high.
£60–80 each *P*

A Doulton figure, 'Florence
Nightingale', HN 3144,
1988, 8½in (21.5cm) high.
£400–450 *P*

A pair of glazed pottery figures of a flower girl and a musician, gold anchor marks, early 19thC, 10in (25.5cm) high.
£240–280 *CaC*

A fairing, inscribed 'Taking the Cream', c1880, 3½in (9cm) wide.
£80–90 *SAS*

A Parian figure of a lady, late 19thC, 10in (25.5cm) high.
£100–120 *GH*

A fairing, inscribed 'Going, Going, Gone', c1880, 3in (8cm) wide.
£75–85 *SAS*

A pair of polychrome decorated squat figures, modelled as musicians, gold anchor marks, 19thC, 8in (20.5cm) high.
£320–350 *CaC*

A figure of a girl with an accordion, c1930, 3½in (9cm) high.
£25–30 *JMC*

A figure of a bathing belle on a fish, 1930s, 3in (7cm) wide.
£45–55 *JMC*

An Arcadian crested china bust, c1920, 3in (9cm) high.
£50–55 *JMC*

A Hummel figure, entitled 'For Father', c1960, 5in (12.5cm) high.
£120–135 *ATH*

A Hummel figure, entitled 'Just Resting', c1970, 4in (9.5cm) high.
£60–70 *ATH*

A Minton jug, decorated with hunting scenes, restored, c1831, 10in (25cm) high.
£60–80 *P(B)*

A Ralph Wood mask jug, , c1790, 5¼in (13.5cm) high.
£250–300 *TVM*

A cottage ware milk jug, unmarked, 1920s, 6½in (16.5cm) high.
£15–20 *LA*

A Staffordshire jug, decorated in relief with classical figures, exhibition mark, c1850, 8in (20.5cm) high.
£120–140 *ALB*

A Sarreguemines pottery character jug, depicting Puck, with happy expression, c1920, 7in (18cm) high.
£120–150 *MEG*

r. A pair of Myott hand-painted jugs, 1930s, 9in (23cm) high.
£100–120 *GH*

A Honiton pottery jug, designed by Charles Collard, with Woodland pattern, 1930s, 7in (18cm) high.
£30–40 *WAC*

A Gibson jug, c1930, 8in (20.5cm) high.
£60–70 *CSA*

A Crown Devon jug, c1930, 7in (18cm) high.
£40–50 *CSA*

A Hackwood & Keeling jug, c1935, 4in (10cm) high.
£20–30 *CSA*

Cottage Ware

A Crown Windsor cottage ware teapot, c1950, 5in (12.5cm) high.
£20–25 *CSA*

A Burlington Devon Cob teapot and biscuit barrel, c1920s, teapot 7½in (19cm) high.
£50–60 each *PC*

A Burlington Devon Cob coffee pot, c1920s, 7½in (19cm) wide.
£60–70 *PC*

A Marutomo ware Thatched Roof jam pot, Japanese, 1920s, 3½in (9cm) wide.
£15–20 *PC*

A Price of Kensington Ye Olde Cottage biscuit barrel, 1930s, 7½in (19cm) high.
£50–60 *PC*

A Shorter & Sons beehive honey pot, 1920s, 6in (15cm) high.
£25–30 *PC*

A Watermill cheese dish, unmarked, 1920s, 7½in (19cm) wide.
£40–50 *LA*

A Price of Kensington three-piece cruet set on stand, 1920s, 7½in (19cm) wide.
£60–70 *LA*

> **Cross Reference**
> Colour Review

l. A Continental teapot and butter dish, 1930s, teapot 6in (15cm) wide.
£15–20 each *PC*

A Ye Olde Cottage teapot, unmarked, 1930s, 8in (20cm) wide.
£30–40 *LA*

Crown Devon

A pair of Crown Devon vases, 1930s, 9¼in (23.5cm) high.
£90–100 *AAC*

A Crown Devon yellow sauce boat and stand, c1928, 5in (7.5cm) wide.
£15–20 *CSA*

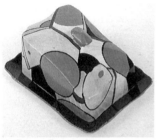

A Crown Devon cheese dish and cover, 1920–30, 3¼in (8cm) high.
£60–80 *MEG*

A Crown Devon preserve jar and cover, entitled 'Berry Inn', c1930, 4in (10cm) high.
£40–50 *CSA*

Crown Devon

Crown Devon was produced by S. Fielding & Co, Staffordshire. The firm was founded in the 1870s, and the name Crown Devon appears on wares from the late 19thC. Pre-WWI Crown Devon was similar in style to Worcester. The 1920s and '30s saw the introduction of lustreware and novelty pieces that were to make the company famous and which provide some of its most collectable pieces today.

A Crown Devon dish, with tube line decoration and flowers, c1935, 9in (23cm) long.
£20–30 *CSA*

A Crown Devon enamelled vase, with gilt rims, c1935, 7in (18cm) high.
£40–50 *CSA*

A Crown Devon lustre vase, with enamelled Chinese landscape scene, c1935, 5in (12.5cm) high.
£30–40 *CSA*

A Crown Devon jug, decorated with enamelled butterfly, c1940, 4in (10cm) high.
£20–30 *CSA*

A Crown Devon lustre vase, decorated with enamelled Chinese landscape scene, on a deep red ground, c1950, 12in (30.5cm) high.
£150–170 *CSA*

r. A Crown Devon vase, decorated in pale turquoise with gilt rims, c1950, 6in (15cm) high.
£15–20 *CSA*

l. A Crown Devon lustre vase, decorated with gilt and enamelled dragon, on a deep red ground, c1950, 6in (15cm) high.
£40–50 *CSA*

Cups, Saucers & Mugs

An Allertons bone china demi-tasse coffee cup and saucer, decorated with black and yellow floral pattern, c1929–42, saucer 4¼in (11cm) diam.
£25–30 *AnS*

An Aynsley coffee can and saucer, c1900, saucer 4¼in (11cm) diam.
£20–25 *WAC*

A Bristol coffee cup, painted with polychrome floral sprays, with simple loop handle, blue painted cross and '12' mark, c1775, 3½in (9cm) high.
£90–110 *HYD*

A Collingwood coffee can and saucer, with green ribboned border, 1924–30, saucer 4¼in (11cm) diam.
£10–12 *WAC*

A Caughley coffee can, with reeded loop handle, printed in underglaze blue with Mother and Child pattern beneath a blue line rim, c1780, 2½in (6cm) high.
£200–220 *DN*

A Cauldon coffee can and saucer, 1905–20, saucer 4¼in (11cm) diam.
£45–55 *WAC*

A Davenport buff earthenware coffee can and saucer, painted with river landscape within gilt line borders, c1805, saucer 4¼in (11cm) diam.
£200–220 *DN*

A Leeds creamware mug, c1850, 3½in (9cm) high.
£40–50 *MEG*

The Antique Shop
01789 292485

*Specialists in
Dolls, Teddy Bears,
Fishing Tackle, Glass,
Porcelain, Jewellery, Oriental,
Silver and Collectables*

**30 Henley Street
Stratford Upon Avon
Opposite The Jester**

l. A Kelsboro Ware cup and saucer, decorated in black and white, 1950s, saucer 6in (15cm) wide.
£12–15 *GIN*

r. A Minton trio, decorated with roses, c1830, bowl 5¾in (14.5cm) diam.
£140–160 *DAN*

A New Hall coffee can, with ring handle, bat printed with a country house scene in coloured enamels within gilt line borders on a pale blue ground, c1810, 2½in (6.5cm) high.
£80–90 *DN*

A Paragon tea set, decorated in pink, green, gold and yellow enamel, and 6 enamel and silver spoons, with original box.
£400–450 *AnS*

A Pinxton coffee can and saucer, decorated in coloured enamels with a wooded river landscape, c1795, saucer 5in (12.5cm) diam.
£600–700 *DN*

A Royal Standard coffee can and saucer, 1929–40, saucer 4¾in (12cm) diam.
£25–30 *WAC*

A set of 6 Royal Crown Derby coffee cans and saucers, decorated in Imari style with flowers and leaves within flower panelled borders, in silk-lined fitted case, printed marks in red for 1931 and 1932, pattern No. 2712/2 in red, saucer 4in (10cm) diam.
£200–250 *HOLL*

A Sèvres cabinet cup, with white enamel pique, jewelled enamel decorations and gilt scroll work, some damage, blue underglaze interlaced 'L' mark, initialled 'F' and impressed 'A', c1900, 3¾in (9.5cm) high.
£250–300 *HCC*

A Spode coffee can, decorated with a band of orange flowers within a gilt background, pattern No. 984, c1810, 2½in (6.5cm) high.
£125–135 *AnS*

A Victorian transfer printed mug, depicting street urchins, inscribed 'How's Business' and 'Slack', 4in (10cm) high.
£50–65 *ANV*

A Spode hand-painted coffee can and saucer, c1889, saucer 4¼in (11cm) diam.
£45–55 *WAC*

A Paragon/Star China Co coffee can and saucer, c1913, saucer 4½in (11cm) diam.
£30–35 *WAC*

r. A porcelain mug, decorated in coloured enamels with overlapping playing cards, c1860, 4¼in (11cm) high.
£275–325 *DN*

Denby

A Denby green glazed Queen Anne tea set, some restoration, c1920, teapot 5¼in (13.5cm) wide.
£100–120 *KES*

A Denby commemorative vase, produced as a tribute to Disraeli, the Earl of Beaconsfield, with impressed fleur-de-lys and 'Elliott' London, mark on base, c1900, 5½in (12.5cm) high.
£200–225 *KES*

A Denby jug, commemorating the coming of age of Wilfred Hugh Julian Gough, Caer-Rhûn, inscribed in Welsh text, dated '1909', 7in (18cm) high.
£50–65 *KES*

l. A Denby Stoneware Arctic Footwarmer, with screw stopper and 2 carrying holes with wires, with inscribed 'Denby Stoneware, Regd. No.', 1920–30, 8in (20cm) high.
£150–170 *BBR*

A Denby dog trough, with raised tube-lined lettering, some damage, mid-1920s, 4in (10cm) diam.
£35–45 *KES*

A Denby Cottage Blue coffee filter, early 1930s, 9in (23cm) high.
£60–75 *KES*

A Denby mug, designed by Glyn Colledge, slight damage, signed, 1950s, 5¼in (13.5cm) high
£20–25 *MAC*

A Denby vase, designed by Glyn Colledge, c1950, 10in (25.5cm) high.
£60–70 *RAC*

r. A Denby vase, designed by Glyn Colledge, c1950s, 12½in (32cm) high.
£130–150 *RAC*

Doulton

Doulton was founded in 1815, when 22 year-old potter John Doulton went into partnership with John Watts and took over a small factory in Lambeth, South London. Doulton and Watts specialised in salt-glazed stoneware, manufacturing bottles, flasks, storage jars and other domestic ceramics. Their great prosperity, however, came with the creation of even more utilitarian products.

The huge population explosion in London in the 19th century had resulted in massive overcrowding and a dangerously over-burdened and polluted water supply. Between 1831 and 1854 there were three cholera epidemics, and as new construction works took place to modernise the capital, Doulton and Watts began to manufacture sewer pipes. Henry Doulton (John's son) established a separate firm devoted to drain pipes.

Henry Doulton was a great innovator, whose inventions included the first glazed ceramic kitchen sink and the ceramic screw top for hot water bottles. His own company was a huge success, supplying pipes for the Houses of Parliament and major buildings across the globe, and in 1854 the two firms amalgamated to form Doulton & Co.

Doulton's Art Pottery was launched in 1871. Major designers included George Tinworth and the Barlow sisters, Hannah and Florence, and by the mid-1880s there were over 300 men and women, many recruited from nearby Lambeth School of Art, producing ornamental ceramics.

In the 1880s Henry Doulton set up another factory in Burslem, Staffordshire. From 1889 the chief modeller at Burslem was Charles Noke. Noke was responsible for many of the ranges that were to make Doulton internationally famous. He produced lines such as Series ware and Kings ware and developed remarkable glazes including Flambé, Sung and Titanian. Noke pioneered the production of figurines, recruiting the services of artists and sculptors, such as Leslie Harradine, who created a huge number of successful figures for Doulton in the 1920s and '30s, some of which are still in production today. Noke was also responsible for the revival of character jugs, beginning with John Barleycorn produced in 1934.

The Lambeth factory closed down in 1954, and Doulton concentrated their activities at Burslem, merging with other companies to become the largest producer of ceramic products in the United Kingdom.

A Royal Doulton stoneware jardinière, decorated with stylised flowers on a blue ground, early 1900s, 7½in (19cm) high.
£220–250 *TMA*

A Royal Doulton trio, decorated with Hydrangea pattern, c1908, 7½in (19cm) diam.
£40–50 *HEI*

A set of 6 Royal Doulton napkin rings, depicting Dickensian characters Sam Weller, Tony Weller, Mr Micawber, Fat Boy, Pickwick and Sarah Gamp, with original labels and cloth covered box, 1939–60, 3in (7.5cm) high.
£1,500–1,700 *CAG*

These boxed sets were produced in limited numbers between 1939 and 1960, primarily for export to the USA. This example is rare and has never been used, hence its price range.

A Royal Doulton ceramic bowl, c1910, 7½in (19cm) diam.
£85–95 *RAC*

l. A Doulton Lambeth slipcast pin tray, in the form of a kookaburra, 1920s, 2¾in (7cm) high.
£150–200 *P*

Bunnykins

l. A Royal Doulton Knockout
Bunnykins, 1985–88,
4in (10cm) high.
r. A Royal Doulton Downhill
Bunnykins, 1985–88,
2⅛in (6.5cm) high.
£110–130 each *P*

A Royal Doulton
Sweetheart Bunnykins,
1992, 4in (10cm) high.
£25–30 *TAC*

l. A Royal Doulton Ace Bunnykins, DB42,
1986–89, 3¼in (8.5cm) high.
£120–150
c. A Royal Doulton Out For A Duck Bunnykins,
DB160, produced especially for U.K.I. Ceramics
Ltd, special edition 1250, c1995, 4in (10cm) high.
£100–120
r. A Royal Doulton Aussie Surfer Bunnykins,
DB133, produced exclusively for Royal Doulton,
Australia, c1994, 4in (10cm) high.
£80–90 *P*

Cross Reference
Nursery Ware

A Royal Doulton
Bedtime Bunnykins,
1994, 4in (1cm) high.
£25–30 *TAC*

A Royal Doulton School-
master Bunnykins, DB60,
1987, 4in (10cm) high.
£16–18 *P*

Bunnykins

Bunnykins models are attracting an
ever-growing following, with even
the most recent figures escalating
rapidly in value. Like Hummels
(p175), Bunnykins were conceived
by a nun, Barbara Vernon Bailey,
daughter of Doulton's managing
director, Cuthbert Bailey, who
submitted her designs from the
convent. The characters, inspired
by bedtime stories that her father
had told her as a child, were
launched in 1934 and the
Bunnykins design remains a
popular nursery ware pattern
today. The first Bunnykins models
were produced in 1939 though
manufacture was halted by the war
making these early models
extremely rare. In the 1970s, Albert
Hallam modelled a new series of
Bunnykins figures and in the 1980s
designs were created by Harry
Sales. To coincide with Bunnykins'
Diamond Jubilee in 1994 eight new
figures were released, and as we
approach the millenium, demand
continues to grow, in particular for
limited edition models which can
sell out almost instantly.

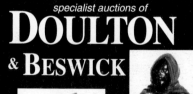

Figures

A Doulton Lambeth figure, depicting a farmer with a scythe, by L. Harradine, c1920, 6in (15cm) high.
£300–350 *P*

A Doulton figure, 'Covent Garden', damaged, HN1339, 1929–38, 7in (18cm) high.
£125–150 *P*

A Royal Doulton figure, 'Miss Demure', HN1440, 1930–49, 7½in (19cm) high.
£120–150 *HYD*

A Royal Doulton figure, 'Victorian Lady, designed by L. Harradine, M2, 1932–45, 4in (10cm) high.
£165–185 *SnA*

Royal Doulton Figures

All Doulton figures carry the Royal Doulton lion & crown backstamp on their base. In addition to this most, but not all, figures carry a registration number, an HN number and the figure's name on their base. The style of these extra marks provides useful hints for the precise dating of figures.

A Royal Doulton figure, 'Suzette', HN1696, 1935–49, 7in (18cm) high.
£250–300 *P*

A Doulton Figure in a pink dress, 'The Ballerina', HN2116, 1953–73, 6½in (16.5cm) high.
£225–250 *P*

A Royal Doulton figure, 'Pearly Boy', HN1547, 1933–49, 5½in (14cm) high.
£125–150 *SnA*

A Royal Doulton figure, 'Loretta', HN2337, 1966–81, 8¼in (21cm) high.
£35–40 *CaC*

r. A Royal Doulton Tolkien figure, entitled 'Frodo', 1980–84, 4¼in (11cm) high.
£75–85 *TP*

A Royal Doulton figure in a green dress, 'Francine', HN2422, 1972–81, 4¾in (12cm) high.
£90–100 *SnA*

Jugs

A Doulton Lambeth
stoneware jug, with
blue trim and incised
decoration, by Hannah
Barlow, c1873,
6¼in (16cm) high.
£500–600 *SnA*

A Doulton Lambeth
brown salt-glaze
stoneware jug,
in the form of a
landlord sitting on
a barrel, impressed
mark, 1877–80,
10¼in (26cm) high.
£150–180 *P(B)*

A Royal Doulton
stoneware jug, with
plain silver rim,
decorated by George
Tinworth, 1879,
9¼in (23.5cm) high.
£650–750 *Bea(E)*

A Doulton Lambeth
brown salt-glazed
stoneware jug, c1890,
5½in (14cm) high.
£45–50 *RAC*

A Doulton jug,
decorated with roses,
c1930, 3½in (9cm) high.
£15–20 *CSA*

A Doulton Lambeth
stoneware jug, c1890,
4½in (11.5cm) high.
£20–30 *CSA*

A Doulton Lambeth
chiné gilt jug, with blue
and white flowers,
c1895, 9½in (17cm) high.
£50–70 *SnA*

*Chiné was patented by
John Slater. Dampened
lace was pressed into
the wet clay which was
destroyed in the firing,
leaving a pattern
behind which was then
coloured and gilded.*

Cross Reference
Colour Review

A Doulton Burslem
blue and white jug,
c1910, 9in (23cm) high.
£100–125 *CSA*

A Doulton Series
ware jug, c1935,
5in (12.5cm) high.
£30–40 *CSA*

A Royal Doulton
embossed jug, entitled
'Old Curiosity Shop',
c1950, 5½in (14cm) high.
£30–40 *CaC*

Character Jugs

A Royal Doulton character jug, 'Scaramouche', D6558, 1962–67, 7in (18cm) high.
£350–400 GH

A Royal Doulton character jug, 'Town Crier', c1975, 4in (10cm) high.
£40–50 CSA

A Royal Doulton character jug, 'The Poacher', D6429, c1980, 6½in (16.5cm) high.
£50–60 GAK

Two Royal Doulton character jugs, *l.* 'Capt. Ahab', D6500, 1959–84, 8½in (21.5cm) high. *r.* 'Yachtsman', D6626, 1971–80, 8in (20.5cm) high.
£100–120 HYD

A Royal Doulton Churchill jug, with VE Day newspaper handle, D6934, 1960s, 4in (10cm) high, and a Churchill Toby jug.
£35–45 CaC

Plates

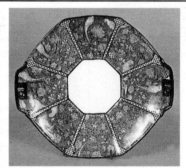

A pair of Royal Doulton plates, in the form of flowerheads, decorated with primroses and pink glaze, c1900, 8½in (21.5cm) diam.
£8–10 CaC

A Royal Doulton sandwich plate, decorated with Parrot pattern, c1908, 10in (25.5cm) wide.
£30–35 HEI

A Royal Doulton blue and white plate, depicting Dickens and characters from his books, c1920, 10½in (26.5cm) diam.
£60–70 BRU

Cross Reference
Plates

r. A Royal Doulton Discovery commemorative plate, 1984, 6¼in (16cm) diam.
£10–15 GIN

Vases

A Doulton blue and white vase, c1880, 9in (30cm) high.
£180–200 *RAC*

A pair of Doulton Lambeth ovoid vases, with short necks, each incised with leaves and leaf scrolls on a pale blue ground, decorator's monogram 'W.W.', impressed marks for 1883, 7½in (19cm) high.
£500–600 *HOLL*

r. A Doulton Burslem vase, painted with flowers on a white ground, signed by John Slater, c1890, 7½in (19cm) high.
£150–200 *CSA*

l. A Doulton Lambeth stoneware vase, decorated with stylised flowers and foliage in blue and green glazes on a buff coloured ground, by Frank A. Butler, impressed factory mark and '1877', 'FAB' incised monogram, 20½in (52cm) high.
£500–600 *WW*

A pair of Royal Doulton stoneware vases, decorated with scolling stylised floral and foliate branches in yellow brown and green on a mottled beige ground, by Mark V. Marshall, c1880, 11½in (29cm) high.
£600–700 *HCH*

A Royal Doulton black and gold vase, c1890, 11in (28cm) high.
£85–100 *RAC*

A Doulton chiné vase, decorated with turquoise flowers, marked, 1885–1939, 3in (7.5cm) high.
£30–35 *MAC*

A Doulton vase, with blue and brown glaze, early 20thC, 3½in (9cm) high.
£30–40 *MAC*

A Doulton Lambeth pot, with wavy edge, decorated with blue flowers on a brown ground, initialled 'SC', 1918–20, 12in (30.5cm) diam.
£25–35 *SnA*

Fairings

Fairings are small porcelain groups that were made as fairground prizes and cheap gifts. The golden age of the Victorian fairing was 1860–1900, when large fairs were in their heyday. Fairings reflected popular taste. Subjects tended to be humorous and often vaguely risqué, with many scenes centred around the bedroom and the trials of love and marriage. Captions often included puns. In addition to purely (or perhaps impurely) decorative figure groups, fairings also took the form of vases, match and spill holders, and other small domestic items. Though fairings seem a typically English product, most were in fact manufactured in Germany, where the major producer was the firm of Conta & Boehme in Possneck.

Price ranges are affected by rarity, quality and subject matter. Though fairings were produced in their thousands, they were not valued and were often simply disposed of, hence their rarity today. Early pieces tend to be better modelled than late 19th century examples and the clarity of the caption is important.

Conta & Boehme fairings are very desirable. From the late 1870s their wares were marked on the base with an arm wielding a dagger and often had a serial number incised, and later impressed, on the base. The factory's early and best pieces, however, were not marked. Some subjects (eg transport) are more collectable than others, and pairs or companion pieces attract a premium.

'During the 1970s fairings made huge prices, and many were restored,' explains Andrew Hilton from Special Auction Services. 'Today people want pieces in original condition, but a small chip will affect prices far less than in other areas of the ceramics market. Fairings have been reproduced so it is important to check for signs of genuine ageing.'

This section concludes with 20th century fairings and souvenir ware, again made predominantly overseas for the UK seaside holiday trade in the 1920s and '30s and which are still very affordable today.

A fairing, entitled 'A Swell', repaired, late 19thC, 4in (10cm) wide.
£80–100 *SAS*

A Victorian fairing, entitled 'The last in bed to put out the light', 3in (7.5cm) wide.
£30–35 *TAC*

A fairing, entitled 'Between two stools you fall to the ground', late 19thC, 3¼in (8.5cm) wide.
£200–240 *SAS*

A fairing, entitled 'Can you do this, grandma?', late 19thC, 3½in (9cm) wide.
£160–180 *SAS*

A fairing, entitled 'God save the Queen', late 19thC, 3¼in (8cm) wide.
£140–160 *SAS*

A fairing, entitled 'How happy could I be with either', late 19thC, 3½in (9cm) wide.
£120–140 *SAS*

A fairing, entitled 'He don't like his Pants', late 19thC, 3½in (9cm) wide.
£480–550 *SAS*

A fairing, entitled 'Mr Jones, remove your Hat', late 19thC, 3½in (9cm) wide.
£100–120 *SAS*

A fairing, entitled 'Trespassing', restored, late 19thC, 4in (10cm) high.
£110–120 *SAS*

A fairing, entitled 'If you please Sir', restored, late 19thC, 3½in (9cm) wide.
£100–120 *SAS*

A fairing, entitled 'Now Ma-rm say when?', slight damage, late 19thC, 4in (10cm) high.
£100–120 *SAS*

A fairing, entitled 'Shamming sick', slight damage, late 19thC, 3½in (9cm) wide.
£160–180 *SAS*

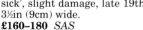
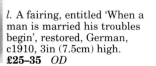

l. A fairing, entitled 'When a man is married his troubles begin', restored, German, c1910, 3in (7.5cm) high.
£25–35 *OD*

A fairing, entitled 'Married for money', German, c1880, 3½in (9cm) wide.
£100–120 *OD*

A fairing, entitled 'The Orphans', late 19thC, 4in (10cm) high.
£100–120 *SAS*

> **Cross Reference**
> Colour Review – Fakes

A fairing, entitled 'Shall we sleep first or how?', German, slight damage, late 19thC, 3½in (9cm) wide.
£55–65 *SAS*

A fairing, entitled 'Twelve months after marriage', repaired, late 19thC, 3½in (9cm) wide.
£25–30   *SAS*

A fairing, entitled 'Who said Rats?', some damage, late 19thC, 3½in (9cm) wide.
£100–120   *SAS*

A fairing match striker, modelled as a black and white cat, c1890, 4in (10cm) high.
£35–40   *OD*

A fairing, entitled 'Who is coming?', damaged, late 19thC, 3½in (9cm) wide.
£90–110   *SAS*

A fairing, entitled 'You careless fool', late 19thC, 4in (10cm) high.
£85–100   *SAS*

A fairing vase, in the form of a pink pig against a green tree, late 19thC, 6in (15cm) high.
£50–60   *SAS*

20th Century

A fairing ashtray, depicting a teddy, inscribed 'A Present from Blackpool', 1920–30s, 3in (7.5cm) wide.
£5–10   *JMC*

A fairing, in the form of a gnome with a key in a horseshoe, inscribed 'Souvenir of Margate', 1920–30s, 2¾in (7cm) high.
£12–18   *JMC*

l. Two fairings, *l.* depicting a clown with a ring, inscribed 'Souvenir of Felixstowe', c1920, 2½in (7cm) high.
r. depicting a chef, inscribed 'A Present from Whitley Bay', c1920, 3in (7.5cm) high.
£20–30 each   *OD*

A fairing, in the form of a dove and key on a horseshoe, with orange and green decoration, inscribed 'A Present from Brighton', 1920–30s, 2¾in (7cm) high.
£15–20   *JMC*

A fairing, in the form of a little devil with wedding rings, inscribed 'Souvenir from Paignton', 1920–30s, 2¼in (5.5cm) high.
£12–16 *JMC*

A wedding fairing, in the form of gold coloured keys and a shoe, inscribed 'Souvenir of Ramsgate', 1920–30s, 2¼in (5.5cm) high.
£15–20 *JMC*

A fairing, in the form of an aeroplane and wedding bells within a horseshoe, inscribed 'A Present from Skegness', 1920–30s, 2¾in (7cm) high.
£15–20 *JMC*

A wedding fairing, in the form of a dove with a nest of eggs within a gold coloured horseshoe, inscribed 'Souvenir of Sheerness', 1920–30s, 2½in (6.5cm) high.
£15–20 *JMC*

A fairing, in the form of a bathing belle in a wicker chair, inscribed 'Souvenir of Southend-on-Sea', c1930, 2¾in (7cm) high.
£25–35 *JMC*

A fairing, in the form of a kitten in a boot, lined with orange, inscribed 'A Present from Southend-on-Sea', 1920–30s, 3½in (9cm) wide.
£12–15 *JMC*

r. A fairing egg cup and saucer, with green salt and pepper pots, Japanese, 1930s, saucer 4¼in (11cm) diam.
£10–15 *JMC*

A fairing, in the form of a yellow duckling on a boat, inscribed 'Souvenir of Westcliff-on-Sea', 1920–30s, 2½in (6.5cm) high.
£10–15 *JMC*

r. A fairing cruet set, with brown and buff salt and pepper pots, on a brown tray decorated with a cat, 1930s, 5in (12.5cm) wide.
£8–10 *JMC*

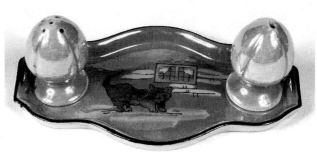

Animals

A fairing group of 3 terrier dogs, 1920–30s, 2¾in (7cm) wide.
£10–12 *JMC*

A fairing lustre model of a buff-coloured camel, German, 1920–30s, 3½in (9cm) wide.
£15–20 *JMC*

A fairing ashtray, in the form of a goldfish, 1920–30s, 3in (7.5cm) high.
£10–12 *JMC*

A fairing in the form of a green and orange bucket with a bear, 1930s, 2¾in (7cm) high.
£15–20 *JMC*

A fairing ashtray depicting Calico dog, entitled 'Snuffers', Japanese, 1930s, 3in (7.5cm) high.
£8–12 *JMC*

A fairing ashtray with a bird, decorated in yellow, blue and orange, Japanese, 1930s, 4in (10cm) wide.
£10–12 *JMC*

Figures

A fairing tape measure holder, in the form of a Welsh lady, inscribed 'Cymru am Byth', 1920–30s, 3¾in (9.5cm) high.
£15–18 *JMC*

A fairing, in the form of a boy scout with a Scottie dog, 1920–30s, 4¼in (11cm) high.
£25–35 *JMC*

Cross Reference
Colour Review

A fairing pepper pot, in the form of a top-hatted figure in a basket, 1920s, 3½in (9cm) high.
£18–22 *JMC*

r. A fairing, in the form of a boy in an orange cap with a dog in a wheelbarrow, 1920–30s, 3¼in (8.5cm) high.
£20–25 *JMC*

A fairing figure, in the form of a boy with orange shoes on a green scooter, 1920–30s, 3¼in (8.5cm) high.
£18–22 *JMC*

Figures

A Bow figure, of a young woman, emblematic of Spring, in white, seated beside a basket of flowers, on mound base, restored, c1755, 4¾in (12cm) high.
£300–350 *DN*

A Pratt ware figure of a woman in a brown coat, carrying a basket, c1800, 4in (10cm) high.
£150–200 *ALB*

A Continental figure of the Muse Clio, late 19thC, 5¾in (14.5cm) high.
£80–100 *MEG*

A Derby porcelain figure, depicting Minerva in floral costume with red and green shawl, late 18thC, 14¾in (37.5cm) high.
£450–550 *AH*

A figure of a girl in a pink dress, holding a ball, 19thC, 5¾in (14.5cm) high.
£25–35 *MEG*

A pair of Nymphenburg figures, after F. A. Bustelli, painted with coloured enamels, restored, impressed marks, late 19thC, largest 5½in (14cm) high.
£150–200 *WW*

r. A Continental porcelain figure, depicting an elderly man reading *The Times*, in pink robe with fir trimmed collar, some damage, late 19thC, 10in (25.5cm) high.
£90–110 *MAW*

A Limoges cherub figure, with salts, on a yellow base, some damage, marked 'HB', late 19thC, 6¾in (17cm) high.
£170–200 *MEG*

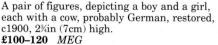

A pair of figures, depicting a boy and a girl, each with a cow, probably German, restored, c1900, 2¾in (7cm) high.
£100–120 *MEG*

A collection of 7 bisque 'Frozen Charlotte' doll figures, including 4 nudes, 2 bathers and a mermaid, c1910, largest 5in (12.5cm) long.
£450–550 *AH*

Parian ware

A Parian ware model, entitled 'Schiller', late 19thC, 19in (48cm) high.
£200–250 *WW*

Schiller was a well-known poet and dramatist of the late 19thC.

r. A Parian ware figure, depicting Paul, c1865, 14in (35.5cm) high.
£180–220 *HYD*

Paul et Virginie *was a popular romance written by Bernadin de St Pierre in 1797. It tells the story of a boy and girl brought up on the rural paradise of Mauritius, who fell in love. Virginie was summoned to France and on her return to the island her ship was wrecked by a hurricane. With a surfeit of feminine modesty, she refused to remove her clothes in order to save herself and drowned. Paul, who had been watching helplessly from the shore, died from grief. This combination of innocent young love and tragic death appealed greatly to the 19thC audience and inspired many sentimental tributes such as these Parian figures.*

A Kerr & Binns Worcester Parian bust of Prince Albert, by E. J. Jones, mid-19thC, 12½in (32cm) high.
£150–200 *WW*

A Parian ware group of 2 children, with a lamb lying at their feet, on oval base, 19thC, 11½in (29cm) high.
£180–220 *AH*

A Continental Parian ware figure, depicting a girl in a pink and blue dress, 19thC, 8½in (21.5cm) high.
£40–55 *MEG*

Russian

A figure of a cobbler wearing blue striped trousers, by A. G. Popov, with high gloss glaze finish, undermarked, 1850–80, 6in (15cm) high.
£350–400 *PC*

A Dulevo figure of a mother washing children, marked, 1930–40s, 8¾in (22cm) high.
£200–250 *SRC*

A Copeland Parian ware figure, depicting a maiden, 19thC, 15in (38cm) high.
£250–300 *HYD*

A Lomonosov group of Russian dancers, with brightly coloured orange and blue costumes, marked 'Made in USSR', c1970, 7in (18cm) high.
£80–90 *AND*

Goss & Crested China
Goss

A Goss mug, entitled 'Jackal', 1862–91, 2¾in (7cm) high.
£35–40   *MAC*

A Goss Burslem ewer, bearing Folkestone crest, 1900–20, 3¾in (9.5cm) high.
£10–15   *G&CC*

A Goss ewer, decorated with Roman armour design, c1880–1900, 5¼in (13cm) high.
£125–150   *G&CC*

A Goss vase, bearing City of Exeter crest, 1900–20, 2½in (6.5cm) high.
£40–50   *G&CC*

A Goss urn and lid, bearing Saffron Waldon crest, 1900–20, 4¾in (12cm) high.
£70–80   *G&CC*

r. A Goss china Durham Abbey knocker cup, c1910, 3in (8cm) high.
£60–80   *G&CC*

A Goss bag vase, with a blue cord, 1900–30, 1¾in (4.5cm) high.
£10–12   *G&CC*

A Goss Chichester ewer, bearing Ceylon crest, 1910–30, 2½in (6.5cm) high.
£10–15   *G&CC*

l. A Goss ring tree, 1910–25, 2¼in (5.5cm) diam.
£30–35   *G&CC*

Crested China

A Goss Bass basket, bearing Colwyn Bay crest, 1910–30, 2½in (6.5cm) high.
£20–25 *G&CC*

A Goss ewer, commemorating the Coronation of George V, 1911, 3in (7.5cm) high.
£15–20 *G&CC*

A Goss model of Portland lighthouse, bearing Blackpool crest, 1920–30, 4¾in (12cm) high.
£80–90 *JMC*

r. An Arcadian ship, entitled 'HMS *Queen Elizabeth*', bearing Brighton crest, 1920–30, 3½in (9cm) high.
£65–75 *JMC*

An Arcadian banjo, bearing Northwich crest, c1910, 6in (15cm) long.
£15–20 *G&CC*

An Arcadian alarm clock, inscribed 'Many are called but few get up', with Petworth crest, 1910–30, 2¼in (6cm) high.
£25–30 *G&CC*

A Carlton china teapot, bearing Kingstown crest, gilt finish, c1900, 2in (5cm) high.
£10–12 *MLa*

A Locke two-handled cup, bearing Devonport crest and Latin inscription, c1900, 1½in (4cm) high.
£25–30 *MLa*

A Locke jug, bearing City of Bath crest, c1900, 1¾in (4.5cm) high.
£35–40 *MLa*

A Locke vase, bearing Durham City crest, c1900, 3in (7.5cm) high.
£60–70 *MLa*

Crested China – Animals

An Arcadian parrot, bearing Bristol crest, 1910–20, 3in (7.5cm) high.
£8–10 *BCO*

An Arcadian pelican, bearing Lyndhurst crest, c1920, 3in (7.5cm) high.
£30–35 *BCO*

A Grafton cockerel, bearing Swindon crest, c1909, 4in (10cm) high.
£20–25 *JMC*

A model of an upright tortoise, bearing Cleethorpes crest, unmarked, 1920–30, 2½in (6.5cm) high.
£50–60 *JMC*

A Carlton Ware goose, bearing Corfe Castle crest, c1920, 3in (7.5cm) wide.
£30–35 *BCO*

l. A Devonia china Scottie dog, 1910–20, 2½in (6.5cm) high.
£10–12 *G&CC*

r. A model of an elephant, bearing Herne Bay crest, unmarked, 1900–20, 2½in (6.5cm) wide.
£15–20 *BCO*

Crested China – Buildings

A collection of crested buildings, 1920s, largest 4in (10cm) high:
l.	Carlton Deller's Café.	**£110–125**
cl.	Savoy Portsmouth Town Hall.	**£55–65**
cr.	Arcadian Rochester Castle.	**£55–65**
r.	Arcadian Temple Bar.	**£55–65** *CCC*

A collection of crested buildings, 1920s, 3–5in (7.5–12.5cm):
l.	Chatham Town Hall.	**£60–70**
cl.	Shelley, Douglas Clock Tower.	**£65–75**
c.	Tuscan, Douglas Tower of Refuge.	**£55–65**
cr.	Carlton Ware, Eddystone Lighthouse.	**£10–12**
r.	Willow, Flamborough Lighthouse.	**£40–45** *CCC*

Crested China – Figures

An Arcadian despatch rider, 1915–20,
3⅛in (8cm) wide.
£85–95 *G&CC*

l. An Arcadian
bust, depicting
Mr Punch, 1920,
3¼in (8cm) high.
£65–75 *G&CC*

An Arcadian golfer's
caddy and bag, bearing
Melton Mowbray crest,
1920s, 3½in (9cm) high.
£75–85 *JMC*

r. A Carlton
Ware figure,
depicting Ye
Maydes, bearing
Cranbrook
crest, 1930s,
4in (10cm) high.
£35–45 *JMC*

An Arcadian policeman,
c1920, 3¾in (9.5cm) high.
£35–45 *G&CC*

A Willow Art model
of Laceby Memorial,
bearing Leeds crest,
1910–25, 6in (15cm) high.
£20–30 *BRT*

A Willow Art
monument, bearing
Great Yarmouth crest,
1925, 6in (15cm) high.
£100–150 *BRT*

Hummels

A Hummel figure of a boy with rabbit, by Goebel, blue mark, 1930s, 4¼in (11cm) high.
£90–110 *TP*

A Hummel figure of a boy playing a violin, by Goebel, 1930s, 5in (12.5cm) high.
£90–100 *TP*

A Hummel figure of a girl in a yellow dress holding a posy of flowers, by Goebel, blue mark, 1930s, 4in (10cm) high.
£65–75 *TP*

A Hummel figure of a child and a bird in a cart, by Goebel, black mark, 1930s, 5¼in (13.5cm) high.
£160–190 *TP*

r. A Hummel figure candle holder, entitled 'Joyous News', marked 'TMK 3', 1955–68, 2in (5cm) high.
£30–40 *ATH*

A Hummel figure, entitled 'Apple Tree Boy', with original label, No. 142/3/0, marked 'TMK3', 1955–68, 4in (10cm) high.
£70–85 *ATH*

A Hummel figure, entitled 'March Winds', No. 43, marked TMK 3, 1955–68, 5in (12.5cm) high.
£75–110 *ATH*

r. A Hummel figure, entitled 'Brother', c1959, 5½in (14cm) high.
£110–130 *BaN*

The production run of this figure lasted from 1934–91 and had 7 different date marks. It has also been known as 'Our Hero'. The older mould style comes with a blue coat.

A Hummel figure, entitled 'Chef', by Goebel, 1960–72, 5in (12.5cm) high.
£90–110 *TP*

A Hummel figure, entitled 'Chick Girl', by Goebel, blue mark, 1960–72, 3½in (9cm) high.
£80–90 *TP*

Hummels

In 1935 William Goebel launched a series of figurines at the Leipzig fair. Sentimental models of country children in national dress, these were named Hummels after their creator, the Franciscan Sister Maria Innocentia Hummel. Such is their popularity that many of the original pieces are still in production today. The various backstamps produced by the manufacturer provide a guide to dating.

William Goebel 'Porzellanfabrik' Rodental, Germany, manufactured sculpted and moulded pottery as well as porcelain figures. They are most famous for their production of figures taken from the drawings of Sister Hummel, which were first brought to the attention of Franz (son of William) in 1934.

A Hummel annual plate, entitled 'Goose Girl', 1974, 7½in (19cm) diam, with original box and certificate.
£90–110 *ATH*

A Hummel bell, entitled 'Lets Sing', 1978, 6½in (16.5cm) high, with original box and certificate.
£65–85 *ATH*

This piece was a first edition of the first annual bell.

A Hummel figure, entitled 'Ride into Christmas', by Goebel, blue mark, 1981, 4½in (11.5cm) high.
£115–135 *TP*

A Hummel figure, entitled 'Little Tooter', by Goebel, 1988, 3¼in (8.5cm) high.
£55–65 *TP*

r. A Hummel figure, entitled 'Birthday Present', by Goebel, blue mark, 1989, 4in (10cm) high.
£65–75 *TP*

This is a first issue by Erste Ausgabe.

A Hummel figure, entitled 'Little Hiker', by Goebel, 1989, 3¼in (8.5cm) high.
£65–75 *TP*

Jugs

Three relief-moulded buff-coloured jugs, with white twisted serpent handles and spouts, some restoration, with Brameld pad on base of smallest, early 19thC, largest 6½in (16.5cm) high.
£200–250 *MEG*

A Bow sparrowbeak jug, with loop handle, painted with polychrome floral sprays, slight damage, c1752, 7in (18cm) high.
£80–100 *HYD*

A bellarmine jug, with salt-glazed handle, decorated with bearded mask to neck and medallion to body with over-all mottled orange peel effect, minor damage and repairs, c1650, 9⅓in (24cm) high.
£100–120 *BBR*

These large beer jugs were manufactured in Flanders from the 16thC and in Britain from the 1670s. The mask is said to be a caricature of Cardinal Bellarmino (1542–1621), a great defender of the Roman Catholic church and one of the leaders of the Counter Reformation – hence the name of the pot. In Britain, they were also called greybeards.

A Staffordshire Pratt ware jug, in the form of a cottage, c1820, 3½in (9cm) high.
£100–125 *JO*

A Bovey Tracey creamware jug, covered in green sparkle slip, painted with foliage in cream and brown, inscribed below spout 'J. & S. Gale, 1818', 6½in (16.5cm) high.
£700–800 *Bea(E)*

Shards of similar items have been excavated at the site of the Bovey Pottery, and are illustrated in A Potwork in Devonshire *by Brian Adams and Anthony Thomas.*

A Minton grey jug, decorated with Silenus pattern, c1831, 7½in (19cm) high.
£90–100 *P(B)*

A brown salt-glazed puzzle jug, with eagle handle, restored, c1840, 8½in (21.5cm) high.
£120–140 *BBR*

r. A Staffordshire jug, decorated in brown, yellow and green with a hunting scene, c1830, 6¼in (16cm) high.
£150–200 *ALB*

A Ridgway buff-coloured jug, with pewter lid, c1835, 9in (23cm) high.
£150–175 *ALB*

A Copeland Parian ware jug, decorated with foliate scrolls and female masks, c1840, 11in (28cm) high.
£300–350 *P(B)*

A Bell pottery jug, relief-moulded with blue, pink and cream lustre finish, c1840, 8¼in (21cm) high.
£65–80 *MEG*

A set of 3 Copeland Spode jugs, depicting figures of hunters, hounds and trees in relief moulding on blue ground, 19thC, largest 6in (15cm) high.
£230–260 *TMA*

A blue and white jug, decorated in relief with a hunting scene, 1840–50, 7¼in (18.5cm) high.
£120–140 *P(B)*

A Charles Meigh Minster jug, relief-moulded with panels depicting religious figures, c1842, 7½in (19cm) high.
£180–200 *MEG*

Charles Meigh produced some of the finest relief-moulded jugs of the mid-19thC. A great Gothic designer, he created a number of pieces based on religious and mythological themes.

A Jones & Walley buff-coloured jug, decorated with Good Samaritan pattern, c1841, 8¾in (22cm) high.
£90–110 *P(B)*

A pottery jug, relief-moulded with tree trunk handle, decorated with a gypsy scene and pink interior, slight damage to rim, mid-19thC, 7½in (19cm) high.
£65–80 *MEG*

Cross Reference
Breweriana

A Charles Meigh jug, with pewter lid, decorated with blue and white relief moulding in Amphitrite pattern, c1856, 10⅝in (27cm) high.
£80–100 *P(B)*

l. A Staffordshire York Minster jug, with relief-moulded religious scenes, exhibition mark, 1846, 10in (25.5cm) high.
£125–150 *ALB*

A Coalport 'Goat and Bee' jug, c1860, 4in (10cm) high.
£125–175 *ALB*

An enamelled jug, cream with brown relief-moulded prunus decoration, damaged and repaired, 19thC, 6½in (16.5cm) high.
£30–40 *MEG*

A pair of Punch and Judy character jugs, decorated in red and yellow, 19thC, 11in (28cm) high.
£300–350 *MAW*

Two Mocha ware jugs, c1870, largest 8in (20.5cm) high.
£100–120 each *SMI*

Named after the mocha stone, an ornamental quartz, Mocha ware was made from the 18th–20thC. The mossy decoration was made by dabbing the still wet pot with a liquid pigment known as tea, and said to contain tobacco juice, manganese and urine, which then fanned out on the damp surface into frond-like patterns. Mocha ware was a cheap and utilitarian pottery, much used in public houses, and in the 19thC such pieces would have cost under a shilling.

A Dudson buff stoneware jug, relief-moulded with a beehive set amongst sprays of flowers, c1870, 10½in (27cm) high.
£125–150 *DAN*

A brown-glazed jug, patent No. 452078, late 19thC, 5in (12.5cm) high.
£50–65 *ANV*

A Mason's Ironstone jug, decorated with blue, red and gilt pattern, damaged, late 19thC, 10in (25.5cm) high.
£120–150 *RAC*

A Brannam pottery jug, with fish-shaped spout, decorated in blue on a grey ground, late 19thC, 5½in (14cm) high.
£60–80 *MEG*

A Foley cream jug and sugar bowl, the lobed bodies enamelled with royal coat-of-arms, the reverse with flowers of the union and gilt rims, by Wileman, inscribed, c1897, jug 4in (10cm) high.
£50–60 *SAS*

r. A set of 3 Crown Devon Fieldings jugs, decorated with sprays of flowers, tinted orange with gilt rims, c1900, largest 6½in (16.5cm) high.
£120–140 *AAC*

A Ridgway jug, decorated with Chinese Japan pattern, c1900, 4½in (11.5cm) high.
£40–50 *CSA*

A James Kent jug, decorated with flowers and leaves on a green ground, c1935, 8in (20.5cm) high.
£30–40 *CSA*

A Vulcan ware jug, decorated in pink, green, blue and yellow with a flower and fern pattern, c1935, 9in (23cm) high.
£40–50 *CSA*

A Buckley pottery jug, minor chips to rim, c1910, 8in (20.5cm) high.
£30–40 *IW*

A Myott jug, hand-painted with orange and brown decoration, inscribed 'ITR', c1930, 6¾in (17cm) high.
£30–40 *WAC*

A Samford ware jug, decorated in green, yellow and black with Fantasy pattern, c1930, 9in (23cm) high.
£30–40 *CSA*

l. A Watts pottery pitcher, decorated in red and green with an apple motif, 1940s, 5½in (14cm) high.
£50–60 *MSB*

An Aller Vale jug, decorated with a cockerel, c1925, 5½in (14cm) high.
£30–40 *CSA*

A Kelsboro Ware jug, hand-painted with black and white pattern, designed by Jim Hayward, mark on base, 1950s, 6in (15cm) high.
£20–30 *GIN*

A stoneware Toby jug, depicting George Ohr designed by Roger Law and Pablo Bach, 1996, 8¼in (21cm) high.
£1,100–1,250 *RDG*

Majolica

Victorian majolica, inspired by 16th century Italian *maiolica*, is a type of earthenware moulded in relief and painted with colourful translucent glazes. In tableware, as in ornamental pieces, bold shapes predominated – jugs were modelled like fish and plates shaped like shells. Manufacturers include Minton, who coined the anglicised trade name majolica, George Jones, Wedgwood and a number of smaller manufacturers. Prices for majolica have risen sharply recently with bold shapes appealing to the current market.

Two Minton majolica jardinières and stands, decorated with ochre, brown, blue and green glazes, impressed marks, 1860–70, largest 7in (17.5cm) diam.
£300–350 *WW*

A Minton majolica jardinière and stand, relief-moulded with strawberry plants on a pink ground, slight damage, impressed mark, 19thC, 9½in (24cm) diam.
£900–1,100 *RBB*

A French majolica base of a centre piece, c1870, 12¾in (32.5cm) high.
£350–400 *SSW*

A Continental majolica plate, c1880, 12in (30.5cm) diam.
£200–250 *ARE*

A pair of Italian majolica plates, each painted in coloured enamels with mythological figures, late 19thC, 10¼in (26cm) diam.
£200–250 *HOLL*

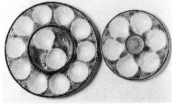

Two majolica oyster dishes, c1900, largest 13in (33cm) diam.
l. **£80–100**
r. **£30–40** *MLL*

A pair of majolica fish-shaped jugs, with loop handles, each brightly decorated in grey, puce, green and orange, slight damage, late 19thC, 9½in (24cm) high.
£50–60 *HOLL*

A majolica jug, with leaf scroll handle, in the form of a cob of corn, late 19thC, 9½in (24cm) high.
£120–150 *HOLL*

A majolica shell-shaped stand, splashed in green, brown and ochre, on 3 dolphin supports, slight damage, 19thC, 9in (23cm) wide.
£90–120 *HOLL*

A majolica jug, in the form of a parakeet, late 19thC, 7½in (19cm) high.
£130–150 *SSW*

Maling

A Maling ware dish, decorated with pink and yellow flowers on a blue ground, c1928, 7½in (19cm) wide.
£70–80 *CSA*

A Maling ware lustre bowl, with floral decoration on a dark blue ground, No. 6190, 1920–30s, 8½in (21.5cm) diam.
£150–180 *MAR*

A Maling ware dish, decorated with Pink Godetia pattern, on a white ground with gilt rim, c1953, 12in (30.5cm) long.
£70–80 *CSA*

Martin Brothers

A Martin Brothers imp singer, covered in a mottled dark brown glaze, slight damage and repair, incised marks, on an ebonised wood base, c1900, 4½in (11.5cm) high.
£950–1,100 *S*

A Martin Brothers vase, with buff and blue washed ground, incised with aquatic creatures, the base incised 'Martin Bros, London and Southall', c1897, 9in (23cm) high.
£2,000–2,500 *HYD*

A Martin Brothers ewer, decorated with aquatic creatures in shades of buff and green, the base incised 'Martin Bros, London', late 19thC, 5¼in (13.5cm) high.
£750–850 *HYD*

Mason's Ironstone

A pair of Mason's Ironstone octagonal-shaped jugs, each with serpent handle, printed in Chinese style with black figures, on an iron red 'Y' diaper ground, printed marks in black, c1830–40, 6½in (16.5cm) high.
£200–250 *HOLL*

A Mason's Ironstone rectangular-shaped inkstand, with gilt loop handle, 2 wells with covers and a sander above a pen tray, decorated in blue, iron red and gilt with flowers and leaves in Chinese style, on 3 paw feet, damaged, c1815–20, 7¼in (18.5cm) wide.
£320–350 *HOLL*

A set of 6 Mason's Ironstone soup plates, printed in blue and painted in colours with flowers and birds, in the Chinese *famille rose* style, printed mark in blue, mid-19thC, 8in (20.5cm) diam.
£200–250 *MSW*

Midwinter

A set of 5 grey Larry the Lambs, designed by Nancy Great-Rex, c1930, largest 8½in (21.5cm) high.
£25–100 each according to size *AND*

A Midwinter Stylecraft teapot and cream jug, designed by Jessie Tait, decorated with Fiesta pattern, in shades of yellow, green and black on a white ground, c1954, largest 3½in (9cm) high.
£30–60 each *AND*

A Midwinter vase, brown with white interior, with wire insert, impressed mark, 1950s, 5in (12.5cm) high.
£40–50 *GIN*

A Midwinter Stylecraft teapot, sugar bowl and milk jug, c1955, and Fashion plate, designed by Sir Peter Scott, decorated with Wild Geese pattern, c1958, plate 6in (15cm) wide.
Tea set £70–80
Plate £18–20 *AND*

Two Midwinter Stylecraft coffee jugs:
l. decorated with Magnolia pattern, on a white ground with green lid,
r. decorated with Cornfield pattern, on a white ground with orange lid, c1955, 8in (20.5cm) high.
£25–30 each *GIN*

Two Midwinter Fashion plates, decorated with Plant Life pattern, by Sir Terence Conran, in shades of green and terracotta on a cream ground, c1956, largest 9¾in (25cm) wide.
£20–30 each *AND*

Two Midwinter plates, designed by Jessie Tait:
l. decorated with Toadstools pattern, c1956, 12in (30.5cm) long,
r. decorated with Cuban Fantasy pattern, c1957, 10in (25.5cm) wide.
£35–45 each *AND*

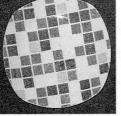

A Midwinter Fashion plate, designed by Jessie Tait, decorated with Patio pattern in yellow and black, c1958, 7½in (19cm) wide.
£15–18 *AND*

A Midwinter tea set, decorated with Reverie pattern, c1968, plate 6in (15cm) diam, with original box.
£50–60 *AND*

l. A Midwinter Stylecraft hors d'oeuvre set, with chrome stand, designed by Sir Hugh Casson, decorated with Cannes pattern, c1960, 17½in (44.5cm) wide.
£100–120 *GIN*

A Midwinter cruet set, designed by Sir Hugh Casson, decorated with Cannes pattern, on a white ground with blue stoppers, c1960, largest 9in (23cm) high.
£100–120 *GIN*

Miniatures

A Staffordshire porcelain miniature cup and saucer, decorated in Imari style on a white ground, with gilt rims, c1830, cup ¾in (2cm) diam.
£60–80 *DAN*

A Chamberlain's Worcester miniature chamber stick, with floral and gilt decoration on a white ground, slight damage, script mark in red, c1800, 2¼in (5.5cm) diam.
£300–350 *MER*

A miniature porcelain vase, with hand-painted floral sprays, and moulded rustic handles decorated with turquoise enamels, unmarked, c1840, 2½in (6.5cm) high.
£120–180 *DAN*

A Victorian porcelain miniature wheelbarrow and spade, decorated with hand-painted floral sprays and gilding, slight damage, c1880, 5in (12.5cm) long.
£120–160 *DAN*

A Coalport miniature mug, depicting a robin on a central medallion with yellow ground and gilt rims, c1881–91, 1⅜in (3.5cm) diam.
£100–125 *WAC*

A Royal Worcester miniature two-handled mug, decorated with pink flowers on a buff ground and gilt rims, c1899, 1⅜in (3.5cm) diam.
£75–85 *WAC*

A Royal Crown Derby miniature mug, decorated with pink flowers, blue upper border and gilt rims, c1907, 1¾in (4.5cm) diam.
£120–150 *WAC*

A Crown Staffordshire miniature sugar bowl, decorated with purple flowers and gilt rims, c1906, 2in (5cm) wide.
£45–55 *WAC*

A Royal Worcester miniature mug, decorated with pink flowers on a buff ground, with gilt rims, c1916, 1¼in (3.5cm) diam.
£75–85 *WAC*

A Royal Crown Derby miniature coal scuttle, decorated in pattern No. 6299, c1918, 2¾in (7cm) high.
£300–350 *MER*

l. A Royal Worcester miniature tyg, decorated with gilt and hand-painted fruit in purple and orange on a white ground, monogrammed 'H. E.', c1930, 1⅝in (4cm) high.
£90–100 *WAC*

Moorcroft

The Moorcroft centenary was celebrated in 1997, stimulating even more interest in this increasingly popular area. Values of early Moorcroft, such as Florian ware, continue to rise and some prices have gone up by as much as 50 per cent over the past five years. With a limited number of old pieces coming on to the market, more collectors have been turning to later and contemporary Moorcroft. When Moorcroft launched its centenary range of ceramics at Liberty's in London in March 1997, this new collection sold out instantly.

At Christie's recent Moorcroft auction, buyers were attracted not just by more traditional ware, but by ceramics from the 1980s and 1990s, in particular small run trial pieces and special commissions made for the Moorcroft Collector's Club. Popular modern-day designers include Rachel Bishop and Sally Tuffin, and many pieces made over the past decade are already fetching far more than their original retail price.

A William Moorcroft Florian ware vase, decorated with Narcissus pattern, in shades of yellow and blue, c1900, 9in (23cm) high.
£2,200–2,600 *RUM*

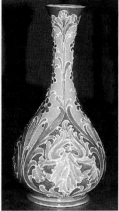

A William Moorcroft Florian ware vase, decorated with Iris pattern, in shades of pink and green, c1902, 8in (20.5cm) high.
£650–750 *RUM*

A William Moorcroft Florian ware trough-shaped bowl, decorated with Poppy pattern, in shades of blue and green on a white ground, c1903, 13in (33cm) long.
£1,000–1,250 *NP*

A William Moorcroft vase, decorated with Liberty Pomegranate pattern, in shades of orange, purple and green, on a wooden base, c1912, 10in (25.5cm) high.
£1,400–1,800 *RUM*

A William Moorcroft mustard pot and lid, decorated with Claremont pattern, with red, purple and green toadstools against a green ground, slight damage, stamped 'Moorcroft Burslem 1914', 2½in (6.5cm) high.
£550–650 *P(Ba)*

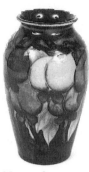

A Moorcroft vase, decorated with Wisteria pattern, in shades of yellow, pink and green on a blue ground, c1918–29, 4¼in (11cm) high.
£250–300 *CEX*

A William Moorcroft two-handled vase, decorated with Wisteria pattern, in shades of orange, yellow and brown on a blue ground, c1925, 8in (20.5cm) high.
£1,000–1,200 *NP*

A William Moorcroft vase, decorated with Chevron Landscape design in the Eventide palate pattern, in shades of blue and orange, c1926, 9in (23cm) high.
£2,500–3,000 *RUM*

A William Moorcroft coffee can and saucer, decorated with Pomegranate pattern, in shades of orange on a green ground, c1928, 2½in (6.5cm) high.
£375–425 *NP*

A Walter Moorcroft pot, decorated with Anemone pattern, in shades of blue, green and pink on an ink blue ground, c1930, 4in (10cm) high.
£180–220 *CEX*

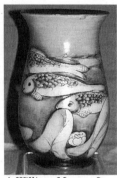

A William Moorcroft saltglaze vase, decorated with Fish pattern, in shades of beige and grey, c1930, 8in (20.5cm) high.
£1,200–1,400 *RUM*

A William Moorcroft salt-glazed tobacco jar, decorated with Fish pattern, in shades of blue and green on a cream ground, c1935, 6in (15cm) high.
£300–350 *NP*

A Walter Moorcroft vase, decorated with African Lily pattern, in shades of terracotta and yellow on a green ground, c1950, 5in (12.5cm) high.
£300–400 *RUM*

A Walter Moorcroft vase, decorated with Spring Flowers pattern, in shades of blue, orange and pink on a white ground, c1955, 12in (30.5cm) high.
£500–600 *RUM*

A Walter Moorcroft vase, decorated with Dahlia pattern, in shades of orange, purple and green on blue ground, c1955, 5in (12.5cm) high.
£300–400 *RUM*

> **Cross Reference**
> Colour Review

r. A Walter Moorcroft vase, decorated with Leaves In The Wind pattern, in autumn shades on a white ground, c1960, 4⅛in (11.5cm) high.
£80–100 *NP*

A Walter Moorcroft vase, decorated with Anemone pattern, in shades of pink and green on a white ground, c1960, 4½in (11.5cm) high.
£150–200 *NP*

A Walter Moorcroft vase, decorated with Anemone pattern, in shades of pink and green on a blue ground, painted mark 'WM', impressed mark, c1970, 8in (20.5cm) high.
£160–200 *HYD*

A Walter Moorcroft plate, decorated with Clematis pattern, in shades of purple and green on a white ground, c1970, 10in (25.5cm) diam.
£200–225 *NP*

A Walter Moorcroft ginger jar, decorated with Hibiscus pattern, in shades of pink and green on a white ground, c1970, 6in (15cm) high.
£200–230 *NP*

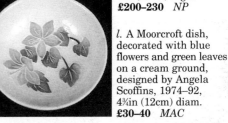

l. A Moorcroft dish, decorated with blue flowers and green leaves on a cream ground, designed by Angela Scoffins, 1974–92, 4¾in (12cm) diam.
£30–40 *MAC*

A Walter Moorcroft vase, decorated with Geranium pattern, in shades of pink and yellow on a cream ground, c1985, 7in (18cm) high.
£80–100 *NP*

A Moorcroft vase, decorated with Dragon pattern, in shades of green on a cream ground, designed by Trevor Critchlow, c1988, 9½in (24cm) high.
£350–400 *NP*

A Moorcroft vase, designed by Sally Tuffin, decorated with Dandelion pattern, in shades of yellow and green, limited edition of 250, c1996, 5in (12.5cm) high.
£250–300 *NP*

A Moorcroft vase, designed by Sally Tuffin, decorated with Spring Blossom pattern, in shades of pink and green on a pale pink ground, c1989, 14in (35.5cm) high.
£350–400 *NP*

A Moorcroft vase, designed by Rachel Bishop, decorated with Inca pattern, in shades of green, brown and yellow, 1995–96, 4in (10cm) high.
£150–200 *NP*

l. A Moorcroft vase, designed by Sally Tuffin, decorated with Carp pattern, in shades of orange, green and buff, limited edition of 100, c1991, 27in (68.5cm) high.
£3,000–3,500 *NP*

FURTHER READING

Paul Atterbury, *Moorcroft – A Guide to Moorcroft Pottery 1897–1993,* Richard Dennis & Hugh Edwards, Reprinted 1996

Keith Murray

A Keith Murray vase, finished in green matt glaze with concentric lines, 1930s, 6¼in (16cm) high.
£175–200 *BEV*

A Keith Murray vase, finished in green matt glaze, 1930s, 7in (18cm) high.
£175–200 *BET*

Keith Murray

Born in New Zealand, Keith Murray (1892–1981) moved to England as a child. He studied at the Architectural Association in London and in the 1930s, when building work was scarce, established himself as a glass and ceramics designer. From 1933 he was employed by Wedgwood. Murray's matt-glazed pottery was architectural in style and cool in colour, and became an icon of British modernism in the 1930s. Murray designed the new Wedgwood factory in Barlaston, Staffordshire, in 1940, and after WWII returned predominantly to architectural practice.

A Keith Murray vase, finished in straw-coloured matt glaze, 1930s, 7¼in (18.5cm) high.
£200–225 *BEV*

A Keith Murray tankard, finished in white matt glaze, 1930s, 5in (12.5cm) high.
£25–30 *BEV*

A Keith Murray vase, finished in white matt glaze, 1930s, 8in (20.5cm) high.
£145–165 *BEV*

A Keith Murray vase, finished in white matt glaze with concentric lines, 1930s, 6½in (16.5cm) high.
£175–200 *BET*

A Keith Murray box, finished in white matt glaze, 1930s, 7¼in (18.5cm) high.
£50–65 *BET*

A Keith Murray vase, finished in white matt glaze, 1930s, 11in (28cm) high.
£225–250 *BEV*

A Keith Murray vase, finished in black matt glaze, 1930s, 4½in (11cm) high.
£550–600 *BEV*

l. A Keith Murray vase, finished in moonstone colour, 1930s, 6½in (16.5cm) high.
£375–400 *BEV*

Cross Reference
Colour Review –
Contemporary Ceramics

Pendelfins

A Pendelfin model of a rabbit, entitled 'Peeps', c1966, 3½in (9cm) wide.
£6–8 *MAC*

A Pendelfin model of a dog, entitled 'Tammy', 1957–87, 3½in (9cm) high.
£18–22 *MAC*

A Pendelfin model of a rabbit, entitled 'Lucy Pocket', 1960–67, 4in (10cm) high.
£55–65 *MAC*

r. A Pendelfin model of a rabbit, entitled 'Crocker', 1980–89, 5in (12.5cm) high.
£45–50 *TP*

A Pendelfin model of a rabbit, entitled 'Muncher', 1965–83, 5in (12.5cm) high.
£18–22 *MAC*

A Pendelfin model of a rabbit, entitled 'Totty', 1971–81, 3½in (9cm) high.
£18–22 *MAC*

A Pendelfin model of a rabbit, entitled 'Nipper', 1981–89, 4in (10cm) high.
£40–50 *TP*

A Pendelfin model of a rabbit, entitled 'Charlotte', 1990–92, 3½in (9cm) high.
£30–40 *TP*

Plates

A delft polychrome plate,
c1770, 9in (23cm) diam.
£100–150 *ALB*

A Sèvres plate, decorated with
flowers, c1770, 9½in (24cm) diam.
£150–200 *ALB*

A Meissen King's plate,
c1780, 9½in (24cm) diam.
£175–200 *ALB*

A Worcester Barr, Flight
& Barr plate, decorated in
Imari palate with flowers and
leaves in shades of red, blue
and gold, impressed
and printed factory mark,
1807–13, 9½in (24cm) diam.
£200–220 *WW*

An H. & R. Daniel Savoy shaped
dessert plate, pattern No. 8777,
c1840, 9½in (24cm) diam.
£80–100 *BSA*

A Nantgarw dessert plate,
decorated in Sèvres style,
with a posy of flowers within
a wavy gilded and blue line
border, impressed mark,
c1818–22, 9½in (24cm) diam.
£300–350 *HOLL*

A Minton bone china plate,
painted to the centre with a
kestrel perched upon a leafy
branch, the pierced and moulded
border decorated with blue and
orange enamel with gilded details
and scalloped rim, probably by
Joseph Smith, slight damage,
impressed registration mark,
mid-19thC, 9¼in (23.5cm) diam.
£80–100 *WW*

A Copeland cabinet plate, the
centre painted with a monogram
in the form of roses, within
pierced borders, with panels of
fruit and flowers, printed mark,
1860s, 9in (23cm) diam.
£650–750 *P(B)*

*This plate bears a written label
on the reverse stating that this
is from the dessert service
ordered by HRH the Prince of
Wales before his marriage.*

r. A Minton plate, in the manner
of Christopher Dresser, with blue
border, c1872, 11in (28cm) diam.
£250–300 *NCA*

A set of 4 china plates, hand-
painted with roses, gold leaves
and trim, Rouen, France,
c1870, 10in (25.5cm) diam.
£100–125 *MSB*

A Brown, Westhead & Moore plate, brown transfer-printed, c1882, 9in (23cm) diam.
£25–35 *OD*

A Copeland Spode cabinet plate, decorated with figures in a landscape with blue and gilt panel of daisies, printed mark, late 19thC, 10in (25.5cm) square.
£80–100 *P(B)*

A Stavangaflint triangular-shaped plate, hand-painted with blue and green herb pattern on a white ground, Norway, 1960s, 7in (18cm) diam.
£15–25 *PC*

A Crown Derby porcelain plate, the centre painted with a stag in a mountain landscape, within a pink border decorated with raised gilt ivy trails, printed and impressed marks, late 19thC, 9¼in (23.5cm) diam.
£80–100 *WW*

A Gouda plate, decorated in a green and blue abstract pattern on an orange ground, with blue lined rim, restored, c1910, 12in (30.5cm) diam.
£65–75 *RAC*

A Falcon ware dish, decorated with flowers and leaves in shades of red, yellow, green and blue on a white ground, c1930, 12in (30.5cm) diam.
£90–110 *LUC*

l. A set of 8 Sarreguemines fish plates and one dish, with pink and grey tinted borders, on a white ground, c1930, dish 21¼in (54cm) long.
£150–175 *MLL*

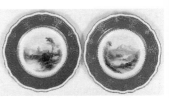

A pair of Copeland cabinet plates, painted to the centre with Hampton Court and Loch Ard respectively, within maroon and gilt borders, titled to reverse, 19thC, 9in (23cm) diam.
£130–160 *P(B)*

A set of 8 Cauldon plates, decorated in Imari style with blue, red and gold, 1890s, 10in (25.5cm) diam.
£150–200 *MSB*

A Ridgway's meat plate, decorated with Homemaker black and white pattern, 1955–67, 12in (30.5cm) wide.
£25–30 *GIN*

A Figgio plate, decorated with black line drawing of Norema factory, Norwegian, 1982, 8in (20.5cm) diam.
£8–10 *GIN*

Poole Pottery

Poole Pottery became the company's trade name in 1963. Established in 1873 as Carter & Co, the firm operated from the Poole Pottery in Dorset. In 1921 it expanded, taking the combined names of its partners, Charles Carter, his son Cyril Carter, Harold and Phoebe Stabler and John Adams, to become Carter, Stabler & Adams.

John Adams designed most of the shapes. Many of the patterns were provided by his wife Truda (subsequently married to Cyril Carter), who was responsible for creating the floral decorated ware that was to become identified as Poole Pottery. Pots were dipped in matt glaze and then hand-painted with stylised flowers and plants, using pastel colours and a free brushstroke. Colours and glaze were then fused in a final firing. This gently modern and attractive pottery was extremely successful in the 1930s when it retailed through shops

such as Heal's and Liberty's and became the trademark line of the company.

Poole successfully combined art and commercial pottery. In the 1950s, design director Alfred Read and senior thrower Guy Sydenham created a series of handsome vases, experimenting with elegant and innovative forms and subtle abstract decoration. In 1958, Robert Jefferson was engaged as chief designer at Poole, pioneering new shapes and colours for the 1960s.

Style from the 1960s and '70s is now fashionable, particularly with young collectors, and this section concludes with hand-painted studio ware from this period, which is now attracting considerable interest. Still active today, the Company retains its policy of combining art and industry producing studio collections as well as functional ware.

A Carter, Stabler & Adams coffee pot and cups and saucers, decorated in shades of yellow, brown and blue on a cream ground, impressed backstamp, 1920s, coffee pot 9in (23cm) high.
Coffee pot **£65–75**
Cups **£40–50 each** *HarC*

Coffee and tea sets of this period are rare.

A Carter, Stabler & Adams vase, painted by Nellie Bishton, with Grape pattern in shades of purple, red and green with yellow rim, impressed backstamp, 1920s, 6in (15cm) high.
£80–100 *HarC*

A Carter, Stabler & Adams pottery charger, painted with stylised dancing nymph, entitled 'Leipzig Girl', slight damage, initials in black, Carter Stabler Adams monogram, 1926–27, 17½in (44.5cm) diam.
£800–900 *AAV*

l. A Carter, Stabler & Adams vase, designed by Truda Adams, decorated with Persian deer pattern in shades of yellow, mauve and green, c1930, 11in (28cm) high.
£450–500 *RDG*

r. A Carter, Stabler & Adams baluster-shaped vase, designed by Truda Carter, painted in coloured enamels with a broad band of flowers and leaves, beneath a geometric band, impressed mark and incised 'No. 203' and decorator's monogram, 1930s, 8¼in (21cm) high.
£160–180 *HOLL*

A Carter, Stabler & Adams vase, designed by Truda Adams, decorated with blue, orange, mauve and green stylised flowers, slight damage, c1930, 14½in (37cm) high.
£700–800 *RDG*

A Carter, Stabler & Adams vase, designed by Truda Adams, decorated with Blue Bird pattern, 1930s, 6in (15cm) high.
£75–100 *RDG*

A Carter, Stabler & Adams jug, designed by Truda Carter, decorated with a geometric pattern in blue, black, beige and lime green, painted by Eileen Prangnell, 1930s, 8in (20.5cm) high.
£300–350 *HarC*

A Carter, Stabler & Adams cylinderical-shaped vase, decorated with stylised flowers and leaves in an abstract design on an off-white ground, decorator's initials 'X & Y O', c1935, 12in (30.5cm) high.
£120–140 *GAK*

r. A Carter, Stabler & Adams shell, designed by John Adams, with blue and vellum Picotee glaze effect, 1930–60s, 11in (28cm) wide.
£20–30 *HarC*

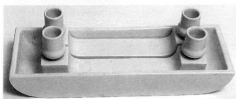

l. A Poole Pottery vase, designed by John Adams, decorated in Everest pattern, 1930s, 7in (18cm) high.
£90–110 *HarC*

A Carter, Stabler & Adams off-white three-piece candlestick set, designed by John Adams, 1930s, dish 11in (28cm) wide.
£75–85 *WAC*

A Carter Stabler & Adams ashtray, modelled as a boat, with vellum glaze with blue waves, probably designed by John Adams, 1930s, 7in (18cm) wide.
£65–75 *HarC*

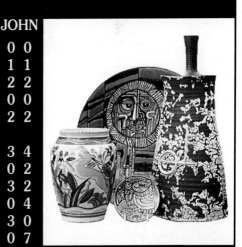

A Carter, Stabler & Adams plate, designed by Olive Bourne, decorated with Sugar for the Birds pattern, 1950, 12¼in (31cm) diam.
£450–500 *RDG*

A Carter, Stabler & Adams plate, commemorating the coronation of Queen Elizabeth II, 1953, 8in (20.5cm) diam.
£30–40 *HarC*

A Carter Stabler & Adams bowl, designed by Guy Sydenham, in black Freeform design with vellum interior, hand-thrown, signed, 1958, 7in (18cm) high.
£130–150 *HarC*

l. A Poole Pottery charger, designed by Tony Morris, decorated with an abstract design painted in shades of dark green, orange and light green, 1960s, 16½in (42cm) diam.
£1,300–1,500 *AAV*

This charger was found in a car boot sale, and was then auctioned for possibly the record price paid for such an item.

A Poole Pottery vase, from the Delphis range, painted with yellow and black design on an off-white ground, 1960s, 6in (15cm) high.
£50–60 *HarC*

A Poole Pottery vase, from the Delphis range, painted with stylised flowers in shades of blue and mauve, 1960–70s, 9in (23cm) high.
£75–100 *HarC*

A Poole Pottery bowl, from the Studio range, painted in vivid blue, orange and red glaze, 1960s, 6in (15cm) diam.
£50–70 *HarC*

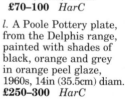

A Poole Pottery plate, designed by Truda Carter, decorated with the CS pattern, Traditional Range, 1960s, 13in (33cm) diam.
£70–100 *HarC*

l. A Poole Pottery plate, from the Delphis range, painted with shades of black, orange and grey in orange peel glaze, 1960s, 14in (35.5cm) diam.
£250–300 *HarC*

A Poole Pottery vase, from the Delphis range, decorated in shades of terracotta, 1960s, 8in (20.5cm) high.
£80–100 *HarC*

This shape was only produced for a couple of years and this design is prone to cracking around the rim.

r. Two Poole Pottery dishes, decorated with blue, orange and red colours in abstract designs, 1960–70s, 8in (20.5cm) wide.
£50–60 each *HarC*

A Poole Pottery plate, from the Delphis range, painted in shades of orange, yellow and green, signed by Janet Laird, 1967, 16in (40.5cm) diam.
£300–350 *HarC*

A Poole Pottery vase, from the Delphis range, painted in shades of blue and red by Pamela Bevens, 1960–70s, 5in (12.5cm) high.
£120–140 *HarC*

Four Poole Pottery dishes, from the Delphis range, decorated in shades of blue, mauve, pink, and orange abstract designs with orange peel glaze, 1960–70s, 7in (18cm) wide.
£60–80 each *HarC*

A Poole Pottery model of a duck, designed by Barbara Linley Adams, finished in brown on a beige ground, 1970s, 3in (7.5cm) high.
£10–20 *HarC*

This is from a large range of animals finished in different glazes.

A Poole Pottery vase, from the Delphis range, decorated with abstract design in shades of orange and blue, 1960–70s, 9in (23cm) high.
£75–100 *HarC*

r. A Poole Pottery vase, designed by Sally Tuffin, decorated with a pheasant design in shades of blue and brown, 1996, 7¾in (20cm) high.
£100–125 *RDG*

Quimper

l. A Quimper wall horn, decorated with a figure on a cream ground, marked, c1885–90, 10½in (26.5cm) high.
£180–200 *VH*

A pair of Quimper barrel-shaped vases, marked, c1895, 12in (30.5cm) high.
£425–475 *VH*

A Quimper bowl, decorated with blue and orange abstract pattern on a cream ground, 1950s, 5in (12.5cm) diam.
£12–15 *RAC*

A Quimper jam pot, decorated with trees and figures on a cream ground, 1950s, 3in (7.5cm) high.
£20–25 *RAC*

A Quimper bowl, decorated with stylised flowers and leaves in shades of orange and green with a blue rim, 1950s, 7in (18cm) diam.
£25–30 *RAC*

A Quimper tureen, decorated with stylised flowers and leaves in shades of orange and green with a blue rim, 1950s, 5in (12.5cm) high.
£40–50 *RAC*

Radford

A Radford trio, decorated with pink and yellow flowers and leaves, on a cream ground, c1935, cup 2½in (6.5cm) high.
£20–30 *CSA*

Cross Reference
Colour Review

A Radford jug, decorated with blue, lilac and red flowers on a cream ground, c1945, 11in (28cm) high.
£50–60 *CSA*

A Radford vase, decorated with pink, lilac, red, blue and yellow flowers on a pink speckled ground, c1950, 10in (25.5cm) high.
£30–40 *CSA*

A Radford vase, decorated with blue and red flowers on a blue speckled ground, c1955, 10in (25.5cm) high.
£30–40 *CSA*

Charlotte Rhead

A Charlotte Rhead basket, decorated with Persian Rose pattern, with a green handle, c1935, 5½in (14cm) high.
£75–100 *HEA*

A Bursley Ware ewer, designed by Charlotte Rhead, decorated in shades of blue, mauve and grey with stylised foliage, on a mottled pale blue ground, printed mark, 1930s, 9½in (24cm) high.
£170–200 *GAK*

A Crown Ducal ewer, designed by Charlotte Rhead, decorated and painted with stylised flowers in orange, black and yellow with gilt detail on a beige speckled ground, printed marks, signed and impressed '145', 1930s, 10in (25.5cm) high.
£230–260 *GAK*

A Crown Ducal ribbed ewer, designed by Charlotte Rhead, with loop handle, tube lined with a band of fruits and leaves picked out in green, brown and yellow, on a brown ground, printed mark in green, painted signature and 'No. 5802', c1935, 8in (20.5cm) high.
£170–200 *HOLL*

A Crown Ducal ovoid vase, designed by Charlotte Rhead, decorated in shades of brown and orange on a speckled beige ground, pattern No. 4968, c1937, 7in (18cm) high.
£220–250 *PC*

A Bursley Ware bowl, designed by Charlotte Rhead, second period, decorated in shades of blue, yellow and brown with turquoise rim, pattern No. TL2, 1940s, 9in (23cm) diam.
£120–150 *PC*

Charlotte Rhead

Some Bursley Ware items, designed by Charlotte Rhead and made by H. J. Wood Ltd, are described as 'first period' and 'second period' as she worked for the company on two occasions from 1913–20 and 1943–7.

A Bursley Ware vase, designed by Charlotte Rhead, second period, decorated in shades of yellow, brown and orange, pattern No. TL5, 1940s, 6in (15cm) high.
£100–120 *PC*

A Bursley Ware lamp base, designed by Charlotte Rhead, second period, decorated in shades of yellow and mauve, pattern No. TL30, 1940s, 7in (18cm) high.
£220–280 *PC*

A Bursley Ware vase, designed by Charlotte Rhead, second period, decorated in shades of pink, blue and beige, pattern No. TL 76, 1940s, 8½in (21cm) high.
£170–200 *PC*

A Bursley Ware vase, designed by Charlotte Rhead, second period, decorated with pink and blue flowers on a white ground with a brown rim, pattern No. TL4, 1940s, 12½in (32cm) high.
£350–400 *PC*

Royal Winton

A Royal Winton jug, depicting a pixie in a red suit on a brown and green ground, c1930, 3½in (9cm) high.
£20–30 *CSA*

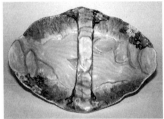

A Royal Winton basket, decorated with Woodland Stream pattern, in shades of green and beige with red and blue flowers, c1930, 8in (20.5cm) long.
£50–60 *CSA*

A Royal Winton Chintz ware dish, decorated with Sweet Pea pattern, in shades of yellow, pink and blue flowers on a cream ground, c1935, 10in (25.5cm) long.
£60–70 *CSA*

A Royal Winton Chintz ware cruet set, decorated with English Rose pattern, with pink and blue flowers on a cream ground, c1940, 5in (12.5cm) long.
£60–70 *CSA*

Two Royal Winton green sauce boats, with yellow floral handles, c1930, 5in (12.5cm) long.
£30–35 each *CSA*

A Royal Winton Chintz ware preserve jar, with silver-plated cover, decorated with Summertime pattern, in shades of pink, yellow and blue on a white ground, 1930s, 4½in (11.5cm) high.
£80–100 *BEV*

A Royal Winton Chintz ware sugar bowl and lid, decorated with Sweet Pea pattern, in shades of pink, blue and green on a cream ground, 1930s, 3¼in (8.5cm) high.
£85–95 *BET*

A Royal Winton Chintz ware dish, decorated with Sunshine pattern, in shades of pink, green and orange on a white ground, 1930s, 5½in (14cm) wide.
£50–55 *BEV*

A Royal Winton Chintz ware dish, decorated with Estelle pattern in shades of pink and yellow flowers on a cream ground, c1935, 10in (25.5cm) long.
£50–60 *CSA*

A Royal Winton toast rack and sauce boat, decorated with mauve pansies on a white ground, c1960, sauce boat 6in (15cm) long, toast rack 4in (10cm) high.
£10–15 each *CSA*

l. A Royal Winton Chintz ware dish, decorated with Old Cottage pattern, with pink and blue flowers on a grey ground, c1935, 5in (12.5cm) long.
£20–30 *CSA*

Shelley

A Shelley porcelain tea set, comprising 39 pieces, decorated with Cottage pattern, depicting a garden scene, on a white ground with blue banding, pattern No. 11604, c1927.
£550–650 *AH*

A Shelley Art Deco porcelain part tea set, decorated with Blue Iris pattern on a white ground, pattern No. 11561, slight damage, c1927.
£700–800 *Bea(E)*

A Shelley candlestick, decorated with orange, yellow, green and black pattern, 1940s, 6in (15cm) diam.
£45–50 *RAC*

A Shelley Chintz ware coffee cup and saucer, decorated with Regent pattern, in shades of yellow, blue and pink flowers, c1932, 2½in (6.5cm) high.
£35–40 *BEV*

A Shelley butter dish, decorated with Crocus pattern, in shades of pink and blue on a white ground, c1930, 4½in (11.5cm) long.
£15–20 *CSA*

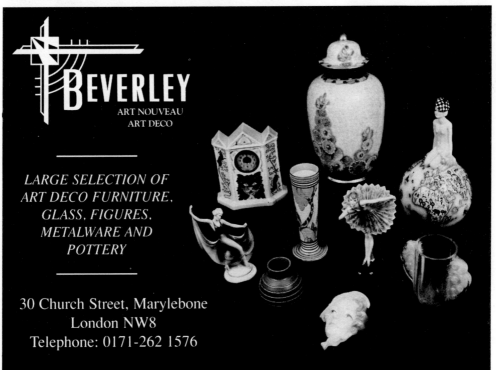

Mabel Lucie Attwell

A Shelley cruet set, depicting a pixie and toadstools, in red, green and white, designed by Mabel Lucie Attwell, 1926–45, 5½in (14cm) wide.
£300–350 *WWY*

A collection of 3 Shelley figures of Boo-Boos, designed by Mabel Lucie Attwell, 1926–1945, 3¼in (8.5cm) high.
£300–350 each *WWY*

Boo-Boos was the name for the series of elves in green suits devised by Mabel Lucie Attwell for Shelley nursery ware in 1926.

Cross Reference
Baby Collectables

A Shelley figure, in the form of a golfer, designed by Mabel Lucie Attwell, 1926–45, 6¼in (16cm) high.
£600–700 *WWY*

A pair of Shelley figures, in the form of a bride and groom, designed by Mabel Lucie Attwell, 1926–45, 6in (15cm) high.
£800–950 each *WWY*

Shorter

A Shorter tulip-shaped posy vase, in shades of yellow and green, on a brown base, c1935, 5in (12.5cm) high.
£20–30 *CSA*

A Shorter petal-shaped basket, in shades of red and green, c1950, 5in (12.5cm) high.
£25–30 *CSA*

FURTHER READING
Irene and Gordon Hopwood, *The Shorter Connection*, Richard Dennis Publications, 1992

A Shorter beehive-shaped honey jar, depicting a brown bee on a pale blue hive, c1935, 4½in (11.5cm) high.
£20–30 *CSA*

Clarice Cliff designed and decorated some Shorter wares in the 1930s.

A Shorter daffodil-shaped posy vase, with yellow petals on green leaves, c1935, 4in (10cm) high.
£10–15 *CSA*

A Shorter petal-shaped dish, with green and red petals, c1950, 7in (18cm) wide.
£10–12 *CSA*

Staffordshire

A Staffordshire porcelain miniature tea service, each piece painted in coloured enamels with sprays of flowers and leaves, slight damage, probably Hicks & Meigh, 1825–30.
£400–450 *DN*

A Staffordshire porcelain stand, with pierced border, painted in coloured enamels with a named view of 'Lambton Castle', within a gilt cartouche, on a turquoise ground, painted title in black, c1840, 9¾in (25cm) wide.
£300–350 *DN*

A Staffordshire egg, depicting Queen Victoria and Prince Albert dancing the polka, 1840s, 2⅛in (5.5cm) long.
£650–750 *TVM*

A Staffordshire plate, with black transfer printed with a religious scene, c1840, 6½in (16.5cm) diam.
£20–25 *SER*

A Staffordshire Pratt ware model of a deer, under-glazed in shades of fawn and green, c1790, 6in (15cm) long.
£600–650 *JRe*

Animals

A Staffordshire pottery model, depicting a recumbent doe with sponged ochre details, on green oval base, late 18thC, 6in (15cm) wide.
£340–380 *RBB*

A Staffordshire stirrup cup, in the form of a fox's mask, with black snout, 19thC, 5in (12.5cm) long.
£140–160 *P(O)*

A Staffordshire pottery cow creamer, decorated in red and white on a green moulded base, 19thC, 7in (18cm) long.
£120–150 *HCH*

A pair of Staffordshire spill vases, modelled as red and white cows with seated milkmaids, slight damage, 19thC, 8½in (21.5cm) high.
£475–525 *TMA*

l. A Staffordshire cow creamer and cover, sponged with multi-coloured glazes on a green moulded base, probably North Country, early 19thC, 5½in (14cm) long.
£420–500 *HYD*

A Staffordshire group, depicting 2 sheep beneath a tree with multi-coloured flowers for leaves, c1835, 3in (7.5cm) wide.
£300–360 *JO*

Staffordshire Animals

Animals were one of the most popular subjects with the Staffordshire potteries. As well as traditional farmyard animals and domestic pets, the opening of the first zoological gardens in the 19thC and the popularity of travelling circuses stimulated demand for exotic beasts: lions, elephants etc. New designs were created and old ones adapted: zebras, for example, were often made in moulds originally intended for horses and appeared complete with flowing equine manes and tails. The favourite subject of all, however, was the dog, in particular the King Charles spaniel and the so-called 'comforter' or lap dog, which were produced in their thousands.

A pair of Staffordshire models of red and white spaniels, each with collar and padlock, slight damage, 19thC, 8in (20.5cm) high.
£240–280 *TMA*

A pair of Staffordshire brown-glazed greyhounds, late 19thC, 2½in (6.5cm) high.
£100–130 *SPU*

A pair of Staffordshire quill stands, modelled as 2 dalmations with yellow collars, on blue bases, mid-19thC, 6in (15cm) high.
£100–120 *CaC*

A Staffordshire white miniature porcelain poodle, c1840, 1¾in (4.5cm) wide.
£180–220 *DAN*

A Staffordshire spill vase, modelled as a black and white zebra with a man in a blue coat, c1865, 7in (18cm) high.
£125–150 *JO*

A pair of Staffordshire pottery spill vases, depicting a lion and lioness, the rustic pattern trunk encrusted with snakes and shells, c1850, 11in (28cm) high.
£1,500–1,800 *CAG*

A Staffordshire spill vase, modelled as a family of swans in their nest, on a white base, c1860, 4¾in (12cm) high.
£100–120 *JO*

r. A pair of Staffordshire pottery cockerels, each with facial features detailed in red and black, 19thC, 11¾in (30cm) high.
£800–900 *P(B)*

A pair of Staffordshire pottery models, in the form of zebras, each on a green oval foliage encrusted base, 19thC, 5in (12.5cm) high.
£250–300 *HCH*

Figures

A Staffordshire pearlware reclining figure of Cleopatra, her dress painted in blue and iron red with flowers and leaves, the green glazed mound base moulded with flowers and leaves, slight damage, 1800–10, 11½in (29cm) long.
£275–325 *DN*

A Staffordshire group, entitled 'Death of Nelson', depicting the Admiral supported by 2 officers, all wearing blue coats, 1840s, 19thC, 8½in (21.5cm) high.
£250–300 *P(O)*

l. A Staffordshire white figure, in the form of a child in a gown with a poodle, flanked with pink flowers, c1840, 6in (15cm) high.
£100–120 *SER*

A Staffordshire model, of the Duke of Wellington on horseback, wearing a black cocked hat, black robe and iron red jacket, painted throughout in colours, on a green and iron-red washed base, restored, 19thC, 12in (30.5cm) high.
£200–230 *GAK*

A Staffordshire figure, depicting a clock seller in a brown overcoat and cream coloured suit, on a cream base, c1840, 7½in (19cm) high.
£180–230 *GEM*

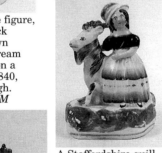

A Staffordshire quill holder, in the form of a girl with goat, in shades of pink, brown, beige and green, c1850, 5in (12.5cm) high.
£100–125 *SER*

l. A Staffordshire figure of Robinson Crusoe, in grey coat with a yellow hat, c1840, 6in (15cm) high.
£160–200 *RWB*

Production of Staffordshire Figures

A clay figure was made from which a mould was taken in 2 parts, front and back. The 2 halves were bound together and fired resulting in a hollow figure ready for painting. As more moulds were made from the original model, so quality of detailing deteriorated.

Flatback figures, intended to be placed against a wall, had all the modelling and painting on the front. The reverse side was almost completely flat and undecorated.

Bright primary colours were popular, in particular cobalt blue. Victorian painted figures are often well-detailed with feathered eyebrows, stranded hair and rouged cheeks, features which tend to be missing from later copies. Figures were often gilded, the soft honey gold being replaced by a sharper, brighter gilding from the 1880s.

A Staffordshire pottery figure, entitled 'Louis Kossuth', wearing a black hat with pink plume and blue frock coat, on a titled base, 19thC, 10¾in (27.5cm) high.
£320–360 *AH*

A Staffordshire pottery figure, entitled 'Liberte', depicting a soldier in orange tunic holding a banner, on leaf and scroll decorated base, 19thC, 9in (23cm) high.
£180–220 *AH*

Houses, Castles & Cottages

A Staffordshire pastille burner, modelled as a castle, decorated with green and pink foliage on a white ground, 4¼in (11cm) high.
£500–550 *JO*

A Staffordshire model of a castle, decorated with green and pink foliage, on a pink ground and a white base, c1850, 3½in (9cm) high.
£75–85 *SER*

A Staffordshire pastille burner, modelled as a cottage with a thatched roof, decorated in coloured enamels and gilt, c1835, 5½in (14cm) high.
£220–260 *JO*

A Staffordshire pastille burner, modelled as a castle, gilt decorated with pink and green foliage on a white ground, c1835, 4in (10cm) wide.
£150–200 *JO*

> **Miller's is a price GUIDE not a price LIST**

l. A Staffordshire pastille burner, modelled as a cottage, decorated in multi-coloured enamels and gilt on a white ground, c1840, 4in (10cm) wide.
£150–200 *ALB*

A Staffordshire money box, modelled as a cottage, decorated with coloured enamels on a white ground, c1860, 4¾in (12cm) high.
£85–95 *SER*

A Staffordshire cottage, entitled 'Windsor Lodge', decorated with red and yellow flowers on a white ground, 5¼in (13.5cm) high.
£200–220 *JO*

A Victorian Staffordshire pastille burner, modelled as a cottage, decorated with green foliage and red chimneys on a white ground, late 19thC, 4in (10cm) high.
£120–150 *TVM*

Whistles

A Staffordshire whistle, The Cleric, in a blue robe on a yellow base, 19thC, 2¼in (5.5cm) high.
£150–180 *TVM*

A Staffordshire whistle, in the form of a white bird on a green branch, 19thC, 2⅖in (6.5cm) high.
£120–150 *TVM*

r. A Staffordshire whistle, in the form of an admiral, 19thC, 3¼in (8.5cm) high.
£150–200 *TVM*

Staffordshire whistles were produced as decorative items.

A Staffordshire whistle, in the form of a pierrot, in an orange overcoat, on green moulded base, 19thC, 3½in (9cm) high.
£150–200 *TVM*

A Staffordshire whistle, in the form of a cream-coloured bird with red wings, 19thC, 1¾in (4.5cm) high.
£100–120 *TVM*

A Staffordshire whistle, in the form of a white owl on a green branch, 19thC, 2⅖in (6.5cm) high.
£150–180 *TVM*

A Staffordshire whistle, in the form of a green bird, 19thC, 3in (7.5cm) high.
£120–150 *TVM*

SylvaC

Two SylvaC pottery book ends, in the form of rabbits, coloured in beige and green, slight damage, 1930s, 5in (12.5cm) high.
£18–20 *MEG*

A SylvaC wall pocket, depicting a rabbit, coloured in beige and green, 1930s, 7¾in (20cm) high.
£30–35 *MEG*

A SylvaC rabbit, coloured in yellow and orange, No. 305, c1930, 5½in (14cm) high.
£55–65 *TAC*

Teapots

A creamware teapot, painted with chinoiserie design in iron-red, blue and gilt, cover damaged, late 18thC, 4in (10cm) high.
£300–350 *RBB*

A Minton Amherst teapot, decorated with Japan pattern in shades of blue, red and gilt on a white ground, c1880, 4¼in (11cm) high.
£160–170 *AMH*

A Staffordshire teapot, hand-painted with pink flowers and gilt foliage, on a black ground, c1890, 6in (15cm) high.
£60–70 *CSA*

Teapots

The teapot was a Western invention, dating from the late 17thC. The earliest silver teapots mirrored the shape of coffee pots, soon replaced by the now traditional globular form. By the 18thC, the Chinese were producing porcelain teapots for the export market, which were then copied by British potteries. As tea became established as the national drink, so increasing attention was lavished on the teapot in terms of shape and decoration, and novelty designs became increasingly popular.

A teapot, inscribed 'Lynmouth', decorated in shades of brown and blue on a cream ground, c1940, 4in (10cm) high.
£35–40 *RAC*

An Avonware teapot, with brown and green lid on a yellow body, c1940, 4in (10cm) high.
£20–25 *CSA*

r. A teapot, in the form of a beige rabbit, marked 'Bunny', c1930, 8in (20.5cm) high.
£60–75 *DKH*

A chrome and ceramic tea and coffee set, with milk jug, sugar bowl and tray, 1950s, tray 12½in (32cm) diam.
£60–70 *GIN*

Wade

The Wade factory was founded in 1922 in Burslem, Staffordshire, by George Wade. The firm consisted of three potteries in England – A. J. Wade Ltd, George Wade & Son Ltd and Wade Heath & Co – and in the 1940s the company also established a factory in Ireland. Before WWII Wade concentrated on mainly utilitarian pottery and produced a comparatively small amount of gift ware.

Rare decorative pieces from the 1930s, such as the Snow White and the Seven Dwarfs figure set (see below), can fetch very high prices today. It was not until after the 1950s, however, and once wartime restrictions were lifted, that the company launched its most famous decorative range. Wade Whimsies were introduced at the British Industries Fair in 1954. These first animal models were sold in boxed sets of five for 5s 9d and, to the pottery industry's surprise, were an instant hit with children and their parents. In order to stimulate demand and to encourage buyers to purchase new designs, sets were produced for a limited period only. Generations of children have now grown up with Wade Whimsies. They were extremely popular as party favours and have appeared as free gifts with everything from Christmas crackers, to tea, to crisps.

Value depends on rarity. The more commonplace examples can still be purchased for pocket-money prices (a couple of pounds or less), while rarer figures are more costly. If a model still has its original box, its value can be increased by as much as 50 per cent.

A Wade glazed figure, entitled 'Queenie', in shades of pink, with a green fan, 1930s, 4in (10cm) high.
£200–220   *P*

A Wade pottery group of Snow White and Seven Dwarfs, in multi-coloured glazes, slight damage, 1938, Snow White 7in (18cm) high.
£1,100–1,300   *Bea(E)*

These models were produced in 1938 to coincide with the launch of Walt Disney's Snow White and the Seven Dwarfs. A different issue of the same 8 characters was also produced in 1981. The later set retailed at £39.50 and is now worth about £500.

A Wade model of a pelican, with a yellow beak, 1946–53, 7in (18cm) wide.
£275–300   *P*

The original retail price of this model was 6/6d.

Two Wade pint mugs, each depicting a vintage car, 1957–86, 7in (18cm) high.
£10–15 each   *RAC*

A Wade model of a penguin, decorated with shades of white and grey, marked 'Wade Made in England', c1950, 2½in (6.5cm) high.
£425–450   *P*

A Shamrock Pottery model of an elephant, c1959, 3in (7.5cm) wide.
£35–40   *MAC*

Some of Wade's Irish pieces were marked 'Shamrock Pottery'. The pink elephant was an obvious and humorous reminder of the perils of drink.

Two Wade ashtrays, decorated with animals and inscribed 'London Zoo', l. blue, r. green, c1979, 5in (12.5cm) diam.
£8–10 each   *RAC*

Wade Whimsies

Two Wade Whimsie dogs, a setter and a spaniel, 1971–72, 1½in (4cm) high.
£2–3 each *P*

Three Wade Whimsies, 1969–72, largest 1¼in (3cm) high:
l. Brook Bond Oxo Ltd otter,
c. Wade goldfish,
r. Brook Bond Oxo Ltd beaver.
£2–3 each *P*

Two Wade Whimsies, a fawn and an owl, 1971–72, 1½in (4cm) high.
£2–3 each *P*

Two Wade Whimsies, a field mouse and bear cub, c1972, 1½in (4cm) high.
£2–3 each *P*

A Wade Whimsie kitten, 1971–72, 1½in (4cm) high.
£2–3 *P*

Three Wade Whimsies, a hippo, a giraffe, and a chimpanzee, c1973, largest 1½in (4cm) high, in original yellow boxes.
£2–3 each *P*

Three Wade Whimsies, in the form of lions, c1973, 1½in (4cm) high.
£2–3 each *P*

Three Wade Whimsie friars, c1983, 1½in (4cm) high:
l. Brother Crispin,
c. Brother Francis,
r. Brother Angelo.
£15–20 each *TRE*

These 3 figures are hard to find and so command higher prices than the others in the set.

Two Wade Whimsies, a fox and an alsation, c1973, 1½in (4cm) high.
£2–3 each *P*

Three Wade Whimsie friars, c1983, 1½in (4cm) high:
l. Brother Benjamin,
c. Father Abbot,
r. Brother Peter.
£5–8 each *TRE*

The K. P. Friars set was commissioned by K. P. Foods as a crisps promotion. Father Abbot was free with tokens, the other 5 figures could be obtained with tokens and a small sum of money.

Two Wade Whimsies, a pine marten and a squirrel, c1974, largest 1½in (4cm) high.
£2–3 each *P*

l. A Wade Whimsie, The Three Bears, 1970–71, 1½in (4cm) high.
£18–20 *HEI*

Wedgwood

A Wedgwood creamware chocolate pot, cover and stand, 18thC, 4½in (11.5cm) high.
£180–210 MEG

A Wedgwood black basalt crocus pot and tray, in the form of a hedgehog, slight damage, 19thC, 7in (18cm) high.
£500–550 TMA

A Wedgwood creamware drainer, the pierced base painted with fruiting vine, on 3 peg feet, impressed mark, c1800, 8in (20.5cm) diam.
£120–140 HYD

A Wedgwood jasper ware pot pourri vase, decorated with white Grecian figures and leaves on a blue ground, restored, mid-19thC, 12in (30.5cm) high.
£250–275 BRU

A Wedgwood buff-coloured game dish, moulded with game and festoons of vines, the cover with hare finial, with liner, 19thC, 9in (23cm) wide.
£230–260 E

A Wedgwood plate, decorated with flowers and insects on a white ground, mid-19thC, 5in (12.5cm) diam.
£10–12 BSA

A Wedgwood blue pottery mug, depicting Sir Winston Churchill in white, and with inscription, c1941, 3in (7.5cm) high.
£85–95 W&S

A Wedgwood Festival of Britain mug, decorated in shades of blue, buff, black and white, 1951, 2½in (6.5cm) high.
£140–160 W&S

A Wedgwood majolica game pie dish, with liner and lid, brown glazed and applied with game and fruiting vine, hare finial, impressed date mark for 1864, slight damage, 9in (23cm) wide.
£500–600 TMA

Cross Reference
Commemorative

r. A Wedgwood Children's Story plate, entitled 'Tom Thumb', 1981, 6in (15cm) diam.
£15–20 MAC

Wemyss

A Wemyss bulb bowl, decorated with crocuses in shades of yellow, purple and green on a white ground, c1890, 8½in (21.5cm) wide.
£400–450 *RdeR*

A Wemyss Gordon plate, painted with red gooseberries and green leaves, with green rim, 1890–1900, 8in (20.5cm) diam.
£250–300 *RdeR*

A Wemyss biscuit jar and cover, painted with oranges on a cream ground, c1900, 5in (12.5cm) diam.
£180–200 *RdeR*

A Wemyss canted rectangular comb tray, painted in coloured enamels with black cockerels within a green line border, impressed mark and printed retailer's mark in puce for T. Goode & Co, damaged and repaired, c1900, 10in (25.5cm) wide.
£140–160 *HOLL*

A Wemyss bowl, decorated with mallard ducks on a white ground with green rim, impressed 'Wemyss Ware, R.H. and S', c1900, 5in (12.5cm) high.
£750–850 *AG*

A Wemyss match striker, decorated with pink and green flowers on a cream ground, c1900, 4in (10cm) high.
£200–250 *RdeR*

r. A Wemyss black and white pig, c1930, 7in (18cm) long.
£350–450 *RdeR*

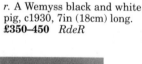

A Wemyss pomade pot and cover, painted with pink roses and foliage, within green line borders, impressed 'Wemyss', c1900, 4½in (11.5cm) diam.
£400–450 *S*

r. A Wemyss flower holder, in the form of a goose, decorated in green, puce and yellow, the wings picked out in blue, green, brown and yellow, on round base, impressed mark, restored, c1900, 7¼in (18.5cm) high.
£220–250 *HOLL*

A Wemyss Kenmore vase, painted with irises within green line borders, impressed 'Wemyss' and painted with the retailer's mark for Thomas Goode & Co, c1900, 14½in (37cm) high.
£800–900 *L*

Worcester

A Worcester teabowl and saucer, decorated in black, with boys riding bulls, workman's marks, slight damage, c1756, teabowl 4in (10cm) diam.
£400–500 *DN*

A Worcester fluted sauceboat, with loop handle, the interior painted in Chinese style, in underglaze blue with boats in a wooded river landscape, the exterior with a broad band of flowers, scrolls and butterflies, c1775, 8in (20.5cm) long.
£400–500 *DN*

A Royal Worcester figure of a Scotsman, seated wearing a beret and kilt, picked out in coloured enamels and gilt, on canted base, printed mark in puce for 1889 and registration mark for 1881, 6¼in (16cm) high.
£400–500 *DN*

A Worcester basket, the interior painted in coloured enamels with flowers and leaves within a puce scroll band, the flared sides pierced with interlinked roundels and applied with flowerheads, small repair, c1760, 6½in (16.5cm) diam.
£600–700 *DN*

A Worcester coffee can, c1805, 2½in (6.5cm) high.
£70–80 *BSA*

l. A Royal Worcester figure of John Bull, picked out in coloured enamels and gilt, on canted base, slight damage, modelled by James Hadley, printed mark in puce for 1884 and registration mark for 1881, 7in (18cm) high.
£250–300 *DN*

r. A Grainger's Worcester coffee can and saucer, decorated with gold and black pattern, 1889–1902, saucer 4½in (11.5cm) diam.
£25–35 *WAC*

A Worcester coffee cup and saucer, with turquoise border and pearl pattern, slight restoration, c1770, saucer 2¾in (7cm) diam.
£100–120 *DAN*

A Chamberlain's Worcester teacup and saucer, with gadrooned rim, painted in coloured enamels with roses, pansies and leaves, on gold ground bands, within gilt stiff leaf borders, painted mark in iron red and pattern No. 924, c1816–20, cup 3½in (9cm) high.
£300–350 *DN*

FURTHER READING
John Sandon,
The Dictionary of Worcester Porcelain, Vol I 1751–1851,
Antique Collectors' Club

A Chamberlain's Worcester 35-piece tea set, decorated with gilt and dark blue border on a white ground, c1820, teapot 7in (18cm) high.
£1,200–1,300 *ALB*

A pair of Royal Worcester wall pockets, blush ivory decorated with gilt, printed marks and date code for 1891, 8in (20.5cm) high.
£180–220 *P(B)*

A Royal Worcester blue and white bowl, some restoration, c1890, 9in (23cm) diam.
£225–250 *RAC*

A Royal Worcester coffee can and saucer, decorated with black and gilt pattern, c1916, saucer 3¾in (9.5cm) diam.
£85–95 *WAC*

A Royal Worcester vase, by James Stinton, painted with a cock pheasant, above a band of blush ivory stiff-leaves and flowers on a circular foot, No. 1047, printed mark with date code for 1907, 9in (23cm) high.
£550–650 *P(B)*

A Royal Worcester figure, in the form of a Beefeater, with green belt and brown shoes on a cream ground, c1890, 10in (25.5cm) high.
£325–350 *TH*

Cross Reference
Figures

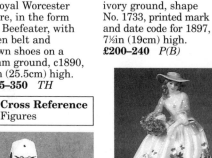

A Royal Worcester vase, decorated with flowers on a blush ivory ground, shape No. 1733, printed mark and date code for 1897, 7½in (19cm) high.
£200–240 *P(B)*

A Royal Worcester figure, entitled 'Magnolia Bud', shape No. 3144, printed marks and date cipher for 1936, 4½in (11.5cm) high.
£110–130 *GAK*

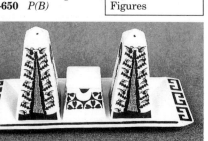

A Royal Worcester cruet set, decorated with black and white pattern, designed by Scottie Wilson, transfer mark, c1940s, 4in (10cm) high.
£160–180 *GIN*

A Royal Worcester figure, entitled 'Sweet Violet', decorated in shades of pink, white and violet, 1980–90s, 7in (18cm) high.
£85–95 *HEI*

A Royal Worcester pie funnel, in the form of a blackbird on a white funnel, c1950s, 4in (10cm), in original box.
£18–20 *MAC*

CLOCKS

Novelty clocks are becoming increasingly popular with collectors. 'I think that they are one of the best investments you can make at the moment in terms of clocks,' says Peter Dixon, specialist dealer and collector. 'Look out for clocks with interesting escapements, novelty pendulums, automata (mechanical figures) and moving parts – anything with an unusual design.'

Prices can range from under £50 for a 1950s novelty alarm clock, decorated with a farmyard or nursery rhyme scene, and up to thousands of pounds for a Victorian automaton clock. 'Even with the good 19th and early 20th century examples, prices are still relatively inexpensive compared with traditional antique bracket clocks,' advises Dixon, 'and frankly a novelty clock is much more interesting.'

Working order is crucial when it comes to value, as restoration can be expensive. 'All clocks can be repaired,' says Dixon, 'it is just a question of how much this will cost. If a timepiece is valuable, it is worth fixing. With a less expensive piece, if the repairs cost more than the clock is worth, there is not much point in restoring it.'

A gilt-brass clock, depicting Little Red Riding Hood, with later movement, c1870, 8½in (21.5cm) high.
£300–320 *CHe*

A French brass carriage clock, the movement with lever platform escapement and push repeat striking on a gong, with enamel dial, in a corniche case, 19thC, 7in (17.5cm) high.
£375–450 *P(B)*

An American cast iron 30-hour clock, entitled 'Topsy', c1865, 17in (43cm) high.
£700–800 *CHe*

A clock and 6-branch candelabra, the clock styled out of 150mm artillery shell from the Franco Prussian war, and candelabra styled from bayonets, c1870, 32in (81.5cm) high.
£1,000–1,250 *HEY*

A brass carriage clock, with shaped handle, the 8-day movement with enamelled dial, late 19thC, 7in (18cm) high.
£150–200 *Mit*

A German spelter clock, in the form of a dog, with 30-hour movement, c1880, 6in (15cm) high.
£400–500 *CHe*
When this clock ticks the tail wags and the tongue laps.

A French brass carriage clock, the movement with lever platform escapement and push repeat striking on a gong, the backplate numbered '8380', with enamel dial, in a gorge case, 19thC, 6¾in (17cm) high, with leather travelling case.
£700–800 *P(B)*

A German 30-hour alarm clock, with oak case, c1890, 9½in (24cm) high.
£150–170 *TPA*

A French drumhead mantel clock, modelled as a wine keg with spelter maiden, inscribed 'Bacchante' on marble base, late 19thC, 14½in (37cm) high.
£110–130 *CaC*

A marble and slate drumhead mantel clock, with white enamel dial and Roman numerals, on rectangular scroll and stepped base, late Victorian, 10in (25.5cm) high.
£120–140 *CaC*

A clock, with picture of castle, designed by Chauncy Jerome for New Haven Clock Co, c1890, 36in (91.5cm) high.
£220–250 *OT*

A German silver-plated mantel clock, with 30-hour movement, c1900, 6in (15cm) high.
£85–110 *TIH*

An Austrian wooden clock, c1900, with later quartz movement, 8¼in (21cm) high.
£85–95 *TPA*

A French spelter clock, modelled as a windmill, with porcelain dial, c1890, 12in (30.5cm) high.
£600–700 *CHe*

r. A German brass clock, modelled as a wheelbarrow, c1900, 6½in (16.5cm) wide.
£120–130 *CHe*

l. A French mahogany mantel clock, with 8-day barrel movement, brass and enamel dial, c1900, 11in (28cm) wide.
£100–125 *TIH*

A silver clock, depicting John Bull, inscribed 'Wake Up', marked, c1909, 6in (15cm) high.
£300–350 *CHe*

A German wooden clock, modelled as a dog, c1920, 7½in (19cm) high.
£100–120 *CHe*

A German clock, modelled as a Scottie dog, the revolving eyes telling the time, c1920s, 6in (15cm) high.
£280–300 *CHe*

A Scottish Art Nouveau clock, by Westclox, with resin surround, 1920s, 5½in (14cm) high.
£15–20 *GIN*

An enamel clock, painted with blue and white flowers, c1930s, 8¾in (22cm) square.
£50–60 *ANV*

A German bronzed-white-metal mystery clock, c1920, 30in (76cm) high.
£600–650 *TPA*

An oak-veneered clock, with 8-day striking movement, restored, c1922, 17in (43cm) wide.
£85–95 *TIH*

A wood and chrome clock, modelled as a galleon, c1930, 16½in (42cm) high.
£80–100 *CHe*

This clock has electric bulbs inside which light up the portholes.

A factory time clock, by Blick, c1920, 38in (96.5cm) high.
£200–250 *JUN*

A Bakelite clock, by Ingersoll, c1930s, 5¼in (13.5cm) high.
£35–45 *RAD*

A metal-framed clock, by John Francis, 1930s, 6in (15cm) square.
£8–10 *GIN*

An aircraft clock, with 8-day movement, from an American Air Force WWII B17B bomber, restored, c1943, 4in (10cm) square.
£120–135 *TIH*

A ceramic clock, modelled as a black horse, 1950s, 8in (20.5cm) high.
£15–20 *WAB*

A Bakelite alarm clock, by Metamec, on chrome feet, restored, c1950, 5½in (14cm) high.
£35–45 *TIH*

A Smiths nursery alarm clock, depicting *The Hare and the Tortoise*, 1950s, 7in (18cm) diam.
£100–110 *CHe*

An alarm clock, depicting a farm scene, inscribed 'Smiths Alarm', 1950s, 4½in (11.5cm) high.
£30–35 *CHe*

An American alarm clock, by Westclox, with pixies on a see-saw, c1950, 4½in (11.5cm) high.
£30–35 *CHe*

A Chinese alarm clock, depicting Mao Tse-tung and his Little Red Book, from the Cultural Revolution, late 1960s, 7in (18cm) high.
£45–50 *CHe*

A clock on a plastic stand, 1950–60s, 6¼in (16cm) high.
£30–35 *RAD*

l. An alarm clock, by Westclox, depicting a Sputnik, c1960s, 4⅛in (11cm) high.
£30–35 *CHe*

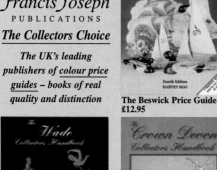
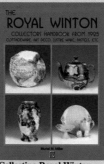

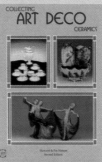

A pair of Torquay
Pottery vases,
early 20thC,
12in (30.5cm) high.
£250–300 RAC

A Losol ware Jazette
pattern biscuit barrel,
c1930, 7in (18cm) high.
£100–110 CSA

A Maling ware flower bowl, decorated
with Green Peony pattern, c1930,
9in (23cm) diam.
£90–120 CSA

A Linthorpe moon
flask, attributed to
Christopher Dresser
and Henry Tooth,
c1880, 6in (15cm) high.
£600–700 NCA

A Charles Meigh
ironstone tureen,
decorated with wild
flowers, c1840,
12in (30.5cm) wide.
£330–360 BRU

A majolica asparagus dish,
the leaf moulded dish with
asparagas moulded lining,
19thC, 15in (38cm) long.
£500–550 TMA

r. Three graduated
majolica style jugs
with basket weave
bases, 19thC, largest
8in (20.5cm) high.
£500–600 E

A majolica owl, late
19thC, 9in (23cm) high.
£130–150 SSW

A majolica box and cover, c1870,
6½in (16.5cm) long.
£170–200 HYD

A majolica cake stand, c1880,
9in (23cm) diam.
£100–120 SSW

A Moorcroft teapot, c1955, 6in (15cm) high.
£60–80 *NP*

A Walter Moorcroft bowl, decorated with
Leaf and Berry pattern, c1948,
11in (28cm) diam.
£450–500 *NP*

A Moorcroft Orchid pattern vase,
1930s, 5½in (14cm) high.
£450–475 *CEX*

A William Moorcroft
Hazeldene pattern vase,
c1903, 11in (28cm) high.
£2,500–3,000 *NP*

A William Moorcroft vase, c1905,
restored, 7in (18cm) high.
£700–800 *NP*

A Moorcroft vase, designed
by Rachel Bishop, one of
only 6 produced, c1995,
10in (25.5cm) high.
£450–500 *NP*

A Moorcroft clock, designed
by Sally Tuffin, decorated
with Buttercup pattern,
c1992, 6½in (16.5cm) high.
£150–175 *NP*

A William Moorcraft vase,
decorated with Pomegranate
pattern, c1920,
8in (20.5cm) high.
£400–500 *RUM*

A Keith Murray green circular vase, with matt glaze, 1930s, 6½in (16.5cm) high.
£225–230 *BEV*

A Palissy-style dish, in the form of a frog and snake, Portuguese, c1900, 7in (18cm) diam.
£340–380 *SSW*

A Poole pottery vase, designed by Truda Adams, 1930, 11in (28cm) high.
£400–450 *RDG*

A set of 6 Carter, Stabler & Adams pottery egg cups and base, 1930s, 9in (23cm) wide.
£60–90 *Har*

A Poole pottery vase, designed by Sally Tuffin, 1996, 7¾in (20cm) high.
£100–125 *RDG*

A Pilkington's Old Lancastrian ceramic vase, 1914–38, 9in (23cm) high.
£100–120 *RAC*

A Poole pottery plate, by Arthur Bradbury, 1964, 11in (28cm) diam.
£300–350 *Har*

A ceramic wall plaque, designed by Robert Jefferson, 1960s, 7in (18cm) wide.
£60–80 *Har*

A Poole pottery dish, decorated with Delphis pattern, 1970, 10in (25.5cm) diam.
£75–100 *Har*

A Poole pottery Cathedral plate, designed by Tony Morris, limited edition of 1,000, 1973, 12½in (32cm) diam.
£80–120 *Har*

A Poole pottery vase, decorated with Delphis pattern, 1960–70s, 16in (40.5cm) high.
£100–120 *Har*

A Crown Ducal wall plaque, by Charlotte Rhead, c1932, 12½in (32cm) diam.
£230–260 *PC*

A Crown Ducal wall plaque, by Charlotte Rhead, c1936, 12½in (32cm) diam.
£230–260 *PC*

A Royal Lancastrian bowl, c1920, 8⅜in (21.5cm) diam.
£450–550 *ASA*

A pair of Bursley ware vases, 1940s, 12½in (32cm) diam.
£750–800 *PC*

A Royal Winton shallow lustre bowl, with gilded rim, c1935, 12½in (32cm) diam.
£200–220 *GH*

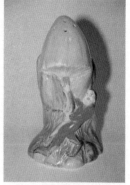

A Royal Winton sifter, c1935, 5½in (14cm) high.
£40–50 *CSA*

A Royal Winton lustre ware and enamelled vase, c1935, 5½in (14cm) high.
£60–70 *CSA*

A Shelley Mabel Lucie Attwell figure, entitled 'Ise Shy', 1926–45, 6in (15cm) high.
£650–750 *WWY*

A Royal Winton Chintz ware plate, decorated with Florence pattern, c1940, 10in (25.5in) wide.
£80–90 *CSA*

A Rubian dressing table set, tray, 1906–33, box 4½in (11.5cm) long.
£25–30 *DgC*

r. A pair of Shelley vases, decorated with tulip pattern, c1930, 8in (20.5cm) high.
£80–90 *CSA*

A Staffordshire cow creamer and cover, the tail flicked over its back to form a handle, 19thC, 6in (15cm) wide.
£260–300 *HYD*

A Staffordshire pottery hen, 19thC, 6½in (16.5cm) high.
£180–200 *TMA*

A pair of Staffordshire figures, entitled 'Old Age' c1825, 7¼in (18.5cm) high.
£400–450 *RWB*

A Staffordshire figure group, 19thC, 10½in (26.5cm) high.
£220–270 *AH*

A Staffordshire group, c1850, 5½in ((14cm) high.
£120–140 *RWB*

A Staffordshire porcelain model of a house, 19thC, 4¼in (11cm) high.
£80–100 *P(B)*

A Staffordshire pepperette, modelled as Falstaff, mid-19thC, 5¾in (14.5cm) high.
£10–15 *CaC*

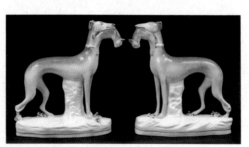

A pair of Staffordshire greyhounds, c1860, 8in (20.5cm) high.
£450–500 *DAN*

A Staffordshire Toby jug, seated on a corner seat, mid-19thC, 10¾in (27.5cm) high.
£200–250 *PC*

A Staffordshire cottage, decorated with flowers, c1870, 9¼in (23.5cm) high.
£200–220 *JO*

A Staffordshire cottage pastille burner, 19thC, 12½in (32cm) high.
£250–300 *ACA*

A Wemyss preserve pot and drip plate, c1900, plate 6¾in (17cm) diam.
£450–500 *RdeR*

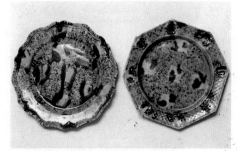

Two Whieldon plates, with moulded relief, c1790, 9in (23cm) diam.
£300–350 *ALB*

A Royal Worcester candle extinguisher, c1885, 3½in (9cm) high.
£475–500 *TH*

A Royal Worcester jug, decorated by Edward Raby, shape No. 1094, printed mark, c1897, 5½in (14cm) high.
£300–350 *P(B)*

A Royal Worcester figure, 'Queen Elizabeth I', c1899, 6½in (16.5cm) high.
£350–375 *TH*

A Locke & Co Worcester ewer, by H. Wall, c1900, 4⅛in (11.5cm) high.
£75–85 *SnA*

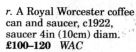

r. A Royal Worcester coffee can and saucer, c1922, saucer 4in (10cm) diam.
£100–120 *WAC*

A Royal Worcester figure, 'Thursday's Child', 1970s, 7½in (19cm) high.
£150–175 *QSA*

A Royal Worcester hand-painted vase, signed 'E. S. Pilsburg', c1916, 5¼in (113.5cm) high.
£200–235 *QSA*

A Royal Worcester candle extinguisher, entitled 'Mandarin', c1929, 3½in (9cm) high.
£225–250 *TH*

A Royal Worcester candle extinguisher, c1930, 3¾in (9.5cm) high.
£200–225 *TH*

A mahogany and brass inlaid mantel timepiece, circular painted dial, on plinth base, 19thC, 13in (33cm) high.
£400–450 *P(B)*

A French 14-day picture clock, oil on canvas, 3-tune music box, signed by Hoffman, c1825, 53in (134.5cm) wide.
£5,000–5,500 *DSP*

A bronze and ormolu mantel timepiece, with turned gilt dial, 19thC, 8¼in (21cm) high.
£550–600 *P(B)*

A brass and copper clock, early 20thC, 7in (18cm) diam.
£10–12 *MAC*

An American cast iron clock, in the form of a black banjo player, c1865, 16in (40.5cm) high.
£700–800 *CHe*

A Smiths Noddy alarm clock, c1950s, 4½in (11.5cm) high.
£30–35 *CHe*

A German brass alarm clock, c1900, 9in (23cm) high.
£100–120 *CHe*

A red enamel clock, 1930s, 6in (15cm) wide.
£25–30 *GIN*

A Smiths Hey-Diddle-Diddle alarm clock, 1950s, 4½in (11.5cm) high.
£30–35 *CHe*

A German painted wood nursery clock, 1950s, 13in (33cm) high.
£80–100 *CHe*

A Walt Disney signed photograph, mounted with colour print and original envelope, 1930s, 20in (51cm) wide.
£120–150 *SAF*

A Walt Disney Donald Duck transfer book, unused, 1940–50s, 6in (15cm) high.
£5–7 *HUX*

A Walt Disney chrome-plated brass Mickey Mouse car mascot, c1930, 4¾in (12cm) high.
£1,000–1,200 *Bon(C)*

Two *Mickey Mouse* annuals, by Dean & Son, 1947–48, 9¾in (25cm) high.
£25–35 *CBP*

A cast iron Mickey Mouse figure, 1950s, 10in (25.5cm) high.
£80–100 *COB*

Two Bakelite bowls, 1930s, 5½in (14cm) diam.
£20–25 each *ORIG*

Walt Disney's 'Lazy Countryside' sheet music, from *Fun and Fancy Free*, 1947, 11in (28cm) high.
£8–12 *CTO*

A Walt Disney *Snow White and the Seven Dwarfs*, 1937, 55in (140cm) wide.
£1,000–1,200 *S(LA)*

A Walt Disney Mickey Mouse alarm clock, by Bradley, German, 1970s, 7in (18cm) high.
£30–35 *TIH*

A EuroDisney mug, made for the ceremonial opening, April 12, 1992, 3in (7.5cm) high, with original box.
£10–15 *COB*

A Walt Disney lunchbox and flask, depicting Mickey Mouse and Donald Duck, Disneyworld scenes, Florida, 1950s, 9in (23cm) wide.
£40–50 *PC*

A Beswick Walt Disney Minnie Mouse figure, 1953–65, 3½in (9cm) high.
£750–800 *P*

A wax doll, with glass eyes, in original clothes, 1860s, 17½in (44.5cm) high.
£250–300 *BaN*

A French bisque swivel-headed doll, with original clothes, slight damage, c1875, 12in (31cm) high,
£3,500–4,000 *EW*

A German bisque shoulder-headed dolls' house doll and bamboo chair, c1880, doll 6in (15cm) high.
£50–60 *BaN*

Twin Armand Marseille dolls, with original clothes, c1910, 16½in (42cm) high.
£650–700 *DOL*

An Armand Marseille bisque-headed Mulatto baby, incised 'AM 341', c1920, 9in (23cm) high.
£250–300 *YC*

A French bisque-headed doll, with jointed composition body, original wig and clothes, c1920, 28in (71cm) high.
£400–600 *BaN*

A German Freundlich series doll, modelled as a soldier, c1925–35, 11in (28cm) high.
£150–170 *DOL*

A Lenci Mexican lady doll, Italian, c1920, 24in (61cm) high.
£800–900 *DOL*

A Lenci felt doll, original clothes and box, c1930, 15in (38cm) high
£500–600 *YC*

A Chad Valley felt doll with original clothes, c1930, 18in (46cm) high.
£250–300 *YC*

A Steiff felt character doll, with glass eyes, c1930, 13¾in (35cm) high.
£300–400 *YC*

A Chad Valley Mabel Lucie Attwell doll, c1930, 15in (38cm) high, with original box.
£250–300 *DOL*

A Maori doll, with baby, c1930–40, 11in (28cm) high.
£65–70 *DOL*

A Bubble Cut Barbie, 1960s, 11½in (29cm) high, with original box.
£200–220 *P(Ba)*

A Pedigree doll, with plastic face, c1950, 17in (43cm) high.
£65–75 *DOL*

Swirl Ponytail and New Look Barbie, c1960, 11½in (29cm) high.
£275–325 *P(Ba)*

A cloth doll, probably French, c1940s, 16in (40.5cm) high.
£90–100 *DOL*

A hard plastic Roddy baby, 1950s, 10in (25.5cm) high.
£25–30 *CMF*

A Pedigree Sindy doll and wardrobe, c1960s, 11¾in (30cm) high.
£60–70 *RAR*

A pair of Peter and Anna Moore dolls, by Pedigree Toys, Canterbury, 1970s, 10in (25.5cm) high.
£200–250 *SVB*

A bone clock and bookshelf, made by Napoleonic prisoners, early 19thC, clock 3½in (9cm) high.
£90–100 *HOB*

A doll's tea set, with 4 gold metal teaspoons, 4 cotton napkins, in a matching box, 1890s, 15½in (39.5cm) wide.
£500–550 *P(Ba)*

A dolls' house, attributed to Silber Fleming, fully furnished including kitchen range, c1900, 28in (71cm) high.
£500–600 *DOL*

A model of a timber-framed Biddenden farmhouse, c1995, 30in (76cm) high.
£750–850 *STE*

A miniature doll's dresser, by Swallow Toys, 1920s, 27in (68.5cm) high.
£100–120 *BaN*

A Meccano cardboard Dolly Varden house and garden, 1936, 18½in (48cm) high.
£700–800 *HOB*

A brass doll's house fireplace, 1920s, 4in (10cm) high.
£25–30 *DOL*

A metal doll's house gas cooker, c1934, 4in (10cm) high.
£30–40 *HOB*

A Victorian doll's house oak bedroom suite, with marble-topped dressing table, wardrobe 9in (23cm) high.
£200–240 *HOB*

A set of Dinky Toy doll's house dining room furniture, in original box, 1936, 10in (25.5cm) wide.
£800–900 *HOB*

John Player & Sons, set of 50, Old England's Defenders, mint condition, 1897.
£800–900 *LCC*

John Player & Sons, set of 50, Football Caricatures, by 'Mac', 1927, 2¾in (7cm) high.
£50–60 *LCC*

B. D. V. cigarettes Godfrey Phillips, set of 36, Old Masters, c1912.
£1–1.50 each *LCC*

W. D. & H. O. Wills, Cricketers 2nd series, 1929.
£50–60 *MAC*

A picture card album, Household Hints, c1936, 6in (15cm) high.
£5–7 *MAC*

Kellogg's trade cards, The Story of the Locomotive 2nd series, set of 16, 1965.
£12–14 set *LCC*

A Kensitas woven-silk cigarette card, flowers in, c1945.
£2–3 *LCC*

Brooke Bond tea cards, set of 50, Transport Through the Ages, 1966.
£4–5 *LCC*

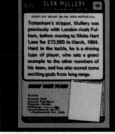

A. & B. C. trade cards, series of 84, Footballers 1970.
£30–40 *LCC*

Topp's trade cards, series of 66, Spitting Image, 1990.
£5–7 *LCC*

A Paramount film poster, entitled *Rear Window,* good condition, 28in (71cm) wide.
£1,500–2,000 *S(LA)*

A poster, entitled 'These Men Use Shell, Journalists You Can Be Sure of Shell', lithograph in colours, 1938, 45in (11.5cm) wide.
£1,000–1,500 *Bon(C)*

A pin-up calendar, by Vargas, 1942, 12in (30.5cm) high.
£90–120 *COB*

A Universal window card, *The Bride of Frankenstein,* good condition, 1935, 22in (56cm) high.
£6,500–7,000 *S(LA)*

Two Warner Bros film posters, *My Fair Lady,* good condition, 1964, 28in (71cm) high.
£1,000–1,200 *S(LA)*

A P & O menu, *Oriana* in Sydney Harbour, 1970, 12in (30.5cm) high.
£4–8 *COB*

A pin-up calendar, by Vargas, c1944, 12in (30.5cm) wide.
£120–150 *COB*

A Robertson's recipe leaflet, 1960s, 6in (15cm) high.
50p–£1.00 *HUX*

Three sweet cigarettes packets, decorated with TV themes, 1965, 2¾in (7cm) high.
£10–15 each *CTO*

A *Man Senior* magazine, November 1955, 12in (30.5cm) high.
£5–7.50 *RAD*

A Festival of Britain 125-piece wooden jigsaw puzzle, complete, c1951, 9½in (24cm) wide, original box.
£40–45 *GIN*

A red velvet hat, 1950s.
£25–30 *Ech*

A hessian and soft metal brooch, modelled as a dog, 1950s, 4in (10cm) high.
£25–30 *SnA*

A pair of lady's shoes, by Raoul Shoe of Paris, 1950s.
£20–25 *Har*

A Midwinter Cannes pattern coffee pot, by Sir Hugh Casson, 1950s, 9in (23cm) high.
£60–75 *GIN*

A Picquot ware aluminium teapot, with wooden handle, 1950s, 5in (13cm) high.
£20–25 *GIN*

A plastic pear-shaped ice bucket, 1950s, 11in (28cm) high.
£15–18 *RAD*

l. A Stratton Regal enamelled goldtone coronation souvenir compact, with opening inner lid inscribed 'TM', 1953, 3in (7.5cm) diam.
£35–45 *PC*

A Russian varnished oak mantel clock, 1950s, 15in (38cm) wide.
£85–100 *TIH*

An Oceanic radio, French, c1955, 18in (46cm) wide.
£120–140 *HEG*

A French porcelain figure of a frog, c1870, 5¼in (13.5cm) high.
£300–350 *BRT*

A porcelain model of 'The Thrower', c1870, 10in (25.5cm) high.
£700–750 *BRT*

A porcelain jug, modelled as a frog on a melon, c1875, 7in (18cm) high.
£200–250 *BRT*

A majolica frog vase, with glass eyes, c1870, 8½in (21.5cm) high.
£250–300 *BRT*

A porcelain frog match striker, c1875, 3½in (9cm) high.
£50–80 *BRT*

A German porcelain dish, modelled as a frog, 1880, 4½in (11.5cm) wide.
£100–150 *BRT*

A Glasform frog, designed by John Ditchfield, 1990, 2¾in (7cm) high.
£30–40 *PC*

A silver frog pincushion, Birmingham, 1907, 2½in (6.5cm) long.
£260–300 *GH*

A green frog candle, the wick on his head, c1910, 4½in (11.5cm) high.
£50–60 *BRT*

A French composition frog group, promoting The Pill, 1980s, 2in (5cm) high.
£8–10 *PC*

A Dartington Pottery dish, designed by Roger Law and Pablo Bach, 1996, 11¾in (30cm) diam.
£700–750 *RDG*

CORKSCREWS

A steel pocket travelling corkscrew,
c1790, 4½in (11.5cm) long.
£50–60   *CS*

Two silver travelling
corkscrews, each with fluted
pattern, *l*. silver handle and
sheath, by Thomas Willmore,
1797, 3¼in (8.5cm) long.
£120–150
r. mother-of-pearl barrel-
shaped handle with silver
bands and silver sheath,
by Samuel Pemberton,
c1790, 3¼in (8.5cm) long.
£140–160   *CS*

A bone-handled corkscrew, with
brush, c1860, 5½in (14cm) long.
£50–60   *CHe*

An all-steel combination 8-tool
bow corkscrew, with faceted
handle, c1820, 3in (7.5cm) long.
£80–90   *CS*

A Thomason double-action
brass corkscrew, with wooden
handle and brush, c1870,
7in (18cm) long.
£100–120   *CHe*

l. A brass
corkscrew, c1860,
6in (15cm) long.
£120–130   *CHe*

An all-steel combination
corkscrew, with
champagne wire nippers
and foil cutter, c1860,
4¼in (11cm) long.
£80–95   *CS*

A German corkscrew,
with double-spring
action, marked 'D.R.G.S.',
c1880, 5½in (14cm) long.
£55–75   *CS*

A wooden-handled
corkscrew, with steel
shaft and brush,
c1860, 6in (15cm) long.
£30–35   *CHe*

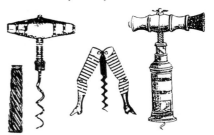

A Wier's double-concertina corkscrew, marked 'Wier's Patent Double No.4283 J.H.S.B.', made by James Heeley & Sons, patented 1884, 4¼in (11cm) long.
£600–700 *CS*

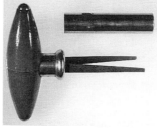

An American two-pronged cork extractor, with wooden handle and sheath, made by Converse and marked 'Patented May 9th 1899', 4in (10cm) long.
£55–65 *CS*

A Prefect concertina corkscrew, c1910, 5in (12.5cm) long.
£20–25 *CHe*

A French ribbed boxwood corkscrew, late 19thC, 4¼in (11cm) long.
£15–18 *BSA*

A silver corkscrew, modelled as a fox with garnet eyes, hall-marked, c1920, 3½in (9cm) wide.
£125–145 *RTh*

A folding bow corkscrew, with grooved helix, late 19thC, 2in (5cm) wide.
£12–15 *BSA*

A Zig-Zag steel-plated concertina corkscrew, c1930, 5½in (14cm) closed.
£35–40 *CHe*

A Chambers bar corkscrew, entitled 'The Don', with clamp fixing, c1910, 12in (30.5cm) long.
£85–95 *CS*

A corkscrew, entitled 'The King Patent 6064', 1904 patent, 6¾in (17cm) long.
£70–90 *CS*

A plated steel corkscrew, with ebonised boxwood handle, late 19thC, 3½in (9cm) long.
£15–18 *BSA*

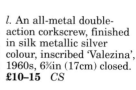

l. An all-metal double-action corkscrew, finished in silk metallic silver colour, inscribed 'Valezina', 1960s, 6¾in (17cm) closed.
£10–15 *CS*

DISNEYANA

Disneyana attracts collectors around the world. Animation cels from celebrated films, period artwork and original ephemera, such as Walt Disney's signature, command huge prices. With mass-produced toys, the golden age for collectors is between 1928 (the year in which Mickey Mouse first appeared in *Steamboat Willie*) and 1938.

Rare tinplate toys such as the Mickey and Minnie on a motorbike (*shown below*) can fetch five figure sums. Other recent auction prices include £15,000 for a Mickey Mouse organ grinder toy dating from the same period. At the other end of the scale, there is also interest in material connected with EuroDisney, such as the plate illustrated. A ticket for the opening day (12 April 1992), which sold for £20 in 1993, can now be worth as much as £70 to confirmed Disney enthusiasts.

Given the profusion of toys and collectables manufactured today, it is unlikely that Disneyana of the 1990s will ever approach the values of pre-WWII material.

A Tipp & Co Mickey and Minnie motorcycle, depicting Mickey in red shorts and Minnie in blue shorts and red collar astride a motorcycle, lithographed in green/cream with red/black lining, TCO logo, with external clockwork motor, slight damage, 1930s, 9in (23cm) wide.
£11,000–12,000 *P*

A Mickey Mouse soft velvet toy, worn condition and repaired, c1930, 6in (15cm) high.
£100–120 *DOL*

A Mickey Mouse silver-plated car or bicycle mascot, slight damage, 1930s, 10in (25.5cm) high.
£150–170 *AAV*

Three Mickey Mouse books, from The Great Big Midget Book range, *Mickey Mouse, The Mail Pilot, Sails for Treasure Island*, with black and white illustrations, ownership inscription to front pastedown of first volume only, original picture boards, published by Dean & Son, 1933–1935, 4½in (11.5cm) high.
£170–200 *DW*

Cross Reference
Animation Art

A Mickey Mouse candle holder, slight damage, 1930s, 5in (12.5cm) high.
£200–300 *TOY*

r. A EuroDisney plate, commemorating the opening ceremony, 1992, with box, 9½in (24cm) diam.
£15–20 *COB*

A Mazda Disneylights 12 bulb lighting set, each bulb holder has a lampshade with colourful transfer of a scene with characters from Disney's *Pinnochio*, in 6 colours, 1950s, box 9½in (24cm) wide.
£120–140 *WAL*

DOLLS

A German wax over papier mâché shoulder-headed doll, with stuffed body and all original clothes, c1840, 19¼in (49cm) high.
£350–400 *YC*

r. Two Native American dolls, dressed in traditional costume, German, 1920–30s, 15½in (39.5cm) high.
£100–150 *DOL*

A wooden peg doll, all original, with hat box and brolly, 1870–80s, 3in (7.5cm) high.
£130–150 *DOL*

A German shoulder-headed doll, with stuffed body and composition limbs, c1890, 26¾in (68cm) high.
£100–120 *YC*

A porcelain pincushion doll, modelled as a clown, c1920, 3in (7.5cm) high.
£35–45 *DKH*

A cut-out doll, complete with dress, Scottish, 1940–50s, 21in (53.5cm) high.
£15–20 *DOL*

A German composition doll, depicting Queen Alexandra, unmarked, possibly Shilling, 1903, 27½in (70cm) high.
£1,000–1,250 *DOL*

A Norah Wellings cloth doll, the pressed felt face with painted features, the velveteen body dressed as a school boy, label to foot, face water marked, 1930s, 11in (28cm) high.
£90–120 *P(Ba)*

Norah Wellings (active 1926–59) was chief designer at Chad Valley before founding her own doll factory in Wellington, Shropshire in 1926. She specialised in cloth dolls, her most collectable creations dating from the 1930s.

Bisque

Bisque (twice fired, unglazed and tinted porcelain) was a popular material for dolls' heads from the mid-19th century to the 1930s. France and Germany were the leading centres of production. Major manufacturers include the French firm Jumeau (1842–99), who pioneered *'Bébés'*, dolls modelled as children rather than fashionable women, and companies such as Armand Marseille (1856–c1925), Kämmer & Reinhardt (1886–c1940s) and Simon and Halbig (c1869–1930), all based in Thuringia, Germany's main porcelain manufacturing region. The mark of a good manufacturer will increase the value of a doll. Dolls tend to be marked either on the back of the head or the shoulder. Marks can sometimes be found on other parts of the body, and period clothes too should be checked for labels. As well as a maker's name or symbol, marks will often include a mould number, which is very important since some moulds are rarer and more desirable than others. Dolls sometimes have two marks: the name of the company that supplied the head and the name of the company that assembled the doll.

Early bisque dolls had closed mouths and moulded eyes and hair. As techniques progressed, dolls became more lifelike with jointed bodies, wigs, open mouths (Simon & Halbig specialised in the production of inset teeth), moving glass eyes and even eyelashes made from human hair, a development introduced by Kämmer & Reinhardt. In 1909 the latter company began to produce character dolls, modelled on real children rather than idealised images of childhood. Their first character doll Kaiser baby, was, it is claimed, based on the Emperor's son, who had suffered from polio as a child and had a crippled hand.

Many of the bisque dolls shown below were expensive at the time, a luxury product aimed at middle- and upper-class nurseries. Today they can cost hundreds and even thousands of pounds. These prices have stimulated demand for less expensive plastic dolls, which are becoming increasingly popular, providing a more affordable starting-point for collectors.

French Bisque

An early Jumeau portrait doll, with all wood eight-ball jointed body, closed mouth, pierced ears, straight wrists, c1880, 15in (38cms) high.
£5,000–6,000 *EW*

FURTHER READING
Alison Becket,
Miller's Collecting Teddy Bears & Dolls
Miller's Publications, 1997

A Jumeau pressed bisque swivel-headed doll, with gusseted kid leather body, separated stitched fingers, closed mouth, fixed blue glass paperweight eyes, pierced ears, blonde real hair wig over original cork pate, dressed in original wedding outfit, impressed '5' and red check mark to rear of head, slight damage, c1870, 15in (38cm) high.
£1,500–2,000 *EW*

A Jumeau bisque socket-headed *bébé* doll, with blue glass paperweight eyes, closed mouth, pierced ears, blonde mohair wig over cork pate, with composition eight-ball jointed body and straight wrists, original spiral spring neck attachment, antique clothes, marked 'J', signed on body and shoes 'E. Jumeau Medaille d'Or Paris 1878', 16in (41cm) high.
£5,500–6,500 *EW*

An Emile Jumeau pressed bisque socket-headed Première *bébé* doll, with blue glass eyes, closed mouth, pierced ears, blonde mohair wig, composition and wood eight-ball jointed body with straight wrists, all original with antique clothes, marked '8' on head, 'Jumeau Medaille d'Or Paris' on body, c1880, 19in (48.5cm) high.
£6,500–8,000 *EW*

A François Gaultier bisque swivel-headed fashion doll, with kid body, stitched fingers, pierced ears and antique blue outfit, F. G. marks on shoulder plate, 1880s, 14in (35.5cm) high.
£2,000–2,500 *EW*

Cross Reference
Colour Review

A Jumeau pressed bisque fortune-telling doll, with fixed blue glass eyes, lambswool wig, gusseted kid body, underskirt containing coloured paper with handwritten soothsayer's messages, c1880, 14in (35.5cm) high.
£1,300–1,600 *BaN*

A Jumeau bisque-headed doll, with open mouth, original wig and clothes, jointed wood and composition body, bearing the Jumeau stamp, 1890, 22½in (57cm) high.
£1,000–1,200 *BaN*

A Bru *bébé* bisque-headed doll, with brown mohair wig, feathered brows, fixed blue paperweight eyes, closed slightly parted mouth, pierced ears, jointed wood and composition body, dressed in original undergarments with later frock, blue stamp to shoulders 'Bébé Bru No. 7', with original shoes and socks, marked 'Déposé', 1866–99, 17in (43cm) high.
£3,800–4,300 *P*

German Bisque

A Bähr & Pröschild bisque shoulder-headed doll, with kid body, marked '309', c1900, 19¾in (50cm) high.
£300–400 *YC*

A Bähr & Pröschild bisque shoulded-headed doll, with blue sleeping eyes, blonde hair wig, kid body, bisque arms and antique clothes, impressed '309', c1890, 15in (38cm) high.
£350–450 *EW*

l. An Armand Marseille bisque-headed girl doll, incised mark 'AM 1894', c1900, 17in (43cm) high.
£300–350 *YC*

A Simon & Halbig bisque-headed doll, with weighted blue eyes, open mouth, 4 upper teeth, pierced ears, long mohair wig, jointed composition and wood body, antique clothing, incised 'SH 1078–6' 1078, c1890, 16in (41cm) high.
£450–550 *EW*

A J. D. Kestner bisque-headed child doll, with kid body, incised 'JDK', c1890, 19¾in (50cm) high.
£500–600 *YC*

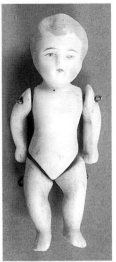

A German all-bisque jointed baby doll, c1900, 3in (7.5cm) high. **£50–80** *BaN*

A J. D. Kestner bisque-headed doll, marked '143', c1905, 17⅝in (45cm) high. **£300–400** *YC*

A J. D. Kestner bisque-headed girl doll, incised 'Germany 124', c1900, 19in (48cm) high. **£700–800** *YC*

l. A J.D. Kestner Gibson girl doll, with rivet jointed kid body and bisque arms, mould 172, c1910, 18in (46cm) high. **£2,500–3,000** *EW*

A Kämmer & Reinhardt bisque socket-headed character Marie doll, with closed mouth, painted eyes, original mohair wig and pate, composition and wood ball-jointed body, antique clothes, mould 101, neck restored, c1910, 9in (23cm) high. **£1,400–1,600** *EW*

A Kämmer & Reinhardt black bisque-headed Kaiser baby, the moulded head with painted brown eyes, eyebrows, open/closed mouth, painted hair, on a five-piece bent limb body, wearing a white baby gown with bib, mould 100, incised '36, K☆R 100', c1900, 14¼in (36cm) high. **£750–900** *Bon(C)*

r. An Armand Marseille bisque-headed doll, with brown eyes, blonde wig, composition body and original clothes, mould 390, c1910, 22in (56cm) high. **£350–400** *BaN*

A Heubach bisque-headed doll, all original, mould 7622, 1910–15, 12in (30.5cm) high.
£250–300 *DOL*

A Gebrüder Knock bisque-headed doll, marked 'GK 165', c1910, 16½in (42cm) high.
£200–250 *YC*

r. A bisque-headed character doll, with composition body, replaced wig, mould PM 914, c1920, 19in (48.5cm) high.
£300–350 *BaN*

A Gebrüder Heubach bisque-headed character doll, with brown mohair wig, blue glass googly eyes with rotating mechanism to back of head, closed smiling mouth, bent limb composition body, dressed in cream woollen outfit, impressed 'Heubach Germany', c1920, 12¼in (31cm) high.
£1,500–2,000 *P*

An Armand Marseille bisque-headed googly-eyed character doll, with wood and composition body, painted shoes and socks, impressed 'A11/0 M 323', c1911, 7in (18cm) high.
£450–550 *EW*

A Kämmer & Reinhardt character doll, with flirting eyes, incised 'S & H, K☆R 126', c1912, 20½in (52cm) high.
£500–600 *YC*

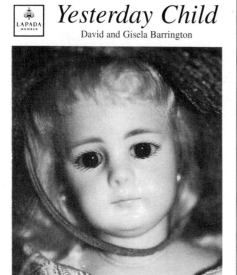

An Armand Marseille bisque-headed girl doll, incised 'AM 390 Germany', c1912, 22½in (57cm) high.
£250–300 *YC*

r. A Gebrüder Heubach bisque-headed character boy doll, dressed in grey trousers and white shirt, incised 'Gebrüder Heubach 7763', c1912, 9in (23cm) high.
£500–600 *YC*

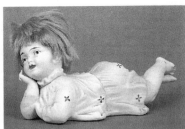

A Hermann Steiner bisque-headed doll, with composition body, 1920s, 14in (35.5cm) high.
£250–300 *BaN*

A German all-bisque girl in a boat, c1925, 7⅞in (20cm) high.
£80–100 *YC*

A German all-bisque figure of a baby, with wig, c1925, 7in (18cm) long.
£60–80 *YC*

r. A Heubach doll, in mauve knitted suit, mould 300, 1920s, 9in (23cm) high.
£160–200 *DOL*

A Georgene Averill Bonnie Babe bisque-headed character doll, with original clothes, made by Alt, Beck & Gottschalck for the K & K Toy Company, c1926, 18in (45.5cm) high.
£550–650 *DOL*

An Armand Marseille doll, all original, in a white dress, red and white jacket and hat, mould 390, 1920s, 25in (63.5cm) high.
£400–450 *DOL*

A German bisque Baby Bud doll, 1920s, 4½in (11.5cm) high.
£90–100 *DOL*

A Käthe Kruse *Du Mein* character doll, the face painted with brown eyes, painted nostrils and mouth, moulded ears, neck sewn to stockinette body, stitched fingers and toes with separately sewn on thumbs, wearing a light green dress, underwear, green velvet coat, shoes and socks, foot stamped 'Käthe Kruse 182', c1928, 19in (48.5cm) high.
£1,300–1,500 *Bon(C)*

Plastic

A plastic Roddy girl doll, with flirty eyes, good condition, 1940s, 16in (40.5cm) high.
£65–75 *DOL*

A pair of plastic twin dolls, with knitted outfits, 1950s, 22in (56cm) high.
£45–55 *HEI*

A Pedigree plastic toddler doll, in pink dress, 1950s, 18in (46cm) high.
£95–115 *CMF*

A Pedigree plastic walking doll, in original clothes, 1950s, 16in (40.5cm) high.
£95–115 *CMF*

A Pedigree walking doll, with flirty eyes, blonde hair and a pink dress, 1950s, 22in (56cm) high.
£85–95 *CMF*

A Rosebud plastic doll, dressed in white dress and blue shoes, 1950s, 16in (40.5cm) high.
£85–95 *CMF*

This black doll is more unusual than the white model, hence the higher price.

A Rosebud hard plastic doll, with bent limbs, in a floral and bear print dress, 1950s, 16in (40.5cm) high.
£45–55 *CMF*

Two Sasha vinyl dolls, *l.* black boy doll, with short curly hair, moulded painted features, dressed in a woollen jumper and corduroy trousers, *r.* girl doll, with long red hair, dressed in a nightgown, 1960–70s, 16in (40.5cm) high.
£200–240 *P(Ba)*

A Pedigree hard plastic doll, dressed in a mauve checked dress, 1960s, 9½in (24cm) high.
£25–30 *CMF*

An OK plastic baby doll, dressed in a yellow dress, Japanese, 1960s, 16in (40.5cm) high.
£18–22 *CMF*

A Sasha vinyl doll, Gregory, by Sasha Morgenthaler, fully jointed with original outfit, c1970, 17in (43.5cm) high.
£140–170 *YC*

Sasha Dolls

Sasha dolls were created by the Swiss designer Sasha Morgenthaler, and were first produced by Trendon Ltd of Stockport, Cheshire in 1965. The hard vinyl dolls came with different skin tones, which varied in shade according to the colour of the hair.

Action Man

Two Action Man dolls, Space Ranger and SAS Commander, together with outfits, 1960–70s, tallest 12in (30.5cm) high.
£45–55 *P(Ba)*

Action Man

In 1964, the American company Hasbro introduced a doll for boys. He was dressed in military costume and had a scarred cheek. His manly visage was based, according to Hasbro, on the faces of 20 real soldiers who had all won medals of honour. GI Joe was a huge success and Palitoy quickly secured the rights for Britain. The US soldier had to be anglicised. One suggestion for a new name was Ace 21 (because the doll had 21 moving parts). This was rejected, however, and in January 1966 Action Man hit the shops. In the late 1960s, anti-Vietnam war feeling severely affected US sales of GI Joe but his British cousin went from strength to strength. By the 1970s it was estimated that there was more than one Action Man for every boy in Britain. By the time production stopped in 1984, over 350 outfits had been created and Action Man had been everything from a deep-sea diver to an astronaut to a footballer.

Complete dress and accessories are very important when it comes to value today, as is condition. Designed for boys and for war-like games, the dolls often suffered a severe battering, particularly vulnerable areas including feet that could be pulled off and rubberised hands, the fingers of which could be twisted and broken. Action Man was relaunched in 1993.

Two Action Man Explorer dolls, together with 5 husky dogs, 1970s, 11in (28cm) high.
£130–160 *P(Ba)*

An Eagle Eye Action Man doll, dressed in police uniform, together with a police motorbike, 1970, 11in (28cm) high.
£30–40 *P(Ba)*

Barbie

A Barbie Skipper doll, by Mattel, dressed in a bridesmaid's outfit, c1963, 9in (23cm) high, with original box.
£175–200 *P(Ba)*

Two Barbie dolls:
l. titian Midge, dressed in a pink evening dress, *r.* brown haired Midge, dressed in 'Gold 'n' Glamour' outfit, mid-1960s, 11½in (29cm) high.
£450–500 *P(Ba)*

First created in 1963 (the same year as little sister Skipper), Midge was Barbie's best friend. The value of these dolls is enhanced by their 1960s clothes.

Two Barbie dolls,
l. with blonde swirl ponytail, dressed in Travel Togethers outfit, *r.* with brunette ponytail, dressed as an air hostess, early 1960s, 11½in (29cm) high, with original boxes.
£400–450 *P(Ba)*

Two Barbie dolls,
l. with blonde swirl ponytail, dressed in 1970s outfit, *r.* dressed in a bridal outfit, 1970s, 11½in (29cm) high, with original boxes.
£240–280 *P(Ba)*

Dolls' Furniture & Accessories

A wooden doll's cot, painted in red, c1860, 17in (43cm) long.
£320–360 *AWT*

A pine doughbox doll's cradle, painted in red, c1860, 20in (50.5cm) wide.
£120–140 *MSB*

A doll's pine bureau, with frieze drawers and 2 cupboard doors, 1880–1910, 4¼in (11cm) high.
£45–55 *MSB*

A doll's pine bed, dated '1889', signed, 17¾in (45cm) long.
£90–110 *MSB*

A collection of miniature grey speckled enamel kitchen equipment, c1900, mug 2in (5cm) high.
£75–80 *SMI*

A miniature mahogany chest of drawers, with 3 drawers, on bracket feet, c1890, 10½in (26.5cm) wide.
£120–150 *BaN*

A wickerwork doll's pram, with rocking hood, wrought iron frame, spoked wheels and beech handle, early 20thC, 24in (61cm) long, together with a wickerwork Moses basket.
£80–100 *Hal*

A Silver Cross coachbuilt doll's pram, 1950s, 25½in (65cm) high.
£85–95 *CMF*

A doll's pine chest of drawers, with 3 drawers, c1910, 9¾in (25cm) wide.
£120–140 *MSB*

A Royale twin dolls' pram, 1950s, 24in (61cm) high.
£80–90 *CMF*

> **Miller's is a price GUIDE not a price LIST**

l. A doll's high chair, with découpage decoration, 1930s, 25in (63.5cm) high.
£25–30 *HEI*

Dolls' Houses

A Victorian doll's house, with red brick effect walls and white painted windows, 1880–90, 42in (107cm) high.
£800–1,000 *HOB*

A French painted wood doll's house, the interior with original papered floor and wall coverings, each room with appropriate furniture, c1880, 29½in (75cm) high.
£2,500–3,000 *P*

A Victorian doll's house, with Gothic windows, filled with an assortment of dolls' furniture and dolls, 1880–90, 48in (122cm) high.
£1,000–1,200 *HOB*

FURTHER READING
Olivia Bristol, and Leslie Geddes-Brown, *Dolls' Houses,* Mitchell Beazley, 1997

r. A Georgian style wooden doll's house, with 4 pillars and balcony to upper floor, 1920s, 33in (84cm) high.
£300–350 *JUN*

A Victorian doll's house, the red brick effect walls with quoin stone edgings and white painted windows, on 4 levels with brick two-storey extension to side, with carrying handles, c1900, 36in (91.5cm) high.
£700–800 *HOB*

A Lines Bros doll's house, with white painted walls and windows, railed balcony over attic window, 1920s, 30in (76cm) high.
£450–500 *DOL*

A wooden doll's house, modelled as a furniture shop in Ashbourne, Derbyshire, on a tiled base, 1980s, 26½in (67.5cm) high.
£1,200–1,500 *SPU*

A doll's house, modelled as a timber-framed Pluckley cottage, with 'thatched' roof, 1995, 30in (76cm) high.
£350–400 *STE*

Dolls' House Furniture

A Victorian marble topped washstand, towel rail and 2 chairs, 4½in (11.5cm) high.
£180–200 *HOB*

A bone table and 2 bone chairs, early 19thC, chairs 2¼in (5.5cm) high.
£160–180 *HOB*

This furniture was made by Napoleonic prisoners-of-war.

A collection of Waltershausen furniture, with transfer-printed designs, late 19thC.
£1,700–2,000 *P*

A collection of Victorian dining furniture, settle 3¾in (9.5cm) high.
Dresser **£60–70**
Settle   **£40–50** *HOB*

A Victorian oak dining table and chairs, with padded seats and backs, chairs 5½in (14cm) high.
£80–90 *HOB*

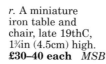

r. A miniature iron table and chair, late 19thC, 1¾in (4.5cm) high.
£30–40 each *MSB*

A suite of Triang furniture, comprising settee, armchairs, side chair and stool, with floral covers, 1930s, 3¾in (9.5cm) high.
£100–120 *HOB*

A Dinky Meccano metal bedroom suite, c1936, tallest 2½in (6.5cm) high.
£150–175 *HOB*

l. A miniature doll's house flat iron, 1930s, ¾in (2cm) long.
£2–3 *DOL*

r. A Dinky Meccano metal kitchen set, c1936, tallest 2½in (6.5cm) high.
£140–160 *HOB*

EPHEMERA

A collection of theatre and music hall bills and programmes, c1870.
£80–100 *DA*

A book of Majestic Private Greeting Card samples, c1912, 10in (25.5cm) wide.
£120–150 *MRW*

A collection of ship and hotel menus, 1920-60s.
£6–10 each *COB*

A Grand Theatre Southampton programme, 1939, 8in (20.5cm) high.
£4–8 *COB*

A French garage receipt for repairs to a Nazi vehicle, 1940, 10in (25.5cm) high.
£20–25 *COB*

A collection of travel brochures, 1930s.
£5–10 each *COB*

A brochure for Ariel motorcycles, entitled '5000 miles non-stop', c1928, 9in (23cm) high.
£20–25 *COB*

A Budget leaflet, 1941–42, 8in (20.5cm) high.
£4–5 *SVB*

FOUR ROSES TRIP PLANNER for the NEW YORK WORLD'S FAIR 1964-65

A Better Tomorrow

The Conservative programme for the next 5 years

r. A government leaflet, Harold Wilson, 1974–75, 8in (20.5cm) high.
£3–4 *SVB*

l. A Conservative programme, Edward Heath, 1970s, 9in (23cm) high.
£3–4 *SVB*

A travel brochure for the World's Fair, 1964–65, 8in (20.5cm) high.
£8–10 *COB*

Autographs

Fred Astaire, a signed
photograph, in later years,
1980s, 6in (15cm) high.
£90–100 *VS*

Fred Astaire and Ginger Rogers,
a signed photograph, modern
reproduction signed in later
years, slight damage, 1980s,
10in (25.5cm) high.
£300–350 *VS*

Maria Callas, a signed
photograph, slight damage,
1960s, 6in (15cm) high.
£300–350 *VS*

Joan Crawford, a signed
photograph, 1940s,
12½in (32cm) high.
£60–70 *VS*

Princess Diana, a signed framed
photograph, by Andrew Soos of
London, in original green leather
frame, with gilt crown and
initial 'D' at head, 1990s,
7in (18cm) high, contained in
original green presentation box.
£1,000–1,500 *VS*

Errol Flynn, a signed
photograph, slight edge knocks,
1950s, 7in (18cm) high.
£300–350 *VS*

Giles, two signed cartoons,
1990s, 11¼in (28.5cm) wide.
£80–100 *SAF*

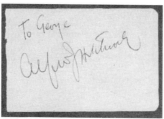

Alfred Hitchcock, an album
page autograph, early 1950s,
4½in (11.5cm) wide.
£90–110 *VS*

Edward Heath, a signed
photograph, 1956,
12in (30.5cm) high.
£12–15 *SAF*

Harrison Ford and Sean Connery, a signed poster, from *Indiana Jones and the Last Crusade*, 1990s, 10in (25.5cm) wide.
£220–260 *VS*

Stan Laurel and Oliver Hardy, a signed photograph, slight damage, 1950s, 7in (18cm) wide.
£300–350 *VS*

Madonna, a signed framed photograph, 1990s, 10in (25.5cm) high.
£110–130 *VS*

l. Charles M. Schultz, a signed coloured sketch of Snoopy, 11½in (29cm) high.
£275–325 *VS*

r. Igor Stravinsky, a signed album page, 1955, 4½in (11.5cm) high.
£170–200 *VS*

R. J. Mitchell, two signed menus, one to celebrate the British victory in the Schneider cup, at Claridge's Hotel, signed to reverse, 1931, 6 x 8in (15 x 20.5cm), the other from the South Western Hotel.
£800–900 *VS*

R. J. Mitchell was the inventor of the Spitfire and Vickers Supermarine S6B seaplane.

James Stewart, a signed original sketch of Harvey, c1990s, 8in (20.5cm) high.
£190–220 *VS*

Mother Teresa, a signed photograph with religious verse, 1980s, 6in (15cm) wide.
£90–110 *VS*

Cigarette & Trade Cards

W. D. & H. O. Wills, Cricketers,
set of 50, 1896.
£2,500–3,500 *LCC*

*Some early sets of cards (such as the
above example) have been reprinted
and cost about £7.50 a set. These
reprints are officially licensed, and
cards are marked on the back and
often include the reprint date. They
could not deceive the expert, but if
sold framed as a picture with the
backs of the cards concealed, could
confuse the beginner. Buyer beware
and remember that the back of a
card can be as important as the front.*

r. W. D. & H. O. Wills, Famous
British Authors, set of 40, 1937.
£50–60 *LCC*

Cohen Weenen & Co.
Celebrities, Gainsborough,
metal frame, c1901.
£90–100 *LCC*

Chairman Cigarettes,
Old Pottery, silk with
card back, c1920.
75p–£1 each *LCC*

Ardath Tobacco, Proverbs,
set of 25, c1936.
£10–15 *LCC*

r. W. D. &
H. O. Wills, The
Sea-Shore, set
of 50, c1938.
£10–12 *LCC*

R. J. Lea Ltd, Chairman Juniors, Film Stars
cigarette card album, 1st series, one missing, 1934.
£15–20 *MAC*

R. J. Lea Ltd, Chairman Juniors, Radio Stars
cigarette card album, part filled, 1935.
£8–10 *MAC*

W. D. & H.O. Wills,
Air Raid Precautions,
set of 50, 1938.
£18–20 *MAC*

John Player & Sons, Zoo
Babies, set of 25, c1938.
£10–15 *LCC*

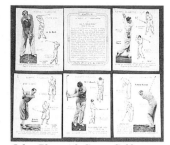

John Player & Sons,
Cricketers, set of 50, 1938.
£35–45 *LCC*

John Player & Sons, Golf,
set of 25, c1939.
£180–200 *LCC*

*Beware of modern reprints
which are available at £7.50.*

W. D. & H. O. Wills,
Speed, set of 50, c1938.
£12–15 *LCC*

Record Tobacco Company,
The Talkie cigarette card,
Sportsmen, set of 25, c1938.
£30–35 each *LCC*

J. A. Pattreiouex, Senior Service, Britain from
the Air, set of 48, c1939.
£8–10 *MAC*

Ardath Tobacco Co
Ltd, Stamps – Rare
and Interesting,
set of 50, c1939.
£60–90 *ACC*

r. John Player & Sons,
Uniforms of the Territorial
Army, set of 50, c1939.
£30–40 *LCC*

Trade Cards

Trade cards have become increasingly popular over the past year. As with cigarette cards, sporting subjects are a favourite with today's collectors, in particular soccer, which, as World Cup fever grips the nation, can only become more desirable. Another theme to watch out for is science fiction. The appeal of such cards is enhanced by the fact that they appeal to both sci-fi and trade card enthusiasts, thus increasing levels of demand.

Fry's Pure Cocoa, With Captain Scott at the South Pole, set of 25, c1912.
£200–250 *LCC*

Barratt & Co. Ltd, Test Cricketers, Series B, set of 48, c1957.
£160–180 *MAC*

Kellogg's Corn Flakes, Motor Cars, set of 40, 1950s.
£90–100 *LCC*

l. Brooke Bond Tea, Famous People, set of 50, c1969.
£3–4 *LCC*

Star Wars collectors cards, first series, c1977.
£2–3 each *Ada*

Topp's, Jurassic Park, c1993.
£7–10 per set *LCC*

Trebor Bassett Ltd, Premier Players, set of 48, c1994.
£5–6 *LCC*

Pin-Ups

The term pin-up is said to date from WWII when servicemen pinned up girlie pictures in their quarters. Pin-up material boomed in the 1940s and '50s. Two of the most famous illustrated pin-ups were the 'Petty Girl' and the 'Varga Girl' created by George Petty and Alberto Vargas respectively, both of whom worked for the American *Esquire* magazine. Their works were extremely popular – 'Varga

Girl' calendars sold over a million copies per annum in the 1940s. America dominated the glamour market but Britain too had its sexy illustrated heroines. 'Jane' first appeared in a cartoon strip in the *Daily Mirror* in 1932. She went on to become the most popular British pin-up during the war and even crossed the Atlantic to appear in the US armed forces paper *Stars and Stripes*.

A pin-up calendar, entitled 'Jane', by Petty, 1945, 4in (10cm) high.
£35–45 *COB*

A pin-up calendar, 'Varga Girl', by Antonio Vargas, 1946, 12in (30.5cm) high.
£75–100 *COB*

A pin-up *Esquire* calendar, by Petty, 1955, 12in (30.5cm) high.
£60–80 *COB*

Posters

A Theatre Royal poster, asking for contributions for the widows and children of an actor who died, 1828, 18in (45.5cm) high.
£35–45 *COB*

l. An Italian poster, entitled 'Anisetta Evangelisti Liquore Da Dessert', designed by Biscaretti, c1925, 55¼in (140.5cm) high.
£170–200 *SLN*

A Leslie's Monthly poster, entitled 'The Golf Walk', by B. Cory-Kilvert, lithographed in colours, c1905, 24in (61cm) high.
£600–700 *Bon(C)*

A poster, entitled 'Do Your Bit – Save Food', by Maurice Randall, lithographed in colours, printed by Hill Siffken and Co Ltd, slight damage, 1914–18, 29¾in (75.5cm) high.
£200–250 *Bon(C)*

FURTHER READING
Janet Gleeson,
Miller's Collecting Prints & Posters,
Miller's Publications, 1997

A poster, entitled 'A Gaiety Girl', by Dudley Hardy, printed by Waterlow and Sons Ltd, c1900, 38½in (98cm) high.
£400–500 *Bon(C)*

A poster, entitled
'Forward! Forward to
Victory Enlist Now',
by Lucy Kemp-Welch,
lithgraphed in
colours, 1914–18,
60in (152.5cm) high.
£650–750 *Bon(C)*

A poster, *Alice in
Wonderland,* depicting
'The Mock Turtle's Story',
by John MacFarlane,
published Macmillan,
lithographed in colours,
slight damage, c1927,
29½in (75cm) high.
£400–450 *DW*

A poster, entitled 'Who
Said Can't', lithographed
in colours, c1929,
43¾in (111cm) high.
£130–160 *Bon(C)*

A film poster, entitled
'*King Kong*', lithograph,
art by Rene Peron,
French, 1933, 63in
(160cm) high.
£2,700–3,200 *S(LA)*

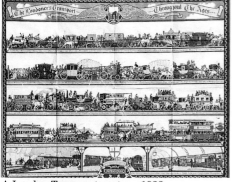

A London Transport poster, c1928,
41in (104cm) high, framed and glazed.
£140–160 *RAR*

A Warner Bros film
poster, entitled '*Angels
With Dirty Faces*', 1938,
41in (104cm) high.
£2,800–3,200 *S(LA)*

A Columbia film
poster, The 3 Stooges,
entitled '*I Can
Hardly Wait*', 1943,
41in (104cm) high.
£2,400–2,800 *S(LA)*

CARELESS TALK
COSTS LIVES   CARELESS TALK
COSTS LIVES

l. A set of 8 posters,
entitled 'Careless Talk
Costs Lives', by Cyril
Kenneth Bird Fougasse,
lithographed in colours,
c1943, 12½in (32cm) high.
£300–400 *Bon(C)*

A Warner Bros film
poster, entitled '*Dial
M For Murder*',
linen backed, 1954,
41in (104cm) high.
£1,200–1,400 *S(LA)*

A Walt Disney poster,
entitled '*Davy Crockett*',
linen backed, 1955,
41in (104cm) high.
£250–300 *S(LA)*

Film Posters

Prices for film posters have risen dramatically
over the past decade. Values depend not only on
the film itself, but on the artist who designed the
poster. Though they were often produced in large
numbers, film posters are rare because they
tended not to be preserved. Posters were only
leased to cinemas, and after the film had been
shown they were returned to the distributors and
often simply destroyed. Since posters tended to
be folded rather than rolled, they can often need
restoration to repair creases and tears. Although
for some collectors, signs that the poster has
been used are part of the attraction of a work.

FANS

An Italian fan, the vellum leaf depicting The Triumph of David, the ivory sticks and guardsticks piqué with silver, slight damage, early 18thC, 10¼in (26cm) wide.
£900–1,100 *Bon(C)*

A paper brisé fan, printed and coloured with figures in abbey ruins, within gilded borders, with tortoiseshell and piqué guardsticks, early 19thC, 6¼in (16cm) wide.
£130–160 *Hal*

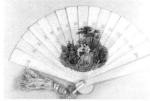

A Victorian ivory brisé fan, painted with 2 young girls seated on a park bench reading a book, one holding a fan, slight damage, c1840, 8in (20.5cm) wide.
£140–160 *Hal*

A French paper leaf fan, with pierced bone guardsticks, one with an oval mirror in gilt frame, mid-19thC, 17¼in (44cm) wide.
£100–120 *HOLL*

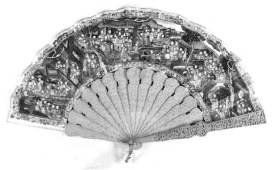

A Cantonese sandalwood fan, the leaf ivory set and painted with a Thousand Faces pattern, the sticks carved with figures and flowers, the reverse leaf painted with peacocks and bright flowers against a gilt ground, mid-19thC, 10in (25.5cm) wide, in fitted case.
£150–180 *Hal*

A Chinese export lacquered fan, the leaves painted in bright colours with figures in a landscape and birds amongst flowers to the reverse, slight damage, Qing Dynasty, 19thC, 11½in (29cm) wide, in fitted box.
£70–90 *P(B)*

A Japanese ivory and lacquerwork brisé fan, decorated in gilt *takamakie* with a landscape of Mount Fuji, Meiji period, 1868–1912, 10in (25.5cm) wide.
£2,400–2,800 *Hal*

A Victorian black ostrich feather fan, with monogram, c1890, 12in (30.5cm) wide, with original Duvelleroy box.
£150–200 *TT*

A cream satin fan, with painted roses and ivory sticks, c1890, 14in (35.5cm) wide.
£55–65 *Ech*

r. A Chinese carved ivory fan, the associated leaf painted in Art Nouveau style in bright colours with figures from a Venetian ball and signed 'Sensani', slight damage, late 19thC, 11in (28cm) wide.
£40–50 *Hal*

A paper leaf fan, with pierced gilded wood sticks and guards, the leaf printed with lithographical scene of figures in a pastoral landscape, repaired, late 19thC, 12in (30.5cm) wide.
£50–60 *HOLL*

A black gauze leaf fan, with ebony sticks, decorated with glass beads, late 19thC, 14in (35.5cm) wide.
£150–165 *PC*

A black peacock feather fan, with sandalwood sticks, late 19thC, 16in (40.5cm) wide.
£70–85 *PC*

A Japanese ivory and shibayama paper fan, painted with figures in a panoramic landscape, the reverse painted with birds, insects and flowers, on a beige background, late 19thC, 12in (30.5cm) wide.
£450–500 *Hal*

A cream lace fan, with ivory sticks, c1900, 8½in (21.5cm) wide.
£65–75 *Ech*

A pink and gold painted fan, with swan's-down trim, decorated with flowers, c1900, 12½in (32cm) wide.
£28–32 *Ech*

A paper fan, entitled 'Souvenir de Café L'Aiglon', c1900, 10in (25.5cm) wide.
£250–275 *PC*

A French paper fan, depicting an aviation scene, c1900, 8in (20.5cm) wide.
£150–175 *PC*

> **Miller's is a price GUIDE not a price LIST**

A wooden fan, depicting birds on a tricycle, c1900, 14in (35.5cm) wide.
£300–325 *PC*

A grey ostrich feather fan, with tortoiseshell sticks, 1920s, 17in (43cm) wide.
£60–70 *Ech*

FIFTIES STYLE

A Festival of Britain edition of *Punch* magazine, April 30th 1951, 11 x 9in (28 x 23cm) high.
£6–7 *GIN*

A Festival of Britain marble plaque, 1951, 12 x 6in (30.5 x 15cm) high.
£35–40 *GIN*

A Festival of Britain bronze-coloured glass liqueur set, c1951, decanter 7½in (19cm) high.
£40–45 *GIN*

A set of Festival of Britain liqueur glasses, with transfer printed logo and gilt rim, 1951, 2½in (6.5cm) high.
£30–40 *GIN*

A wicker and metal bar stool, 1950s, 32in (81.5cm) high.
£25–30 *Har*

A Hille Ltd chair, designed by Robin Day, for the Festival of Britain, 1951, 35in (89cm) high.
£450–500 *GIN*

This chair design was illustrated on Homemaker pottery (see below).

A Ridgway's Homemaker cup and saucer, 1955–67, saucer 5½in (14cm) diam.
£6–8 *GIN*

A pair of towelling bathroom/shower curtains, 1950s, 40in (101.5cm) wide.
£20–25 *JV*

A Ridgway's Homemaker tureen, 1955–67, 9in (23cm) diam.
£65–70 *GIN*

Homemaker

Homemaker is probably the most famous British ceramic design of the 1950s. Conceived by Enid Seeney and produced by Ridgway Potteries, Homemaker sold exclusively through Woolworths 1955–67. Although it retailed for shillings, rarer pieces such as tureens and coffee pots can fetch substantial sums today.

l. An orange musical decanter, modelled as a golf cart, 1950s, 12in (30.5cm) high.
£28–32 *RAD*

A Ridgway's Homemaker pattern cream jug, 1955–67, 4¾in (12cm) high.
£25–30 *GIN*

A Midwinter magazine advertisement, 1950s, 10in (25.5cm) wide.
£10–12 *GIN*

A Ridgway's Homemaker two-tier cake stand, 1955–67, 11in (28cm) high.
£30–35 *GIN*

A Midwinter cruet set, decorated with Riviera pattern, on a turquoise plate, 1950s, plate 8½in (21.5cm) wide.
£55–65 *GIN*

A collection of Midwinter Fashion tableware, decorated with the Chequers pattern, designed by Sir Terence Conran, 1950s, plate 9½in (24cm) diam.
£10–25 *AND*

A James Cooper 12-piece tea set, 1950s, plate 7in (18cm) diam.
£30–40 *RAD*

A Mascot engraved goldtone handbag-shaped compact, with musical movement, c1955, 3in (7.5cm) wide, with original pouch and box.
£60–70 *PC*

A plaster wall plaque, depicting an African woman with a child, 1950s, 19in (48.5cm) high.
£80–90 *GIN*

Two hand-mirror compacts, 1950s: *l.* Coty Vanité Parisienne white plastic compact, for cream powder, with lipstick in handle, 4¾in (12cm) long. *r.* goldtone, with powder compartment beneath mirror, 4¾in (12cm) long, **£45–55 each** *PC*

A set of chrome fire irons, with acrylic handles, c1950, 19in (48.5cm) high.
£35–45 *TIH*

FURTHER READING

Madeleine Marsh, *Miller's Collecting the 1950s,* Miller's Publications, 1997

A brocade puff-ball dress, decorated with pink flowers and brown silk waistband, 1950s.
£30–35 *Har*

FROGS

Frogs have long been a favourite motif in the decorative arts and are a popular subject with many collectors. Throughout history frogs have been a source of superstition and are often associated with witches and fertility. In the ancient world, frogs were a symbol of the foetus and were sacred to Hecate, Goddess of Witchcraft and Queen of the Heavenly Midwives. From this period onwards frogs and toads became a traditional element of the witch's brew, and toads in particular were thought to be sorceress' familiars. In Roman mythology, the frog was associated with Venus, whose reproductive organs were sometimes shown as a fleur-de-lys composed of three frogs. The fleur-de-lys, the French royal coat-of-arms, was in the past represented in heraldry as frogs or toads.

Scholars have associated the fairy tale of the frog who turns into a prince with the fact that the stages of development of the frog, from spawn, to tadpole, to froglet, to fully limbed amphibian, are visible and provide a remarkably clear image of the miracle of evolution. The mating ritual of the frog, which involves a lengthy embrace, has also been suggested as one of the reasons why the frog became an emblem of fertility and licentiousness, and the subject of many songs and poems on the theme of 'Froggy Goes a-Courting'. Like snails and puppy dog's tails, frogs, according to the well-known nursery rhyme, were a major constituent of little boys. Famous frogs and toads in literature include Beatrix Potter's Jeremy Fisher, Toad of Toad Hall and, more recently, Kermit from *The Muppets*.

A bronze frog, 18thC,
4in (10cm) long.
£440–470 *ARE*

A Belleek frog, with
black mark, late 19thC,
4⅜in (12cm) high.
£650–700 *MLa*

A stone salt-glazed frog, c1870,
4in (10cm) long.
£100–150 *BRT*

A wooden netsuke,
modelled as a standing
frog, holding a gourd flask
over his shoulder, signed,
damaged and repaired,
19thC, 2½in (6.5cm) long.
£500–600 *Bon*

A large frog loving cup, 1860s,
6¼in (16cm) high.
£140–160 *MRW*

r. A German porcelain dish,
depicting 2 green frogs removing
a boot, 5in (12.5cm) wide.
£150–200 *BRT*

A German porcelain dish, depicting
fighting frogs in blue jackets,
c1877, 5in (12.5cm) wide.
£150–200 *BRT*

A silver pincushion, modelled as a frog, by A & LL, Birmingham 1910, 1¾in (4.5cm) long.
£200–250 *GH*

An Edwardian ceramic vase, depicting a frog chauffeur in a car, c1905, 5in (12.5cm) long.
£90–110 *BKS*

A green majolica frog vase, c1880, 6in (15cm) high.
£200–250 *BRT*

A pair of Poole Pottery blue frogs, 1920s, 3¼in (8.5cm) wide.
£200–250 *GH*

A tinplate clockwork frog, with glass eyes and a key, 1930s, 1¼in (3cm) long.
£15–20 *PC*

A French white porcelain frog, by TH, marked 'SEZ', 4¼in (11cm) high.
£100–150 *BRT*

A tinplate 'clacker' frog, 1930–40s, 3in (7.5cm) long.
£10–15 *PC*

A set of 3 French ceramic frogs, coloured in green glaze, 1970s, 2in (5cm) high.
£10–15 *PC*

A Corgi Kermit the Frog, in a yellow painted car, paint worn, c1979, 3½in (9cm) long.
£1–2 *PC*

A silk brocade covered rice filled frog, c1979, 6in (15cm) high.
£3–4 *PC*

A ceramic doorstop, entitled 'Old Frog', 1950–60s, 5in (12.5cm) long.
£10–15 *PC*

A green and white glass frog, damaged, 1980s, 1½in (4cm) high.
£2–3 *PC*

A pottery frog, beige with black eyes, 1990s, 1½in (4cm) high.
£1–1.50 *PC*

A Royal Albert model of Beatrix Potter's Mr Jeremy Fisher digging, c1989, 4in (10cm) high.
£65–75 *TP*

A Lalique frog, in shades of blue and green, signed, 1990s, 2in (5cm) high.
£30–35 *PC*

A bronze frog, 1990s, 1½in (4cm) high.
£15–20 *PC*
This is a Past Times *reproduction taken from a Roman model.*

A Country Life Collection frog, by Anything Goes Ltd, Chinese, c1992, 3½in (9cm) high.
£6–8 *PC*

A mug, entitled 'Climbing frog', depicting yellow frogs on a white ground, by McLaggan Smith, Alexandria, Scotland, designed by Tyrrell Katz, 1990s, 3¼in (8.5cm) high.
£6–8 *PC*

Locate the Source

The source of each illustration in Miller's can be found by matching the code letters below each caption with the Key to Illustrations.

A Dartington Pottery high-fired stoneware pot, hand-sculpted with a frog and snake, designed by Roger Law and Janice Tchalenko, 1996, 8¼in (21cm) high.
£1,300–1,400 *RDG*

A Dartington Pottery high-fired stoneware bowl, with moulded frogs, designed by Roger Law and Janice Tchalenko, limited edition of 100, 1996, 5¼in (13cm) high.
£100–120 *RDG*

GAMES

A boxwood cribbage board, on turned brass feet, c1830, 9in (23cm) long.
£35–45 *MRT*

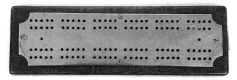

A brass and oak cribbage board, 19thC, 10½in (26.5cm) long.
£20–25 *No7*

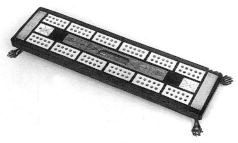

An ivory and boxwood cribbage board, on brass feet, early 19thC, 10in (25.5cm) long.
£80–100 *COT*

A rosewood cribbage board/box, inlaid with mother-of-pearl, mid-19thC, 11in (28cm) long.
£200–250 *COT*

A St George chess set, 19thC, king 3½in (9cm) high.
£75–100 *FB*

A travelling chess set, with red and white ivory pieces, 19thC, 6in (15cm) long.
£150–200 *FB*

A mahogany travelling solitaire board, with ivory pegs, c1870, 9in (23cm) wide.
£150–170 *AMH*

Two leather-bound games compendium boxes, 19thC, 15in (38cm) long.
£100–150 each *FB*

A pair of Victorian ivory finger counters, c1880, 1¾in (4.5cm) diam.
£150–175 *SPU*

A leather presentation set of 2 packs of full colour playing cards, inscribed in gold, commemorating the 60th year of the reign of Queen Victoria, c1897, 3½in (9cm), with leather case inscribed in gold.
£250–300 *PC*

A draughts board, with lidded compartment to each side holding draughtsmen, late 19thC, 14in (35.5cm) long.
£50–60 *FOX*

A boxwood bottle and 3 dice, c1900, 3in (7.5cm) high.
£20–30 *BIL*

A travelling chess set, with red and white ivory figures, c1900, 15¾in (40cm) extended.
£55–65 *WAB*

A Sandown racing game, in mahogany box, by F. H. Ayres, London, c1900, 12in (30.5cm) wide.
£130–150 *MUL*

A Bakelite draughts/chess set, c1920s, each piece 1½in (4cm) diam.
£100–150 *FB*

A wooden jigsaw puzzle of London, 1930s, 6in (15cm) wide.
£20–25 *COB*

A 24-hour chess clock, by H Koopman, Dordrecht, limited edition, c1940, 10in (25.5cm) high.
£150–200 *FB*

A Swiss musical chess table, with inlaid top, c1940, 17in (43cm) high.
£100–120 *FB*

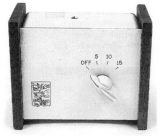

An electric chess timer, c1950, 5in (12.5cm) wide.
£50–60 *FB*

r. A pinball game, by Louis Marx, entitled 'Three Keys to Treasure', with treasure and balls, c1960, 21¾in (55cm) long.
£35–45 *OTS*

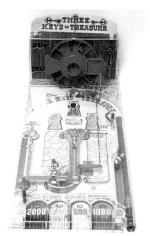

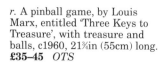

An inlaid wooden chessboard, 1970s, 23in (58.5cm) square.
£40–50 *FB*

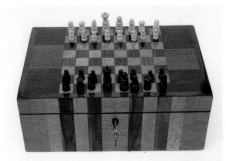

An Indian carved ivory chess set, each piece of architectural design and on a scalloped base, 19thC, 3¼in (8.5cm) high.
£375–425 *HYD*

A William IV inlaid writing slope and chess board, c1830, 14in (35cm) wide.
£350–400 *MB*

A "Victory" Jig-saw Puzzle — a wooden jigsaw, depicting a flying boat, 1930s, 10in (25.5cm) wide.
£15–20 *COB*

A mahjong set, with silver mounts and handle, early 20thC, 9in (23cm) wide.
£275–325 *PSA*

A Dan Dare Bagatelle game, by Chad Valley, c1960, 24in (61cm) high.
£150–200 *CTO*

A Garde world championship chess clock, 1950–60s, 9in (23cm) wide.
£40–50 *FB*

A Waddington's board game, c1958, 10¼in (26cm) high.
£15–18 *OTS*

A Dr Who board game, c1975, 20in (51cm) wide.
£20–30 *Ada*

A Waddington's Railroader board game, c1963, 20in (51cm) wide.
£15–18 *OTS*

A Westrak chess computer, c1980, 14in (35.5cm) long.
£100–150 *FB*

A Bristol wine glass,
1730–80,
5in (12.5cm) high.
£100–125 *JAS*

A glass picture, commemorating the death of
Admiral Nelson, c1808, 17in (43cm) wide.
£1,000–1,200 *TVM*

A glass tea caddy bowl,
c1830, 4¼in (11cm) high.
£220–250 *MJW*

An American glass
candlestick, c1840,
9in (23cm) high.
£250–280 *MJW*

A pair of wine glasses, with wide
ovoid bowls and flat-cut stems,
c1840–50, 5in (12.5cm) high.
£40–50 each *BrW*

A pair of Bristol wine glasses, c1850,
5in (12.5cm) high.
£120–140 *JAS*

A glass decanter, c1857,
11½in (29cm) high.
£400–450 *MJW*

A French glass flask,
c1860, 4in (10cm) high.
£225–245 *MJW*

A pair of Bristol wines, c1860,
5in (12.5cm) high.
£100–120 *JAS*

A cranberry glass decanter,
c1880, 9¾in (25cm) high.
£150–175 *AMH*

A Continental glass decanter, with celery handle, c1880, 6½in (16.5cm) high.
£200–225 *Har*

A Bohemian ruby glass font, with gilded rims and engraved panels, 19thC, 3¾in (9.5cm) high.
£150–200 *TMA*

A glass tazza, decorated in gold with Greek key pattern, c1880, 5¾in (14.5cm) high.
£350–400 *MJW*

A St Louis Art Nouveau amethyst glass vase, with flame enamelling, c1900, 8in (20.5cm) high.
£90–110 *MON*

A WMF lustre glass dish, c1890, 2in (5cm) high.
£145–165 *MON*

An opaline striped glass trumpet-shaped vase, c1890, 15½in (39.5cm) high.
£500–550 *ARE*

A cranberry cut-glass engraved decanter, c1890, 11in (28cm) high.
£175–200 *ARE*

A French enamelled opaline glass vase, late 19thC, 7¼in (18.5cm) high.
£140–160 *GH*

A Loetz glass shell-shaped vase, c1900, 10in (25.5cm) wide.
£225–250 *MJW*

A Gallé glass vase, c1900, 3¾in (9.5cm) high
£600–650 *MON*

A Bagley glass flower holder, decorated with gum leaves, No. 3014, c1936, 11in (28cm) wide.
£90–120 *PC*

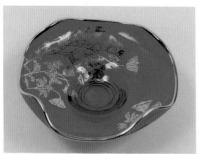

An American ruby glass dish, with silver overlay, 1950s, 6½in (16.5cm) wide.
£60–70 *MON*

A Glasform glass bowl, No. 4032, signed, c1990, 9½in (24cm) diam.
£250–300 *GLA*

A glass vase, 1920s, 7½in (19cm) high.
£40–50 *JAS*

An acid glass powder bowl, 1930s, 5½in (14cm) high.
£65–75 *MSB*

A Siddy Langley vase, 1997, 8in (20.5cm) high.
£90–100 *NP*

A claret jug, with silver-plated mounts and glass eyes, hinge replaced, 1930s, 12in (30.5cm) high.
£375–425 *JAS*

A Gray-Stan barrel-shaped glass vase, with everted rim, 1930s, 10in (25.5cm) high.
£150–200 *CMO*

A glass model of a swordfish, 1960s, 3¾in (9.5cm) long.
£10–12 *GIN*

A Murano glass duck, 1960s, 7in (18cm) high.
£10–15 *RAC*

A Glasform glass vase, with gold trails and lava, No. 4440, signed, 1995, 7in (18cm) high.
£250–300 *GLA*

A Northwood Carnival glass Grape and Cable pattern candle lamp , c1910, 10½in (26.5cm) high.
£400–500 *ASe*

A Northwood Carnival glass Grape and Cable pattern butter dish, in green base glass, c1910, 6in (15cm) wide.
£150–225 *ASe*

A Northwood Carnival glass Leaf and Beads pattern rose bowl, in blue base glass, c1910, 5½in (14cm) diam.
£50–75 *ASe*

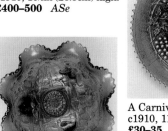

A Northwood Carnival glass Wishbone pattern bowl, c1910, 7½in (19cm) diam.
£65–85 *ASe*

A Carnival glass plate, c1910, 11in (28cm) diam.
£30–35 *DKH*

An Imperial Carnival glass Diamond Lace water set, in purple base glass, c1915, jug 9in (23cm) high.
£500–600 *ASe*

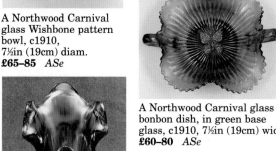

A Northwood Carnival glass bonbon dish, in green base glass, c1910, 7½in (19cm) wide.
£60–80 *ASe*

A Carnival glass bowl, c1910, 6½in (16.5cm) diam. **£10–15** *MAC*

A Fenton Carnival glass Diamond and Rib pattern vase, in green base glass, c1910, 11in (28cm) high.
£15–20 *ASe*

A Brockwitz Carnival glass Curved Star cheese dish, c1930, 8½in (21.5cm) diam.
£80–100 *ASe*

A Carnival glass Grand Thistle Art Deco style water set, c1930, jug 11½in (29cm) high.
£1,000–1,200 *ASe*

Four Victorian miser's knitted purses, with cut steel beads, 12in (30.5cm) long.
£20–40 each *CCO*

A knitting bag, with blue lining and wooden handles, 1940s, 15in (38cm) wide.
£15–20 *Ech*

A beaded bag, with silver metal frame and blue and gunmetal beads, c1920, 8in (20.5cm) long.
£25–30 *Ech*

An American fake leopard skin and Bakelite handbag, 1950s, 11½in (29cm) wide.
£65–75 *RAD*

A Victorian multi-coloured woolwork bag, with tassels, 6in (15cm) wide.
£40–50 *CCO*

A plastic and raffia handbag, 1950s, 6in (15cm) wide.
£15–20 *HarC*

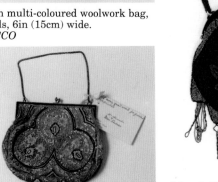

A multi-coloured beadwork and embroidered handbag, with enamel frame and original gift tag, c1930, 7in (18cm) wide.
£40–50 *CCO*

A beaded handbag, with Bakelite frame, 1920s, 12in (30.5cm) long including tassels.
£75–85 *Ech*

An American plastic basket handbag, 1950s, 12in (30.5cm) wide.
£50–60 *RAD*

A plastic handbag, with perspex lid, 1960s, 6in (15cm) diam.
£25–35 *CCO*

A gold mesh evening handbag, 1960, 11in (28cm) wide.
£15–18 *CCO*

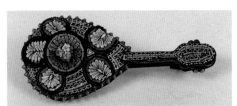

A Victorian mosaic on brass brooch, in the form of a violin, 2in (50mm) wide.
£5–8 *MAC*

A Scottish 9ct gold dirk brooch, set with citrine and agate, c1880, 2in (50mm) long.
£110–125 *SPE*

A micro mosaic brooch, engraved on reverse, 19thC, 1in (25mm) wide.
£175–195 *ANV*

A Scottish silver bracelet, set with agate, with engraved heart clasp, c1880, 7in (18cm) long.
£300–325 *WIM*

A Ruskin two-tone pottery brooch, with silver mount, 1920s, 1¾in (45mm) wide.
£35–45 *SnA*

An Amy Sandheim Arts and Crafts necklace, c1930, 15½in (39.5cm) long.
£700–800 *P*

A Czechoslovakian brooch, with red stone design and filigree metal mount, 1920s, 2¼in (57mm) wide.
£40–60 *SnA*

An American gold-plated Christmas tree brooch, set with rhinestones, 1950s, 2¼in (57mm) high.
£40–50 *BAH*

A Hattie Carnegie yellow metal brooch, c1965, 1½in (38mm) long.
£75–85 *PKT*

A Christian Dior blue crystal necklace, with central flower setting and 5 pendant drops, S-type hook, unsigned, 1950s.
£1,200–1,500 *GLT*

A Butler & Wilson yellow metal brooch, with red and white diamanté, c1984, 3in (75mm) long.
£80–90 *PKT*

Two copper jelly moulds, 19thC,
largest 7½in (19cm) long.
l. **£125–145** *r.* **£100–115** *No7*

A Victorian copper kettle,
13in (33cm) high.
£65–75 *PPe*

A *New Royal Cook Book*,
1930s, 8in (20.5cm) high.
£1–2 *RAD*

Two enamel storage jars, c1900,
8in (20.5cm) high. **£18–20 each** *SMI*

A Cerebos table salt tin,
1930s, 9in (23cm) high.
£15–18 *WEE*

A German coffee grinder,
c1940, 8in (20.5cm) high.
£25–35 *CPA*

A Garfield egg cup, c1978,
2¾in (7cm) high.
£3–4 *MAC*

A Swan electric
toaster, 1930–50s,
8in (20.5cm) wide.
£12–18 *GIN*

A Kenrick mincer, c1950,
11in (28cm) high.
£25–35 *CPA*

A Cornish ware coffee jar,
c1950, 7in (18cm) high.
£60–70 *SMI*

A tea towel, c1961,
30in (76cm) long.
£8–10 *RAD*

Four Cornish ware shakers, 1950s,
largest 5½in (14cm) high.
£25–35 each *SMI*

The Illustrated London News magazine, silver jubilee edition, May 11 1935, 24in (61cm) high.
£8–10 *MAC*

Woman's Life magazine, No. 883, January 1929, 9in (23cm) high.
£4–5 *SVB*

Picture Post magazine, March 1940, 13in (33cm) high.
£2–3 *RAD*

Illustrated magazine, July 1953, 13½in (34.5cm) high.
£2–3 *RAD*

Spick magazine, January 1958, 7in (18cm) high.
£5–7 *RAD*

Harper's Bazaar magazine, February 1957, 13in (33cm) high.
£8–10 *RAD*

Carnival magazine, December 1960, 11in (28cm) high.
£3–4 *SVB*

Playboy magazine, May 1970, 11½in (29cm) high.
£10–12 *RAD*

19 magazine, July 1975, 12in (30.5cm) high.
£5–6 *PPe*

A Chinese grey pottery horse, Western Han Dynasty, circa 206BC–AD24, 15in (38cm) high.
£1,600–1,800 *ORI*

A starburst dish, from the *Diana* cargo, c1816, 11in (28cm) diam.
£100–180 *CFA*

A blue and white baluster vase, c1720, 6in (15cm) high.
£300–350 *ORI*

A Chinese cream jug, Kangxi, 6in (15cm) high.
£400–450 *ORI*

A Canton basin, with *famille rose* decoration, 19thC, 19in (48cm) diam.
£1,200–1,400 *P(B)*

A Chinese porcelain charger, Qianlong, c1780, 18in (45.5cm) diam.
£950–1,000 *ORI*

A Chinese *famille verte* export ware plate, enamelled with butterflies, 19thC, 7½in (19cm) diam.
£15–20 *MEG*

A Chinese vase, c1740, 8in (20.5cm) high.
£340–380 *ORI*

A Japanese Imari bowl, Meiji period, late 19thC, 7in (18cm) diam. **£50–70** *MEG*

A Japanese Imari plate, c1880, 10in (25.5cm) diam.
£125–145 *BRU*

A pair of Canton vases, c1840, 12in (30.5cm) high.
£400–450 *ALB*

A Japanese red and black lacquered cabinet, c1900, 16in (40.5cm) wide.
£240–280 *TMi*

A grey hardstone model of a buffalo, c1900, 3¾in (9.5cm) long.
£100–120 *P(B)*

A Burmese carved wooden horse puppet, with bridle and velour saddle, c1930s, 19in (48cm) long.
£200–250 *PaM*

An Indonesian dowry chest, c1900, 32in (81cm) long.
£200–225 *LHB*

A Japanese black lacquer frame, c1900, 12in (30.5cm) high.
£100–120 *P(B)*

A Japanese silk *haori*, with printed pattern depicting blossoms and chrysanthemums, c1940s.
£30–40 *ASG*

A green glass dump paper-
weight, 19thC, 4in (10cm) high.
£45–55 *FD*

A Clichy garland paperweight,
possibly repolished, c1850,
3in (7.5cm) diam.
£1,200–1,600 *STG*

A Murano paperweight, 1970,
3¼in (8cm) diam.
£35–45 *SWB*

A Paul Ysart paperweight,
Harland Glass Works, Wick,
c1970, 2½in (6.5cm) diam.
£225–275 *STG*

A Wedgwood glass stoat paperweight,
1970s, 6in (15cm) long.
£45–55 *SWB*

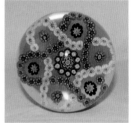

A Baccarat paperweight,
c1850, 2¾in (7cm) diam.
£400–450 *SWB*

A Wedgwood glass elephant paperweight, 1970s, 4¾in (12cm) long.
£30–40 *SWB*

A Perthshire glass Annual
Collection paperweight, dated
'1976', 3in (7.5cm) diam.
£200–230 *STG*

A Perthshire Annual
Collection paperweight,
1979, 3¼in (8cm) diam.
£300–330 *STG*

A Baccarat paperweight, signed
and dated cane, engraved base,
1976, 3in (7.5cm) diam.
£500–550 *STG*

A Wedgwood paperweight,
1983, 4¼in (11cm) high.
£25–30 *SWB*

A Baccarat paperweight, with
scarab beetle, signed and dated
cane, 1985, 3¼in (8.5cm) diam.
£400–480 *STG*

A Terro Lazzarine paperweight, 1992, 3¼in (8.5cm) diam.
£40–50 *SWB*

A Perthshire limited edition paperweight, c1990, 3¼in (8.5cm) diam.
£100–120 *STG*

A Siddy Langley paperweight, 1990s, 3½in (9cm) high.
£25–30 *SWB*

A William Manson paperweight, 1997, 3¼in (8.5cm) diam.
£100–120 *SWB*

A William Manson paperweight, 1997, 3¼in (8.5cm) diam.
£175–200 *SWB*

An Okra paperweight, 'Opal', 1997, 3¾in (9.5cm) diam.
£75–85 *SWB*

Three Bakelite boxes, 1930s, largest 4in (10cm) diam.
Large £50–55
Small £40–45 *BEV*

A Bakelite string ball container, 1930–40s, 3½in (9cm) diam.
£12–14 *GIN*

A pair of Art Deco style urea formaldehyde cream jars, c1935, 2in (5cm) diam.
£8–10 *TIH*

A plastic dressing table set, in original fitted box, 1930–50s, 11in (28cm) wide.
£10–12 *GIN*

An acrylic biscuit jar, formed from acrylic sheets, with Lucite barley sugar twist handle, c1940, 9in (23cm) high.
£75–85 *TIH*

A two-tone green Thermos flask, 1960s, 7in (18cm) high.
£10–12 *GIN*

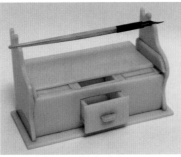

An acrylic inkwell, with pen holder, 2 inkwells and nib drawer, 1940s, 6in (15cm) wide.
£35–45 *TIH*

A plastic picnic set, comprising cups, plates, bowls and cutlery, 1970s, plates 7in (18cm) diam.
£2–3 *TRE*

A plastic Busby money box, 1980s, 5in (12.5cm) high.
£8–10 *GIN*

A plastic lamp, 1970s, 22in (56cm) high.
£30–40 *RAC*

An Art Nouveau glamour postcard, entitled 'Paris', by Hans Christiansen, c1900, 6 x 3½in (15 x 9cm).
£80–90 *SpP*

A Christmas greetings card, by Kosa, Paris, slight edge wear, c1901, 6 x 3½in (15 x 9cm).
£20–30 *SpP*

An Art Deco postcard, by G. Meschini, c1920, 6 x 3½in (15 x 9cm).
£18–20 *SpP*

A postcard from Eltham, depicting a bicycle decorated with violets, c1900, 4 x 6in (10 x 15cm).
£2–3 *THA*

A motoring postcard, by Raphael Kirchner, published by Tuck, c1904, 6 x 3½in (15 x 9cm).
£30–35 *SpP*

A postcard from Ramsgate, entitled 'Fishy Customers', July 23, 1908, 4 x 6in (10 x 15cm).
£3–4 *JMC*

A Birthday Wishes postcard, depicting a Jack Russell, c1915, 4 x 6in (10 x 15cm).
£2–4 *THA*

An American postcard, by Philip Boileau, 1904, 5½ x 3½in (14 x 9cm).
£4–5 *JMC*

A maritime advertising postcard, published by James Walker, c1904, 6 x 3½in (15 x 9cm).
£18–20 *SpP*

A Mabel Lucie Attwell postcard, 1930s, 5½ x 3½in (14 x 9cm).
£3–6 *CMF*

A K.B. (Kolster Brandes) console radio, in an oak case, original condition, with instruction booklet, c1930, 38in (96.5cm) high.
£200–250 *OTA*

A Philips model 636A radio, 1933, 11in (28cm) wide.
£600–700 *OTA*

A Pye model Q3 portable radio, with PVC case, battery-operated, restored, 1950s, 11in (28cm) wide.
£50–60 *TIH*

A Cossor special edition radio, cabinet by Challen, c1947, 31in (78.5cm) high.
£250–300 *OTA*

A Philips model 790A console radio, c1936, 34in (86.5cm) high.
£80–100 *OTA*

A GEC model BC 4050 radio, with Bakelite case, 1930s, 21in (53cm) wide.
£60–80 *OTA*

r. A Baird radio, 1950s, 10½in (26.5cm) wide.
£15–20 *GIN*

A Roberts model RIC 2 radio, 1960s, 10in (25.5cm) wide.
£55–65 *TIH*

A Ferguson model 352 radio, 1960s, 12in (30.5cm) wide.
£85–95 *TIH*

A black and white TV set, 1960s, 12in (30.5cm) wide.
£30–40 *GIN*

GLASS
Animals

A red glass swan ashtray,
1950s, 7in (18cm) long.
£5–7   *GIN*

A pair of pressed glass white
swans, c1890, 3¼in (8.5cm) wide.
£50–65   *ARE*

A glass inkwell, modelled
as Bonzo dog, 1930s,
3½in (9cm) high.
£80–100   *TMA*

A glass pheasant, with blue and yellow
striped body, 1960s, 8in (20.5cm) long.
£10–14   *GIN*

A glass bambi, with blue
and white spotted body,
c1958, 3½in (9cm) high.
£10–12   *PC*

A Murano glass bird,
with multi-coloured
striped body, 1960s,
10in (25.5cm) high.
£15–20   *RAC*

A pair of Davidson's blue pearline posy
baskets, c1890, 7½in (19cm) long.
£80–100   *CSA*

Baskets

A Sowerby pressed glass basket,
c1880, 3in (7.5cm) high.
£60–80   *MJW*

**Miller's is a price GUIDE
not a price LIST**

A Victorian latticino satin
glass basket, with yellow air
twist stripes, mid-19thC,
6½in (16.5cm) high.
£80–100   *AnS*

A Bagley Jetique polka-dot
basket, with clear glass
handle, c1957, 6in (15cm) high.
£25–30   *JMC*

Carnival Glass

Carnival glass is press moulded glass, sprayed while hot with a mixture of oil and metallic salts to give it its distinctive iridescence. The name Carnival was only applied to this glassware from the 1950s; before that it was known by a number of different names including Rubigold, Taffeta, Pompeian, Venetian Art and, colloquially, Poor Man's Tiffany.

It was the great American glassmaker, Louis Comfort Tiffany, who in the late 19th century popularised iridescent art glass. Tiffany's products were costly and aimed at the top end of the market. He tried, and failed, to patent his techniques which, by the early 1900s, were being applied to inexpensive mass-produced pressed-glass.

The golden age of carnival glass was 1908–1930s, and the best producers were in the USA. In 1908 the Fenton Art Glass Co launched 'Iridill', a new range of lustrous glassware aimed at the general public and which sold extremely well in the ten cent stores. Rival manufacturers soon set up production, and major factories included the Northwood Co, the Dugan Co (destroyed by fire in 1931), the Millersburg factory and the Imperial Glass Co. American carnival glass was exported across the world. Carnival glass was also made in other countries. Brockwitz was the leading Continental manufacturer. Australia produced some fine iridescent glass to compete with USA imports, and in Britain carnival glass was made by Sowerby's, who, in the 1920s, sold their glassware across the British Empire. By the 1930s carnival glass had fallen from fashion. It was not until the 1960s that new carnival began to be produced and that old carnival became collectable. Today this colourful glass is extremely popular both at home and abroad, particularly in the USA. American products tend to be the most desirable, and some shapes are more easily found than others.

'A lot of decorative carnival glass was imported to the UK in the first part of the 20th century, but much less domestic ware,' explains collector Alan Sedgwick. 'It's hard to find some items of American carnival glass in the UK such as water sets, butter dishes, jugs and sugar bowls. These practical pieces are far more common in the USA than here.' Equally, while certain patterns such as Grape and Cable appear on many examples, other designs such as Peter Rabbit are rare and, therefore, more costly. Shape and pattern, however, are not the only things that the serious collector is looking for.

'Quality of iridescence is all important,' says Alan Sedgwick, 'poor iridescence, any chips or damage will immediately lower values. You have to remember this was pressed glass and mass-produced. Most things will eventually turn up if you wait long enough, so don't compromise and buy inferior examples unless they are really cheap. The pieces that collectors want and that gain in value are the best ones, in good condition and with the finest lustred surfaces.'

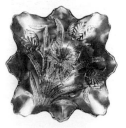

A Brockwitz Curved Star celery vase, in blue base glass, 1930–34, 7in (18cm) high.
£100–150 *ASe*

Blue glass examples are quite scarce, unlike examples with the marigold finish which are plentiful. This vase is also known as the Cathedral Chalice.

A pair of Brockwitz Rose Garden vases, with marigold iridescence, 1930–35, 9½in (24cm) high.
£150–200 *ASe*

Greater use of intaglio patterns were made in Europe whereas most US carnival glass has embossed designs.

A Crown Crystal kangaroo bowl, in black amethyst base glass, Australian, 1924–30, 9½in (24cm) diam.
£300–400 *ASe*

Two versions exist of this bowl, one with a small kangaroo and another with a big kangaroo, probably to represent the Flying Grey and the Big Red kangaroos.

A Dugan Butterfly and Tulip footed bowl, in black amethyst glass, 1910–31, 13in (33cm) wide.
£500–600 *ASe*

FURTHER READING

Raymond Nutley, *Carnival Glass,* Shire Publications, 1986

A Dugan Nautilus bowl, with marigold iridescence on opalescent glass, 1908–15, 6in (15cm) wide.
£200–250 *ASe*

A Dugan scalloped Cherry bowl, with marigold finish, 1910–31, 8in (20.5cm) diam.
£25–35 *MEG*

A Fenton Peter Rabbit plate, in green base glass,1909–15, 9½in (24cm) diam.
£900–1,200 *ASe*

This pattern can also be found on bowls.

A Fenton Stag and Holly footed bowl, in green base glass, 1908–25, 8in (20.5cm) diam.
£55–75 *ASe*

This round shape would possibly denote a bowl for ice cream.

A Fenton Peacock and Urn plate, with Bearded Berry exterior pattern, in blue base glass, 1908–25, 9½in (24cm) diam.
£150–200 *ASe*

A Fenton Vintage bowl, in green base glass, 1908–25, 8in (20.5cm) diam.
£45–55 *ASe*

Grape patterns were very popular in their day and are amongst the most available now.

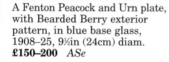

A Fenton Peacock Tail card tray, in amethyst base glass, 1908–25, 7in (18cm) wide.
£45–60 *ASe*

Card trays are distinct from bonbons in that they only have 2 sides turned up.

r. An Imperial Fashion punch set, with marigold iridescence, comprising a bowl base, 6 cups and 6 hooks, 1910–25, bowl 12in (30.5cm) diam.
£80–120 *ASe*

A Fenton red carnival glass butter dish, modelled as a hen, c1925, 6¾in (17cm) high.
£240–300 *MEG*

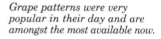

Three Imperial ripple vases, in lavender, purple and helios green, 1910–20, largest 16in (40.5cm) high.
£30–90 each *ASe*

This pattern was a very successful line.

A pair of Imperial Soda
Gold candlesticks, with
smoke iridescence, 1910–25,
3⅓in (9cm) high.
£65–85 *ASe*

A pair of Imperial Premium
candlesticks, with marigold
iridescence, 1910–25,
8⅓in (21.5cm) high.
£40–50 *ASe*

An Imperial Octagon wine set,
with marigold iridescence, 1910–20,
decanter 10⅓in (26.5cm) high.
£100–130 *ASe*

A Northwood Peacock bowl, in
amethyst base glass, 1908–15,
9in (23cm) diam.
£100–125 *ASe*

*This example has been finished
with a type of ruffling referred
to as a piecrust edge. This
bowl has been reproduced,
but the reproductions are
noticeably different as the
moulding is not as crisp.*

A Northwood Spring Time butter
dish, in amethyst base glass,
1908–15, 8in (20.5cm) wide.
£250–300 *ASe*

A Millersburg Seacoast pin tray,
with satin finished iridescence,
on amethyst base glass,
1909–11, 5in (12.5cm) wide.
£225–250 *ASe*

*This is one of the smallest
pieces of carnival glass.*

A Sowerby Hen on the Nest
butter dish, with marigold
iridescence, 1925–35,
5⅓in (14cm) wide.
£35–45 *ASe*

*This item was originally marketed
as 'Chic', and some examples have
very pale iridescence.*

A Sowerby Diving Dolphins
footed bowl, in pale amethyst
base glass, 1925–35,
8in (20.5cm) diam.
£120–150 *ASe*

*This piece was made from
an 1880s mould with a new
plunger bearing the scroll
embossed pattern copied
from Imperial Glass Co.*

r. A carnival glass
Blackberry footed bowl,
with marigold iridescence,
c1920, 8¼in (21cm) diam.
£20–25 *MAC*

A Grape and Cable dish, in
amethyst base glass, early
20thC, 9in (23cm) diam.
£30–40 *MEG*

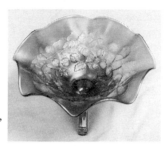

Decanters & Bottles

A Bristol blue glass club-shaped rum decanter, with stopper, c1790, 9¾in (25cm) high.
£250–275 *JAS*

Two clear glass spirit decanters, with flute-cut bases and target stoppers, c1810:
l. 7¼in (18.5cm) high.
£70–80
r. 7¾in (20cm) high.
£110–130 *Som*

A clear glass guest bottle, engraved 'I.W.', c1830, 5¼in (13.5cm) high.
£100–125 *JAS*

A guest bottle was placed by the bed with a favourite nightcap.

A pair of amethyst glass decanters, with stoppers, c1840, 15½in (39.5cm) high.
£1,000–1,100 *AMH*

r. An etched-glass and Dutch silver-mounted decanter, the glass decorated with flowers, the mount embossed with figures, windmills and buildings, 19thC, 9½in (24cm) high.
£625–675 *WeH*

A pair of toddy lifters, with flute cut necks, c1810, 5¼in (13.5cm) high.
£230–260 *Som*

Toddy lifters were used for transferring punch from the bowl into the glass.

A French oil and vinegar bottle, with later engraving, c1825, 10in (25.5cm) high.
£135–155 *JAS*

l. A pair of miniature two-ring clear glass carafes, c1870, 1¾in (45mm) high.
£60–70 *BrW*

Decorative Glass & Curiosities

A Bristol blue glass
lacemaker's lamp, c1790,
10½in (27cm) high.
£750–850 *FD*

A sulphide box lid, depicting
Louis Philippe, probably Baccarat,
c1830, 2⅜in (6cm) diam.
£180–200 *BrW*

A frosted-glass bust, depicting
Napoleon III, inscribed
'Chislehurst 1873' on base,
c1873, 8in (20.5cm) high.
£400–450 *BrW*

A sulphide plaque, depicting
George III in old age, minor
manufacturing flaw, c1820,
4¼in (11cm) diam.
£230–260 *BrW*

A pair of Victorian
blue marbled pressed-
glass obelisks,
on square stepped
bases, some damage,
11in (28cm) high.
£130–150 *DN*

A Waterford crystal globe,
1970s, 12⅗in (32cm) high.
£900–1,000 *WeH*

Two miniature clear glass bellows,
with ribbed notched edges,
c1860, largest 6in (15cm) long.
£40–50 each *Som*

A Victorian blue-tinted glass pipe, with
tapering stem and rounded bowl, trailed
overall with white bands, 17in (43cm) long.
£100–120 *DN*

Two glass swizzle sticks, in the form of golf
clubs, decorated with gold bands, c1900,
5¼in (13cm) high.
£8–10 each *AMH*

A Baccarat engraved plaque,
c1930, 5½in (14cm) high.
£100–125 *BrW*

Domestic Glass

A Silesian stemmed glass salver, with domed and folded foot, c1750, 9in (23cm) diam.
£350–450 *BrW*

An opaline glass sugar bowl, with enamelled floral decoration, c1790, 4¼in (11cm) high.
£85–95 *FD*

A blue glass sugar basin, with cold enamelled floral decoration, on high conical folded foot, c1800, 4¾in (12cm) high.
£230–260 *Som*

A cut glass preserve pot, c1810, 4¼in (11cm) high.
£220–260 *BrW*

A red glass rinser, c1860, 3½in (9cm) high.
£140–170 *MJW*

Wine glass coolers, or rinsers as they are known in the USA, are an unusual item of late 18th and 19thC tableware. They are approximately the same size as a finger bowl with pouring lips on either side of the rim, and were used to rinse or cool wine glasses between each course of a meal.

A Victorian crackle glass jug, 12¼in (31cm) high.
£65–75 *OBS*

A yellow vaseline glass tazza, c1890, 5in (12.5cm) high.
£280–320 *MJW*

A green glass ashtray, in a decorative silver-plated mount, c1930, 1½in (4cm) high.
£35–45 *MON*

A Davidson's blue pearline glass jug, c1890, 2in (5cm) high.
£20–30 *CSA*

r. A French pink opaline glass candlestick, c1880, 6½in (16.5cm) high.
£125–145 *MJW*

Drinking Glasses

A firing glass, mid-18thC, 3½in (9cm) high.
£70–80 *FD*

A double dram glass, with bell bowls, c1750, 3½in (9cm) high.
£250–280 *FD*

A Jacobite glass, engraved with a rose and carnation, c1755, 7in (18cm) high.
£500–600 *JAS*

A set of 6 hock glasses, with decorative hollow stems, late 18thC, 4½in (11.5cm) high.
£250–300 *JAS*

Prunts & Printies

Prunts: are blobs of glass applied to the surface of a vessel as decoration.
Printies: are decorative patterns of shallow, concave, rounded shapes made on cut glass.

A pair of Bristol hock glasses, with green panels, c1850, 5in (12.5cm) high.
£125–150 *JAS*

l. A blue boot glass, c1790, 4¼in (10.5cm) high.
£250–280 *Som*

A clear boot glass or stirrup cup, with band of etched decoration and monogram 'T.E.S', c1800, 3¾in (9.5cm) high.
£70–80 *Som*

A pair of green wine glasses, with cup bowls, knopped stems and plain conical feet, c1830, 5in (12.5cm) high.
£110–130 *Som*

Two green sherry glasses and a wine glass, c1880, tallest 5½in (14cm) high.
£30–55 each *JAS*

A pair of Bohemian amber glass schnapps glasses, with fine engraving, 19thC, 2¼in (5.5cm) high.
£65–75 *JAS*

A pair of glass goblets, cut with printies and engraved with Greek key design, c1880, 6¼in (16cm) high.
£80–90 *BrW*

A set of 6 Bohemian blue glass goblets, c1880, 6½in (16.5cm) high.
£130–160 *MON*

A pressed glass ale glass, c1870–90, 7¼in (18.5cm) high.
£75–85 *JAS*

This decoration was an imitation of the earlier thumb print design.

A Bohemian red glass goblet, c1940, 7¾in (20cm) high.
£100–120 *MON*

A Bohemian green glass goblet, c1945, 7¾in (20cm) high.
£100–120 *MON*

Jelly & Sweetmeat Glasses

A sweetmeat glass, the double ogee bowl on a moulded Silesian stem with base collar and domed folded foot, c1750, 3¼in (8.5cm) high.
£130–150 *Som*

This glass has trapped air threads in the folded foot.

A sweetmeat glass, with ogee-shaped bowl, on collared stem and domed and folded foot, c1740–50, 3¼in (8.5cm) high.
£230–260 *DN*

Sweetmeat Glasses

Sweetmeat glasses were used to serve dry sweetmeats (chocolates, dried fruits etc), as opposed to desserts such as trifle and jelly, which were eaten from jelly glasses.

l. A blue bonnet glass, the double ogee bowl diamond moulded overall, c1780, 3in (7.5cm) high.
£230–260 *Som*

Bonnet glasses were used for sweetmeats.

A jelly glass, the eight-sided panel-moulded flared bowl engraved with a vine band, on beaded knopped stem and domed foot, c1730, 4¼in (11cm) high.
£170–200 *DN*

A jelly glass, with bell-shaped bowl, on opaque spiral twist knop and domed foot, c1760, 4in (10cm) high.
£300–350 *DN*

A set of 8 jelly glasses, with hexagonal moulded bowls and plain conical feet, c1760, tallest 4½in (11.5cm) high.
£800–1,000 *Som*

Plates, Bowls & Dishes

A pair of Bohemian red glass dishes, with clear cut glass centres with scalloped borders and gilt decoration, c1850, 5in (12.5cm) diam.
£240–280 *MJW*

A WMF glass lustre bowl, c1890, 4in (10cm) diam.
£50–65 *MON*

A WMF glass lustre bowl, c1890, 7in (18cm) diam.
£170–180 *MON*

A Bagley frosted green glass plate, with central fish pattern, No. 3123, c1945, 9in (23cm) wide.
£20–30 *PC*

This pattern was available in various colours as well as in clear glass.

A Davidson's yellow pearline dish, c1890, 7½in (19cm) diam.
£60–70 *CSA*

A Jobling opalescent glass dish, c1925, 10in (25.5cm) diam.
£60–70 *CSA*

An American glass two-handled bread and butter plate, with silver decoration, 1950s, 13in (33cm) diam.
£80–100 *MON*

An American two-section red glass dish, with silver overlay, 1950s, 7in (18cm) long.
£60–70 *MON*

A WMF glass lustre plate, c1890, 8½in (21.5cm) diam.
£140–160 *MON*

A René Lalique opalescent glass bowl, entitled 'Coquilles', engraved mark, c1900, 5¼in (13.5cm) diam.
£140–160 *HYD*

A Venetian blue glass dish, with gilt decoration, c1955, 7in (18cm) long.
£20–30 *CSA*

A Vasart pink glass bowl, c1955, 7in (18cm) diam.
£40–50 *CSA*

Rolling Pins

A Nailsea black and white flecked glass rolling pin, early 19thC, 15¾in (40cm) long.
£55–65 *FD*

An amethyst glass rolling pin, with remains of gilt decoration, c1820, 13½in (34.5cm) long.
£125–145 *JAS*

A Victorian Kilner-type glass rolling pin, with rounded ends, 16¼in (41cm) long.
£80–100 *DN*

A Victorian glass rolling pin, with rounded ends, decorated with ruby tinted trailed looped bands, 15in (38cm) long.
£120–140 *DN*

l. A Nailsea green glass rolling pin, with rounded ends, decorated with white trailed looped bands, 19thC, 14½in (37cm) long.
£70–80 *DN*

Salts

An amethyst glass salt, with hollow blown bowl and deep domed foot, c1760, 3¼in (8cm) high.
£360–400 *Som*

r. A boat-shaped glass salt, with step cutting, on diamond foot, c1810, 2½in (6.5cm) high.
£75–85 *FD*

Two fan-cut glass salts, c1800, 3½in (9cm) high.
£55–60 each *FD*

A pink opaline glass salt, c1890, 1¾in (4.5cm) high.
£100–120 *MJW*

FURTHER READING
Mark West, *Miller's Glass Antiques Checklist,* Miller's Publications, 1994

A pair of moulded and cut glass salts, with lemon squeezer feet, c1810, 3¼in (8cm) high.
£100–130 *BrW*

Three cut glass salts, the oval bodies, on diamond-shaped moulded and cut stems, c1810, 3¼in (8.5cm) high.
£75–85 each *Som*

Vases

A burgundy glass
bulb vase, c1840,
7¼in (18.5cm) high.
£80–100 *MJW*

An opaque white glass
bulb vase, with brown
base decorated with
Greek key pattern and
gilding on neck, c1850,
5in (12.5cm) high.
£150–170 *MJW*

A Victorian cranberry
glass vase, with
long fluted stem,
on green tinted base,
12in (30.5cm) high.
£120–150 *PCh*

A pair of cranberry
glass vases, c1880,
7¾in (20cm) high.
£165–185 *AMH*

An opaque white glass
vase, with blue trailed
rim, commemorating
Queen Victoria's
Jubilee, c1887,
5⅛in (14cm) high.
£75–80 *JMC*

A white trailed vaseline
glass vase, c1890,
12in (30.5cm) high.
£200–250 *ARE*

A pink vaseline glass
posy bowl, c1890,
4in (10cm) high.
£150–200 *MJW*

A Jack-in-the-pulpit
green vaseline glass vase,
c1890, 7in (18cm) high.
£150–175 *ARE*

*Jack-in-the-pulpit vases
were shaped and named
after the American flower
of the same name.*

A Victorian opalescent
blue and yellow striped
glass vase, c1890,
4¼in (11cm) high.
£175–200 *ARE*

A pair of blue and yellow
vaseline glass posy holders,
c1890, 4¼in (11cm) high.
£110–130 *ARE*

A pair of green glass
bulb vases, early 20thC,
8in (20.5cm) high.
£70–80 *PCh*

A Gray-Stan blue
marble effect glass vase,
c1920, 7in (18cm) high.
£750–850 *MJW*

*Made at the London
glasshouse of Mrs
Graydon-Stannus
(1920–30s), Gray-Stan
glass is very sought-after
in the current market.*

A French pale brown moulded glass vase, c1925, 9in (23cm) high.
£60–70 *CSA*

A Gray-Stan blue glass vase, c1930, 12in (30.5cm) high.
£420–470 *MJW*

A cameo glass oval trumpet-shaped vase, the rim and sides of raised amber colour, with flowering stems against a cut mottled ground, bearing etched signature 'Richardson' on underside of foot, 1930s, 10in (25.5cm) high.
£220–260 *HCC*

A Lalique thistle-shaped clear glass vase, moulded with a band of birds perched in between ivy, all raised on a waisted circular foot, engraved 'Lalique, France', c1945, 5in (12.5cm) high.
£250–300 *WeH*

A Flavio Poli cased-glass vase, with red interior, 1950s, 9in (23cm) high.
£225–250 *Gar*

r. A Vasart red and blue mottled glass vase, c1960, 11in (28cm) high.
£70–80 *CSA*

A Bagley glass Jetique polka dot handkerchief vase, c1957, 6in (15cm) high.
£10–15 *JMC*

Walking Sticks

A Victorian blue-tinted glass walking stick, with loop handle and corkscrew stem, 36½in (93cm) long.
£120–150 *DN*

A Victorian blue-tinted spirally-moulded glass walking stick, with scroll handle, 52in (132cm) long.
£90–110 *DN*

A Victorian glass shepherd's crook, with spirally-moulded scroll handle, containing blue, pink and green tinted canes, 38in (96.5cm) long.
£140–160 *DN*

A glass walking stick, with red and blue spiral, c1890, 36in (91.5cm) long.
£160–190 *ARE*

A Victorian clear glass walking cane, with ball finial, applied with red, white and blue spiral twist canes, 37in (94cm) long.
£180–200 *DN*

GOLLIES

The golly first appeared in *The Adventures of Two Dutch Dolls and A Gollywog*, written and illustrated by Florence K. Upton in 1895, with verses by her sister Bertha. This was the first of a series of children's books featuring this new and mischievous hero, and by the early 1900s the golly had become a favourite nursery character. Golly toys were produced by numerous manufacturers as well as being homemade, and, like teddies and dolls, the golly became a staple of children's stories,

appearing perhaps most famously in Enid Blyton's *Noddy* books.

In 1914 the jam and marmalade company Robertson's adopted the golly as their trademark, and from 1928 paper gollies were stuck to their glass jars, launching decades of golly collectables. The golly was predominantly a British phenomenon and remained a standard toy until the 1960s when growing social and political awareness and charges of racism led to the golly's demise.

An Austrian painted bronze golly charm, with red trousers and blue jacket, c1900, 1½in (4cm) high.
£100–125 *CMF*

A golly musical rattle, 1920s, 6½in (16.5cm) high.
£18–20 *HUX*

A knitted woollen golly car mascot, with orange ribbon, 1930s, 4in (10cm) high.
£10–12 *CMF*

A golly, made from pipe cleaners, 1930s, 3½in (9cm) high.
£10–12 *CMF*

A hand-made felt golly, c1940, in red jacket with striped trousers, 1940s, 5in (12.5cm) high.
£6–8 *CMF*

Constance Wickham, *My Teddy and Golly Board Book*, illustrated by E. Kennedy, 1940s, 10in (25.5cm) high.
£40–50 *CMF*

Florence K. Upton, *The Golliwogg in War*, c1903, 8in (20.5cm) high.
£65–75 *CMF*

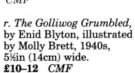

r. *The Golliwog Grumbled*, by Enid Blyton, illustrated by Molly Brett, 1940s, 5½in (14cm) wide.
£10–12 *CMF*

A two-faced golly, 1940s, 8½in (21.5cm) high.
£25–30 *CMF*

A cloth rag bag golly, c1940, 20in (51cm) high.
£35–45 *CMF*

This golly was made from various scraps of cloth including velvet from curtains and blackout cloth.

A Pelham golly string puppet, in striped jacket and beige trousers, 1950s, 13in (33cm) high.
£35–45 *CMF*

A homemade golly, with red and white checked trousers and blue shirt, 1960s, 17½in (44.5cm) high.
£25–30 *CMF*

A golly, made from a clothes peg, 1960s, 5½in (14cm) high.
£8–10 *CMF*

A Bulgarian golly, with label on foot, 1960s, 13½in (34.5cm) high.
£25–30 *CMF*

A Chad Valley golly, in navy jacket with striped trousers, 1960s, 13½in (34.5cm) high.
£25–30 *CMF*

A Dean's Rag Book golly, modelled as Mr Smith, with a white face, 1960s, 12in (30.5cm) high.
£65–75 *CMF*

This unusual golly is rare, hence its price range.

A *Golly's Magic Painting Book*, unused, 1960s, 6½in (16.5cm) high.
£6–7 *HUX*

r. Two golly road safety brochures, 1960s, 7¾in (19.5cm) wide.
£6–7 each *HUX*

l. A collection of Robertson's plaster golly musicians, 1960–70s, 3in (7.5cm) high.
£8–10 each *HUX*

A Robertson's golly plastic apron, 1970s, 20in (51cm) long.
£15–18 *CMF*

A hand-knitted woollen golly, with blue jacket, 1970s, 20in (51cm) high.
£15–18 *CMF*

A nylon golly, with red trousers and blue jacket, 1970s, 17in (43cm) high.
£18–22 *CMF*

A Robertson's plastic inflatable golly, 1980s, 21in (53.5cm) high.
£25–30 *HUX*

A nylon golly, with red trousers, yellow shirt and blue jacket, 1970s, 35in (89cm) high.
£35–45 *CMF*

Badges

A Robertson's golly badge, 1950s, 1in (25mm) diam.
£6–8 *SVB*

A golly badge, 1960s, 1in (25mm) diam.
£6–8 *HUX*

r. Two Golden Shred golly badges, depicting a golfer and a tennis player, 1960s, 1½in (40mm) high.
£10–15 each *HUX*

A collection of golly badges, 1970–80s, 2in (50mm) high.
£3–5 each *HUX*

HANDBAGS

The handbag is more or less 300 years old. From the Middle Ages onwards, purses were suspended from belts, and loose fabric pockets attached to tapes were worn both above and underneath skirts, which were slit at the sides to allow easy access. The handbag as we know it today did not emerge until the late 18th century. The new high-waisted, slim-line, neo-classical dresses, made of daringly diaphanous material, hugged the body, and made bulging pockets a sartorial impossibility. A new accoutrement emerged for the *à la mode* lady; a little drawstring bag, carried on a wrist strap and known as a reticule. Though cynics called them ridicules, the fashion stuck, and the handbag became an essential female accessory.

The handbags in this section date from the 1900s to the 1960s. Prices depend on age, shape (the more interesting the better), designer and condition (check the interiors of bags for staining and damage). Whereas collectors of 19th and early 20th century beaded purses tend to buy for display, collectors of less fragile items often use their collectables. The 1950s was a golden age for bag design (look out for perspex box bags and decorative baskets) and there is growing interest today for bags from the 1960s, in particular anything glamorous and space-age. Though at the top end of the market you can pay hundreds of pounds for a vintage Hermes, it is still possible to buy fun and usable handbags for under £10. Check out charity shops, car boot sales and vintage clothes dealers.

A Victorian red velvet bag, with plated frame and pinch clasp, 5in (12.5cm) high.
£25–30 *CCO*

A Victorian crocheted draw string purse, with cut steel decoration, 13½in (34.5cm) high.
£75–85 *Ech*

A late Victorian chain link bag, with tassel, 10½in (26.5cm) high.
£55–65 *Ech*

A French cut-steel multi-coloured bag, with metal clasp, early 1900s, 5in (12.5cm) wide.
£40–50 *CCO*

A Continental silver gilt purse, with import mark for London 1902, sponsor's mark Samson Mordan and Co, c1902, 4¼in (11cm) wide.
£250–275 *TC*

An Edwardian embossed leather bag, 8¼in (21cm) wide.
£40–50 *TT*

A cut-steel bag, with mother-of-pearl button, c1910, 2in (5cm) high.
£24–28 *CCO*

r. A yellow and black beaded evening bag, 1920s, 10in (25.5cm) high.
£10–15 *PC*

A yellow and red chain mail bag, with plastic clasp, 1920s, 5in (12.5cm) high.
£20–25 *PC*

A chain-work purse, with metal frame, in shades of red and yellow, 1920s, 5in (12.5cm) high.
£30–35 *Ech*

A beaded purse, with tortoiseshell frame, decorated with blue and yellow flowers, some damage, 1920s, 7in (18cm) high.
£20–25 *Ech*

A beaded bag, with silver-plated frame, decorated with black and red bugle beads, 1920s, 9in (23cm) high.
£30–35 *Ech*

A black satin embroidered bag, with bone handles, decorated with a pink rose, lined with pink grosgrain, 1920s, 11in (28cm) high.
£15–18 *Ech*

A tapestry bag, decorated with a geometric pattern in shades of blue, camel and black, c1930, 10in (25.5cm) wide.
£18–22 *PC*

A beaded and embroidered bag, c1930, 7in (18cm) high.
£15–18 *CCO*

A black leather bag, with yellow Bakelite clasp, 1930s, 9in (23cm) high.
£18–20 *PC*

A raffia work purse, decorated with flowers in shades of brown and green, 1930s, 5in (12.5cm) high.
£15–20 *SUS*

A fabric evening bag, with floral bordered lining, 1930s, 8in (20.5cm) wide.
£30–40 *TT*

A blue and white beaded bag, c1930, 7in (18cm) wide.
£15–20 *CCO*

A velvet purse, decorated with tan and brown embroidered woollen flowers, 1930s, 10¼in (26cm) wide.
£20–25 *SUS*

A Waldy quilted leather bag, 1940s, 7½in (19cm) wide.
£55–65 *LBe*

Waldy, who made handbags for the Queen, had a small factory in Tottenham Court Road, London.

A tan crocodile leather bag, with yellow perspex handle, c1940, 9in (23cm) high.
£30–40 *PC*

A navy blue leather bag, with chrome clasp, c1940, 8in (20.5cm) high.
£35–40 *PC*

A brown snakeskin bag, with chrome clasp, c1940, 6½in (16.5cm) high.
£40–45 *PC*

A mesh evening bag, 1940s, 8¼in (21cm) wide.
£30–40 *TT*

A brown snakeskin bag, with metal clasp, 1940s, 7in (18cm) high.
£40–45 *Har*

A multi-coloured sparkle bag, with expanding handle, c1940, 9in (23cm) wide.
£4–6 *CCO*

A circular white satin purse, decorated with beads, resembling a spider's web, with zip fastening, 1960s, 5½in (14cm) diam.
£4–6 *BOH*

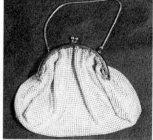

A white beaded purse, with gilt-metal clasp and handle, 1960s, 5½in (14cm) wide.
£20–25 *BOH*

l. A Pandora plastic sequinned bag, with satin lining, 1960s, 5in (12.5cm) high.
£4–6 *BOH*

A silver-plated purse, 1960s, 7in (18cm) wide.
£55–60 *RAC*

JEWELLERY
Bracelets

A Victorian silver bracelet, c1890, 7½in (19cm) long.
£350–400 *WIM*

A Victorian silver bangle, with gold inlay, engraved with flowers, c1870, 1¾in (45mm) wide.
£300–350 *WIM*

A Victorian ivory bracelet, with gold metal elephant, 3in (75mm) wide.
£18–22 *HEI*

A Russian 15ct gold chain bracelet, c1890, 6in (15cm) long.
£800–900 *WIM*

An Arts and Crafts bracelet, with 5 oval plaques embellished with foliage and set with rose quartz cabochons, with matching brooch, a pair of drop earrings and a ring, c1925, bracelet 7in (18cm) long.
£250–300 *P*

A 15ct gold gate bracelet, c1914, 7in (18cm) long.
£850–950 *WIM*

A 9ct gold chain bracelet, with padlock, c1918, 7in (18cm) long.
£450–500 *WIM*

Brooches & Pins

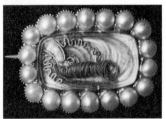

A gold mourning brooch, the outer rim set with pearls, the centre with plaited human hair, c1810, 1¾in (45mm) wide.
£100–120 *DIC*

A gold mourning brooch, set with pearls, in the shape of a basket, c1820, 1in (25mm) wide.
£200–250 *DIC*

A Victorian gold and ceramic scarf pin, painted with a mastiff, by William Bishop Ford, signed on reverse, 1in (25mm) diam.
£220–250 *AH*

l. A Victorian 15ct gold brooch, with inset central diamond and shell patterned edges, c1880, 2in (50mm) wide.
£600–700 *WIM*

FURTHER READING

Stephen Giles,
*Miller's Jewellery
Antiques Checklist*
Miller's Publications, 1997

A Victorian 15ct gold brooch, inset with a central pearl and diamonds, the outer rim cut with keyhole pattern, c1890, 1½in (38mm) wide.
£800–900 *WIM*

A Ruskin flambé glaze ceramic brooch, in a silver mount, late 19thC, 2in (50mm) wide.
£50–60 *SnA*

A sterling silver wing brooch, naturalistically fashioned with detailed plumage, marked with 'B', wings motif and 'Sterling', probably American, c1900, 4in (10cm) long.
£110–130 *P*

Name Brooches

Two Victorian silver name brooches, largest 1¾in (45mm) wide.
£35–40 each *SPE*

Two Victorian silver name brooches, largest 1¾in (45mm) wide.
£35–40 each *SPE*

Two silver name brooches, 1880–1920, 1½in (38mm) wide.
£45–65 each *FMN*

The value of these brooches depends on the name depicted, some are very popular and difficult to obtain.

Four Victorian silver name brooches, largest 1¾in (45mm) wide.
£35–40 each *SPE*

Five Victorian name brooches, 1¾in (45mm) wide.
£35–40 each *SPE*

Costume Jewellery

A yellow metal brooch and clip-on earrings set, modelled as inter-twined snakes, with open mouths and red glass eyes, the undersides painted in white, signed 'Art', c1970, brooch 3in (76mm) long.
£50–60 *PKT*

A Hattie Carnegie yellow metal openwork brooch, set with fixed and dropped pale blue diamanté and small round white glass beads, signed, c1950, 2¼in (57mm) long.
£95–110 *PKT*

A Ciner yellow metal brooch, in the form of a butterfly with pink veined glass wings, small multi-green stone body and pearl head, signed, c1960, 1½in (38mm) wide.
£120–135 *PKT*

l. A Coro pin, in the form of a fish, set with coloured stones, 1960s.
£200–250 *GLT*

A Marcel Boucher yellow metal openwork brooch, depicting a small dog, set with blue stone eyes, the head on a spring and wobbles as the brooch is moved, signed, c1955, 2in (50mm) wide.
£75–85 *PKT*

An Alice Caviness silver metal necklace, with 11 silver metal leaf drops highlighted in black, clasp replaced, signed, c1945, 14in (35.5cm) long.
£75–85 *PKT*

A Chanel pearl necklace and bracelet set, the bracelet with 6 glass leaf, bead and pearl posies, the necklace with a single posy with pearl and glass droplets, signed 'France', 1930s, necklace 14in (35.5cm) long.
£1,000–1,500 *GLT*

A Butler & Wilson yellow and white metal brooch, depicting a bird's head, set with white diamanté, signed, c1980, 3in (76mm) wide.
£120–140 *PKT*

A Chanel enamel brooch, in the form of a bouquet of red flowers with blue glass crystal centres and green leaves, signed 'Chanel', 1930s.
£450–500 *GLT*

A Christian Dior bracelet, brooch and earring set, made by Kramer, with white and lemon crystals in a chrome-plated setting, signed, 1950s, bracelet 7in (18cm) long.
£500–600 *GLT*

A Christian Dior yellow metal necklace, set with various shaped autumn-coloured diamanté and tiny pearl drops, made in Germany by Henkel & Grosse, signed, c1962, 14in (35.5cm) long.
£190–220 *PKT*

Costume Jewellery

The value of costume jewellery depends principally on the name of the designer. Always check on the back of a piece for a mark or signature. Some names to look out for include:

Boucher: US costume jewellery company, founded by former Cartier designer, Marcel Boucher, who emigrated from France to USA in 1925.

Hattie Carnegie (1886–1956): US fashion designer.

Coco Chanel (1883–1971): One of the first French couturiers to design costume jewellery as part of her fashion collections.

Coro: US company, founded in the early 1900s, one of the pioneers in creating affordable costume jewellery for the mass market.

Christian Dior (1905–57): Paris fashion designer and creator of the 'new look'.

Eisenberg: Chicago-based fashion house and jewellery manufacturer, established 1880.

Miriam Haskell (1899–1981): New York costume jewellery designer, particularly celebrated for *faux* pearls.

Joseff of Hollywood: Los Angeles company founded in 1930s, provided costume jewellery for Hollywood movies as well as retail pieces.

Kramer: New York company founded in 1943, manufactured Dior jewellery for the US market.

Elsa Schiaparelli (1890–1973): Italian fashion designer and creator of the colour 'shocking pink' which became her trademark.

Trifari: Rhode Island costume jewellery firm, founded in 1918, known for their imaginative high quality designs and celebrated for creating the jewellery worn by Mamie Eisenhower at the Presidential inauguration ball.

Weiss: US company established in 1942, known for high quality rhinestones.

An Eisenberg necklace and bracelet, set with rhinestones, signed, 1940s, necklace 14in (35.5cm) long.
£500–600 *GLT*

A Miriam Haskell 4-strand silver pearl and glass bead necklace, signed, 1950s, 14in (35.5cm) long.
£400–500 *GLT*

A Florenza yellow metal hinged bracelet, decorated with flower patterns set with white diamanté and pearls, with a central black cabochon stone, signed, c1955.
£100–120 *PKT*

A Miriam Haskell 3-strand silver baroque pearl necklace and earrings, the centre pendant and earrings set with pink and blue cut glass crystals, signed, 1960s.
£500–600 *GLT*

A Grosse yellow metal brooch, set with a single naturally-shaped green stone and 3 cloudy white tear drops, signed, c1966, 2in (50mm) long.
£50–60 *PKT*

A Hobe gilt-brass brooch, in the form of a basket, set with rhinestones, American, 1940s, 2in (50mm) diam.
£90–110 *PGH*

A pair of Hobe yellow metal earrings, set with baguette, oval and round diamanté, signed, c1960, 1¼in (32mm) diam.
£75–85 *PKT*

A Holly Craft yellow metal brooch and pair of earrings, set with variously shaped green diamanté, with green diamanté and pearl overlays, signed, c1953, 2in (50mm) long.
£165–185 *PKT*

A Joseff of Hollywood silver 'slave' bracelet, set with green crystals in silver mounts and chains, script, signed, 1930s.
£650–750 *GLT*

A Kramer bracelet, set with pink diamanté, the centre with baguette and marquis-shaped pink diamanté, signed, c1965, 7in (18cm) long.
£125–150 *PKT*

A Kramer brooch and earring set, the brooch set with round and marquis-shaped pink diamanté, with 2 aurora tear drops, the earrings set with various sized round and marquis-shaped pink diamanté with clip-on fastenings, signed, c1970, brooch 2in (50mm) diam.
£70–80 *PKT*

A Monet gilt pin brooch, with central amethyst crystal, American, signed, 1950s, 1½in (38mm) diam.
£40–50 *PGH*

A Napier yellow metal brooch, in the form of a bunch of grapes, set with tear drop shaped amethyst, signed, c1970, 2in (50mm) long.
£50–60 *PKT*

A Roberts Original yellow metal brooch, in the form of a spray of flowers, with pink enamelled petals and green enamelled leaves, the flower centre set with a pearl, signed, c1965, 3in (76mm) long.
£40–50 *PKT*

An Ora silver metal bracelet, with 7 segments, each joined with cruciform links, set throughout with white diamanté, signed, c1970, 7in (18cm) long.
£60–70 *PKT*

An Elsa Schiaparelli silver-plated metal bracelet, set with dark blue glass crystals, signed, 1940s, 7in (18cm) long.
£500–600 *GLT*

A St Labre silver metal brooch and pair of earrings, with metal leaves, set with green diamanté surrounded by matt black stones, the earrings of similar design with clip-on fastenings, signed, c1970, brooch 3in (76mm) long.
£40–50 *PKT*

An Elsa Schiaparelli yellow metal brooch, set with aurora crystals, signed, c1965, 3in (7.5cm) wide.
£175–200 *PKT*

A Sherman brooch, with clear rhinestones on rhodium-plated setting, American, 1930s, 2in (50mm) wide.
£60–80 *PGH*

A Vendome necklace and earring set, the three-strand necklace with yellow and orange Venetian beads interspersed with white aurora faceted beads and matching earrings, made for Coro, signed, c1965, necklace 15in (38cm) long.
£75–95 *PKT*

A Schreiner ruffle pin, set with green, orange and white stones, 1950s.
£150–200 *GLT*

A Trifari sunburst pendant, with *faux* topaz in yellow metal setting, signed, c1970, 2in (50mm) wide.
£60–70 *PKT*

A Vendome brooch, set with centre *faux* blister pearl, surrounded by pink diamanté, with an outside ring of large, faceted, smoky grey diamanté, signed, c1965, 3in (7.5cm) diam.
£65–85 *PKT*

l. A pair of Weiss earrings, set with faceted white diamanté, signed, c1950, ¾in (20mm) diam.
£55–65 *PKT*

A Schreiner pendant style necklace and pair of earrings, set with red, blue and green crystals in metal and oxydised mounts, signed, 1960s.
£400–500 *GLT*

A pair of Trifari earrings, set with centre single large white diamanté surrounded by smaller baguette diamanté in silver-coloured metal, signed, c1970, 1in (25mm) wide.
£35–40 *PKT*

A Weiss gold metal brooch, with a centre faceted amethyst diamanté, surrounded by marquis amethyst diamanté with green diamanté leaves, signed, c1965, 3in (7.5cm) long.
£85–100 *PKT*

Cuff Links

A pair of Victorian silver cuff links, in the shape of shamrocks, set with green agate.
£45–50 *SPE*

A pair of gold-plated brass cuff links, c1900.
£25–30 *JBB*

A pair of Edwardian 9ct gold cufflinks, Chester 1907.
£60–70 *TAC*

A pair of Indian silver cuff links, with painted ivory miniature under glass, c1900.
£100–125 *JBB*

A pair of cuff links, depicting a boxer dog, c1900.
£30–40 *JBB*

A pair of silver cricketing cuff links, 1930s.
£35–45 *JBB*

Necklaces & Pendants

An Arts and Crafts pendant and necklace, attributed to Sibyl Dunlop or Dorrie Nossiter, the faceted pear-shaped drop held within a mount of vine-leaves and berries set with cabochons of chalcedony, the whole suspended on chains interspaced with faceted beads and further mauve-stained chalcedony beads, c1925, pendant 2½in (6.5cm) long.
£850–1,000 *P*

A Victorian 15ct gold collar, c1880, 17½in (44.5cm) long.
£1,600–1,900 *WIM*

A Roman glass fragment pendant, with gold mount, 1990s, 1¼in (30mm) high.
£250–300 *JFG*

An Arts and Crafts enamelled necklace, with plaques shaped as stylised roses and picked out with green, blue and white enamels, terminating with enamelled batons with omega-shaped hook, c1895, 57½in (146cm) long.
£350–400 *P*

r. A white gold pendant, set with central pearl and rubies, c1935, 1in (25mm) diam.
£750–850 *GEM*

An Arts and Crafts pendant, with an oval plaque of lapis lazuli contained at the top within a simple foliate mount, c1925, 2¼in (6cm) long.
£200–220 *P*

Scottish Jewellery

In the second half of the 19th century, Queen Victoria's love of Balmoral, her passion for Scotland, its people and its customs, helped stimulate the fashion for Scottish jewellery. Miniature dirks (daggers) and Highland shoulder brooches were fashioned from silver and set with local agates (known as Scottish pebbles), with cairngorm (yellow quartz originally found on the Cairngorm mountains in Scotland) and with slivers of granite. Edinburgh was the principal centre of production, but as the craze for Scottish jewellery grew and spread across Europe it was also manufactured in Birmingham.

A Victorian Scottish silver brooch, in the shape of an owl and crescent moon, set with agate, 1½in (40mm) diam.
£40–50 PSA

A Victorian Scottish silver and citrine brooch, 1¾in (45mm) diam.
£60–70 SPE

A Scottish silver and hardstone brooch, 1860–80, 2in (50mm) diam.
£350–400 WIM

A Scottish silver and hardstone brooch, 1860–80, 1¾in (45mm) diam.
£350–400 WIM

A Scottish silver and hardstone bar brooch, 1860–80, 2½in (65mm) wide.
£425–475 WIM

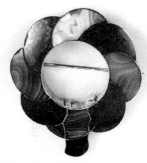

A Scottish silver and hardstone brooch, 1860–80, 2¼in (55mm) wide.
£350–400 WIM

A Scottish silver brooch, set with citrine thistles, 1860–90, 2in (50mm) diam.
£120–135 WIM

r. A Scottish silver pin, set with citrine and agate, 1¾in (45mm) wide.
£25–30 SPE

l. A Scottish 9ct gold brooch, set with citrine centre, ¾in (20mm) diam.
£50–60 SPE

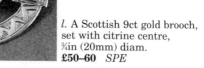

KITCHENWARE

A bell metal skillet, inscribed on handle 'T. P. B. Water', 18thC, 6½in (16.5cm) diam.
£150–175 *ANV*

A set of 3 Army & Navy graduated copper saucepans, late 19thC, largest 8in (20.5cm) diam.
£140–170 *MEG*

A copper saucepan lid, with handle, 19thC, 7in (18cm) diam.
£25–30 *No7*

A beech grain measure, c1850, 17in (43cm) diam.
£60–80 *COM*

A Victorian one gallon size copper measuring jug, 11½in (29cm) high.
£145–165 *ANV*

A pewter scoop, 19thC, 4in (10cm) long.
£5–6 *No7*

A Holts egg whisk, with side handle, c1890, 8in (20.5cm) long.
£25–35 *SMI*

A set of brass kitchen scales, c1890, 18in (45.5cm) wide.
£240–280 *CHe*

r. A green painted food safe, late 19thC, 29in (73.5cm) high.
£125–175 *CPA*

For smaller houses that did not have walk-in larders, the food safe provided a storage cupboard for fresh produce and meat. Gauze grilles allowed the air to circulate and freestanding safes often had legs to raise them off the ground out of the reach of rats and mice.

An oak cutlery tray, 19thC, 13in (33cm) long.
£85–100 *SMI*

Two miniature whisks, c1920, 6in (15cm) long.
£15–20 each *SMI*

A packet of Stag jam pot covers, 1930–40, 7½in (19cm) wide.
£3–4 *RAD*

l. A cream can, with brass lid, c1920, 4in (10cm) high.
£30–40 *SMI*

A green glass mixing jug, with beater and lid, c1920s, 12in (30.5cm) high.
£35–45 *MSB*

An American wood and leather cranberry scoop, c1920, 18in (45.5cm) long.
£130–150 *YAG*

A Tala icing set, c1940, syringe 6in (15cm) long, with tin box.
£10–15 *SVB*

r. An aluminium steam boat, by Tung Meng Co Ltd, Singapore, 1950s, 12in (30.5cm) diam.
£30–35 *No7*

A brass iron trivet, inscribed '60th Year of H.M. Reign', 1897, 5in (12.5cm) wide.
£60–80 *SMI*

An Aga double-oven white enamelled cooker, CB model, c1950, 38in (98cm) wide.
£2,500–2,700 *DOR*

In unrestored condition this would be worth £150–200. This one has been completely reconditioned (re-enamelled and re-chromed) hence the price. Thanks partly to the novels of Joanna Trollope, originator of the so-called 'Aga Saga', the Aga cooker has become one of the objects of desire of the 1990s, a symbol of middle-class rural life and comfort.

Bread

A sycamore bread board, carved with flowers and leaves, 19thC, 13in (33cm) diam.
£80–120 *SMI*

A collection of late Victorian, bread knives, with carved handles, 13in (33cm) long.
£25–30 each *SMI*

A sycamore bread board, decorated with carved lattice work and wheat sheaves, 19thC, 14in (35.5cm) diam.
£150–180 *SMI*

A bread board, c1910, 6½in (16.5cm) diam.
£35–40 *SMI*

A Sycamore carved bread board, 1920s, 12in (30.5cm) wide.
£25–30 *SMI*

Butter & Cheese

A Tyrolean elm cheese box, c1820, 8in (20.5cm) diam.
£65–85 *CPA*

A butter stamp in sleeve, 19thC, 3½in (9cm) diam.
£80–90 *No7*

Butter Markers

Butter stamps and rollers were used to decorate butter and also served as a trademark to distinguish one farm's produce from another.

r. An Italian cheese former, 19thC, 2¼in (5.5cm) high.
£20–22 *No7*

Cheese was wrapped in gauze or muslin, placed into the ring and then left to mature.

A butter roller, carved with a cow on the roller, 19thC, 7in (18cm) long.
£55–65 *SMI*

Two animal butter markers, 19thC, 4in (10cm) diam.
£55–65 each *SMI*

An oak cheese press and liner, 19thC, 8in (20.5cm) diam.
£80–90 *MTa*

A Shaker straw cheese drainer, c1890, 4in (10cm) high.
£190–220 *AWT*

Shaker items are very collectable, particularly in the USA. This humble, homemade, domestic product is very rare, hence its high price range.

l. A Continental pine iron-bound butter churn, 1880s, 39in (99cm) high.
£40–50 *HRQ*

An American cast iron and marble cheese scale and cutter, late 19thC, 20in (51cm) diam.
£220–250 *MSB*

A French terracotta cheese dish, c1890, 7in (18cm) diam.
£25–35 *CPA*

l. A Buttercup Dairy Co 5lb ceramic butter pot, c1910, 9in (23cm) diam.
£80–100 *SMI*

A ceramic cheese dish, handpainted with blue flowers on a white ground, c1930, 4in (10cm) high.
£20–25 *RAC*

A Maypole Dairy Co Ltd ceramic butter pot, with handle, c1910, 7in (18cm) diam.
£60–80 *SMI*

l. A ceramic butter slab, by Thomas Steen Ltd, Scale Makers, Burnley, c1930, 16½in (42cm) diam.
£150–200 *SMI*

Ceramics

A Derbyshire salt-glazed pipkin, c1840, 5½in (14cm) high.
£50–70 *IW*

A Davenport meat dish, with draining channels, mid-19thC, 21in (53cm) long.
£50–60 *CaC*

A Mochaware ceramic colander, c1870, 10in (25.5cm) diam.
£85–100 *SMI*

A late Victorian yellow ware colander, 9in (23cm) diam.
£30–40 *SMI*

A Royal Doulton banded milk jug, c1900, 10in (25.5cm) high.
£55–60 *SMI*

Two chef pie funnels, 1910–20, largest 5in (12.5cm) high.
£25–30 each *SMI*

Three milk savers, c1900–20, largest 6in (15cm) high.
£25–35 each *SMI*

Milk savers stopped milk from boiling over.

Two Cornish Ware storage jars, with blue and white bands, black shield mark, 1920–60s, 5¾in (14.5cm) high.
£25–35 each *AL*

FURTHER READING

Christina Bishop,
Collecting Kitchenware,
Miller's Publications, 1995

l. A Grimwades pudding basin, 1920s, 4in (10cm) high.
£65–75 *SMI*

An Allinson's rolling pin, 1930s, 18in (45.5cm) long.
£90–100 *SMI*

Two grey elephant pie funnels, 1930s, 4in (10cm) high.
£15–25 each *SMI*

Choppers & Crushers

Eighteenth century choppers were often very decorative, with carved handles and engraved and pierced iron blades. By the 19th century manufacture had become industrialised and designs were far simpler. Major centres included Sheffield in Yorkshire, where steel-bladed choppers were mass-produced along with other tools.

The choppers illustrated were used for chopping herbs and vegetables. Curved choppers were designed to be used with wooden bowls or mortars, and flat-bladed examples with chopping boards.

Two steel herb choppers, c1850, 7in (18cm) high.
£35–40 each *SMI*

A brass and steel herb chopper, with wooden handle, 19thC, 7in (18cm) high.
£45–50 *SMI*

A metal chopper, with wooden handle, 19thC, 6¼in (16cm) wide.
£15–20 *No7*

A metal herb chopper, with copper handle, 19thC, 4¾in (12cm) wide.
£30–35 *No7*

Three Victorian brass-handled herb choppers, largest 7in (18cm) wide.
£65–80 each *SMI*

A metal herb chopper, with wooden handle, 19thC, 6¼in (16cm) high.
£25–30 *No7*

Condition

Condition is important when it comes to value. Avoid pitted blades and check that handles have not been replaced. The design of the handle (particularly if decorative) affects price, and curved choppers are worth more if they come complete with their original bowl.

A wooden herb chopping block, c1870, 17in (43cm) wide, with original chopper.
£75–100 *JUN*

An American metal tobacco or sugar cutter, on wooden base, c1870, 7½in (19cm) high.
£280–320 *AWT*

A wooden herb crusher, c1900, 7in (18cm) long.
£15–20 *AWT*

Coffee Grinders & Makers

A Romanian coffee grinder, with original orange paint, c1860, 11in (28cm) high.
£85–100 *CPA*

A cast iron and brass coffee grinder, by Kenrick, c1870, 5in (12.5cm) high.
£70–80 *CHe*

A Tower Brand aluminium coffee percolator, 1930–40s, 8½in (21.5cm) high.
£1–3 *GIN*

A Cona chrome and glass coffee machine, 1950–60s, 10in (25.5cm) high.
£15–20 *GIN*

A German wooden coffee grinder, by Armin Trosser, c1940, 8½in (21.5cm) high.
£25–35 *CPA*

A Kenrick metal coffee grinder, c1950, 7in (18cm) high.
£25–35 *CPA*

Coffee Grinders

In 1815, the iron founder Archibald Kenrick patented a new box-type cast iron coffee grinder. His design was copied by numerous manufacturers and became the standard pattern for coffee grinders throughout the century. Coffee beans were placed in the brass bowl. This is the most vulnerable part of the grinder and should be checked for cracks.

Eggs

A Victorian egg bowl, inscribed 'New Laid Eggs', by Parnell & Son, Bristol, 10in (25.5cm) diam.
£120–150 *SMI*

Four Cornish Ware blue and white striped egg cups, c1950, 2in (5cm) high, and an egg separator c1930, 4in (10cm) diam.
£20–25 *SMI*

An Aynsley porcelain egg cup, decorated with Pagoda pattern, c1891, 2¼in (5.5cm) high.
£15–18 *AnS*

r. A wooden egg box, c1945, 7in (18cm) high.
£25–30 *SSW*

Enamel Ware

A set of 4 French storage jars, c1910, largest 7½in (19cm) high.
£60–70 *CPA*

A blue enamel salt box, c1900, 10in (25.5cm) high.
£35–40 *SMI*

A Victorian enamel hot water jug, with pewter lid and cane handle, 12in (30.5cm) high.
£35–45 *SMI*

r. A blue enamel cake tin, c1900, 9½in (24cm) diam.
£25–35 *SMI*

Kettles

A copper flat-back kettle, with side handle, 19thC, 5in (12.5cm) high.
£60–70 *ANV*

A brass kettle, with faceted spout, c1820, 11in (28cm) high.
£200–220 *ANV*

A brass kettle, with white ceramic handle, late 19thC, 10in (25.5cm)high.
£150–165 *ANV*

A Victorian cast iron and enamel kettle, 8in (20.5cm) wide.
£45–55 *SMI*

A brass kettle, with bound cane handle, late 19thC, 9¾in (25cm) high.
£60–80 *MEG*

An American copper kettle, with brass handle, 19thC, 13½in (34.5cm) high.
£160–190 *MSB*

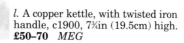

l. A copper kettle, with twisted iron handle, c1900, 7¾in (19.5cm) high.
£50–70 *MEG*

Moulds

A tin jelly mould, 19thC,
5in (12.5cm) high.
£25–30 *No7*

A copper jelly mould,
c1860, 5in (12.5cm) high.
£100–120 *SSW*

An tin ice cream mould,
19thC, 5¾in (14.5cm) high.
£40–50 *No7*

Three copper moulds, 19thC,
largest 2½in (6.5cm) high.
£15–18 each *No7*

Two copper ring moulds, 19thC:
l. 4½in (11.5cm) diam. **£55–65**
r. 6in (15cm) diam.   **£15–20** *No7*

An ironstone asparagus mould,
c1880, 7½in (19cm) long.
£90–110 *MSB*

A Continental copper mould,
late 19thC, 7in (18cm) diam.
£40–50 *FOX*

A Royal Doulton Paisley Flour
shortbread mould, 1920–30s,
7½in (19cm) diam.
£35–45 *SMI*

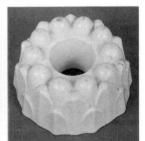

Two Shelley ceramic swan-
shaped jelly moulds, c1920,
largest 9in (23cm) long.
£180–200 each *SMI*

A Shelley ceramic rabbit-
shaped jelly mould, c1920,
10in (25.5cm) long.
£150–180 *SMI*

A Shelley ceramic
jelly mould, 1920–30,
6in (15cm) diam.
£15–20 *No7*

Spice Containers

A tole ware spice tin and central nutmeg grater, with brass handle, 19thC, 7in (18cm) diam.
£28–32 *No7*

A fruitwood spice container, 19thC, 9in (23cm) high.
£170–200 *GAK*

A set of painted pine spice drawers and salt box, c1810, 16in (20.5cm) high.
£175–275 *CPA*

A set of stained oak spice drawers, c1920, 9in (23cm) wide.
£80–120 *SMI*

r. A chrome toaster, 1930s, 7in (18cm) wide.
£40–50 *JUN*

Toasters

A Universal toaster, 1920s, 9in (23cm) wide.
£45–55 *JUN*

An Ediswan 841 toaster, 1930s, 9in (23cm) wide.
£35–40 *JUN*

A J. A. Brooke toaster, c1940, 7in (18cm) wide.
£30–40 *JUN*

A Swan 703 aluminium toaster, 1950s, 8in (20.5cm) wide.
£25–30 *JUN*

A chrome toaster, with green base, 1950s, 8in (20.5cm) wide.
£30–40 *JUN*

Toasters

The first electric toaster was made by the General Electric Company (USA) in 1913. Early models had no thermostat and burnt toast was a regular problem. This was resolved, to some extent, when American mechanic Charles Strite invented the automatic pop-up toaster in 1927.

r. A chrome toaster, c1960, 7¼in (18.5cm) wide.
£30–35 *GIN*

Vacuum Cleaners & Brushes

'Is your cleaner a museum piece?' demanded one early Hoover advertisement. 'If so, change now to the latest model.' Today obsolete vacuum cleaners have indeed become museum pieces (the Science Museum in London houses a fine collection) and also attract small numbers of collectors.

The first vacuum cleaner – 'the Puffing Billy' – was invented by Englishman Cecil Booth in 1901. The huge appliance arrived at the door by horse and cart, suction pipes were then passed through a window and operated by the white uniformed employees of Booth's British Vacuum Cleaner Company. This was such a novelty at the turn of the century that ladies would hold tea parties so that guests could watch the house-cleaning process. Booth's machine could scarcely be described as a labour-saving appliance, and it was an American, W. H. 'Boss' Hoover, who in 1908 patented the design for the upright bag and stick vacuum cleaner, the ancestor of today's familiar models. Hoover also pioneered the technique of door-to-door demonstrations and soon their products became known worldwide.

Vintage vacuum cleaners tend to appeal to collectors interested in design technology. Since the market is at present small, prices tend to be low, and good hunting grounds include car boot sales, junk shops and vacuum cleaner repairers, who often sell reconditioned old machines.

A Victorian japanned brush, 27in (68.5cm) long.
£35–40 *SMI*

A Victorian badger hair adjustable brush, 29in (73.5cm) long.
£20–25 *SMI*

r. A Vorwerk Multiplex vacuum cleaner, Type 13, 1950s, 54in (137cm) high.
£55–65 *GIN*

A late Victorian badger hair brush, 22in (56cm) long.
£15–20 *SMI*

l. A Whirlwind vacuum cleaner, Model-E, 1930s, 50in (127cm) high.
£15–25 *JUN*

A Hoover vacuum cleaner, model No. 750, c1930, 50in (127cm) high.
£25–35 *JUN*

A Hoover vacuum cleaner, c1930, 50in (127cm) high.
£25–30 *JUN*

A Hoover 100 Dustette hand-held vacuum cleaner, 1930s, 20in (51cm) long.
£25–35 *JUN*

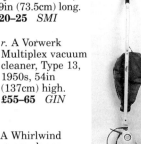

Washing & Ironing

A collection of wooden lace crimping boards, c1850, largest 8in (20.5cm) long.
£55–65 each *SMI*

A Beatty Red Star manual washing machine, early 1900s, 22in (56cm) high.
£200–250 *JUN*

A Beatty electric washing maching, with copper tank, c1930, 21in (53.5cm) diam.
£150–200 *JUN*

r. A Chappee No. 6 flat iron, c1910, 6in (15cm) long.
£10–12 *GIN*

A box iron, with original No. 2 slug, c1880, 2in (5cm) wide.
£125–150 *SMI*

A J. & J. Siddons cap iron, c1900, 3in (7.5cm) wide.
£35–40 *SMI*

A wooden ironing board, c1920, 43in (109cm) wide.
£40–50 *AL*

Three J. & J. Siddons irons, c1900, largest 3½in (9cm) wide.
£35–40 each *SMI*

A French sleeve iron, c1900, 12in (30.5cm) long.
£50–60 *SMI*

A Prilect travelling iron, 1950s, 5½in (14cm) long, with tin box.
£20–25 *PPe*

LIGHTING

An American papier maché lantern, modelled as a black cat's head, c1910, 6in (15cm) high.
£90–100 *AWT*

A brass hand-held paraffin lamp, c1880, 5¼in (13cm) high.
£15–20 *PC*

An engineer's brass space lamp, c1900, 5¼in (13cm) long.
£30–40 *PC*

r. A green plastic flash light, c1954, 4in (10cm) high.
£10–12 *JUN*

Candlesticks

A pair of brass candlesticks, with knopped stems and swirl bases, one split, 18thC, 8¼in (21cm) high.
£240–260 *P(B)*

A pair of George III brass candlesticks, c1800, 9in (23cm) high.
£165–185 *ANT*

A George III silver chamberstick, by William Bateman, with gadrooned rim and detachable sconce, complete with snuffer, marked for London 1808, 5in (12.5cm) diam.
£450–500 *GAK*

A Hukin & Heath electroplated chamberstick, in the manner of C. Dresser, the central cylindrical column flanked by an ebonised rod handle and detachable wick holder, stamped H&H 4876, c1880, 4¼in (11cm) high.
£300–350 *P*

A brass chamberstick, c1890, 2¼in (5.5cm) high.
£50–60 *CHe*

r. A pair of Arts and Crafts candlesticks, c1890, 14¼in (36cm) high.
£100–120 *GBr*

A pair of Edwardian brass portable candle holders, glass missing, 10in (25.5cm) high.
£20–25 *PPe*

A pair of WMF electroplated candelabra, each supporting 3 sconces on an ornate openwork frame cast with leaf and grape decoration, stamped maker's mark, c1900, 15in (38cm) high.
£375–425 *P*

A pair of brass candlesticks, c1915, 7¼in (18.5cm) high.
£300–320 *SUC*

Ceiling & Wall Lights

A brass saloon paraffin lamp, in gimbals, c1880, 11in (28cm) high.
£180–220 *PC*

A pair of cast brass double wall lights, c1900, 10in (25.5cm) high.
£600–650 *CHA*

A pair of brass lamps, by M. E. Stroud London, with Holophane crinoline moulded glass shades, c1913, 10in (25.5cm) diam.
£200–250 *DOR*

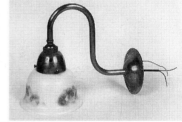

A pair of brass wall lamps, with milk glass shades, transfer printed with rose pattern, c1920, 10in (25.5cm) wide.
£160–190 *ML*

A double cherub light fitting, with original gilt finish, c1920, 24in (61cm) wide.
£600–700 *CHA*

Electric Lighting

Always check that electric lighting conforms to the current safety regulations.

r. A brass gas ceiling pole light, with milk glass coolie shade, 1920s, 22½in (57cm) high.
£90–100 *ML*

l. A French gilded brass chandelier, with reproduction glass shades, 1920s, 12½in (32cm) high.
£325–375 *ML*

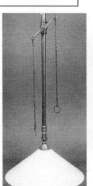

A set of 4 Art Deco wall lights, c1928, 11in (28cm) high.
£1,200–1,400 *DRU*

Table Lamps

A French glass and silver-plated electric lamp, modelled as a basket of fruit, c1890, 7½in (19cm) high.
£1,000–1,300 *PC*

A pair of Victorian silver-plated candle lamps, the domed chased bases and stems with crimped flange edges, with drip pans and pink satin glass shades, c1880, 14in (35.5cm) high.
£550–650 *GAK*

A Doulton oil lamp, c1900, 22½in (57cm) high.
£550–650 *MEG*

A porcelain oil lamp, the base modelled as a snowy owl, replacement shade ring, late 19thC, 20½in (52cm) high.
£320–400 *PC*

A brass table lamp, the base modelled as a boy, 1920s, 18in (45.5cm) high.
£180–220 *LIB*

A Snoopy table light, 1970s, 21in (53.5cm) high.
£20–25 *DUD*

An adjustable desk lamp, with marble effect finish, 1950s, 19in (48.5cm) high.
£30–45 *JUN*

Switches

Two Edwardian brass-topped electric light switches, largest 3½in (9cm) diam.
£15–25 each *JUN*

Two brass-topped light switches, 1930s, 3¼in (8.5cm) diam.
£8–10 each *JUN*

LUGGAGE & TRAVEL GOODS

A Victorian tin trunk, dated '25 Feb, 1875', 23in (58.5cm) wide.
£40–50 *AL*

A leather top hat box, with brass fittings, c1900, 11in (28cm) high.
£100–150 *JUN*

A leather military instrument case, c1900, 5in (12.5cm) square.
£25–30 *COB*

A wooden trunk, c1910, 36in (91.5cm) wide.
£30–40 *AL*

A leather trunk, with brass fittings, c1920, 36in (91.5cm) wide.
£45–55 *AL*

Two leather collar boxes, 1930s, largest 8in (20.5cm) diam.
£30–35 each *RIS*

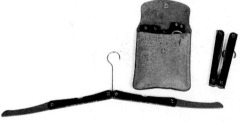

A set of 5 tin and cardboard folding travel hangers, in leather pouch, c1936, 5in (12.5cm) high.
£8–10 *GIN*

A canvas suitcase, with leather and metal fittings, initialled 'J. K.', 1940s, 26in (66cm) wide.
£50–55 *RIS*

A leather briefcase, with brass fittings, 1950s, 16½in (42cm) wide.
£40–45 *RIS*

Picnic Hampers

Picnic hampers were fitted out with crockery, cutlery, food containers and, eventually, a Thermos flask. The vacuum flask was invented by Scottish scientist Sir James Dewar in 1892. Early examples were expensive and the inner flasks were individually blown by glass makers. It wasn't until some 20 years later that the Thermos company (named after *therme*, the Greek word for heat) mechanised production and began to mass-produce affordableThermos flasks.

The development of motoring stimulated the production of picnic hampers as more families went on day trips. Particularly fine hampers can be found from the 1920s and 1930s, when Bakelite provided a colourful and practical addition to the more traditional ceramic and metal fittings. By the 1950s, Bakelite was being replaced by other types of plastic, though since hampers often tended to be luxury items, quality, even of later hampers, can be high. Price depends on age, condition and completeness of the fittings.

A Sirram picnic hamper, complete with contents, 1920s, 15in (38cm) wide.
£150–175 *PPH*

A Sirram picnic set, with Bakelite plates and cups, some pieces missing, 1920s, 19in (48.5cm) wide.
£150–175 *DRJ*

r. A Sirram picnic hamper, 1930s, 19in (48.5cm) wide.
£150–175 *PPH*

A Brexton picnic hamper, complete with contents, 1930s, 17½in (44.5cm) wide.
£250–275 *PPH*

A Sirram picnic set, 1930s, 23in (58.5cm) wide.
£150–175 *PPH*

A Brexton willow picnic hamper, 1950s, 23½in (58.5cm) wide.
£100–125 *PPH*

r. A Sirram picnic hamper, 1960s, 19½in (49.5cm) wide.
£65–75 *PPH*

l. A Brexton picnic hamper, 1960s, 23in (58.5cm) wide.
£100–120 *PPH*

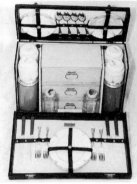

MAGAZINES & COMICS
Magazines

However fascinating vintage magazines might be in terms of nostalgia and social history, a large percentage of 20th century magazines can still be purchased for well under £10 each. A magazine can be judged by its cover and its value will be enhanced if it is designed by a well-known artist, features a famous photograph or a particularly desirable personality (eg Marilyn Monroe). First issues of magazines are desirable, as are commemorative numbers celebrating major national events such as coronations. Recently, there has been growing interest in vintage fashion and interior decoration journals, since the pictures and articles can provide a valuable research tool for identifying period items.

The current popularity of pin-up material among collectors has stimulated demand for girlie magazines, in particular examples featuring the nubile creations of famous illustrators such as George Petty and Alberto Vargas, both of whom worked for *Esquire* magazine.

Visitors to antique fairs or auctions will have seen vintage magazine advertisements framed and sold as pictures. Though this is clearly one way of profiting from a magazine, it destroys the journal itself as a historical entity. Magazines in mint condition should be left intact, and, as with books, unless a magazine is badly damaged, it is usually best not to remove the illustrations.

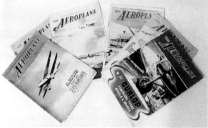

A collection of *The Aeroplane* magazines, 1930s, 14in (35.5cm) high.
£4–6 each *COB*

l. Harper's Bazaar magazine, December 1957, 12¾in (32.5cm) high.
£8–10 *RAD*

Home Notes magazine, January 1925, 9in (23cm) high.
£4–6 *SVB*

A collection of *British Chess* magazines, bound in volumes, 1881–97, 8in (20cm) high.
£50–100 each *FB*

This is the longest running magazine in Britain.

Esquire magazine, October 1951, 13¼in (33.5cm) high.
£10–12 *RAD*

l. Illustrated magazine, December 1955, 13½in (34.5cm) high.
£2–3 *RAD*

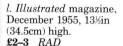

Harper's Bazaar magazine, June 1958, 11½in (29cm) high.
£8–9 *RAD*

l. The Illustrated London News, May 1935, 24in (61cm) high.
£8–10 *MAC*

Two *John Bull* Magazines,
1950s, 9in (23cm) high.
£1–2 each *RAC*

Lenz magazine, June
1964, 7in (18cm) high.
£7–8 *RAD*

A collection of *Lilliput* magazines,
No. 1–150, lacking 3 issues
(September 1943, December 1947
and October 1949), as issued with
original wrappers, staples rusted,
1940s, 8in (20.5cm) high.
£120–160 *DW*

Three *Meccano* magazines,
1950s, 12in (30.5cm) high.
£2–3 each *RAC*

My Weekly magazine, July
1931, 12in (30.5cm) high.
£4–5 *SVB*

Man's magazine, American,
April 1965, 10⅜in (26.5cm) high.
£1–2 *RAD*

Man Senior magazine,
August 1953, 12in
(30.5cm) high.
£7–8 *RAD*

News Review magazine, June
1948, 18½in (47cm) high.
£2–3 *PPe*

l. Picture Post magazine,
June 1957, 13in (33cm) high.
£5–8 *PPe*

Nova magazine, June 1973,
13½in (34.5cm) high.
£3–4 *RAD*

Picture Post magazine,
February 1940, 13in
(33cm) high.
£2–3 *RAD*

Playboy magazine,
February 1973,
11½in (29cm) high.
£10–12 *RAD*

The Queen magazine,
April 1961, 12½in
(32cm) high.
£8–10 *RAD*

Span Extra magazine,
Summer 1958, 7in
(18cm) high.
£7–8 *RAD*

Spick magazine,
No. 41, 1957,
7in (18cm) high.
£6–7 *RAD*

Spick and Span Extra
magazine, Autumn
1956, 7in (18cm) high.
£6–7 *RAD*

Girlie Magazines

The girlie magazine industry blossomed in the 1950s. In 1953, Hugh Heffner launched *Playboy* Magazine in the US and within a few years sales were verging on one million per issue, Playmate of the Month had become a national institution, and *Playboy* was attracting some of America's leading contemporary writers. British girlie papers were far less glamorous and sophisticated. *Spick and Span* magazines launched in 1953 and 1954 respectively, were comparatively tame publications, with minimal articles, modest poses and much airbrushing.

r. Woman and Home
magazine, July 1953,
12in (30.5cm) high.
£4–5 *SVB*

l. Swank magazine, July
1961, 11in (28cm) high.
£2–4 *SVB*

True Story magazine,
November 1939,
12in (30.5cm) high.
£4–8 *SVB*

l. Woman magazine, April
1948, 12in (30.5cm) high.
£5–6 *SVB*

Vogue magazine, July
1957, 13in (33cm) high.
£8–10 *RAD*

*r. Woman's
Illustrated* magazine,
February 1951,
12in (30.5cm) high.
£2–3 *RAD*

Comics

Amazing Spider-Man 1 comic, slight damage, 1963.
£650–750 *CBP*

Amazing Spider-Man 2 comic, 1963.
£140–160 *CBP*

Avengers comic, good condition, 1963.
£325–375 *CBP*

Beano comic, No. 21, first Christmas issue, 1938.
£150–200 *CBP*

The Broons comic, 1962, and *Oor Wullie*, 1969.
£40–50 *CBP*

Dandy comic, No. 9, 1938.
£300–350 *CBP*

Dandy Monster comic, 1950.
£120–150 *CBP*

Eerie comic, No. 8, 1952.
£50–60 *CBP*

l. More Fun comics No. 59, National Periodical Publications, some damage, September 1940.
£500–550 *S(NY)*

The Flash comic, No. 137, 1963.
£80–100 *CBP*

A collection of *Famous Funnies* comic books, Nos. 20–21, 29–35, 37, 39–82, March 1935, May 1941, good condition.
£1,200–1,400 *S(NY)*

l. Gem comic, Nos. 287–312, double Christmas issue, 1913.
£140–160 *CBP*

r. Justice League of America comic, No. 1, slight damage, 1960.
£400–450 *CBP*

A collection of *Jungle Comics*, Nos. 82, 84–98, 100–138, 140–160, 162–163, good condition, October 1946, September 1950.
£2,000–2,400 *S(NY)*

Knockout Fun comic, Book 1, 1st annual of Deed-A-Day Danny, 1941.
£100–120 *CBP*

Lois Lane comic, No. 13, 1959.
£45–55 *CBP*

Murderous Gangsters comics Nos. 2 and 3, 1951.
£140–160 *CBP*

Superman comic, No. 34, slight damage, 1945.
£250–270 *CBP*

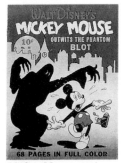

Mickey Mouse comic, No. 16, The Walt Disney Company, slight damage, 1941.
£750–850 *S(NY)*

A complete 2 year volume of *Wizard* No. 944–1014 comics, 1941–42.
£575–625 *CBP*

Superman comic No. 147, 1962.
£50–60 *CBP*

l. World's Best Comics, No. 1 with *World's Finest Comics*, No. 22, National Periodical Publications, slight damage, Spring 1941, May/June 1946.
£900–950 *S(NY)*

X-Men comic, No. 1, slight damage, 1963.
£275–325 *CBP*

MEDALS
Historical

A Charles II coronation gold medal, 1661, by Thomas Simon, slight rim indentation, 29mm diam.
£1,200–1,500 *DNW*

An Edmund Halley, astronomer, bronze medal, 1744, by J. Dassier, from his series of famous contemporaries, inscribed on reverse, 55mm diam.
£80–120 *EIM*

r. A John Philip Kemble, actor, bronze medal, 1798, by J. Hancock, inscribed on reverse, 36mm diam.
£40–60 *EIM*

l. A Captain Cook, Investigator of Oceans, silver medal, 1780, by L. Pingo, 43mm diam.
£300–400 *EIM*

An Admiral Cornelius Tromp silver medal, Naval Action against the English, 1666, by W. Muller, 78mm diam.
£800–875 *BAL*

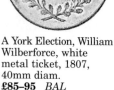

A York Election, William Wilberforce, white metal ticket, 1807, 40mm diam.
£85–95 *BAL*

r. A Westmoreland Election, Henry Brougham, silver ticket, 1818, by G. Mills, inscribed to reverse, 36mm diam.
£40–50 *BAL*

A Joshua Reynolds, President of the Royal Academy of Arts, silver medal, 1773, by J. Kirk, depicting a female artist seated at an easel on reverse, 31mm diam.
£150–200 *EIM*

An Anti-Slavery white metal medal, 1787, with enchained kneeling slave, inscribed 'Am I Not A Man and A Brother', 33mm diam.
£100–125 *BAL*

A Death of the Earl of Effingham silver medal, 1791, by J. Milton, with Britannia seated on globe on reverse, 35mm diam.
£100–120 *DNW*

A Phoenix Park, Dublin, white medal, 1841, by W. Woodhouse, with giraffe on face and conjoined busts on reverse, 32mm diam.
£30–40 *EIM*

A Royal National Lifeboat Institute, George IV, gold medal, 1841.
£1,300–1,500 *Gle*

This medal was awarded to Coastguard Commander Charles Steel for rescuing 3 women and one man shipwrecked at Scilly on 4th January, 1841.

A Westmoreland Kendal Agricultural Society silver ploughing medal, 1847, by S. C., with plough on face and inscribed 'To John Forsythe adjudged The Best Ploughman 1847' on reverse, 54mm diam.
£145–165 *BAL*

A Spencer's Captive Balloon, Souvenir of Ascent aluminium medal, 1868, unsigned, inscribed on reverse, 38mm diam.
£80–100 *EIM*

A Nasser-Ed-Deen, Shah of Persia, Visit to the City of London bronze medal, 1873, by A. B. Wyon, 77mm diam.
£150–175 *BAL*

A Brighton Aquarium Cat Show silver medal, 1885, by J. Restall, depicting 3 cats on face and inscribed to reverse, 38mm diam.
£60–80 *EIM*

l. A London College of Chemistry and Pharmacy silver medal, c1880, unsigned, inscribed on reverse, 55mm wide.
£40–60 *EIM*

A Richmond Camera Club
bronze medal, 1890,
unsigned, inscribed to
reverse, 50mm high.
£30–40 *EIM*

An Islington Agricultural
Hall silver-gilt medal, c1890,
inscribed on reverse,
unsigned, 52mm diam.
£80–100 *EIM*

A Birmingham and Midland
Counties Bulldog Club silver
medal, 1899, by T. Ottley, with
a bulldog standing in classic
pose, inscribed on reverse,
45mm diam.
£55–65 *BAL*

A Motor Union of Great
Britain and Ireland silver
medal, c1904, by H. Herkomer,
inscribed on reverse,
69mm diam.
£300–400 *EIM*

A Edinburgh Veterinary Medical
Society silver medal, 1907–08, by
A. Kirkwood, depicting a native
in traditional dress holding the
paw of a lion, inscribed to
reverse, 51mm diam.
£85–100 *BAL*

An Oxford Aviation Meeting
silver medal, 1914,
unsigned, inscribed on
reverse, 38mm diam.
£120–150 *EIM*

A National Pig Breeders
Association silvered bronze
medal, 1923, by Herbert Maryon,
depicting a pig with inscription
under 'Awarded to Colonel C. W.
Sofer-Whitburn', classical scene
to reverse, 46mm diam.
£50–60 *BAL*

A Stockton Darlington
Railway aluminium medal,
1825–1925, by J. Gaunt,
depicting Stephenson's
Rocket on face and George
Stephenson on reverse,
38mm diam.
£40–60 *EIM*

l. A Commissioning of RMS
Queen Mary bronze medal, by
G. Bayes, depicting New York
on reverse, 70mm diam.
£80–120 *EIM*

Military Medals

In terms of personal history family medals are priceless, but what makes a military medal valuable in financial terms and desirable to collectors?

'The most important factor is scarcity,' says specialist Jim Bullock. 'You've also got to look at the recipient (the person who was awarded the medal), what regiment they served in, and the campaign fought.'

The more celebrated and unique the event, the more desirable the medal, and within the same war prices for decorations can vary tremendously. 'Let's take the Crimea as an example,' says Bullock. 'A medal belonging to a bombadier in the Royal Artillery might fetch around £150–200, but one given to a cavalry officer who took part in the famous and tragic Charge of the Light Brigade could be worth £7,000 or more. Similarly, the Distinguished Flying Medal from WWII, if presented to someone for long service, might be worth £600–700, but if it was awarded to an RAF pilot for his part in the famous Dam Busters raid, values shoot up to between £4,000–5,000.'

Glamour and fashion affect the value of medals. *Zulu,* the classic film of 1964, starring Michael Caine, has been a major influence in inspiring demand for the South Africa 1877–9 medal awarded to a soldier who fought at Rorkes Drift, currently worth around £7,000. Most people, however, are unlikely to have such rarities lurking in the family home. 'One of the most common medals,' explains Bullock, 'is the WWII Africa Star, which was awarded to everyone who served in Africa, wasn't inscribed with the recipient's name, and is only worth around £5. WWI British War and Victory medals were also produced in their millions and fetch around £10 although a medal will be worth more if its recipient died on the first day of the Battle of the Somme.'

Condition is not as important with medals as it is with coins. 'A bugle boy might have been awarded his first medal at the age of 15 and then wore it for decades throughout a long and distinguished military career, so you have to expect a little bit of wear and tear,' says Bullock. This same bugle boy might have ended up with a whole row of decorations on his chest, and these various medals should be kept together. 'It's a cardinal sin to take one medal away from another,' concludes Bullock. 'Medals are worth more as a group and give the whole story of the man. It's this sense of history that is the real fascination of medal collecting.'

A Waterloo silver medal, 1815.
£600–650 *WAL*

Awarded to Thomas Novis, 1st Reg Dragoon Guards, who was wounded at Waterloo.

A Baltic silver medal, 1854–55.
£60–80 *RMC*

Awarded to J. White.

An Indian General Service medal, 1854–95, with bar 'Chin-Lushai 1889–90'.
£100–110 *RMC*

Awarded to Pte J. Stevely, King's Own Scottish Borderers.

A South Africa silver medal, 1877–79.
£450–500 *WAL*

Awarded to 1098 Pte H. Cooper, 2nd Dragoon Guards.

An Afghan medal, 1878–80.
£60–80 *RMC*

Awarded to the 25th Regiment.

An Egypt medal, with bar 'Gemaizah 1888', and a Khedives Star.
£130–150 *RMC*

Awarded to Stoker W. Shannon, Royal Navy.

A Distinguished Service Order (George V), Queen's South Africa medal, British War medal, 1989–1902, Victory medal with Mentioned in Dispatches emblem, Territorial War medal and Territorial Decoration (George V), 1914–18.
£800–875 *RMC*

A Military Cross (George V), British War medal, Victory medal, 1914–18 and Defence medal, 1939–45.
£375–400 *RMC*

Awarded to Capt H. T. Sampson, Royal Field Artillery.

l. A British War medal, 1914–18, Victory medal, Defence and a Civil Defence medal, 1939–45.
£40–50 *RMC*

Awarded to Pte C. R. Hart, Norfolk Regiment and Civil Defence.

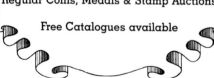

A Distinguished Service Cross (George VI), 1944–45, reverse engraved, France and Germany Star, 1939–45, and Defence and War medals, together with recipient's passport, Chinese ID card, 4 copies of the *London Gazette* listing award, letter from Admiralty dated '18.4.1945' regarding award and transmission letter from Buckingham Palace.
£450–500 *WAL*

Awarded to Commander Frank Scurr, DSC, RNR, Normandy 1944–45.

r. A Queen's and a United Nations Korea medal, 1950–53.
£65–80 *RMC*

Awarded to Gnr D. B. Harvey, Royal Artillery.

MEN'S TOILETRIES

A rosewood and brass-banded military shaving set, with contents, 1860–70, 7in (18cm) long.
£140–160 *SPU*

A Wardonia gentleman's Bakelite shaving set, 1930s, 5in (13cm) wide.
£10–12 *Ech*

A Victorian mahogany shaving case, with contents, 8½in (21.5cm) long.
£140–160 *SPU*

A Wardonia Bakelite shaving set, 1950s, 3½in (9cm) wide.
£15–20 *SVB*

A ceramic moustache cup, transfer-printed in colours, with gilded decoration, c1930, cup 4in (10cm) high.
£15–20 *WEE*

The moustache cup was a 19thC invention, the guard over the rim designed to protect a gentleman's moustache whilst drinking.

A Hygex personal brush, 1950s, 5in (13cm) wide, with original box.
£5–8 *SVB*

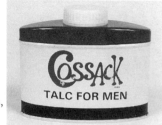

r. A tin of Cossack talcum powder, 1960s, 3½in (9cm) high.
£6–8 *HUX*

A nickel-plated shaving mirror and stand, c1900, 15in (38cm) high.
£90–100 *JUN*

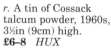

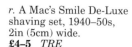

r. A Mac's Smile De-Luxe shaving set, 1940–50s, 2in (5cm) wide.
£4–5 *TRE*

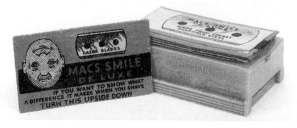

MILITARIA

A bronze and brass powder flask, c1870, 8in (20.5cm) long.
£65–75 *WAB*

A silver snuff box, the lid chiselled with an oak leaf and acorn pattern, initials to lid 'W.M.B.', foliate engraved decoration overall, gilt interior, London 1864, 2½in (6.5cm) wide.
£475–525 *WAL*

An engraved inscription to the base reads 'W. M. Boase Esqre MD from Gordon H. L. Pellew XIth Hussars, in remembrance of many acts of kindness during a long minority 13th Septr 1866'.

An Abyssinian shield, 19thC, 18in (45.5cm) diam.
£250–300 *GV*

A black leather gas mask handbag, 1939, 9in (23cm) high.
£15–20 *PC*

A WWI British tank driver's mask, leather-covered front, narrow metal eye slits, chain mail mouth guard, chamois lined, with cord ties, c1916, 7in (18cm) wide.
£200–250 *PC*

A painted brass side drum, of the 2nd (City of London) Regiment, The Royal Fusiliers, with badges, titles and battle honours to 1918, 14in (35.5cm) diam.
£250–300 *WAL*

On September 3, 1939, Great Britain and France declared war on Germany. Two days later Queen Elizabeth was photographed carrying her gas mask on an official visit to the Red Cross in London. This was an important publicity stunt, since in spite of fears of gas raids, many people were reluctant to carry the cumbersome masks with them. Masks were supplied in cardboard boxes, but the more stylish, and wealthier people commissioned specially-designed handbags. The distribution and checking of gas masks was one of the responsibilities of the wardens of the ARP (Air Raid Precautions).

An ARP poster, 'Looks to You, for the Women's Voluntary Services', 1939, 15in (38cm) high.
£40–50 *PC*

An aluminium and red and blue plastic cigarette case, c1945, 5½in (14cm) wide.
£35–45 *TIH*

This is an example of items made by Italian and German prisoners-of-war in North Africa during WWII utilising available materials, eg mess tins and old aeroplanes etc.

A Nazi grey cloth car pennant, with embroidered Nazi eagle, white roped border, metal bar inner frame, some wear, c1940, 12in (30.5cm) wide.
£150–175 *WAL*

Badges & Plates

A Victorian silver Royal
Sussex 1st Vol Battalion
helmet plate, 4in (10cm) high.
£120–140 *PC*

A gilt-metal and silver officer's
shako plate, The Buffs, East
Kent Regiment, c1870,
2½in (6.5cm) high.
£150–200 *PC*

A post-1902 3rd (Queen
Alexandra's Own) Gurkha
Rifles officer's silver pouch belt
badge, Birmingham 1912.
£240–260 *WAL*

A Victorian gilt and silver-
plated York & Lancaster
Regiment officer's helmet
plate, 4in (10cm) high.
£350–380 *WAL*

A Calcutta Scottish silver plaid
brooch, c1920, 4in (10cm) wide.
£180–200 *PC*

r. A Highland Light Infantry
silver dirk belt plate, bearing
'71' in the curl of the bugle,
by Wilson & Sharp Ltd,
Edinburgh, marked
'Regimental' on the back,
Edinburgh 1927, some wear.
£80–100 *WAL*

A 15th Battalion Canadian
Expeditionary Forces
bronze cap badge, 1914–19,
3in (7.5cm) high.
£30–40 *PC*

**Miller's is a price GUIDE
not a price LIST**

l. A formation sign 14th Army (Burma) officer's bullion cloth
badge, c1940. **£10–12**
r. A pair of Eastern Command cloth badges, 1944–47.
£8–12 *PC*

A 16th Lancers white metal
and brass cap badge, c1958.
£8–10 *PC*

Edged Weapons

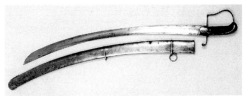

A 1796 pattern cavalry trooper's sword, with steel stirrup hilt and leather grip, original steel scabbard, blade 32¼in (82cm) long.
£250–300 *GV*

A Nepalese kukri, with horn hilt and silver-mounted velvet-covered scabbard decorated with flowers and animals, c1900, blade 10¼in (26cm) long.
£240–280 *GV*

A Japanese tanto, the *saya* and *tsuka* covered with figures in a landscape, Meiji period, 1868–1911, 10in (25.5cm) long.
£325–375 *GV*

A cavalry trooper's heavy sword, with straight fullered blade, iron pommel and wooden grip, c1780, 40½in (103cm) long.
£500–600 *WSA*

A 1788 pattern 17th Light Dragoons sword, with curved bi-fullered single-edged blade, steel stirrup and ebony grip, well worn, 1788, 35½in (90cm) long.
£1,400–1,600 *WAL*

This sword belonged to Capt William Jephson who was appointed Cornet August 1780, Lieutenant in July 1787 still in the 17th Regiment of Light Dragoons.

A British 1834 pattern Rifle Volunteer's sword, c1842, 38in (96.5cm) long.
£150–200 *GV*

A Malayan kris, with chiselled brass cup, wooden garuda hilt and grained wooden sheath with ivory tip, 19thC, 14¼in (36cm) long.
£120–140 *WAL*

l. An Indian bone-handled *pesh kabz*, with leather-covered wood scabbard, c1870, 13in (33cm) long.
£50–70 *GV*

A Scottish dirk, with carved basket-weave hilt, orange stone mounts and companion knife and fork, 19thC, 18⅝in (47.5cm) long.
£450–500 *GV*

A French 1874 pattern gras bayonet, with scabbard, dated '1879', 25½in (65cm) long.
£40–50 *WSA*

A Nazi officer's dirk, with etched double fullered blade, gilt mounts, white grip, gilt sheath with bullion dressed knot and hanging straps, by Eickhorn, c1940, 15¾in (40cm) long.
£300–350 *TMA*

Helmets & Caps

A cabasset, formed in one piece with pear stalk finial to crown, brass rosettes around base, good condition, c1600, 7½in (19cm) high.
£200–240 *WAL*

An officer's khaki service dress cap, with red felt band and bullion insignia, c1935.
£40–45 *FAM*

A Civil Defence beret, 1939, 9in (23cm) wide.
£20–25 *PC*

A 36th Division officer's khaki slouch hat, silk puggaree with purple flash, liner marked 'Failsworth Hats Ltd, 1945' with ink name 'Lt C. F. Hobdell' and 'Major C. F. Hobdell', minor wear and age marks, 1940s.
£110–130 *WAL*

A Royal Artillery Militia officer's blue cloth ball-topped helmet, with silver-plated 'M' below the cannon and velvet backed chinchain and ear rosettes, in a round tin case, good condition, 1902–08.
£500–550 *WAL*

A German Luftwaffe NCO's cap, with regimental stamps inside, c1937.
£180–200 *FAM*

A Civil Defence side cap, c1940, 12in (30.5cm) wide.
£20–25 *PC*

A 1st Aid Post helmet, c1940, 11½in (29cm) diam.
£15–20 *PC*

A Gloucestershire Regiment officer's blue cloth peaked forage cap, with black lace headband, gilt badge and leather and silk lining, slight service wear, late 19thC.
£300–350 *WAL*

This cap is initialled inside 'JDC': James Duff Coghlan, Lt 1871, Capt 1881 seconded to Commissariat Dept, Retired Maj 1889.

An Imperial German Württemberg NCO's peaked cap, with navy blue crown, scarlet band and piping, both cockade badges, maker's label 'Otto Knecht Heilbronn', early 20thC.
£100–120 *WAL*

A Royal Artillery Mk1 helmet, with regimental flash, c1940.
£20–25 *FAM*

A German Luftwaffe blue/grey serge and brown sheepskin cap, c1940.
£80–90 *FAM*

Uniform & Military Dress

An Imperial German Zeppelin crew navy blue jacket, with cloth badges to left sleeve of Zeppelin oval badge and single chevron in yellow cloth, black cloth lining stamped in red print 'B.A.K. 18.3.04.2 I.W.2.A 1616 04' with cloth name tag 'Bruggemann', c1900.
£550–600 *WAL*

r. An ARP vicar's armband, with a white cross and red lettering on blue cloth, c1939, 15in (38cm) long.
£30–40 *PC*

A pair of RAF black leather flying boots, with sheepskin lining, late 1930s.
£90–110 *FAM*

A pair of RAF leather and suede escape boots, with sheepskin lining, c1940.
£80–100 *FAM*

The tops of these boots can be removed to make them into shoes.

A light khaki wool army pullover, c1943.
£15–20 *FAM*

A Women's Voluntary Service green cloth armband, with red lettering, c1940, 7in (18cm) wide.
£15–20 *PC*

ARPs

Air Raid Wardens were volunteers and approximately one in 6 of them were women. Their jobs ranged from ensuring that blackout procedures were properly enforced, to providing first aid to the wounded and investigating unexploded bombs.

A khaki wool collarless army shirt, c1943.
£15–20 *FAM*

l. An ARP overcoat, c1942, 34½in (87.5cm) long.
£15–20 *PC*

A Civil Defence Guildford male warden's jacket, c1944, 19½in (49.5cm) long.
£40–45 *PC*

MONEY BOXES

A Victorian pig money bank, c1860, 8in (20.5cm) long.
£55–65 *BEV*

A cast iron Little Joe money bank, c1880, 5½in (14cm) high.
£70–80 *CHe*

A pottery money box, decorated with a child feeding hens with greyhound head handles, marked 'Ernest 29th April 1890', 4in (10cm) high.
£125–150 *ANV*

An American cast iron money box, c1881, 5in (12.5cm) high.
£100–140 *MRW*

l. A Scottish brown glazed Johnny Souter money box, c1880, 4½in (11.5cm) high.
£45–50 *ANV*

A cast iron dog money box, c1900, 5½in (14cm) wide.
£60–80 *CHe*

A celluloid dog money box, 1920s, 5in (12.5cm) high.
£10–15 *RAC*

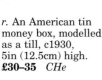

A George V coronation money box, 1911, 7in (18cm) high.
£90–100 *CHe*

r. An American tin money box, modelled as a till, c1930, 5in (12.5cm) high.
£30–35 *CHe*

A tin money box, modelled
as a fireplace, 1930s,
4¾in (12cm) high.
£55–60 *CHe*

A brass money
box, modelled as
a post box, c1930,
4¾in (12cm) high.
£20–25 *CHe*

Two Rye Pottery money boxes, modelled as
owls, designed by David Sharp, 1947–56,
5½in (14cm) high.
£15–20 each *GIN*

A Rye Pottery squirrel
money box, designed by
David Sharp, 1947–56,
8½in (21.5cm) high.
£30–35 *GIN*

A brass money box,
in the form of a
telephone box,
souvenir from
Kenilworth, c1950,
5½in (14cm) high.
£35–40 *CHe*

A tin money box,
modelled as a clock,
1950s, 3½in (9cm) diam.
£18–22 *WAB*

A money box, with
a wobbly head on
a spring, 1950s,
5in (12.5cm) high.
£16–18 *RAD*

A blue plastic piggy bank,
1960s, 6½in (16.5cm) long.
£5–7 *DUD*

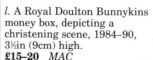

A Liverpool Trustee Savings
Bank money box, 1970–80,
4½in (11.5cm) high.
£4–5 *GIN*

l. A Royal Doulton Bunnykins
money box, depicting a
christening scene, 1984–90,
3½in (9cm) high.
£15–20 *MAC*

A plaster Snoopy Bristol &
West money box, 1970s,
5in (12.5cm) high.
£5–10 *PPe*

A ceramic mug, depicting a 2-2-0 locomotive, 'Fury', c1840, 3½in (9cm) diam.
£340–380 *SRA*

Les Gamineries de Toto, published by Van Leer & Co, c1900, 9¾in (25cm) high.
£80–100 *SRA*

The Railway Train, c1880, and *The Railway Engine*, c1900.
£200–250 *SRA*

Sheet music for 'After Dark, Galop', c1870, 13½in (34cm) high.
£160–200 *SRA*

A GWR 150 piece jigsaw puzzle, 'The Railway Station', 1930s.
£220–260 *SRA*

The Train Scrap Book, 1920–30s, 10¼in (26cm) wide.
£80–100 *SRA*

Sheet music for 'Oh! Blow the Scenery on the Railway', c1910, 14¼in (36cm) long.
£60–80 *SRA*

My Book of Trains, c1920, 10¾in (27cm) high.
£40–50 *SRA*

A Railwaymen's Convalescent Home souvenir book, c1905, 7in (18cm) long.
£7–10 *BAf*

A collection of railway signs, consisting of a nameplate, cabside number plate, works plate and bunker letters, c1955.
£2,700–3,000 *SRA*

A Midland Railway signal instrument, c1910, 18in (45.5cm) high.
£70–80 *SRA*

A British Railways (Southern) poster, 1963, 40in (101.5cm) high.
£110–130 *RAR*

A set of 5 Beatles liquorice records, in original sleeves, 1960s, 4¾in (12cm) high.
£220–250 *SAF*

A Beatles car seat cover, Dutch, 1960s, 30in (76cm) high.
£150–200 *BTC*

A Beatles mirror and brush set, and a paperweight, 1960s, mirror 8½in (21.5cm) high.
£50–60 *SAF*

A Thermos *Yellow Submarine* lunch box, 1960s, 9in (23cm) wide.
£150–200 *CTO*

Joyce Bond, 'Soul and Ska', EP record, 1968.
£60–80 *TOT*

Suzy and the Red Stripes, alias Linda and Paul McCartney, 'Seaside Woman', limited edition record, c1977, 10½in (26.5cm) wide.
£25–30 *CTO*

An Airfix Monkeemobile kit, c1967, 10in (25.5cm) long.
£80–100 *CTO*

Elvis Presley's Gretsch Chet Atkins Country Gentleman Guitar, Serial No. 24755, 1965.
£36,000–40,000 *Bon*

Elvis Presley's blue and white wool jacket, worn in the film *Speedway*, with verification of authenticity, 1968.
£7,000–8,000 *Bon*

Two Jimi Hendrix hand bills, *l.* Grand Ballroom, c1969, *r.* Fillmore auditorium, 7in (18cm) high.
£100–130 each *CTO*

Elvis Special 1968, 10in (25.5cm) high.
£8–10 *SVB*

A mid-Georgian mahogany apothecary's box, with 4 drawers, bottles not original, 19thC, 8in (20.5cm) wide.
£550–650 *TMA*

A pair of French enamelled opera glasses, with original leather case, early 19thC, 4in (10cm) wide.
£300–350 *BIG*

A Victorian apothecary's box, by E. Gould and Son, with various medicine bottles, 10in (25.5cm) wide.
£250–300 *HYD*

A Campbell-Stokes Mk 2 brass sunshine recorder, by Casella, c1930, 8in (20.5cm) long.
£550–650 *RTw*

A Victorian model single cylinder horizontal steam engine, 16in (40.5cm) long.
£200–250 *JUN*

A Spartan 'Viking' fan, with steel blade and guard, 1920s, 12in (30.5cm) high.
£20–25 *MRo*

A Larm-U electric fire alarm, with original box, 1930s, 4in (10cm) square.
£20–25 *JUN*

A copper and brass three-bar electric fire, 1920s, 21in (53.5cm) high.
£50–70 *JUN*

A Gilda electric hairdryer, 1950s, 21in (53.5cm) high.
£100–130 *JUN*

An oak-cased barograph, with lacquered movement, by Negretti and Zambra, c1920, 16in (40.5cm) wide.
£650–700 *RTw*

An Olivetti adding machine, with handle, 1960s, 11in (28cm) long.
£15–18 *GIN*

Sheet music for 'The Baby's Opera A Book of Old Rhymes', by Walter Crane, 1877, 7in (18cm) square.
£90–100 *RAC*

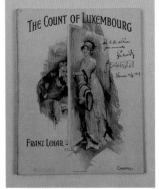

Sheet music for 'The Count of Luxembourg', by Franz Lehar, first edition, 1939, 11in (28cm) high.
£200–220 *HB*

Two volumes of sheet music for 'The Great Operas', with leather-bound and gilded covers and hand coloured plates, c1890, 10in (25.5cm) high.
£600–700 *HB*

Sheet music for 'The Apostles', by Edward Elgar, dated 'November 1913', 10in (25.5cm) high.
£500–600 *HB*

Sheet music for 'Isn't it Romantic', from *Sabrina Fair*, 1954, 11in (28cm) high.
£2–3 *RAD*

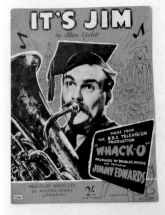

Sheet music for 'It's Jim', by Alan Yates, from *Whack-O*, 1950s, 8½in (21.5cm) high.
£2–3 *SVB*

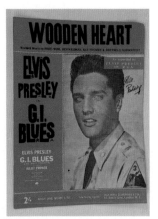

Sheet music for 'Wooden Heart', from *GI Blues*, 11in (28cm) high.
£7–8 *RAD*

Sheet music for 'I Believe', from *It happened in Brooklyn*, 10in (25.5cm) high.
£3–4 *RAD*

Two Victorian maritime pictures in shellwork frames, 21in (53.5cm) high.
£120–140 each *BSA*

A ship's log, by G. Bening, c1930, 19in (48.5cm) long.
£250–300 *NC*

An electric table lamp, in the form of a galleon, 1930s, 11in (28cm) high.
£45–55 *ML*

A Bakelite and plated ship's souvenir jam container, c1950, 3in (7.5cm) high.
£20–30 *NC*

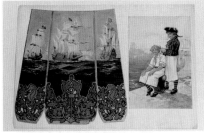

Artwork for a ship's menu, 1920s, 16in (40.5cm) high.
£50–75 *COB*

A 3 circle micrometer sextant, by Henry Hughes, 1944, 10in (25.5cm) high.
£400–500 *NC*

A Royal Navy silk effect vanity bag, 1930s, 10in (25.5cm) wide.
£30–40 *COB*

A Russian mahogany double-cased chronometer, c1989, 9in (23cm) square.
£800–1,000 *NC*

A collection of six ships badges, 1950–80, largest 10in (25.5cm) high.
£10–30 each *NC*

A brass passageway lamp, 1960s, 8in (20.5cm) high.
£50–60 *GWA*

A Russian star globe, with English lettering, c1956, 10in (25.5cm) square.
£350–400 *NC*

A late Georgian copper wine
funnel, 8½in (21.5cm) high.
£50–70 *MEG*

A brass pouring pot, with side
handle, mid-19thC, 7½in (19cm) high.
£150–200 *ANT*

A set of 4 silver salts and
spoons, boxed, late 19thC,
6in (15cm) wide
£245–275 *WAC*

A set of brass scales, with
malachite pans, by Asprey,
c1870, 7in (18cm) wide.
£300–320 *CHe*

A set of 12 fruit knives and
forks, with ivory handles,
c1880, 10in (25.5cm) long.
£240–280 *PSA*

A gold-plated scent case, in
the form of a house, c1890,
6in (15cm) high.
£400–450 *LBr*

A silver-gilt pincushion, in the
form of a crown, on a domed
silver base, Birmingham 1910,
3¾in (9.5cm) diam.
£130–160 *GH*

A silver sugar bowl and
tongs, Birmingham 1885,
3⅛in (9cm) diam.
£250–270 *AMH*

A cold-painted bronze robin,
1920–30, 1¼in (3cm) high.
£25–35 *MAC*

A silver pincushion, in the form
of a billiard table, 1910, 3½in (9cm) long.
£320–360 *GH*

A silver and gilt salt set
with spoons, Birmingham
1903, 6¼in (16cm) long.
£170–200 *WAC*

Receive 12 issues for the price of 10 or 25 issues for the price of 20

To take advantage of this special offer, or to send a gift subscription, just complete the form below. Or call our CREDIT CARD HOTLINE on 01795 414713

BBC HOMES & ANTIQUES MAGAZINE SUBSCRIPTION ORDER FORM

☐ *I would like to subscribe to* **BBC Homes & Antiques** *magazine for 12 issues at £22.00*
☐ *I would like to subscribe to* **BBC Homes & Antiques** *magazine for 25 issues at £44.00*

Your details (essential)

Title.................Full Name ....

Address...

.........................Postcode ....Daytime Tel No ....

I wish to pay for ....subscriptions at the total price of.............................

I would like to pay by ☐ Cheque   ☐ Credit Card (☐ Visa ☐ Access)   ☐ Switch/Delta/Connect

Please make cheques/postal order payable to **BBC Homes & Antiques Magazine**

Card number ☐☐☐☐☐☐☐☐☐☐☐☐☐☐☐☐☐☐☐☐

Valid from ☐☐☐☐   Expiry date ☐☐☐☐   Switch issue number ☐☐

Signature.................................Date ....

☐ *I would like to send a gift subscription to* **BBC Homes & Antiques** *magazine for 12 issues at £22.00*
☐ *I would like to send a gift subscription to* **BBC Homes & Antiques** *magazine for 25 issues at £44.00*

Gift recipient's details (Please continue on a separate sheet if necessary)

Title.................Full Name ....

Address...

.........................Postcode ....

Offer ends December 31st 1998

NB Please continue to buy the magazine until you receive your subscription acknowledgement letter.

Please state your credit card billing address on a separate sheet if different from above. Subscription rates quoted are for UK delivery only. Normal UK subscription rate is £26.40. Europe/Eire £41.80. Rest of world £61.20. BBC Worldwide Publishing offers you the opportunity to receive information from other organisations about its products and services. Please tick here if you do *not* wish to participate. ☐

Please send this form with your payment to:
BBC Homes & Antiques, FREEPOST SCE505, Woking, Surrey GU21 1BR.

HAJM198

Subscribe today

BBC Homes & Antiques is the only magazine that specialises in blending the best of old and new in the home and offers you a wealth of inspiration. Inside each issue you'll find our monthly feature 'Starting a Collection' written by Judith Miller as well as an eight page *Antiques Roadshow* Price Guide and lots of expert advice.

Subscribe today and you'll receive each issue delivered to your door FREE of postage and packaging before it's on sale in the shops

A Crimplene Op-Art mini-dress, 1960s.
£18–20 *TCF*

A Jeff Banks floral print crepe shirt, 1960s.
£6–9 *BOH*

A vinyl coat, 1960s, 26in (66cm) long.
£20–25 *BOH*

A long sleeved mini dress, 1960s, 34in (86.5cm) long.
£10–15 *BOH*

A Double Two man's polyester and cotton shirt, 1970s, 28in (71cm) long.
£10–15 *BOH*

A cotton skirt, by Highlight, 1970s, size 12.
£10–12 *BOH*

A Paco Rabanne tunic top and matching mini skirt, late 1960s.
£900–1,100 *CSK*

A pair of Dolcis leather platform shoes, 1960s.
£15–20 *Har*

A plastic handbag, in the form of a *Madoni* magazine, 1970s.
£25–30 *PB*

A *Yellow Submarine* poster, artwork by Peter Max, 1968, 41in (104cm) high.
£900–1,100 *S(LA)*

A Whitefriars glass in the form of stacked bricks, 1960s, 8¼in (21cm) high.
£60–80 *PLB*

A Carlton Ware money box, 1960s, 6½in (16.5cm) wide.
£30–35 *PLB*

A Holmegaard bottle vase, by Otto Brauer, Scandinavian, 1960s, 10in (25.5cm) high.
£45–55 *PLB*

A Joe Colombo plastic Boby trolley, c1970, 21in (53.5cm) high.
£75–95 *PLB*

A Pierre Paulin lounge chair, on castors, 1968, 33in (84cm) wide.
£900–1,100 *CSK*

A Zanker Fabach plastic fan heater, 1970s, 10½in (26.5cm) diam.
£85–95 *PLB*

A Panasonic Model R70 Panapet radio, Japanese, 1960–70s, 4¼in (11cm) diam.
£30–40 *PLB*

An Italian moulded plastic 'frog' chair, 1970s, 25in (63.5cm) high.
£30–35 *Har*

An orange Trimphone, 1970s, 8in (20.5cm) long.
£45–55 *PLB*

ORIENTAL
Ceramics

A Yüeh celadon jar, Western Jin Dynasty, circa 265BC–AD316, 10in (25.5cm) high.
£800–850 *ORI*

Celadon is a semi-translucent glaze derived from iron, ranging in colour from putty to sea green and used on Chinese stoneware. Celadon ceramics were greatly admired and copied in the East, and the word itself is said to derive from Salah-ed-din (Saladin), the Sultan of Egypt, who in 1171, sent 40 pieces of this ware to the Sultan of Damascus.

A Chinese blue and white provincial bowl, Ming Dynasty, c1368–1644, 5in (12.5cm) diam.
£80–100 *ORI*

A pair of Chinese blue and white plates, Kangxi period, c1710, 11in (28cm) diam.
£600–700 *Wai*

A pair of *Kraak porselein* dishes, Wanli period, c1573–1620, 8in (20.5cm) diam.
£600–630 *ORI*

A blue and white ribbed porcelain tea bowl and saucer, decorated with crabs amongst peonies, Kangxi period, c1700, saucer 5in (12.5cm) diam.
£110–120 *ORI*

Three Chinese pottery models of horses heads, Han Dynasty, 206BC–AD220, largest 6¾in (17cm) high.
£300–360 *WW*

Cross Reference
Colour Review

r. A Chinese blue and white porcelain yen yen, depicting scholars in a garden scene, Kangxi period, c1710, 17½in (44.5cm) high.
£1,400–1,500 *ORI*

Yen yen is a term for a long-necked vase with a trumpet mouth.

A Chinese *famille verte* moulded dish, Yongzheng period, c1730, 9in (23cm) diam.
£250–270 *ORI*

A Chinese blue and white teapot, with replaced silver lid, Qianlong period, c1770, 3½in (9cm) wide.
£100–120 *ORI*

A Chinese export foot warmer, decorated in iron red palette, 18thC, 11in (28cm) diam.
£200–300 *Wai*

An Imari tea bowl and saucer, from the *Nanking* cargo, decorated with a pine tree pattern, 1750, saucer 4⅓in (11.5cm) diam.
£180–250 *RBA*

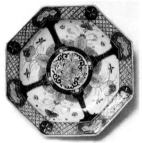

A Japanese Imari dish, c1840, 4¼in (11cm) diam.
£130–150 *ALB*

A Chinese *famille rose* yin yang artist's stem bowl, c1800, 2¼in (5.5cm) high.
£170–210 *MEG*

l. An encrusted brown glazed storage jar, from the *Diana* cargo with lug handles, 1816, 36in (91.5cm) high.
£600–750 *RBA*

r. A Nabeshima ware blue and white dish, c1830, 8in (20.5cm) diam.
£650–750 *Wai*

Nabeshima ware is Japanese porcelain produced at Okawachi, near Arita, at the pottery founded by Nabeshima, Prince of Kaga in the mid-17thC.

A blue and white tea bowl and saucer, from the *Nanking* cargo, decorated with a pagoda riverscape, c1750, 4½in (11.5cm) diam.
£230–260 *RBA*

A Nanking blue and white platter, c1790, 10in (25.5cm) wide.
£120–150 *BRU*

A Chinese *famille rose* tea caddy, Qianlong period, c1780, 6in (15cm) high.
£160–180 *ORI*

An Imari vase, decorated in green, yellow and red over underglaze blue, with gilding, mid-19thC, 8½in (21.5cm) high.
£70–100 *MEG*

A pair of Japanese Imari ball vases, 19thC, 6½in (16.5cm) high.
£45–60 *MEG*

A pair of Canton *famille rose* vases, with twin handles to the neck, painted with panels of figures and precious objects, 19thC, 13¾in (35cm) high.
£2,000–2,400 *P(B)*

A Chinese vase, decorated with birds and flowers, rim damage, late 19thC, 10½in (26.5cm) high.
£110–140 *MEG*

A Malaysian Nyonya bowl, with goldfish design in orange and green malacca glaze, minor chips, Qing Dynasty, Guangxu period, 1875–1908, 3½in (9cm) diam.
£45–65 *MEG*

A Japanese Imari charger, decorated in enamelled colours with a screen against an iron red trellis ground, within blue border of cranes in clouds, late 19thC, 21¾in (55.5cm) diam.
£450–550 *DN*

A pair of Japanese Imari porcelain vases, decorated with garden scenes, c1880, 8in (20.5cm) high.
£140–170 *BRU*

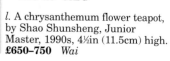

A Chinese brush washer, painted with a bird on a peony branch, signed by the artist Hongshun, with artist's seal, 1930s, 3½in (8.5cm) diam.
£300–400 *Wai*

A Japanese export vase, decorated with red, black and blue enamels on soft orange ground, minor rim chips, c1900, 6½in (16.5cm) high.
£15–20 *MEG*

l. A chrysanthemum flower teapot, by Shao Shunsheng, Junior Master, 1990s, 4½in (11.5cm) high.
£650–750 *Wai*

Lacquer

A scarlet lacquered casket, with hinged doors, decorated with figures beside pavilions, restored, 19thC, 13¼in (33.5cm) high.
£100–120 *Bon*

Sculpture & Carvings

A pale green jade plaque, carved and pierced in the form of a butterfly, on a folding stand, Qing Dynasty, 19thC, 3¾in (9.5cm) wide.
£80–100 *P(B)*

l. A Japanese ivory okimono of a peasant, standing on an oval base holding a pumpkin, with 2 pumpkins at his feet, signed Ichgyoku, Meiji period, c1868–1912, 7in (18cm) high.
£240–280 *P(B)*

A Japanese lacquer model of a pagoda, the central circular section with 4 pairs of double doors between reticulated panels, below a frieze of dragons, the stepped square base with a balustrade at each corner, beneath a roof with a stupa finial, the whole decorated in gold and black, the insides of the doors painted with immortals, slight damage, Meiji period, 1868–1912, 17¼in (44cm) high.
£240–280 *WW*

An ebony netsuke, carved as a Noh mask of an old man, signed Tomokazu Yama, 19thC, 3½in (9cm) high.
£230–260 *Bon*

A collection of Japanese painted and lacquered Noh theatre masks, c1900, 9in (23cm) high.
£750–850 *CAG*

Noh is the stylized classic drama of Japan, developed in the 15thC or earlier, using music, dancing, chanting, elaborate costumes and themes, from religious stories or myths.

A horn netsuke, depicting an Oriental figure dressed in a cloak of leaves with a frog on his back, c1900, 2in (5cm) high.
£275–325 *AnS*

A Japanese ivory box, carved with a growling lion, c1900, 4½in (11.5cm) wide.
£90–110 *WeH*

Textiles

A pair of Chinese yellow silk sleeve panels, embroidered with a trailing design of narcissus and bamboo, late 19thC, 20in (51cm) high.
£120–130 *PBr*

A silk kimono, decorated with red, green and yellow clouds and abstract flower pattern on a white background, 1920s.
£200–250 *ASG*

A hand-woven orange silk *obi*, embroidered with a white orchid, 1930s, 131in (332.5cm) long.
£40–50 *ASG*

A pair of oriental embroidered lotus boots, 19thC, 4in (10cm) long.
£50–55 *BaN*

Foot-binding for women was common practice in China from the 10thC until 1949, when it was banned by Chairman Mao. Girl's feet were bandaged from early childhood onwards and only unwrapped for bathing or as part of the sexual ritual. The ideal was to achieve a 'golden lotus' foot, measuring only 3in (7.5cm). Their tiny, contorted feet were considered objects of great beauty, and were shod in beautifully embroidered and decorated shoes to show them off.

Kimonos

Derived from Chinese robes, kimonos have been worn by Japanese men and women from the early Nara period (645–724) onwards. The full length, open-sleeved robe has neither buttons nor ties, but is secured by an *obi*, a broad sash, wound round the waist and tied at the back. Very wide *obis* were not adopted until the 18thC, when women also began to wear the short *haori* coat, which has remained a traditional element of Japanese costume.

A red silk tie-dyed *haori*, with white flower and cloud pattern, 1930s.
£200–250 *ASG*

A rose and blue silk kimono, hand-painted with flowers, stained, 1920s.
£50–60 *ASG*

A black silk ceremonial formal kimono, with Samurai family crests, hand-painted with flying birds and cloud pattern on bottom, 1930s.
£245–285 *ASG*

All ceremonial kimonos are hand-painted and often use the batik method of dyeing.

An orange silk *haori*, with white tie-dyed flying kite pattern, c1940s.
£50–60 *ASG*

OSBORNES

An Osborne plaque, entitled 'Chained Bible, Canterbury', early 1900s, 3½in (9cm) high.
£25–30 *JMC*

An Osborne plaque, entitled 'A Canterbury Pilgrim the Prior', 1920s, 5½in (14cm) high.
£30–35 *JMC*

An Osborne plaque, entitled 'Poets' Corner, Westminster Abbey', 1904, 9in (23cm) wide.
£50–55 *JMC*

This plaque was re-issued in 1930 with the figures in foreground and on the right omitted.

An Osborne plaque, entitled 'St Paul's Cathedral', 1910–39, 4½in (11.5cm) high.
£10–15 *GIN*

l. An Osborne plaque, entitled 'Windsor Castle', 1918, 3in (7.5cm) wide.
£20–30 *RAC*

Osborne Plaques

Osborne plaques were produced in Faversham, Kent, between 1899–1965. The plaques show highly detailed relief representations of buildings, historical events and personalities. They were handmade from plaster, finished with wax and then hand-painted. The finish was given the trade name Ivorex.

An Osborne plaque, entitled 'William Shakespeare 1564–1616', 1920s, 6¾in (17cm) diam.
£40–50 *JMC*

An Osborne free-standing plaque, entitled 'Lady Godiva', 1930s, 6¾in (17cm) high.
£150–170 *JMC*

An Osborne plaque, entitled 'Bunyans Cottage, Elstow', 8¼in (21cm) wide.
£10–12 *MAC*

A newspaper cutting from the Bedfordshire Times *dated 1st November, 1944, is attached to the reverse, relating how a lorry had crashed into the cottage, causing severe damage.*

Two Osborne figures, entitled 'Sairey Gamp' and 'Mr Pickwick', part of a series of 8 Dickens characters, 1940s, 4½in (11.5cm) high.
£55–65 each *JMC*

An Osborne plaque, entitled 'Scriptorium Cloister, Gloucester Cathedral', 1940s, 6½in (16.5cm) high.
£35–40 *JMC*

PAPER MONEY

A Mauritius Commercial Bank $20 note, 1839.
£40–50 *NAR*

A Newton Provincial Bank £5 note,
cancelled with punch holes, 1841.
£40–50 *WP*

A Haverfordwest Bank £1 note, cancelled with
punch holes, 1880.
£30–40 *WP*

A South African Mafeking Siege £1 note, 1900.
£500–600 *NAR*

A Durham Bank £5 note,
cancelled with cut, 1891.
£5–8 *WP*

A Bank of England £1 error note,
with extra paper, 1940.
£70–80 *WP*

A Bank of England 10/- note, 1940–48.
£10–15 *NAR*

A Nottingham and Nottinghamshire Banking Company Limited £5 note, 1944.
£100–125 *NAR*

A Bank of England £5 note, signed by L. K. O'Brien, 1956.
£70–80 *WP*

This was the last year the white £5 notes were issued.

A National Commercial Bank of Scotland £1 note, dated 16th September 1959.
£7–9 *WP*

A National Commercial Bank of Scotland £20 note, first issue, 1959.
£40–50 *WP*

A Bank of England 10/- note, with D38N prefix, 1960–1970.
£20–25 *WP*

D38N was the last prefix number used on 10/- notes.

Did you Know?

In 1694 The Bank of England was founded by William Paterson. One year later the Bank released its first printed notes. These were immediately copied by a clever forger and were quickly withdrawn. The Bank then used a new marbled paper and also introduced the practice of cutting notes in half. One half was given to the customer and when it was returned to the Bank it could be checked against its twin. Unsurprisingly, none of these early marbled notes appear to have survived!

Forgery continues to this day, aided and abetted by the development of the colour photocopier. If you are unfortunate enough to receive a fake note, it should be given in to the Bank of England.

A Bank of England specimen £10 note, 1964.
£700–800 *WP*

A States of Jersey 10/- note, with Padgham, Treasurer of the States, signature, c1963.
£7–8 *WP*

A Bank of Ireland specimen £100 note, c1980.
£80–90 *WP*

Two Bank of England £10 error notes, miss-cut with extra paper, 1994.
£120–140 *WP*

A Bank of England £20 error note, with inverted serial numbers, 1993.
£90–100 *WP*

The States of Jersey £1 note, dated '9th May 1995', commemorating the 50th anniversary of the liberation of Jersey.
£2.50–3.50 *WP*

Paper Money

Paper money should be in mint condition with no folds or ink annotations to command premium prices.

PAPERWEIGHTS

The first recorded glass paperweight was made by an Italian in Venice in the 1840s. It was a millefiori weight, (from the Italian for 'thousand flowers'), formed from cut sections of rods of glass which have been shaped, covered with various colours and then stretched. The French glassworks, notably Baccarat, St Louis and Clichy, soon improved and developed the lampwork technique, in which flowers, insects, reptiles etc are hand-formed from molten coloured glass. When French manufacture declined in the 1850s, French makers moved to the USA, which became an important centre of production. The brief golden age of classic paperweights was 1845–55, after which weights were made only intermittently.

The craft was revived in the 1930s when Paul Ysart, born in Barcelona of Bohemian parents, started making lampwork and millefiori weights in Scotland. Baccarat and St Louis in France regenerated their classic skills in the 1950s, and in 1969 Perthshire Paperweights started producing high-quality weights. Today fine paperweights are again being manufactured by studio glass makers both in Europe and the USA.

A Baccarat pansy paperweight, with a star cut base, mid-19thC, 2¾in (70mm) diam.
£180–220 *WW*

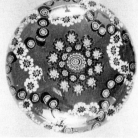

A Clichy paperweight, with 2 linked millefiori garlands around central millefiori, canes broken, c1850, 3in (75mm) diam.
£500–600 *STG*

A Baccarat pansy and bud paperweight, with green leaves and stem, c1855, 3in (75mm) diam.
£950–1,200 *STG*

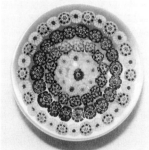

A Baccarat concentric paperweight, with a central white rose, 1845–60, 2½in (65mm) diam.
£400–450 *SWB*

A Vasart paperweight, with flowers set on a green background, c1955, 4in (10cm) diam.
£20–30 *CSA*

r. A Murano paperweight, with brightly coloured flowers, c1970, 3in (75mm) diam.
£35–45 *SWB*

l. A Strathearn paperweight, with flowers on green and red background, c1970, 2¾in (70mm) diam.
£15–20 *CSA*

A Chinese white painted paperweight, depicting a landscape, c1950, 2in (50mm) diam.
£40–50 *SWB*

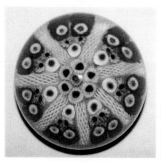

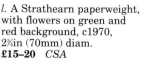

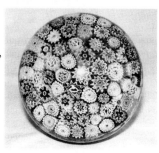

A Modena glass paperweight, with a blue and green coloured base, 1970s, 6in (15cm) high.
£14–16 *HEI*

A Wedgwood panda paperweight, 1970s, 3½in (9cm) high.
£40–50 *SWB*

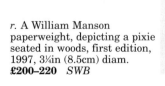

A Perthshire millefiori inkwell paperweight, pre-1994, 5½in (14cm) high.
£200–220 *STG*

A Whitefriars glass paperweight, signed with Whitefriars cane, with certificate, 1977, 3½in (9cm) diam.
£200–250 *STG*

This is one of 4 designs produced by Whitefriars Glass for the Queen's Silver Jubilee.

A glass paperweight, with yellow flower, unmarked, 1960–70, 2¼in (55mm) diam.
£8–10 *MAC*

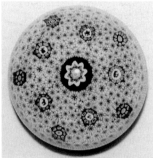

A Perthshire carpet ground paperweight, No. 40 of edition of 300, c1994, 2½in (64mm) diam.
£100–125 *SWB*

r. A William Manson paperweight, depicting a pixie seated in woods, first edition, 1997, 3¼in (8.5cm) diam.
£200–220 *SWB*

A St Louis paperweight, with red rose and green stem, limited edition of 350, signature on cane, 1978, 3¼in (8.5cm) diam., with certificate.
£350–400 *STG*

A polar bear glass paperweight, possibly attributed to Wedgwood, 1970s, 5½in (14cm) wide.
£15–20 *MAC*

A Perthshire floral spray paperweight, with central pink flower, 1984, 2½in (64mm) diam.
£125–145 *SWB*

PLASTICS

A Bandalasta fruit bowl, 1920s,
6½in (16.5cm) diam.
£20–25 *REN*

A phenolic inkstand, 1930s,
9in (23cm) wide.
£60–70 *BEV*

Chronology of Plastics Invention

The word plastic comes from the Greek word *plastikos*
meaning to mould.
1907: Leo Baekeland produced phenol formaldehyde, the
first truly synthetic plastic, which came to be known as
Bakelite or oxybenzylmethyleneglycolanhydride.
Compression moulded with fillers this gives the classic
Bakelite mottled product, cast with pigments to resemble
onyx, jade, marble and amber. It has come to be known as
phenolic resin.
1924: Rossiter produced urea thiourea formaldehyde,
marketed as Linga Longa or as Bandalastaware by
British Cyanides.
1930: Catalin Corporation produced Catalin, (Marblette),
a refined phenolic, often opaque, marbled, translucent or
richly coloured.
1933: ICI produced polythene.
1938: Du Pont produced nylon.
1939–45: War effort produced PVC, melamine, polyethylene,
polystyrene and acrylic.

A brown Bakelite paper holder,
1930s, 7in (18cm) wide.
£80–100 *BEV*

A Smiths cream Bakelite
wind-up clock, 1930s,
8in (20.5cm) wide.
£30–40 *TIH*

A Lindenware brown Bakelite
smoker's companion, c1925,
6in (15cm) wide.
£50–60 *TIH*

A brown Bakelite ashtray,
1930s, 4½in (11.5cm) diam.
£2–4 *GIN*

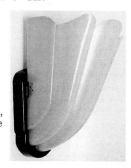

r. An Art Deco wall lamp,
with brown Bakelite base
and pink plastic shade,
1930s, 8in (20.5cm) high.
£35–40 *TIH*

A red Bakelite dice, with
inset compass, 1930s,
2½in (64mm) high.
£35–40 *BEV*

An Art Deco style plastic biscuit
jar, in blue/black geometric
design, c1935, 6in (15cm) high.
£55–65 *TIH*

A Bakelite cigarette box,
1930s, 6½in (16.5cm) long.
£18–20 *GIN*

A brown Bakelite electric bed warmer, by R. A. Rothermel Ltd, 1930s, 13in (33cm) long.
£20–30 *JUN*

A mottled Bakelite torch, by Stadium, c1940, 5in (12.5cm) long.
£16–18 *TIH*

A brown Bakelite electric bed warmer, by Veret Ltd, c1930, 10in (25.5cm) high.
£20–25 *TIH*

r. An Art Deco style green urea formaldehyde toothbrush holder, 1940s, 7in (18cm) long.
£10–12 *TIH*

A pair of urea formaldehyde salad tongs, with elephant-shaped handles, 1940s, 10in (25.5cm) long.
£10–15 *TIH*

A peach-coloured acrylic hand-painted toast rack, 1940s, 7in (18cm) long.
£12–14 *TIH*

A pink and green acrylic money box, with a green Scottie dog and lucite base, 1940s, 6in (15cm) long.
£40–50 *TIH*

An orange and clear acrylic cigarette box, 1940s, 7in (18cm) long.
£30–40 *TIH*

A pair of plastic trinket boxes:
l. blue and yellow,
r. yellow and cream,
1950s, 4½in (11.5cm) high.
£20–25 each *TIH*

Locate the Source

The source of each illustration in Miller's can be found by matching the code letters below each caption with the Key to Illustrations.

l. A black Bakelite ice bucket, with white lid, 1940–50, 7in (18cm) high.
£25–30 *GIN*

A plastic 'handkerchief' basket, 1950s, 10in (25.5cm) wide.
£10–12 *GIN*

A plastic teapot stand, painted by Sir Peter Scott, depicting birds on a blue background, 1950s, 6½in (16.5cm) diam.
£3–4 *GIN*

A white plastic lampshade with chain, 1950s, 13½in (34.5cm) diam.
£10–12 *GIN*

A cream-coloured plastic bowl, 1950s, 9½in (24cm) diam.
£7–8 *GIN*

A Palitoy plastic key ring, modelled as Archie Andrews, with opening mouth, c1950, 2in (5cm) long.
£15–20 *SVB*

A Melaware 24-piece yellow and white dinner service, 1960s, plates 9in (23cm) diam.
£20–25 *GIN*

A plastic burgundy and grey Thermos flask, 1950–60, 10in (25.5cm) high.
£5–7 *GIN*

A turquoise plastic Thermos flask, 1960s, 14in (35.5cm) high.
£18–20 *TIH*

A wire and plastic plant stand, 1960s, 19in (48.5cm) high.
£10–15 *GIN*

An Emsla yellow plastic cake plate, with cover, German, 1970s, 9in (23cm) diam.
£2–3 *GIN*

l. A Gaydon Melmex orange butter dish, 1960–70, 7½in (19cm) wide.
£10–12 *GIN*

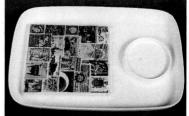

A set of 6 plastic drink and sandwich trays, made in Hong Kong, 1950–60, 10in (25.5cm) wide.
£6–7 *GIN*

POSTCARDS

The first British postcard appeared on the market on 1 October, 1870. It wasn't pretty pictures that attracted early purchasers – the card was plain and buff-coloured – but price. Already printed with a halfpenny stamp, the postcard cost half the price of a letter to send, and although fears were expressed about postmen reading private messages, postcards soon caught on. Initially the Post Office stipulated that one side had to be left completely undecorated for the stamp and address, and any illustrations had to be combined with the message. These regulations were lifted in 1902, opening the way for the picture postcard and creating a new collecting craze.

No Edwardian drawing room was complete without a case of stuffed birds, a potted aspidistra, and an album of postcards filled with pictures of actresses and prominent public figures, seaside views and comic scenes. 'The golden age for the postcard was the Edwardian era, from 1902 up until WWI,' says Ken Lawson of Specialised Postcard Auctions. 'The cards then were extremely high in quality and give a real sense of history: how the world once looked and how quickly things change.'

Popular subjects today include Art Nouveau cards by artists such as Alphonse Mucha (1860–1939) and Raphael Kirchner (1876–1917), and good sets of 'what the butler saw' style 'glamour' pictures, with encouragingly chubby Edwardian misses performing a card-by-card striptease. Topographicals (rural and urban views) are a favourite with many collectors. The slow shutter speeds of early cameras made capturing movement difficult, and photographers would often set up while streets were still comparatively quiet. Today collectors are prepared to pay more for pictures showing people and some form of vintage transport.

The comic postcard was a great British speciality, illustrated by such famous artists as Donald McGill (1875–1962), Mabel Lucie Attwell (1879–1964), and Louis Wain (1860–1939).

Some of the most poignant postcards date from WWI. Soldiers at the front purchased silk cards embroidered with sentimental messages and patriotic flags to send to their families back home. Because of wartime restrictions messages were movingly brief and to the point: 'love to you and the kids and don't forget Mum ... somewhere in France.'

Postcards can be picked up from car boot sales, flea markets and specialist dealers. There are fairs across the country and the collectors' magazine *Picture Postcard Monthly*. As well as collecting vintage examples, some collectors are also beginning to focus on more modern cards, particularly those featuring events and personalities (Falklands War and Margaret Thatcher cards are sought after) that somehow sum up the spirit of their time.

Advertising

An Art Nouveau advertising poster-type postcard, by M'lle H. Dufau, unused, c1910.
£50–55 *SpP*

An Art Nouveau advertising poster-type postcard, by A. Beaume-Miller, unused, c1910.
£45–50 *SpP*

Two advertising postcards, depicting children, c1900.
£12–14 each *MRW*

Beauties & Glamour

A French Art Nouveau coloured litho print vignette panel study postcard, by Eva Daniell, signed, series 176, unused, c1900.
£60–70 *SpP*

An American glamour postcard, by Philip Boileau, entitled 'Tomorrow', c1907.
£4–5 *JMC*

A glamour postcard, by T. Corbelle, c1917.
£3–4 *JMC*

r. A set of 4 French postcards, unused, c1920.
£110–130 *SpP*

An Art Nouveau monogrammed glamour study, by Josef Hoffmann, from Stilistisches, Philipp & Kramer, series XXXIII No. 3, some wear, c1900.
£15–20 *SpP*

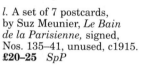

l. A set of 7 postcards, by Suz Meunier, *Le Bain de la Parisienne,* signed, Nos. 135–41, unused, c1915.
£20–25 *SpP*

An American glamour postcard, by Charles Scribner's Sons, entitled 'Anticipation', c1910.
£4–5 *JMC*

A French coloured litho print vignette postcard, signed by Raphael Kirchner, Dell'Aquila, unused, c1900.
£85–100 *SpP*

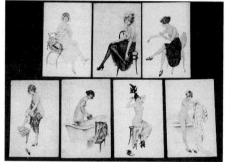

Comic Cards

A Louis Wain postcard, entitled 'Manx Kippers for Tea', c1910.
£20–30 *MRW*

A set of 6 Tucks litho print vignette postcards, by Percy V. Bradshaw, with Jersey overprints, entitled 'The Cockney Yachtsman', signed, Series 1768, Nos. 1–6, unused, c1910.
£45–50 *SpP*

A Louis Wain Tucks Dressing Dolls' Fairy Tales postcard, series V, c1900.
£200–220 *VS*

Cross Reference
Colour Review

A Davidson Bros postcard, entitled 'His First Sea Dip', 1911.
£4–5 *THA*

r. Two comic postcards, depicting seaside scenes, 1908.
£4–6 each *MRW*

A Mabel Lucie Attwell postcard, 1930s.
£3–6 *CMF*

A Mabel Lucie Attwell postcard, 1930s.
£3–6 *CMF*

r. A postcard, entitled 'Prehistoric Motoring', c1926.
£4–6 *MRW*

Greetings Cards

Two Christmas postcards, c1900.
£4–6 each *MRW*

Topographical & Transport

A postcard, entitled 'Good Wishes For Your Birthday', decorated with violets, c1915.
£3–4 *THA*

Two hunting scene Christmas postcards, 1930s.
£4–6 each *MRW*

r. A postcard showing Wylye Railway Station, published by Wilkinson, c1905.
£20–25 *SpP*

A postcard showing Ruislip Station, unused, c1905.
£25–30 *SpP*

r. Two postcards depicting exterior and interior views of a garage at Pershore, Worcestershire, 1920s.
£20–30 each *MRW*

Two postcards showing railway engines, 1940s.
£2–3 each *MRW*

Two Japanese postcards, 1920s.
£4–6 each *MRW*

World War I

A WWI woven postcard
showing devastated buildings
at Louvain, Belgium.
£15–18 *SpP*

l. Two WWI
silk embroidered
Christmas
postcards.
£2–6 each *MRW*

Two WWI embroidered
silk postcards, sent
home from France
by the soldiers.
£3–4 each *MAC*

A WWI embroidered naval
postcard, entitled 'Greetings
from HMS *Royalist*',
some mount shrinkage.
£25–35 *SpP*

Postcards

The value of a postcard can be enhanced by
stamp and postmark, subjects which also
appeal to philatelic collectors. The postmark
provides a clue to dating although it is
important to remember that a card could be
published long before it was ever posted.

r. An embroidered
WWI South Wales
Borderers postcard,
from Egypt.
£40–45 *SpP*

An embroidered
Grenadier Guards
postcard, with WWI crest
design and title above
and below, unused.
£50–55 *SpP*

*Woven silks can be worth
more if they depict a
specific regiment.*

A military poster-type
postcard, entitled 'Your
Country Needs You and
What have You got to
say?', depicting
Kitchener, signed Alfred
Leete, unused, 1914–18.
£20–25 *SpP*

RADIOS, GRAMOPHONES & TAPE RECORDERS
Radios

A Weston Electric Co crystal set, with instructions on lid, c1922, 7in (18cm) high.
£100–150 *OTA*

A Gecophone BC 2820 wireless, in wooden case on bracket feet, c1920, 10¾in (27.5cm) wide, with original box and earphones.
£550–650 *L&E*

A Burne-Jones Magnum crystal set, 1930, 10in (25.5cm) wide, with headphones.
£150–200 *OTA*

This set was made for the Wireless for the Blind Fund, a charity shop set up to provide free radio sets for the blind. This set had a 'permanent' type detector, with a single adjuster to eliminate the fiddly cat's-whisker, and the tuning dials have markings in braille only.

l. A National Wireless Co National Gnat crystal set, 1923–24, 4in (10cm) high, with a pair of S. G. Brown headphones.
£100–125 *OTA*

An Ekco C25 console radio, c1931, 40¼in (102cm) high.
£350–400 *GM*

A Gecophone BC 3240 radio set, with walnut cabinet, c1931, 18in (45.5cm) wide, with matching speaker.
£150–200 *OTA*

This is one of the last radio sets to be made without a built-in speaker.

A VE301 Nazi propaganda radio, 1933, 18in (45.5cm) high.
£150–180 *HEG*

r. An Ekco AC85 black Bakelite and chrome radio, c1934, 20in (51cm) wide.
£350–400 *OTA*

Radios in these colours are rare.

A GEC D159 radio, with mahogany-veneered case, restored, 1936, 15in (38cm) high.
£165–185 *TIH*

A Philco Model 444 People's Set radio, with black Bakelite cabinet, 1936, 16in (40.5cm) high.
£100–150 *HCC*

An Ever Ready Model C valve portable radio, 1930s, 12½in (32cm) high.
£75–85 *GIN*

r. An American Westinghouse 'refrigerator' radio, c1946, 11in (28cm) high.
£100–120 *HEG*

l. A Murphy A46 radio, with walnut-veneered case, 1936, 18in (46cm) wide.
£100–120 *GM*

A Marconi portable radio, 1930s, 10½in (26.5cm) wide.
£55–65 *GIN*

A McMichael model 487AC console radio, 1948, 32¼in (82cm) high.
£80–100 *GM*

A Murphy V144 radio, with two-tone Bakelite case, c1949, 10¼in (26cm) wide.
£10–20 *OTA*

r. A GEC battery-portable radio, with green mottled Bakelite case, 1947, 14in (35.5cm) high.
£150–180 *HEG*

A Bush DAC904 radio, with brown Bakelite case, c1950, 11in (28cm) wide.
£80–120 *OTA*

A SNR receiver, in green and black shaded case with sinuous curved gold Perspex grille and matching mirror-glass dials, 1950, 12in (30.5cm) wide.
£600–700 *CSK*

An Ekco U215 cream plastic radio, 1952, 11in (28cm) wide.
£45–60 *OTA*

A Decca Deccette portable radio, 1952, 10in (25.5cm) high, with mains unit.
£100–120 *HEG*

A Pye Cambridge International PE80 valve radio, 1953, 22⅜in (58cm) high.
£100–120 *GM*

A HMV/Marconi press button station select radio, with brown Bakelite and cream trim, c1960, 19in (48.5cm) wide.
£100–120 *TIH*

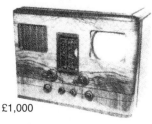

A Murphy model B385 battery radio, with light brown leatherette case, restored, 1961, 10in (25.5cm) wide.
£60–70 *TIH*

A Dansette Dorchester battery radio, with light blue PVC case, restored, c1960, 12in (30.5cm) wide.
£50–60 *TIH*

A Dynatron Commodore radio, with twin aerials, c1963, 9in (23cm) high.
£20–25 *PC*

An Ever Ready Sky Baron transistor radio, c1965, 7in (18cm) high.
£35–45 *PC*

A Dansette Chorister battery-operated radio, mid-1960s, 6in (15cm) high.
£20–25 *GIN*

A National UFO speaker, c1965, 7in (18cm) high.
£20–30 *PC*

This is an unusual extension loudspeaker intended to amplify sound from sub-miniature radios.

A Hacker Herald RP35 radio, with grey PVC case, 1960s, 11in (28cm) wide.
£55–65 *TIH*

A Ferguson 384 radio, with brown Bakelite case and cream trim, late 1960, 18in (45.5cm) wide.
£75–85 *TIH*

A Defiant radio, c1970, 9in (23cm) high.
£10–15 *PC*

A Panasonic Tune-A-Loop radio, c1975, 5in (12.5cm) diam.
£40–50 *PC*

Designed to be worn on the wrist, this white version is less desirable than those in brighter colours.

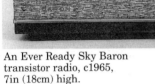

A miniature promotional radio for the Winter Olympics, 1980, 5in (12.5cm) high.
£20–30 *PC*

Gramophones & Tape Recorders

A HMV hornless Model 1 gramophone, c1919, 15in (38cm) square.
£120–150 *OTA*

A Victor horn gramophone, c1910, base 11in (28cm) square.
£750–850 *OTA*

A Peter Pan portable gramophone, Swiss, 1920, 7in (18cm) long.
£300–350 *JUN*

A Regal gramophone, with an oak case, c1928, 19in (48.5cm) long.
£100–120 *OTA*

An Edison Bell gold-plated gramophone, c1928, 20in (51cm) square.
£200–220 *HEG*

A Grundig ABS Phono Boy plastic and stainless steel portable record player, by Mario and Dario Bellini, designed 1968, 8½in (21.5cm) high.
£450–550 *S*

l. A Braun AG white aluminium and plastic stereo system TS45, by Dieter Rams, c1963, 11in (28cm) wide, with speakers.
£500–600 *S*

Microphones

A German Minifon cassette dictation machine, 1960s, 7in (18cm) long.
£18–20 *JON*

A Streamline aluminium microphone, labelled 'Turner Dynamic, Cedar Rapids, Iowa, USA.' c1940, 10in (25.5cm) high.
£250–300 *CSK*

A Reslo Ribbon RV microphone, c1960, 9in (23cm) high.
£40–45 *JON*

RAILWAYANA

A LNER John Rabon & Sons leather bound tape, with brass fittings, c1920–30, 66ft (20m).
£35–40 *CHe*

A SR white glazed lavatory pan, c1890, 17in (43cm) high.
£15–20 *HAX*

Books & Games

A Boyhood of Famous Men game, by J. Grubb Islington, in wooden box, 1880s, 6in (15cm) wide.
£220–250 *SRA*

l. A *British Railways Rule Book,* 1950, 5in (12.5cm) long.
£7–10 *SVB*

A LMS Pullman blanket, 1940s, 60in (152.5cm) square.
£18–22 *HAX*

l. A L&NWR Fletchers double line block and bell signal box instrument, c1900, 24in (61cm) high.
£90–110 *SRA*

A London Underground fire bucket, Piccadilly Circus, 1990, 12in (30.5cm) diam.
£10–12 *HAX*

The Railway ABC, published by Ernest Nister, cover depicting a 0-4-2 tank locomotive, and *The Wonderbook of Trains,* c1910, 7½in (19cm) wide.
£40–50 *SRA*

An enamel pictorial convex plaque, mounted on polished golden brown wooden shield with green baize on reverse, depicting an instructor showing a young boy how to use a green flag, 1963, 7¼in (18.5cm) wide.
£40–50 *SOL*

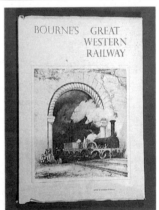

John C. Bourne, *Great Western Railway,* reprint of 1846 edition, with dust cover, 1970, 21in (53.5cm) high.
£35–45 *HAX*

Ceramics

A bowl, the side displaying 2 early 2-2-2 locomotives, tender and 2 coaches, hairline crack to the base, 1850s, 6½in (16.5cm) diam.
£80–90 *SRA*

A teapot and lid, by Arthur Robson, one side depicting a coloured coat-of-arms, the other printed in black 'Railway Centenary, Shildon, 27th September 1825–1925' and a bust of 'Timothy Hackworth 1786–1850 Inventor of the Steam Blast Pipe', 1925, 7in (18cm) high.
£230–260 *SRA*

A porcelain mug, with oval vignette coloured scene on both sides, one side depicting a blue 2-2-2 locomotive with 2 pink coaches emerging from a tunnel, the other with 2 young children, triangular chip to rim, 1840s, 5in (12.5cm) high.
£550–650 *SRA*

r. A porcelain jug, decorated with a transfer print of the entrance to the Liverpool Manchester Railway, 1840s, 5in (12.5cm) high.
£375–400 *SRA*

l. A Midland Railway salt-glazed ink bottle, the side impressed 'Midland Railway Co, Derby', c1900, 7½in (19cm) high.
£40–45 *SRA*

Lamps

An LMS railway handlamp, c1925, 12in (30.5cm) high.
£60–70 *JUN*

A GNR railway signal lamp, with brass Rauceby station plate, c1900, 17in (43cm) high.
£120–150 *JUN*

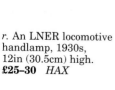

r. An LNER locomotive handlamp, 1930s, 12in (30.5cm) high.
£25–30 *HAX*

Nameplates

An LMS cast-brass curved nameplate, Hood, 1935, 29in (73.5cm) long.
£7,200–7,600 *SRA*

This nameplate was carried on the right side of the LMS Jubilee 5 x P/6 P Class 4-6-0 locomotive, LMS 5654, built at Crewe as Works No. 215 in February 1935. It was withdrawn in June 1966 and cut up by Wards of Beighton, Sheffield.

A GWR curved brass and steel nameplate, 'Princess Louise', 1914, 68in (172.5cm) long.
£7,000–7,500 *SRA*

The Princess Louise Victoria Alexandra Dagmar, Duchess of Fife, and later The Princess Royal, was the elder daughter of King Edward VII and Queen Alexandra.

A BR diesel locomotive nameplate, Haliolidae, raised letters on black background and with yellow on red Shell logo, 1965, 51½in (131cm) long.
£700–800 *SOL*

This nameplate originates from locomotive No. 47196 previously D1846, built at Crewe May 1965, renumbered 1974, named October 1988, but name removed June 1991.

A cast brass and enamelled steel nameplate, Royal Mail, displaying the coloured house flag and bearing on either side 2 cast brass arms, face restored, 1941, 74in (188cm) wide.
£15,000–16,000 *SRA*

This plate was carried by the Southern Railway Merchant Navy Class 4-6-2 Pacific locomotive, SR 213C, built at Eastleigh in September 1941, withdrawn in July 1967.

An SR cast brass nameplate, 'Ventnor', 1892, 34in (86.5cm) wide.
£3,500–4,000 *SOL*

Number Plates

A CLC bridge number plate, 'C.L.Ry. 86', 1865, 17½in (44.5cm) wide.
£35–45 *SOL*

r. An L&NWR enamel shed-plate, '34', slight restoration, c1920, 5in (12.5cm) wide.
£140–160 *SRA*

Station Signs

A BR(W) brown and cream enamel doorplate, 'Station Master', 1950s, 18in (45.5cm) wide.
£45–55 *SRA*

A Great Eastern Railway metal sign, 'Beware of the Trains', c1910, 23½in (59.5cm) wide.
£40–50 *SOL*

A BR(S) white on green enamel sign, 'Parcels and Left Luggage', 1950–60, 24in (61cm) wide.
£30–40 *SOL*

An SR double-sided enamel station sign, 'Woolston Station', 1930s, 20in (51cm) wide.
£100–120 *COB*

A London Underground red enamel sign, 1950s, 22in (56cm) square.
£25–30 *HAX*

Totems

A BR(S) white on green enamel totem, 'London Road (Guildford)', 1950s, 36in (91.5cm) wide.
£500–600 *SOL*

Only 2 totems ever had lower case letters on the small lower panel, hence the price of this rare example.

A green on white enamel totem, 'Tonbridge', 1950s, 36in (91.5cm) wide.
£200–250 *HAX*

Works Plates

l. A LNER works plate, 'LNER 1873 Doncaster Works 1929', 9in (23cm) wide.
£180–200 *SRA*

ROCK & POP

A set of 4 colour photographs of Abba, signed in blue pen by each member, mounted, framed and glazed together, 1970s, 47in (119.5cm) wide.
£450–550 *Bon(C)*

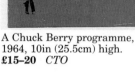
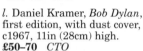

A silver and turquoise Navajo Indian finger ring, owned and worn by Jimi Hendrix, 1960s.
£650–750 *Bon(C)*

A Chuck Berry programme, 1964, 10in (25.5cm) high.
£15–20 *CTO*

l. Daniel Kramer, *Bob Dylan*, first edition, with dust cover, c1967, 11in (28cm) high.
£50–70 *CTO*

A poster for Jimi Hendrix at the Saville, designed by Hapshash and the Coloured Coat, 1967, 30in (76cm) wide.
£200–250 *CTO*

Cross Reference
Colour Review

A Boy George doll, by Sharpegrade Ltd, 1984, in original box, 12in (30.5cm) high.
£50–60 *TBoy*

A copy of *International Times*, with the obituary of Jimi Hendrix, 1970, 17in (43cm) high.
£10–15 *CTO*

A Michael Jackson doll, 1984, 12in (30.5cm) high, with original box.
£40–50 *TBoy*

International Times

International Times was Europe's first underground newspaper. Trailblazers in the hippie revolution, the magazine was responsible for organising events such as The Technicolor Dream, a 14-hour 'love-in' at Alexandra Palace. Issues recording important events are particularly desirable. Other collectable magazines from the period include *Oz*.

There is a strong demand today for psychedelic posters from the 1960s. Leading artists include the Americans Stanley Mouse and Rick Griffin, and British painters and musicians Nigel Waymouth and Michael English, who worked together under the name 'Hapshash and the Coloured Coat'. Their elaborate and idiosyncratic silkscreen designs are among the most sought after of all psychedelic posters.

A pair of Roller Derby boots, worn by Elton John, with 'EJ 76' transfers on the ankles, together with an Adidas football shirt with 'Elton' and '1' on the back and 'Comets' on the front, c1976.
£120–150 *Bon(C)*

A purple electric guitar with black hardware, by B. C. Rich, together with a Sonor drumskin and sticks, both signed by Gene Simmons, Peter Criss, Peter Stanley and Ace Frehley from Kiss, 1970–80.
£750–850 *Bon(C)*

A black and white promotional photograph, signed by Manic Street Preachers, c1993, 10in (25.5cm) wide.
£120–150 *CTO*

Rickey disappeared in 1995, since when there have been several reported sightings but he has not been discovered as yet.

A colour photograph of The Monkees, signed by each band member, with a concert pass for their Japan gig and an album cover entitled 'The Monkees Live 1967', framed and glazed, 1960s, 27in (68.5cm) high.
£100–120 *Bon(C)*

A RIAA Hologram platinum sales award, presented to Epic to commemorate the sale of more than 1,000,000 copies of the Oasis cassette and CD '(What's The Story) Morning Glory?', 1990s.
£700–800 *Bon(C)*

A Virgin promotional poster, featuring a portrait of Sid Vicious of The Sex Pistols holding a beer bottle and listing song titles, 39in (99cm) high.
£170–200 *Bon(C)*

A tour programme for Wham Club Fantastic 1983, signed by George Michael, Andrew Ridgely and backing singers, Pepsi and Shirlie.
£120–150 *Bon(C)*

Part of an LP cover, by The Small Faces, signed and with comments by Ian McClagan, c1968, 12in (30.5cm) diam.
£40–45 *CTO*

The Beatles

One of the most collectable names in rock and pop is The Beatles. Thanks to their enormous popularity in the 1960s, they are the band who have probably inspired the most memorabilia and who really started the fashion for rock merchandising.

Beatles-related objects appeal to a wide range of collectors. 'It tends to be those with a living memory of the band, the 30–50 somethings, who buy the more expensive one-off items,' says Paul Wane of Tracks, dealer in rock and pop memorabilia. 'Younger collectors tend to go for the less expensive mass-produced material.' As Wane explains, there is an established hierachy in Beatles collectables. Top of the pops are personal items that belonged to members of the band, for example instruments or clothing. 'If you have something like a jacket which belonged to John Lennon, what you also want is a contemporary photograph of him wearing it, which both confirms its authenticity and sets it in historical context.' Next in line are signatures. 'Beatles signatures are always desirable,' says Wane, 'but collectors are becoming a lot more finicky about whether or not there is a personalised inscription, about condition and also medium; a signed concert programme, LP cover or photograph is worth more than a page from an autograph book.' In the 1960s, there was

such a demand for Beatles signatures that they were faked by their management and fan club, and the high price for genuine Beatles signatures today has also led to modern-day fakes. 'There is a lot more expertise today, and specialists have got very good at identifying false signatures,' says Wane. 'But if you're buying, you've got to be careful. Go to reputable dealers and always ensure that they are prepared to take items back if any problems emerge.'

After signatures comes ephemera related to concerts (tickets, flyers, posters etc) and novelty merchandise. Condition is an increasingly important factor. 'These are modern antiques,' insists Wane, 'and rock and pop enthusiasts apply exactly the same criteria in terms of rarity, condition and completeness as do collectors in more traditional fields.'

Although Beatles collectables were manufactured in profusion, particularly at the height of Beatlemania (1964–5), many of the products were ephemeral, and rare survivors, such as the Beatles talcum powder tin illustrated in this section, can fetch high prices. 'Supplies of '60s material are dwindling,' concludes Wane. 'Because of this, collectors are now turning to more modern material, for example CDs and other promotional items relating to newly released compilations of Beatles music.'

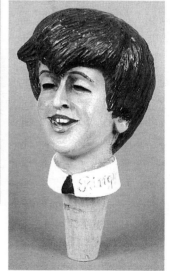

A Cavern Club membership card, signed by Paul McCartney and Ringo Starr, 1962–63.
£150–200 *BTC*

A programme for The Beatles Finsbury Park Christmas Show, early 1960s, 10⅞in (27.5cm) high.
£40–50 *BTC*

l. A cinema foyer poster for The Beatles 'Help' film, Mexican, c1965, 16in (40.5cm) wide.
£30–40 *CTO*

A German Ringo cork stopper, 1960s, 5in (12.5cm) high.
£100–125 *BTC*

A framed concert ticket, for a
Beatles show at the Odeon
Theatre, Llandudno, 1960s,
3in (7.5cm) wide.
£60–80 *SAF*

A set of 4 glass tumblers, by
Joseph Long Company Ltd, each
with gold rim and an individual
colour portrait of each member of
The Beatles, in original box, 1960s.
£700–800 *Bon(C)*

A Beatles style doll, by
Rosebud, 1960s, 8in (20.5cm)
high, in original packet.
£20–25 *BTC*

r. A chenille tailored jacket,
worn by John Lennon in
1966 on tour in Hamburg,
by Hung On You, London,
with orange broad stripe
and white buttons to cuffs
and front.
£4,000–4,500 *Bon(C)*

A Beatles vinyl record-shaped
seat, 1960s, 14in (35.5cm) diam.
£150–175 *BTC*

A Beatles necklace, with mini record pendant,
1960s, 12in (30.5cm) long.
£30–40 *SAF*

A Beatles comb, 1960s, 15in (38cm) long.
£50–75 *BTC*

A set of 4 Beatles Subbuteo figures, 1960s,
box 11½in (29cm) wide.
£100–150 *BTC*

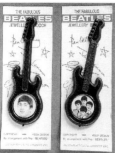

Two plastic Beatles guitar badges, 1960s, cards 5½in (14cm) high.
£8–10 each *BTC*

A Beatles tie pin, 1960s, card 6in (15cm) long.
£15–20 *BTC*

A tour programme of The Beatles 1965 UK tour, with a cover from the American cartoon show of The Beatles, 1960s.
£60–70 *CTO*

A Beatles Fan Club letter, with a ticket for the 1965 show at Shea Stadium, Flushing NY, USA, c1965, 8in (20.5cm) high.
£10–15 *BTC*

A tin of Beatles talcum powder, by Margo of Mayfair, 1965, 7¼in (18.5cm) high.
£150–200 *HUX*

A set of 4 black and white two-sided Beatles coat hangers, manufactured by Saunders Enterprises, die-cut bust photos with hook-on top, 1960s.
£450–500 *Bon(C)*

l. A set of 12 Cavern Club stickers, 1960s, 2in (5cm) diam.
£15–20 *CTO*

Six Beatles CD singles, Japanese, 1980s.
£6–10 each *TOT*

Elvis Presley

A collection of Elvis Presley's personal copies of his first 5 Sun record releases, 1954–5.
£16,000–18,000 *Bon*

Among the most historic rock 'n' roll recordings of all time are Elvis' first 5 recordings for Sam Phillips' Sun records. This set includes the extremely rare sample copy of 'Blue Moon of Kentucky' and is made rarer still as they are all signed and come from Elvis' personal collection.

Elvis Presley, 'Elvis Sings Christmas Songs', EP, with Christmas card cover, second issue, 1957.
£55–65 *CTO*

The second issue is rarer than the first issue.

Elvis Presley, 'Love Me Tender', EP, HMV label, 1956.
£50–60 *CTO*

Elvis Presley, 'Don't/Wear My Ring Around Your Neck', 45rpm disc, with cover, RCA label, very good condition, 1950–60.
£1,500–2,000 *Bon*

This promotional record was sent to disc jockeys to help them remember Elvis while he was away serving in the army.

A colour photograph of Elvis Presley, aged 2, signed and dedicated in black ink, in original frame, 1970, 11in (28cm) high.
£4,500–5,000 *Bon*

This photograph came from the estate of Norman Taurog, Elvis' friend and the director of 9 of his greatest films. This is perhaps the only time that Elvis signed Priscilla's and Lisa's names, adding to the interest of this piece.

Elvis Presley, 'By Request of Japanese Fans', box of 4 LPs, RCA label, c1980.
£80–100 *TOT*

A poster for *Kissin' Cousins*, signed 'Elvis Presley' in black ink, c1964, 41in (102cm) high.
£1,400–1,800 *Bon*

A poster for *Elvis On Tour* film, signed, MGM, 1972, 41in (102cm) high.
£700–800 *Bon*

A pair of flared denim jeans, decorated with silver roses, medallions and braid, worn by Elvis, 1970s.
£1,000–1,200 *Bon*

A colour photograph of Elvis Presley, wearing the Elvis Today suit on stage at Nassau Coliseum, New York, signed in black pen, 1973, 10in (25cm) high.
£500–600 *Bon*

Records

David Bowie, 'Do Anything You Say', single, advance promotion copy, Pye label, c1966.
£100–120 *TOT*

Screamin' Jay Hawkins, 'I Put a Spell on You', 7in single, Direction label, 1969.
£15–18 *TOT*

The Rolling Stones, 'The Last Time', Italian White Label Decca, jukebox promotional issue, c1965.
£10–15 *TOT*

r. Jimmy Witherspoon, 'At the Renaissance', EP, 1964.
£10–15 *ED*

l. Original soundtrack of *'Sweet Charity'*, UK MCA label, with gatefold sleeve, 1970s.
£25–30 *TOT*

Marlene Dietrich, 'Marlene, The Great Dietrich Sings in German, with the orchestra of Burt Bacharach', EP, HMV label, 1964.
£6–7 *ED*

Eartha Kitt, 'Eartha Kitt Revisited', EP, London, 1960.
£6–8 *ED*

'The Marvellous Marvelettes', LP, UK Tamla-Motown label, c1965.
£100–120 *CTO*

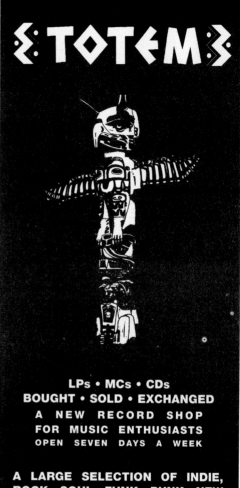

SCENT BOTTLES

A Victorian silver triple loop twist scent bottle, Birmingham 1899, 5in (12.5cm) long.
£250–300 *AAV*

A cut glass scent bottle, with silver top, Birmingham 1902, 3in (7.5cm) high.
£50–55 *PSA*

l. A pair of cut glass perfume bottles, with silver tops, Birmingham 1903, 4½in (11.5cm) high.
£250–280 *PSA*

A clear glass 2 compartment heart-shaped bottle, with silver-gilt mounts and stoppers, c1882, 3¼in (8.5cm) high.
£620–680 *Som*

One compartment in a double bottle was often used for scent and the other for smelling salts.

A Lalique perfume bottle, made for Worth, c1920, 4in (10cm) high, in original box.
£80–90 *RAC*

René Lalique, 1860–1945, designed many perfume presentations. The shape of this bottle was inspired by the Empire State Building.

An Avon perfume bottle, in the form of a rabbit, 1970s, 3in (7.5cm) high.
£5–10 *RAC*

A Ronson perfume atomiser, inscribed 'Marcel Franck Le Super-Kid', French, 1930s, 2in (5cm) high.
£55–65 *PC*

A Lanvin perfume bottle, 1930s, 3in (7.5cm) high, in original box.
£40–50 *RAC*

The value of commercial scent bottles is increased by the presence of the box and if the bottle still contains its original perfume.

SCIENTIFIC INSTRUMENTS

A brass pantograph, with ivory casters and accessories, signed 'W. & S. Jones, Holborn, London', in a mahogany case, early 19thC, 27½in (70cm) wide.
£170–190 *DN*

A Victorian brass compass, 1¾in (45mm) diam.
£75–85 *SPU*

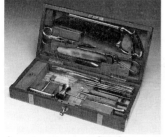

A postmortem set, fitted in a brass-bound mahogany case, late 19thC, 14in (35.5cm) wide.
£220–260 *TMA*

A brass military compass, c1918, 3in (7.5cm) diam.
£40–50 *COB*

A Victorian bronze sextant, with a rosewood grip, the arc inscribed 'H. Hughes, 59 Fenchurch St, London', in a mahogany case with accessories, and trade label, the lid with a brass presentation plate, 6½in (16.5cm) radius.
£850–950 *WW*

Presented to Captain Francis Robert Beauvois for the management of his vessel the Ocean Spray. The lid has a brass presentation plate from the Concordia Insurance Company.

A Carl Zeiss Jena medical microscope, No. 9751, with additional lenses in brass cases, in mahogany carrying case, late 19thC, 15½in (39.5cm) high.
£250–300 *PCh*

A Victorian silver-cased pocket barometer, the engraved silvered two-gradient dial with an altimeter 0–1500, with maker's name James Joseph Hicks, London 1883, 3½in (9cm) diam.
£500–550 *JIL*

James Joseph Hicks was a famous barometer maker, born in London.

A thermograph, with tin lid and cast iron base, by L. Maxant, France, c1910, 14in (35.5cm) wide.
£80–100 *RTw*

A MkIII prismatic brass compass, restored, c1940, 2¼in (5.5cm) diam.
£250–275 *GWA*

l. A Russian meteorological office barograph, in black plastic case, c1960, 9in (23cm) wide.
£350–400 *RTw*

SCRIPOPHILY
Africa

A share certificate for the Egyptian Shipping Company, for 1 share, light green and blue with underprint of feluccas, dated '1925'.
£55–65 *GKR*

A share certificate for the Electricity & Ice Supply Company, for 5 shares, illustrated with vignettes of electricity generating equipment and power lines, dated '1939'.
£25–30 *GKR*

l. A share certificate for the Connemara Mining Company of Ireland, for 5 shares, decorated with coat-of-arms, vignette and Gothic script, dated 'July 1852'.
£65–75 *GKR*

China

A Canton Kowloon Railway £100 bond certificate, 5% gold loan, in pink/black, dated '1907'.
£130–150 *GKR*

This railway is still the main link between Hong Kong and mainland China – completed in 1911 but bonds remained in default for almost 50 years.

Europe

A 500 pesetas share certificate for Banco de Cataluña, with underprint of coat-of-arms, dated '1929'.
£20–25 *GKR*

> **Cross Reference**
> Paper Money

A Stabilisation and Development Loan £100 bond for the Kingdom of Romania, with vignette of Transylvanian Castle, on which Bram Stoker's *Dracula* was based, in blue and black, dated '1929'.
£30–35 *GKR*

A 500 pesetas share certificate for Compañia Trasmediterranea, a Madrid-based shipping company, dated '1977'.
£16–18 *GKR*

Great Britain

A share certificate for Clarence Railway Company, for one share, with a blue embossed paper seal depicting a horse-drawn train, sailing boat in background and coat-of-arms, dated '1828'.
£500–600 *P*

Miller's is a price GUIDE not a price LIST

A share certificate for the Herne Bay Pier Company, for one share, printed on vellum with affixed blue seal, dated '1842'.
£125–145 *SCR*

Construction of the pier began in 1831, following the establishment of Herne Bay as a 'watering place'. The original pier, five-eighths of a mile long, was rebuilt in 1873 and lengthened in 1898.

South & Central America

A $100 share certificate for Compañia Mexicana de Petroleo 'El Tigre', green/black with printed revenue stamps, dated '1929'.
£16–18 *SCR*

l. A 500 francs share certificate for Compagnie du Port de Rio de Janeiro, designed by G. Fraipont, illustrating the port installations, lighthouse and various marine themes, issued 1912.
£100–120 *GKR*

USA

A £250 stock certificate for State of Carolina, some cancellation cuts taped, dated '1838'.
£150–200 *P*

A stock certificate for Chicago, Burlington & Quincy Railroad, orange and black, 1900.
£20–25 *SCR*

SEWING

A French wedge-shaped ivory *nécessaire*, fitted with a pair of scissors and a silver gilt thimble, crested within a garter and bearing a monogram, mid-19thC, 4in (10cm) long.
£150–180 *P(O)*

A Victorian novelty needlework tape/pincushion, contained within a mother-of-pearl shell, 2¼in (5.5cm) wide.
£50–70 *TMA*

A silver shoe pincushion, Birmingham 1890, 3⅓in (8.5cm) wide.
£120–130 *PSA*

A vegetable ivory and ivory tape measure, c1870, 2in (5cm) high.
£60–70 *BIL*

A silver pincushion, in the form of a standing pig, maker S. & Co, Birmingham 1904, 3⅓in (8.5cm) wide.
£130–150 *GH*

A silver pincushion, in the form of a swan, maker C. & K., Birmingham 1907, 3in (7.5cm) wide.
£230–260 *GH*

A silver pincushion, in the form of a fledgling bird, by S. M. & Co, Chester 1905, 2in (5cm) long.
£80–100 *GH*

A silver pincushion, in the form of a standing bulldog, maker A. & L. Ltd, Birmingham 1906, 2¾in (7cm) wide.
£300–350 *GH*

l. A silver pincushion, in the form of a standing camel, maker A. & L. Ltd, Birmingham 1907, 2½in (6.5cm) wide.
£270–310 *GH*

l. A silver and mother-of-pearl pincushion, in the form of an elephant and cart, Birmingham 1909, 3½in (9cm) long.
£550–650 *AMH*

A silver pincushion, in the form of a hedgehog, maker A. & L. Ltd, Birmingham 1908, 2in (5cm) wide.
£250–280 *GH*

SHEET MUSIC

In the 18th and early 19th centuries it was still commonplace to copy out music by hand. Making music was one of the necessary accomplishments of a young lady, and families would have books in which popular tunes and songs of the day were laboriously inscribed by the daughters of the house. 'Elizabeth is very cruel about my writing music,' noted Jane Austen in a letter to her sister Cassandra in 1799, 'and as a punishment for her, I should insist upon always writing out all hers for her in future, if I were not punishing myself at the same time.' With improved printing processes in the Victorian period, ready-printed sheet music became popular and affordable. Handsome and colourful hand-lithographed covers were used to promote sales and entice purchasers. Major Victorian cover artists included figures such as Alfred Concanen, John Brandard and James Montgomery Flagg, whose names often appeared on the song sheets. These would sometimes be collected in volumes, providing the equivalent of a 19th century record collection.

By the 20th century, and once radio and talking pictures were popular, it was no longer cover artists who were used to promote printed music, but stars. Vast numbers of song sheets were produced featuring songs from favourite Hollywood musicals, decorated with pictures of leading actors and actresses. As piano playing became less popular after WWII, the design of song sheets declined in quality, although 1960s sheet music is sought after for its pictures of the new generation of pop stars.

Enthusiasts often centre their collection around a certain theme: show tunes, WWI songs etc. This section, for example, includes a selection of Victorian song sheets devoted to railway subjects, with fine lithographed covers. Such material is hugely desirable to railway enthusiasts, hence its high value. Price is affected both by the image on the cover and condition. Song sheets were often trimmed (so as to fit into folders), written on and mended with sticky tape when torn. With rare song sheets, professional help should be sought when removing tape and cleaning. Since the printing ink can bleed, sheets should be stored in acid-free tissue paper. At the top of the range, rare sheet music with fine illustrations, or perhaps signed by the composer, fetches high sums. At the other end of the scale it is still possible to pick up 20th century song covers from flea markets and antique shops for under £5. Framed up, these can make attractive period pictures.

Sheet music for 'Dies Irae', composed by F. P. Ricci, signed on the title page by Samuel Wesley, 1850, 13in (33cm) high.
£120–150 *HB*

r. Victorian sheet music for 'Johnny The Engine Driver', by G. W. Hunt, published by John Alvey Turner, London, 14¼in (36cm) high.
£60–70 *SRA*

l. Piano sheet music for 'March Indienne', by A. Sellenick, 1879, 12in (30.5cm) high.
£20–30 *HB*

Victorian sheet music for 'The Kiss in the Railway Train', by Watkin Williams and C. H. Mackney, published by B. Williams, London, 13in (33cm) high.
£120–140 *SRA*

Victorian sheet music for 'The Muddle-Puddle Porter', written and composed by George Grossmith Jnr, published by Hopwood & Crew, London, cover artist A. B. Berridge Bros, 13¾in (35cm) high.
£70–80 *SRA*

Sheet music for 'The Railway Bell(e) and Railway Guard', by Harry Clifton, published by Hopwood & Crewe, London, 1860s, 13½in (34.5cm) high.
£120–140 SRA

Sheet music for 'The Electric Polka', by T. Berry, published by Charles Horn, London, 1860s, 13in (33cm) high.
£70–80 SRA

Victorian sheet music for 'The Excursion Train Galop', by Frank Musgrave, published by Boosey & Sons, London, 13¾in (35cm) high.
£180–200 SRA

Sheet music, *Francis & Day's Rag-Time Album*, published by Francis, Day & Hunter, London, 1920s, 11in (28cm) high.
£5–6 SVB

The Strand a musical portfolio of copyright songs and music, published by George Newnes Ltd, London, 1920s, 14in (35.5cm) high.
£10–12 SVB

Piano sheet music, *When The Children Play*, by E. Markham Lee, published by Murdoch Murdoch & Co, London, 1920s, 10in (25.5cm) high.
£3–5 SVB

Sheet music, *Feldman's 24th Song Annual*, published by B. Feldman & Co, London, 1920s, 11in (28cm) high.
£5–6 SVB

Sheet music, *The Sing-as-we-go Song Book*, edited by Gracie Fields, 1933, 9¼in (23.5cm) high.
£2–3 RAD

The booklet was presented free with Woman's World *magazine.*

Sheet music for 'Farewell To Dreams', by Gus Kahn and Sigmund Romberg, 1937, 11in (28cm) high.
£2–3 RAD

Sheet music for 'It Can't Be Wrong', by Kim Gannon and Max Steiner, published by Chappell & Co Ltd, London, 1944, 9½in (24cm) high.
£2–3 RAD

Sheet music for 'One Night of Love', by Gus Kahn and Victor Schertzinger, published by The Sterling Music Publishing Co Ltd, London, 1934, 12in (30.5cm) high.
£2–3 RAD

Sheet music for 'Jealousy', by Winifred May and Jacob Gade, published by Lawrence Wright, 1942, 12½in (32cm) high.
£1–2 RAD

Sheet music for 'The Harry Lime Theme', by Michael Carr and Jack Golden, published by Chappell & Co Ltd, London, 1950, 11in (28cm) high.
£2–3 *RAD*

Sheet music for 'Angry', by Dudley Mecum, Jules Cassard, Henry and Merritt Brunies, published by Keith Prowse Music Publishing Co Ltd, London, 1950s, 11in (28cm) high.
£2–3 *RAD*

Sheet music for 'I Could Have Told You', by Carl Sigman and Arthur Williams, published by Gale & Gayles Ltd, London, 1954, 11in (28cm) high.
£2–3 *RAD*

Sheet music, *Tennessee Ernie Album of Favourite Songs*, published by Campbell, Connelly & Co Ltd, London, 1950s, 11in (28cm) high.
£5–6 *SVB*

Sheet music for 'I've Grown Accustomed to Her Face', by Frederick Loewe, published by Chappel & Co Ltd, incomplete, 1956, 11in (28cm) high.
50p–£1 *RAD*

Sheet music for 'Goodness Gracious Me!', by David Lee and Herbert Kretzmer, published by Essex Music Ltd, 1960, 11in (28cm) high.
£3–4 *RAD*

Sheet music for 'Return To Sender', by Otis Blackwell and Winfield Scott, published by The Manor Music Co Ltd, London, 1962, 11in (28cm) high.
£7–8 *RAD*

Sheet music for 'Go Now', by Larry Banks and Milton Bennett, published by Belinda (London) Ltd, London, 1963, 11in (28cm) high.
£3–4 *SVB*

Sheet music for 'I Just Can't Help Believin', by Cynthia Weil and Barry Mann, published by Chappell & Co Ltd, London, 1968, 10in (25.5cm) high.
£7–8 *RAD*

Sheet music for 'Boy', by Geoff Stephens and Howard Blaikley, published by Meteor Music Publishing Co Ltd, London, 1968, 11¼in (28.5cm) high.
£3–4 *RAD*

Sheet music for 'Think It All Over', by Chris Andrews, published by Sunbury Music Ltd, London, 1969, 11in (28cm) high.
£2–3 *RAD*

Sheet music for 'The Good Old Bad Old Days', by Leslie Bricusse and Anthony Newley, published by The Peter Maurice Co Ltd, London, 1971–2, 11in (28cm) high.
£1–2 *RAD*

SHIPPING

A late Georgian bronze-barrelled naval signal cannon, with slightly flared muzzle, turned reinforcers, integral conical trunnions, swollen cascabel, on a bleached hardwood stepped truck with 4 wheels and steel fittings, barrel 29in (73.5cm) long.
£1,300–1,600 *WAL*

A cast iron 10lb cannon ball, 18thC, 3½in (9cm) diam.
£10–15 *NC*

A woolwork commemorative picture, late 19thC, 23in (58.5cm) wide.
£150–200 *NC*

A brass tobacco box, commemorating Admiral Lord Nelson, with battles listed on reverse, early 19thC, 2in (50mm) diam.
£380–420 *TVM*

A steamer chair, from the Liverpool Steamship Co, c1880.
£200–250 *NC*

A wooden fid, for splicing rope, late 19thC, 11¾in (30cm) long.
£25–30 *BSA*

A ship's copper and brass masthead lamp, c1900, 24in (61cm) high.
£200–250 *JUN*

Funnel-topped ship's lamps were designed for paraffin. The fluted cap was added protection since it allowed the rain to run off. Later ships' lights were made for electricity and tops were flat.

A pair of Chinese painted and carved wood book ends, carved in relief with ships and pagodas, c1900, 7½in (19cm) high.
£55–65 *TIH*

A black and white photograph of the *Titanic* leaving Belfast, a modern copy from the original negative of 1912, 9in (23cm) wide.
£10–12 *COB*

l. A pair of copper and brass ship's lanterns, with swing handles, and plaques for 'Port' and 'Starboard', by Wm Harvie, Glasgow, late 19th/early 20thC, 19in (48.5cm) high.
£250–300 *WW*

Two Centuries of Shipbuilding, published by Scotts of Greenock, full leather-bound edition, 1920, 11in (28cm) high.
£65–75 *BAf*

A Union Steamship Co china plate, flag mark stamped on reverse, c1920, 9½in (24cm) diam.
£45–55 *COB*

A Royal Naval Officer of the Watch type single draw telescope, c1920, 24in (61cm) extended.
£150–200 *NC*

A Norwegian pattern rotary fog horn, 1930s, 21in (53.5cm) wide.
£100–150 *NC*

l. A silver-plated souvenir loving cup, from SS *Oxfordshire*, Bibby Line, 1920s, 1½in (38mm) high.
£18–20 *BAf*

A ship's saloon chair, from SS *Mulbera*, British India Steam Co, 1922.
£250–300 *NC*

This chair was designed to be bolted to the deck in bad weather.

A souvenir butter knife, from RMS *Strathnaver*, P & O Line, 1930s, 6in (15cm) long.
£12–18 *BAf*

r. A postcard depicting HMS *Queen Mary*, 1936, 5½in (14cm) wide.
£2–5 *COB*

A souvenir powder compact, from the aircraft carrier HMS *Furious*, 1940s, 2in (50mm) diam.
£18–25 *BAf*

A souvenir petrol lighter, from the troopship SS *Empire Fowey*, 1940–50s, 2in (50mm) high.
£20–25 *BAf*

A US Navy clock, by the
Chelsea Clock Co, Boston,
1940–50s, 8in (20.5cm) diam.
£125–175 *NC*

A bridge pedestal
telegraph, by
A. Robinson & Co,
Liverpool, 1940–50s,
38in (96.5cm) high.
£700–800 *BAf*

Two ships in a bottle, made by a sailor,
c1950, 11in (28cm) long.
£30–40 *NC*

A Siebe-Gorman diver's torch, c1950,
10in (25.5cm) long.
£50–60 *NC*

A brass porthole, 1950s,
14in (35.5cm) diam.
£100–120 *NC*

Two wood and steel ship's
blocks, c1950, 15in (38cm) high.
£20–30 each *NC*

A Union Castle Line chamber
pot, by Ashworth Brothers,
1950–60s, 8½in (21.5cm) diam.
£35–45 *BAf*

An azimuth circle, c1950,
10in (25.5cm) wide.
£30–40 *NC*

*The azimuth circle is placed on
top of the ship's compass and
used for taking land bearings
and coastal observation.*

A brass bell, engraved 'Spearfish
1956', 10in (25.5cm) high.
£300–350 *NC*

l. A Sestrel brass lifeboat
compass, with light attachment,
c1953, 9in (23cm) high.
£130–150 *NC*

A brass and wood ship's wheel,
with wire steering attachment,
1950s, 21in (53.5cm) diam.
£150–200 *NC*

r. A Shaw Savill Line bottle
opener, in the form of an
anchor, c1958, 5½in (14cm) long.
£20–25 *BAf*

A pewter table cigarette lighter, in the form of a U-boat, marked 'U–581', 1960s, 9in (23cm) long.
£15–20 *BAf*

A cardboard bingo card, from SS *Andes*, 1960s, 8in (20.5cm) square.
£15–20 *COB*

A steward's teapot, made for the Cunard Steamship Co Ltd, by George Clews & Co, 1950s, 4½in (11.5cm) high.
£35–45 *BAf*

A Union Castle Line white Bakelite Thermos flask, c1960, 9in (23cm) high.
£25–30 *BAf*

l. A double brass masthead light, c1980, 16in (40.5cm) high.
£100–150 *NC*

r. A padded chair from the restaurant of Cunard liner *QE2*, 1980s.
£100–120 *NC*

A souvenir tray, depicting the maiden voyage of the *QE2*, 1969, 18in (45.5cm) long.
£15–30 *COB*

r. An enamel badge, depicting the RMS *Titanic*, 1990s, 1½in (3.8cm) wide.
£3–5 *MAP*

A lithograph of the SS *Lusitania*, entitled 'The Final Farewell', by Ken Marschall, 1990s, 32in (81.5cm) wide.
£40–50 *MAP*

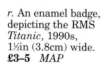

SILVER & METALWARE
Brass & Copper

A brass pestle and
mortar, early 19thC,
pestle 7in (18cm) long.
£70–75 *CHe*

A copper coffee pot, with wooden
handle and acorn finial, c1820,
12½in (32cm) high.
£275–300 *ANT*

A brass warming pan, with
wrought iron handle, hinged
and domed lid, pierced and
chased with a floral pattern,
18thC, 41in (104cm) long.
£150–200 *AH*

A pair of brass watchmaker's
callipers, 19thC, 3¾in (9cm) long.
£25–30 *BSA*

A Victorian brass spitoon,
5½in (14cm) high.
£25–35 *PPe*

A Victorian copper quart
measuring jug, marked 'VR/200
Blackburn', 7½in (19cm) high.
£45–60 *MEG*

A copper and brass hot water
bottle, 1930s, 8in (20.5cm) diam.
£10–12 *PPe*

A group of 3 brass wise monkeys,
1930s, 2⅛in (55mm) wide.
£12–15 *TAC*

A brass adjustable whistle, with
engraved notes 'E', 'F', 'G', and
'A', c1950, 3⅝in (9cm) closed.
£30–40 *WAB*

A brass desk bell, with original
legs and feet clapper, c1900,
4in (10cm) high.
£20–25 *CHe*

Bronzes

A pair of bronze figures of cherubs, c1800, 9in (23cm) high.
£800–1,000 *PC*

A pair of French bronze models of greyhounds, c1810, 6½in (16.5cm) long.
£250–300 *SSW*

A Regency bronze model of a horse, on a gilded base, c1820, 5½in (14cm) high.
£350–400 *WeH*

A Viennese bronze rabbit, c1860, 2¼in (5.5cm) high.
£220–260 *SSW*

A Viennese cold-painted bronze model of a dog, c1860, 5in (12.5cm) wide.
£450–500 *SSW*

A bronze cold-painted cat and kitten group, 1920–30s, largest 1¾in (4.5cm) high.
£85–100 *MAC*

Bronze statuettes

Bronze statuettes became extremely popular in the 19thC, when they decorated many middle-class Victorian homes. The process of mechanical reduction was invented in France by Achille Collas and patented in 1834.

A popular subject for bronzes included miniature versions of famous statues by both contemporary and classical artists, animals and sentimental themes. France produced some of the best 19thC bronzes and it was not until the second half of the 19thC that English foundries developed the technology to rival European manufacturers. Bronzes are often marked with both the signature of the artist and the stamp of the foundry.

Value depends on subject, artist and manufacturer as well as quality, rarity and patination.

A miniature bronze model of a tortoise, signed 'Hagenauer', 1930s, 2in (50mm) long.
£85–95 *WeH*

r. A bronze model of a rearing kid, on a green and black marble base, c1910, 12in (30.5cm) high.
£500–550 *WeH*

A bronze statue, depicting the young Queen Victoria in court dress with sash and decorations, a crown upon her head, finished in silver and gilt, mounted on an onyx base, numbered '113' of 500, 1981, 9½in (24cm) high.
£140–160 *SAS*

Door Furniture

A cast iron door knocker,
18thC, 8in (20.5cm) high.
£300–350 *DOR*

Four sets of nickel-plated metal
door furniture, each comprising
a pair of door handles and a
pair of escutcheons, designed
by Walter Gropius in
1928 for Wehag, handles
4⅛in (11.5cm) long.
£1,000–1,200 *CSK*

*This door furniture was
designed by German architect
Walter Gropius (1883–1969),
founder of the Bauhaus
movement. Gropius was one
of the most significant figures
in the history of modernism.
He turned his design skills
to everything from buildings,
to furniture, to wastepaper
baskets, and even his most
utilitarian works are hugely
collectable today.*

A brass eagle
door stop, c1840,
15in (38cm) high.
£130–150 *SSW*

A brass door
knocker, c1880,
8in (20.5cm) high.
£80–90 *HEM*

A bronze door
knocker, c1890,
6in (15cm) high.
£120–150 *DRU*

Fireplace Furniture

A cast iron fireback, depicting
Warwick Castle, late 19thC,
19in (48.5cm) high.
£40–50 *WEE*

A pair of cast iron andirons, in
the form of an owl with glass
eyes, c1890, 13in (33cm) high.
£200–220 *CHe*

l. A pair of brass
and cast iron
andirons, 19thC,
22in (56cm) high.
£400–500 *RAC*

r. A set of Art
Deco fire irons,
incorporating
an ashtray and
pipe rack, with
chrome stand and
brown Bakelite
base, c1925,
26in (66cm) high.
£75–85 *TIH*

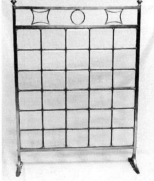

A brass fire screen, with leaded
glass, 19thC, 28in (71cm) high.
£180–220 *ASH*

Silver & Silver Plate

A Georgian silver cream jug, with prickwork scroll panel, c1800, 5½in (14cm) wide.
£180–200 *PSA*

An Old Sheffield silver plate wine coaster, with mahogany base, c1840, 6in (15cm) diam.
£100–125 *JAS*

A silver candle snuffer, by Edward Hutton, London 1891, 3½in (9cm) long.
£325–350 *BEX*

Silver Marks

Hallmarking was first instituted in Britain in 1300. On British silver there are usually 4 basic marks, read from left to right:
1. The 'Hall' or 'Town' mark, the stamp of the Assay office where the quality of the metal was tested.
2. The 'Standard' or 'Quality' mark indicating the standard of the silver – Sterling silver bears the device of the lion passant.
3. The annual date letter, showing the year in which the object was hallmarked.
4. The maker or sponsor's mark, consisting of the symbol or initials of the maker or retailer.

When assessing a piece of silver, the first mark that should be looked up is the hallmark since each Assay office used different date letters to indicate the year of production.

Two silver sovereign cases,
l. Birmingham 1909,
r. W. M. Neale, Chester 1889, 1in (25mm) diam.
£220–260 each *THOM*

r. A silver book mark, Birmingham 1896, 4in (10cm) long.
£35–45 *PSA*

A Dutch silver cow milk jug, naturally modelled with its tail curled to form the handle, a hinged lid with an insect knop, glass bead eyes, .934 standard and export marks, and London import marks for 1891, 11in (28cm) long.
£1,700–2,000 *DN*

l. A Continental silver parrot pepper shaker, c1925, 3in (7.5cm) high.
£500–550 *DIC*

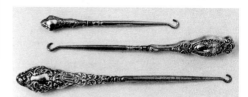

Three silver-handled button hooks, marked Birmingham 1899–1907, longest 4½in (11.5cm).
£20–30 each *GAK*

Button hooks were an essential Victorian accessory for doing up the tiny buttons on boots, gloves and tight-fitting clothing.

Three miniature books:
l. with Art Nouveau silver cover, London 1903, by William Comyns, 2in (5cm) wide.
£120–140
c. Birthday Book, with silver and leather cover, by W. Matthews, Chester 1905, 2in (5cm) wide.
£150–175
r. Tennyson – Poetical Works, with silver cover, by William Comyns, London 1905, 2in (5cm) wide.
£250–275 *THOM*

Cutlery & Tableware

A pair of silver bright-cut sugar tongs, by Hester Bateman, London c1784, 5in (12.5cm) long.
£75–100 *DIC*

A silver fish slice, with pierced and engraved fiddle pattern and fish design, by Benori Stephens, London 1835, 12¼in (31cm) long.
£300–325 *TC*

A silver marrow scoop, with thread edge, by George Adams, London 1843, 9in (23cm) long.
£150–170 *TC*

Used for extracting the marrow from cooked bones, these implements came with a large scoop at one end and a smaller one at the other. Marrow scoops can also be found on the handle end of spoons.

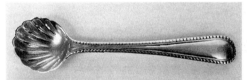

A silver salt spoon, London 1873, 3in (7.5cm) long.
£20–25 *AMH*

Two pairs of silver salt spoons, Birmingham 1852 and 1879, largest 4¼in (11cm) long.
£180–200 each pair *AMH*

A silver and ivory travelling apple corer, c1804, 4in (10cm) long.
£100–120 *PSA*

A silver tea caddy spoon, by Thomas Robinson II and Samuel Harding, London 1809, 3½in (9cm) long.
£150–170 *AMH*

A silver and mother-of-pearl butter knife, by Yapp and Woodward, Birmingham 1846, 7in (18cm) long.
£60–70 *AMH*

A silver and mother-of-pearl fork, by Hilliard and Thomason, Birmingham 1859, 6¾in (17cm) long.
£55–60 *AMH*

A silver sugar crusher, by Thomas Smily, with twisted stem, London 1873, 5½in (14cm) high.
£200–230 *TC*

A silver sifter spoon, with vine leaf decoration by Hilliard & Thomason, Birmingham 1881, 5in (13cm) long.
£200–225 *AMH*

An American sterling silver orange peeler,
by Gorham & Co, c1900, 6in (15cm) long.
£220–250 *BEX*

A silver jam spoon, Sheffield 1898,
6in (15cm) long.
£50–55 *AMH*

A silver King's pattern cheese scoop,
by Goldsmiths & Silversmiths Co Ltd,
London 1925, 8¼in (21cm) long.
£300–330 *TC*

A set of 6 silver spoons, marked for 1934,
3½in (9cm) long.
£50–60 *CHe*

*These spoons are terminated with the traditional
good luck symbol. The Germans reversed this
emblem to transform it into the swastika.*

A silver lemon juice extractor, by Adie Bros,
Birmingham 1930, 3¼in (8.5cm) long.
£150–170 *BEX*

Photograph Frames

l. A silver photograph
frame, by L. Emmanuel,
Birmingham 1893,
8in (20.5cm) high.
£400–450 *THOM*

A silver photograph
frame, by W. Comyns,
London 1892,
6½in (16.5cm) wide.
£420–460 *THOM*

A silver photograph
frame, by W. J. Myatt
& Co, Chester 1905,
8in (20.5cm) high.
£300–350 *THOM*

A silver photograph
frame, by A. & J.
Zimmerman,
Birmingham 1913,
4½in (11.5cm) high.
£165–185 *THOM*

l. A silver photograph
frame, by J. & W.
Deakin, Sheffield 1916,
7in (18cm) high.
£300–340 *THOM*

l. A silver photograph
frame, with 2 scroll
feet and an oak back
and strut, Chester
1918, 9in (23cm) high.
£90–120 *PSA*

Salts

A pair of Victorian silver salts, with embossed scroll and foliate decoration, gadroon edging, lion mask and claw-and-ball feet, London 1859, 3½in (9cm) diam.
£300–340 *Bea(E)*

A pair of silver salts, maker M. H. & Co, Sheffield 1862, 2½in (65mm) diam.
£150–170 *WAC*

A pair of silver and gilt salts, marked 'GM, JM', London 1872, 2¼in (55mm) diam.
£90–100 *WAC*

Caring for Silver Salts

Always empty salt cellars after use as salt corrodes silver, and wash them together with their spoons as soon as possible. Use warm soapy water, rinse meticulously and dry carefully with a soft cloth – keep them in their box and in tissue paper.

A set of silver salts and spoons, Birmingham 1895, salts 3in (7.5cm) wide, in original box.
£120–140 *WAC*

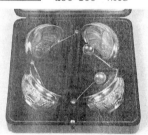

A set of 4 silver salts and spoons, Birmingham 1904–05, salts 2¼in (55mm) wide, with original box.
£250–300 *RAC*

A pair of silver and gilt salts, marked 'M. S.' Birmingham 1917, 5in (12.5cm) high.
£50–60 *WAC*

Toast Racks

l. A George III silver six-division toast rack, by Thomas Hatter, London 1813, 5½in (14cm) long.
£250–300 *PSA*

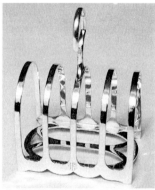

A Victorian silver six-division toast rack, all supported on 4 cast acanthus feet, with centre ringlet carrying handle, by Barnard Bros, London 1846, 6in (15cm) long.
£220–250 *GAK*

r. A silver-plated four-division toast rack, in the form of a car, c1900, 6in (15cm) long.
£250–275 *SFL*

A silver-plated four-division toast rack, by Walker & Hall, c1910, 4in (10cm) long.
£45–55 *ABr*

SIXTIES & SEVENTIES

There is currently huge interest in the 1960s and 1970s. Fashions from these decades are once again popular, and as well as wearing newly-designed flares, platforms and Union Jack mini dresses, young trendies have been patrolling the flea markets and vintage clothes stores to seek out period originals. Auction houses are hosting a growing number of modern design sales, and 1960s and '70s plastic and chrome furniture now regularly appears alongside polished wooden masterpieces from previous centuries. Ever more dealers are focusing on post-war products in every medium causing many antiques fairs to shift their date lines to incorporate more recent objects.

The most collectable works from the 1960s and 1970s tend to be pieces by well-known designers, such as Eero Aarnio, Ettore Sottsass, Joe Colombo etc, as well as objects that have become icons of the period such as the lava lamp and the Globesphere

television, famously modelled on an astronaut's helmet. Space travel, pop art, pop music, film and TV were all important influences on period design, and plastic was a favourite material for creating works that looked colourful, fun and futuristic.

Buyer beware! The 1960s was the decade that pioneered throwaway culture and built-in obsolescence. Period icons, such as paper and inflatable chairs, were designed for the instant gratification of a youth market and were never expected to last. According to specialists in the field, it is hard to find plastics in the good condition that is so crucial to value.

Many objects are still affordable and can be picked up from car boot sales and junk markets. Prices are rising steadily, however, particularly for the best pieces and as we reach the millennium and the 20th century becomes history, 1960s and 1970s style can only become more collectable.

Sixties

A pink plastic bobble sculpture, 1960s, 15in (38cm) high.
£20–25 PLB

A card political beer mat, depicting Harold Wilson, 1960s, 3¾in (9.5cm) square.
50p–£1.00 PC

'The Laurie Johnson Orchestra Plays *The Avengers* And Other Favourites' record, c1965, 12in (30.5cm) diam.
£25–35 CTO

The Avengers was launched in 1961, with Patrick Macnee as Steed – Honor Blackman was succeeded as the female star in 1965 by Diana Rigg. These attractive women, clad in the latest fashions, helped turn the show into a cult.

A James Bond belt buckle, and white metal badge, inscribed 'Special Agent 007', 1960s, badge 1½in (4cm) high.
Belt buckle £130–150
Badge   £40–50 CLW

Created in the 1950s, James Bond became a cinema hero and popular icon in the 1960s. James Bond material is very collectable today and rarities, such as the belt buckle, command high prices.

A pair of Carlton Ware salt and pepper shakers, depicting lions' faces, 1960s, 3½in (9cm) high.
£18–20 PLB

Dolls & Toys

A chrome Newton's cradle, 1960s, 7¼in (18.5cm) high.
£15–17 *GIN*

Two World of Love dolls, Peace and Flower, 1971, 10¾in (27.5cm) high, with original boxes.
£35–40 each *TBoy*

The complete set of dolls also included Love and Soul.

A Sindy No. 1 doll, with weekender outfit, 1962, 12in (30.5cm) high, with booklet and original box.
£120–150 *CLW*

This is the very first Sindy doll. She was launched in 1962 by the Pedigree Doll company to compete with Barbie. Sindy might have had a more adolescent figure than her American rival, but she too boasted an enormous wardrobe and was billed as 'the doll you love to dress'.

Fashion

A suede jacket, with sheepskin collar and press stud fastenings, 1960s.
£18–22 *BOH*

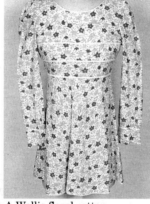

A Wallis floral cotton mini dress, 1960s.
£10–12 *BOH*

A pair of Mary Quant red tights, in original packaging, 1960s.
£4–5 *HUX*

A dolly rocker green mini dress, with matching jacket, designed by Sambo, 1960s.
£15–18 *BOH*

A man's tan leather jacket, with suede cap, 1960s.
Jacket £35–40
Cap £10–12 *Har*

A pair of fur and leather shoes, 1960s.
£15–18 *TCF*

A long cashmere sleeveless cardigan, in burgundy, pink and white, 1960s, 48in (122cm) long.
£30–35 *BOH*

A black wool cloak, with fake fur trim and gold coloured buttons, 1960–65, 34in (86.5cm) long.
£20–25 *BOH*

A pair of Jean Varon cotton culottes, blue printed chiffon over white, 1970.
£20–25 *Har*

A Playfair London black and silver sequinned evening top, lined with silk, 1970s.
£30–35 *BOH*

A multi-coloured patchwork leather jacket, 1970s.
£20–25 *Har*

A Simon navy and white cotton jersey shirt, 1970s.
£6–8 *BOH*

Two plastic fake snakeskin shoulder bags, by Elliott of Bond Street, 1970s.
£4–8 each *Har*

A Harrods strawberry-coloured velvet blazer, 1970s.
£10–13 *BOH*

A pair of Charmaine hot pants, with skinny ribbed jumper, 1970.
£15–20 *Har*

r. A pair of black suede platform shoes, 1970s.
£10–12 *Har*

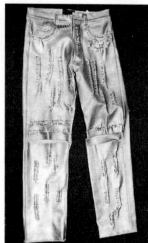

A pair of plastic trousers, with safety pins, by Joe Casely-Hayford, London, late 1970s.
£10–12 *Har*

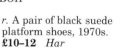

Furniture

A teak laminated side chair, designed by Grete Jalk, manufactured by Paul Jeppesen, Denmark, 1963, 30in (76cm) high.
£4,750–5,250 *CSK*

This chair is a very important designer piece, hence its high value.

A chrome and leather adjustable armchair, 1970s, 37in (94cm) high.
£120–140 *Har*

A child's red and cream corduroy bean bag, in the form of a boxing glove, by Hobart Rose, 1970s, 40in (101.5cm) long.
£65–75 *PLB*

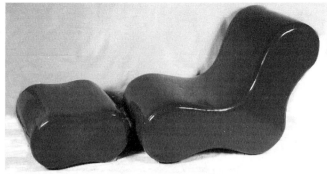

An Alvar red vinyl lounge chair, with matching ottoman, designed by Guiseppe Raimondi, 1967, chair 32in (81.5cm) high.
£1,500–2,000 *CSK*

A white laquered-wood barboy cabinet, designed by Verner Panton, 1963, 28½in (72.5cm) high.
£475–525 *CSK*

A Zanotta inflatable chair, including clear plastic seat, with foot pump, Italian, 1967.
£250–300 *CSK*

Inflatable chairs were subject to punctures and were never intended to be durable. Condition is all important and collectors today prefer to buy old stock, unused and still boxed.

A steel and cane parrot chair, with tubular upright pedestal, 1960s, 69in (175.5cm) high.
£325–375 *CSK*

An Italian chrome and plastic bar stool, 1970.
£40–45 *Har*

Lighting & Electrical Equipment

l. A chrome and glass bubble lamp, 1960s, 17½in (44.5cm) high.
£90–110 *PLB*

The lava or bubble lamp was invented by British engineer Craven Walker in 1963. Initially many shops were reluctant to stock these curious liquid lights but, as psychedelia took hold in the mid-60s, demand boomed and the lava lamp became a colourful icon of '60s style and flower-power culture.

A Joe Colombo white plastic lamp/desk tidy, Italian, 1967, 13in (33cm) high.
£90–120 *PLB*

An Italian Artemide eclipse lamp, designed by Vico Magistretti, 1960s, 9in (23cm) high.
£50–60 *PLB*

A German fibre optic table lamp, 1970s, 18in (45.5cm) high.
£75–100 *Har*

A chrome sputnik light, 1970s, 11in (28cm) diam.
£90–110 *PLB*

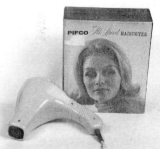

A Pifco hair dryer, 1960s, 9in (23cm) long, with original box.
£18–22 *GIN*

l. A Weltron 200S stereo console housing, with hinged lid enclosing turntable, radio and 8-track components, on a black painted metal pedestal, 1960s, 26in (66cm) high.
£300–400 *CSK*

r. A Brion Vega cube radio, 1970s, 6in (15cm) wide.
£120–150 *HEG*

Watches & Jewellery

An Old England wristwatch, with orange face and black vinyl strap, 1960s, 2½in (6.5cm) diam.
£120–140 *CSK*

Three plastic bangles, in yellow, red and green, 1960s.
£10–15 each *PLB*

SMOKING

A brass tobacco tin, with chased ship design, c1840, 4in (10cm) wide.
£60–80 *PC*

r. A brass repoussé tobacco tin, 1860, 3¼in (8cm) diam.
£30–40 *PC*

A Dutch fruit-wood pipe case, 18thC, 12in (30.5cm) long.
£500–600 *AEF*

An ivory pipe tamper, in the form of a mermaid, c1820, 3¼in (8.5cm) high.
£450–500 *AEF*

A silver matchbox holder, Birmingham 1902, 1¾in (4.5cm) long.
£30–40 *PSA*

A Mappin & Webb match striker, with silver top, c1930, 4in (10cm) high.
£200–220 *CHe*

r. A chrome ashtray, with black metal legs, 1960s, 24in (61cm) high.
£25–30 *TIH*

Lighters

A WWI lighter, c1918, 1in (25mm) high.
£20–25 *RAC*

A spherical silver-plated table lighter, 1960s, 2in (5cm) high.
£8–10 *RAC*

A metal lighter, in the form of a golfer, 1970s, 6in (15cm) high.
£25–35 *RAC*

Vesta Cases

A Victorian silver vesta case, modelled as a recumbent wild boar, marked 'LE', Birmingham 1888, 2¼in (5.5cm) long.
£800–850 *GH*

Vesta Cases

Friction matches – wooden sticks with a phosphorus tip – were produced from the 1820s. As phosphorous is a poisonous product, workers suffered from the fumes, and manufacturers sought to make their products safer. The result was the development of small waxed matches, named after Vesta, the virgin goddess of the hearth in Roman mythology.

Popular from the 1840s these new matches, also known as Lucifers, were successful but still volatile, and were kept in protective metal vesta cases, with a hinged lid and a ridged striking section. Often hung from the watch chain, vesta cases were produced in a huge variety of shapes, the most collectable today being novelty designs.

A brass vesta case, in the form of a boot, c1900, 2in (5cm) long.
£50–60 *GH*

An Austrian enamel vesta case, with concealed portrait of a nude, marked '925', c1900, 3¼in (8.5cm) high.
£1,700–2,000 *SHa*

A silver dog vesta case, modelled as Toby, marked 'SML', Birmingham 1890, 2½in (6.5cm) high.
£700–750 *GH*

A silver vesta case, Birmingham 1901, 1¾in (4.5cm) high.
£35–45 *PSA*

r. A white metal vesta case, in the form of a fox's head, c1910, 2in (5cm) high.
£100–110 *CHe*

l. A silver vesta case, Birmingham 1908, 1¾in (4.5cm) long.
£35–45 *PSA*

A silver vesta case, enamelled with a chisel and inscribed 'Don't [chisel] me out of it', marked 'LE', Birmingham 1895, 1½in (4cm) long.
£320–350 *GH*

A silver vesta case, the lid inscribed 'His Masters Voice', with the dog and horn gramophone trade-mark, the interior inscribed 'With the Compliments of the Gramophone Company Ltd', marked 'SM & Co', Chester 1907, 1¾in (4.5cm) wide.
£700–750 *GH*

SPORT
Baseball

A Moxie bottle label, depicting Ted Williams, on a red background, 1940s, 3½in (9cm) wide.
£10–15 *HALL*

A Fenway Park ticket stub, 1960s, 3¼in (8cm) high.
£250–300 *HALL*

This was Ted Williams' last game.

A leather baseball catcher's mit, 1930s, 12in (30.5cm) diam.
£175–200 *SMAM*

A pair of leather baseball boots, 1930s.
£150–180 *SMAM*

A set of 16 baseball plastic emblems, including Braves and Dodgers, on original cards, c1952, 2½in (6.5cm) wide.
£70–80 *HALL*

A Transogram plastic baseball, in original package, early 1960.
£25–30 *HALL*

Billiards

A cartoon from *Punch,* entitled 'Officers' Grievances', 1876, 7in (18cm) high.
£35–45 *BRA*

A mahogany carousel cue stand, with spring clips, holds 18 cues, c1900, 48in (122cm) high.
£850–950 *ABC*

Billiards

Billiards first became popular in the 16thC, and by the 17thC it was an expected diversion in country houses. The 19thC saw the development of the modern game as we know it. In 1826, the first slate bed table was made for Whites Club by John Thurston, who was also the first to introduce rubber as opposed to felt cushions on the table.

The 19thC also witnessed the introduction of the leather-tipped cue, and in 1868 American inventor John Wesley Hyatt produced the first thermo-plastic ball. As plastic technology developed, composition balls gradually replaced traditional ivory balls.

A mahogany portable life pool scorer, c1890, 19in (48.5cm) high.
£350–450 *BRA*

A golden oak combined billiard and dining table, by E. J. Riley, c1900, 72in (183cm) long, closed.
£2,500–3,000 *BRA*

Two sets of billiard balls, in original boxes, c1900, 7in (18cm) long.
£40–50 each *BRA*

A box of wafers for cue tips, in original box, c1920, 2in (5cm) diam.
£5–10 *BRA*

A selection of billiard table and accessory manufacturers' plaques, 1860–1930.
£4–6 each *BRA*

An E. J. Riley *Billiards for Modern Homes* trade catalogue, 1932–3, 10in (25.5cm) wide.
£40–50 *BRA*

Three Victorian billiard table irons, stamped, 10in (25.5cm) long.
£50–60 each *BRA*

Boxing

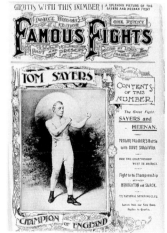

A collection of *Famous Fights* magazines, with numerous black and white illustrations of boxers and fights, volumes 1–5, Nos. 1–52 bound as one, c1901–02, 12in (30cm) high.
£170–200 *DW*

Billy Edwards, *The Portrait Gallery of Pugilists of England, America, Australia*, with 96 plates, published by London & Philadelphia, c1894, 13in (33cm) high.
£200–230 *DW*

A pictorial magazine, depicting the stories of Randolph Turpin and Sugar Ray Robinson, by Frank Butler, 1950s.
£4–5 *MAC*

Cricket

A cricketers' brass measure, c1920, 4⅛in (11.5cm) diam.
£45–50 *CHe*

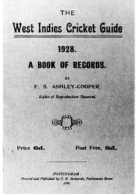

A signed album page of *Cricket Australia*, with other non-related items, c1926.
£160–180 *VS*

The above is signed by members of the side which played at Nottingham on 12–15th June 1926, including Collins, Mailey, Andrews, Bardsley, Ellis, Oldfield, Macartney, Sydney Smith etc. This match was played for only one hour on the first day.

l. F. S. Ashley Cooper, *The West Indies Cricket Guide, A Book of Records*, with original printed wrappers, 1928, 7in (18cm) high.
£50–60 *DW*

A miniature cricket bat, c1910, 5½in (14cm) long.
£12–15 *BIL*

A cricket bat, signed by Surrey and Yorkshire players, 1985, 33in (84cm) high.
£40–50 *WAB*

Croquet

An Edwardian mahogany croquet mallet stand, c1900, 36in (91.5cm) high.
£150–175 *MUL*

A presentation croquet mallet, with ebonised handle and ivory head, c1870, 30in (76cm) long.
£100–120 *MSh*

A Dutch wooden snuff box, carved in the shape of a shoe, 19thC, 4½in (11.5cm) long.
£200–250 *AEF*

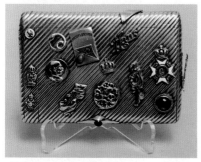

An Imperial Russian officer's cigarette case, St Petersburg, marked '84', c1890, 4in (10cm) wide.
£1,000–1,250 *SHa*

A bronze bear match striker, with glass eyes, 19thC, 3in (7.5cm) high.
£150–180 *BaN*

A Victorian silver and enamel vesta, maker SM, London 1886, 2in (5cm) high.
£1,300–1,500 *GH*

A brass vesta, modelled as a human skull, c1915, 2in (5cm) high.
£55–75 *GH*

A base metal vesta, in the form of Mr Punch, 1890s, 2½in (6.5cm) high.
£75–95 *GH*

A German enamelled cigarette case, painted in the manner of Raphael Kirschner, maker's mark for Fritz Bemberg of Pforzheim, c1900, 3½in (9cm) high.
£750–850 *P*

An Austrian enamel vesta, c1900, 3½in (9cm) high.
£2,000–2,250 *SHa*

A Continental white metal and cloisonné vesta, 1920s, 1¾in (45mm) high.
£120–150 *GH*

A chrome aeroplane lighter, with Sarome pocket lighter as cockpit, 1950s, 8in (10.5cm) long.
£75–85 *FAM*

A Ronson enamel and chrome lighter, with felt case and box, 1950–60, 3in (7.5cm) high.
£30–40 *FAM*

A leather quiver of arrows, with 10 arrows, c1920, 24in (61cm) long.
£65–75 *RTh*

A *New York Yankees* yearbook, by Jay Publishing, c1956, 6 x 5in (15 x12.5cm)
£60–80 *HALL*

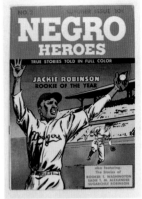

Negro Heroes comic book, issue No. 2, featuring Jackie Robinson – Rookie of the Year, c1950, 8 x 6in (20.5 x 15cm) long.
£100–125 *HALL*

A complete set of 20 Fleer Gum baseball pennants, 1960s, 8in (20.5cm) wide.
£50–60 *HALL*

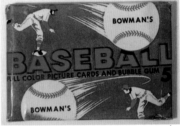

A pack of 7 Bowman baseball cards, unopened, 1954.
£75–95 *HALL*

A Muhammad Ali action figure, The Champ, in original package, 1976, figure 8in (20.5cm) high.
£50–60 *HALL*

Two jars of Riloid billiard cue tipping cement, c1910, 3in (7.5cm) high.
£15–20 each *BRA*

A collection of cricket memorabilia, 1940–50s, largest 8½in (21.5cm) high.
£50–60 *MAC*

A humorous billiard cartoon, from *Punch*, 1927, 7in (18cm) wide.
£60–70 *BRA*

A French table croquet set, c1860, in a pine box, 15½in (39.5cm) wide.
£65–85 *CPA*

An original print, depicting a fishing fly, by G. Kelson, c1880, 6in (15cm) square.
£55–65 *RTh*

An enamel sign, 1910, 10in (25.5cm) high. **£180–200** *JUN*

A Hardy Jack Scott lure, unused in original box, c1930, 4in (10cm) wide. **£65–75** *RTh*

A Malloch Traill salmon prawn lure, carded, c1930, 4in (10cm) high. **£35–40** *RTh*

A Farlow's enamelled steel tea tray, decorated with salmon flies, c1950, 15in (38cm) diam. **£15–20** *OTB*

A set of 4 silver memo holders, each containing a salmon fishing fly, Chester 1912, 1¾in (45mm) diam. **£700–750** *AMH*

A Welsh International jersey, No. 9 to back, worn and signed by Dean Saunders (Nottingham Forest), 1996/97 season. **£110–130** *P(C)*

A Brazil football shirt, and 2 World Cup 1994 pennants, signed by Pele, pennant 30in (76cm) long. **£120–140** *SAF*

The Sun newspaper page, signed by Les Ferdinand and Alan Shearer, and a poster signed by David Grinola, 1990s. **£14–18** *SAF*

A velvet Gloucestershire RFU cap, embroidered with badges and date badges from 1891–1901. **£160–200** *P(C)*

With the All Blacks in Springbokland by M. F. Nicholls, 1928. **£50–50** *P(C)*

A Royal Bradwell Sports Series mug, 1920s, 3in (7.5cm) high. **£70–80** *AAV*

A Farnell Winnie The Pooh bear, c1920, 18in (46cm) high.
£1,000–1,200 *TED*

A Bing gold plush teddy bear, with boot button eyes, swivel head, pads replaced, c1910, 14in (35.5cm) high.
£1,000–1,200 *BaN*

A Bing teddy bear, with button on arm, c1925, 17in (43cm) high.
£2,500–3,000 *TED*

A Knickerbocker gold mohair musical teddy bear, label on chest, c1930, 14¼in (36cm) high.
£150–200 *TED*

A Chad Valley Magna teddy bear, c1930, 20in (51cm) high.
£350–450 *TED*

A teddy bear, with kapok-filled body, 1940s, 15in (38cm) high.
£65–75 *HEI*

A Merrythought teddy bear, with stitched nose and claws, c1960, 16in (41cm) high.
£160–180 *TED*

A teddy bear, c1950, uniform not original,15in (38cm) high.
£80–100 *TED*

A Pedigree teddy bear, 1950s, 18in (45.5cm) high.
£240–260 *BaN*

A straw-filled cat, with cloth body, registered oval stamp, c1920, 12in (30.5cm) high.
£70–80 *BaN*

A Norah Wellings cloth elephant, late 1920s, 9in (23cm) high.
£150–180 *BaN*

A fake fur armadillo, 1970s, 9½in (24cm) high.
£10–15 *DOL*

A Pedigree Noddy, with cap bell and bow tie, c1980, 15in (38cm) high.
£10–12 *CMF*

A straw-filled monkey, with glass eyes and padded feet, c1920, 8in (20.5cm) high.
£30–45 *BaN*

Florence and Mr Rusty glove puppets, c1966, largest, 10in (25.5cm) high.
£24–28 *CMF*

An Art Deco feather-filled quilt, 1920s, 55in (140cm) wide.
£100–150 *TT*

An Edwardian patchwork quilt, 102 x 94in (260 x 240cm).
£650–750 *TT*

A child's tartan wool dress, with short sleeves, 1950s.
£15–20 *Har*

A Victorian short silk cape, with tassels to sleeve and bottom edge.
£150–200 *TT*

A Victorian silk princess line dress, with buttoned front and original bustle, 1870–80.
£250–350 *TT*

A rayon sleeveless evening dress, with tasselled hem, 1920s.
£100–150 *TT*

A full-length rayon evening dress and bolero, with velvet belt, 1930s.
£75–85 *Ech*

A pair of Harrods brocade shoes, with gold and silver leather trim, with diamanté buckle, 1930s.
£65–75 *Ech*

A German painted wood Noah's ark and various animals, late 19thC, 23in (58.5cm) long.
£2,200–2,600 *Bon(C)*

A tinplate billiard toy, complete, 1920s, 6in (15cm) high.
£530–580 *P(Ba)*

A Lines Brothers pedal horse, c1910, 41in (104cm) long.
£800–1,000 *JUN*

A wood and metal milk cart, c1925, 15in (38cm) high.
£500–550 *JUN*

A wooden pedal train, 'Leeway Flyer', 1930, 44in (112cm) long.
£200–250 *JUN*

An Alps clockwork celluloid 'Traveling Boy', Japanese, c1950, 4in (10cm) high.
£100–120 *RAR*

Two Hornby wagons, boxed, c1927, 3¼in (8.5cm) high.
l. **£160–180** *r.* **£40–60** *HOB*

A Britains Knights of Agincourt figure, 1954, 4in (10cm) high.
£100–120 *OTS*

A Triang pedal car, c1940, 24in (61cm) long.
£120–150 *BAf*

A Schuco Mercedes, 1950s, 8¼in (21cm) long.
£200–220 *RAR*

A Lesney Massey Harris tractor, c1950, 8in (20.5cm) long.
£120–150 *JUN*

An Austin J40 pedal car, requires restoration, c1940, 59in (150cm) long.
£200–300 *JUN*

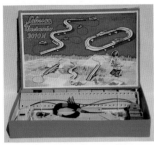

A Schuco Varianto 3010H car set, with saloon car and truck, c1950, 14in (35.5cm) long.
£200–230 *RAR*

A Japanese tinplate car, 1960s, 9in (23cm) long.
£60–80 *JUN*

A Sutcliffe tinplate clockwork Nautilus from *20,000 Leagues Under the Sea*, 1950s, 10½in (27cm) long.
£80–100 *RAR*

A Noddy plastic bagatelle game, 1975, 7½in (19cm) diam.
£10–12 *CMF*

A Distler clockwork tinplate Mercedes convertible, c1950s, 10in (25.5cm) long.
£140–160 *RAR*

An Arnold tinplate remote-controlled car, boxed, 1950s, 10in (25.5cm) long.
£200–220 *RAR*

A Hornby No. 6135 SNCF B0-B0 and 2 coaches, boxed, c1960s, 13in (33cm) wide.
£110–130 *RAR*

A Märklin No. 3071 Tee set, mint and boxed, c1971, 12in (30.5cm) long.
£150–180 *OTS*

A Matchbox MF-1 fire station, mint and boxed, 1960s, 10in (25cm) wide.
£90–100 *RAR*

A Budgie Toys No. 266 delivery sidecar, 1963, 4in (10cm) long.
£80–100 *RAR*

A Snoopy bi-plane, 1960s, 5in (12.5cm) long.
£8–12 *PPe*

Two Pedigree model horses, boxed, 1970s, 14in (35.5cm) wide.
£100–150 each *SVB*

A Corgi Toy No. 268, boxed,
mid-1960s, 5in (12.5cm) long.
£90–110 *P(Ba)*

A Dinky Supertoys No. 503 Foden Flat
Truck, c1947, 7¼in (18.5cm) long.
£70–80 *OTS*

A Dinky Toys No. 071 Volkswagen
Delivery Van, mint and boxed,
c1960, 2¼in (6cm) long.
£35–45 *OTS*

A Corgi Noddy car, with
Noddy, Big Ears and Golly,
1960s, 4in (10cm) long.
£70–80 *P(Ba)*

A Corgi Toys No. 152S Grand
Prix Racing Car, mint and
boxed, c1961, 3½in (9cm) long.
£50–60 *OTS*

A Dinky Toys No. 930 Bedford lorry,
boxed, c1960, 6½in (16.5cm) long.
£65–75 *AAC*

A Dinky Toys No. 065 Morris pick-up,
mint and boxed, c1957, 2½in (6cm) long.
£35–45 *OTS*

A Dinky Supertoys No. 956 Turntable
Fire Escape, c1960, 3¼in (8.5cm) long.
£90–100 *NTM*

A Dinky Toys No. 404 Conveyancer Forklift
truck, c1967, 4in (10cm) long.
£20–25 *AAC*

An Ideal Batman child's play
suit, c1966.
£50–60 *CTO*

An Eaglton Toys battery-
operated robot, boxed,
1960s, 12in (30.5cm) high.
£30–40 *RAC*

A Mattel Space Crawler,
1960s, 14in (35.5cm) wide.
£100–120 *OW*

A *Battlestar Galactica,*
Ovion action figure, carded,
1978, 9in (23cm) high.
£10–15 *OW*

A Japanese clock-
work robot, 1960s,
8½in (21.5cm) high.
£140–160 *P(Ba)*

A *Star Trek* Scotty
action figure, 1984,
8in (20.5cm) high.
£40–50 *OW*

A Palitoy Bradgate
talking Dalek, parts
missing, c1975,
6in (15cm) high.
£40–45 *CTO*

A *Dr Who* action figure, mint and boxed,
1979, 10½in (26.5cm) high.
£80–100 *OW*

A *Buck Rogers* Tiger Man
action figure, boxed, c1979,
9in (23cm) high.
£115–135 *OW*

A Matchbox Thunderbird 2, with
stand, 1992, 6in (15cm) long.
Boxed   £10–15
Unboxed £8–10 *OW*

A *Star Trek* Captain
Kirk doll, 1979,
12in (30.5cm) high.
£50–60 *OW*

A *Star Wars* Chewbacca action
figure, mint condition, boxed,
1978, 12in (30.5cm) high.
£140–160 *TBoy*

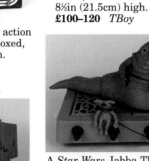

A *Star Wars* remote-controlled robot
R2D2, Italian version, boxed, 1978,
8½in (21.5cm) high.
£100–120 *TBoy*

A *Star Wars* Jabba The Hut playset,
unboxed, c1983, 11in (28cm) high.
£30–35 *CMF*

A *Star Wars* Bobafett
action figure, with all
accessories, 1980s,
12in (30.5cm) high.
£90–120 *TBoy*

An *Empire Strikes Back* At
At, with chin guns, unboxed,
c1979, 18in (45.5cm) high.
£35–45 *CMF*

A *Return of the Jedi* speeder bike
vehicle, c1983, 9in (23cm) long.
£20–25 *CMF*

An *Empire Strikes Back*
sticker album, 1980,
12in (30.5cm) high.
£40–50 *Ada*

A *Star Wars* Bib
Fortuna action figure,
c1983, 4in (10cm) high.
£7–10 *TBoy*

A *Star Wars* radio-controlled Jawa
Sandcrawler, mint condition, boxed,
c1979, 18in (45.5cm) wide.
£400–450 *TBoy*

A *Return of the Jedi* Luke
Skywalker action figure,
c1983, 9in (23cm) high.
£65–75 *TBoy*

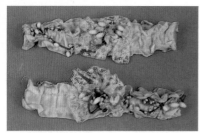

A pair of Victorian silk wedding garters, decorated with lace and flowers.
£45–50 *LB*

A pair of green artificial silk French knickers, 1940s, 17½in (44.5cm) long.
£12–15 *PC*

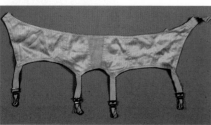

A pink satin suspender belt, 1940s, 27in (68.5cm) long.
£8–10 *PC*

A postcard depicting an underwear shop, by Bamford & Co, c1911, 5½ x 3½in (14 x 9cm).
£4–5 *THA*

A pair of Polka nylons, by Belmont, 1960s.
£4–6 *RAD*

l. A nylon leopard print half slip, 1970s, 19½in (49.5cm) long.
£2–3 *RMA*

A pink silk petticoat, c1930, 27in (68.5cm) long.
£55–65 *PC*

A pink corset, The Dracolena, 1920s, 31in (78cm) long.
£30–40 *PC*

A pair of Striking seamfree micromesh nylons, 1950s.
£4–6 *RAD*

A red nylon bra, unused, with label '5/11d', 1970s, size 32in (81cm) bust.
£3–4 *BOH*

A pair of Sheerest nylons, 1950s, in original packet.
£5–7 *RAD*

A silver pocket watch and chain, by
J. W. Benson, restored, London 1886,
2in (50mm) diam.
£355–385 *TIH*

A Swiss pocket watch,
engraved 'RMSP Asturias',
c1920, slight damage,
5in (12.5cm) high.
£110–130 *BAf*

A lady's 18ct gold fob
watch, with enamelled dial,
1920s, 1½in (38mm) diam.
£280–300 *BWC*

A Waltham gold wristwatch,
1in (25mm) high, c1937.
£170–200 *BWC*

A lady's silver and enamel brooch watch,
by Godwins & Son, London, 1920s,
4in (10cm) high, with original box.
£350–400 *BWC*

A gentlemen's Swiss wristwatch, with day, date and
month apertures, 1920s,
1½in (38mm) diam.
£200–225 *TIH*

A gold and agate desk seal,
c1820, 3in (7.5cm) long.
£2,250–2,500 *STH*

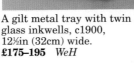

A gilt metal tray with twin
glass inkwells, c1900,
12½in (32cm) wide.
£175–195 *WeH*

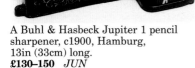

A Buhl & Hasbeck Jupiter 1 pencil
sharpener, c1900, Hamburg,
13in (33cm) long.
£130–150 *JUN*

A German wooden pen
and ink holder, c1870,
10½in (27cm) high.
£250–300 *SSW*

A 'GR' initialled post box,
with enamel collection plate,
1940s, 20in (51cm) high.
£250–300 *JUN*

A fake of a 1930s Carlton Ware bone china figure, colours and modelling coarser than on originals, with post-WWII black script mark, 1993–97, 7in (18cm) high.
Fake, no commercial value
CCI

l. A fairing, 'A mouse! A mouse!', incised marks on base, 19thC, 3in (7.5cm) high. **£80–100**
r. A fake fairing, colours are more stringent than the original, the modelling is clumsy and the script modern, mark not properly incised. **Fake £2–5** *SAS*

A fake Newcastle glass jug, foot formed from the body and not applied as with the original, made in Mexico, c1920–50, 5in (12.5cm) high.
Fake £20–30 *JHa*

A fake Carlton Ware golfer on ashtray and 2 figures, possibly based on heraldic ashtray produced c1900, the original golfer stood on a white/mother-of-pearl ashtray and was not produced as an independent figure, with Cooper black mark, 1994–7, 3½in (9cm) high.
Fake, no commercial value
If original £85–100 *CCI*

A set of fake toucan wall plaques, the colours are flatter than on originals, definite line between orange and yellow bands on the breast as opposed to the colours blending in, the biggest give away is no feet, which appear on the originals shaded in blue, largest 10in (25.5cm) long.
Fake, no commercial value
If original £200–250 *CCI*

A 19thC Samson of Paris porcelain plate, decorated with 'GR' monogram, simulating commemorative pieces produced for the golden jubilee of 1809, 9in (23cm) diam.
£70–90 *SAS*

A fake Carlton Ware seal, on the original model the seal is Guinness coloured and the head on the beer is cream, 1993–7, 3¾in (9.5cm) high.
Fake, no commercial value
If original £100–150 *CCI*

A Carlton Ware drayman pulling a horse and cart, original *left*, fake *right*, which has more muted colours than the original 1960s model and absence of a red-painted swag bag, 1993–7, 5½in (14cm) wide.
l. **£400–500** *CCI* *r.* **Fake, no commercial value**

An embroidered postcard, sent from France during WWI.
£4–5 *MAC*

A Ronson service outfit tin, 1950s, 4in (10cm) long.
£4–5 *FAM*

A silk velvet neck tie, with triangular design, 1930s, 36in (91.5cm) long.
£4–5 *Ech*

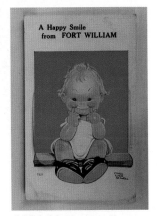

A Mabel Lucie Attwell postcard, 1930s, 5½in (14cm) high.
£3–5 *CMF*

A Snoopy plastic rain hat, 1970s, 9in (23cm) diam.
£3–5 *PPe*

Kellogg Co, International Soccer Stars, set of 12, 1961.
£3–5 *LCC*

The Strand magazine, April 1949, 8in (20.5cm) high.
£4–5 *SVB*

A barrel ashtray, 1950s, 3½in (9cm) high, with original box.
£1–2 *TRE*

A boxed set of Chad Valley dominoes, 1950–60s, 7½in (19cm) long.
£4–5 *TRE*

A plastic and metal chain belt, with silver metal medallion, 1960s, 32in (81.5cm) long.
£3–4 *BOH*

Three plastic Smurf models, 1970s, 2¼in (5.5cm) high.
£4–5 *MAC*

Two candles depicting Margaret
Thatcher and Tony Blair, 1997,
9in (23cm) high.
£8–10 each   *CAN*

*Margaret Thatcher material is already
sought after, but New Labour is the
party who will be inspiring the
political commemoratives of the 1990s.*

A silver-gilt and enamel ring,
in the form of a Tudor rose,
by Vivienne Westwood, 1997.
£150   *PC*

*British designers are currently
dominating world fashion.
Vivienne Westwood, originator of
the punk look, is the 'grand dame'
of British radical style and her
creations are a strong contender
for collectable of the future.*

Two Eggbert figures, Peak Beak and Brand's
Hatch, c1992, 4in (10cm) high.
£10 each   *PC*

*There is huge demand for modern collectables
and Eggberts are a case in point. Created in
1983, the chicks come in many forms, and the
collector's club now has over 3,000 members.
Eggberts are the winner of this year's collectables
of the future competition.*

A *Nightmare Before Christmas*
talking Jack Skellington, 1993,
18¾in (47.5cm) high.
£200–250   *TBoy*

*It is not only the most popular toys
that become collectable. Nightmare
Before Christmas items did not sell
well. This makes them rare and
collectors now pay surprisingly high
prices for these very recent toys.*

A *Toy Story* Buzz Lightyear talking action figure, 1996,
13in (33cm) high. **£25.00**   *PC*
Teletubbies figures, **£13–15 each** *CtC*

*Every Christmas there is a 'must have' toy. In 1996 it was
Buzz Lightyear and in 1997 it is the Teletubbies. In 30 years
time will today's children be buying back the toys of their
youth from antique dealers? Watch this space and remember
toys are at their most collectable when mint and boxed.*

A *Star Wars* Tazo collector's
pack, 1997, 8½in (22cm) high.
£2.50–3
Tazos 10–40p each   *PC*

*These Tazos came free with
Walkers crisps in 1997 but
are already being sold by
science fiction dealers.*

Three *101 Dalmations* McDonald's Happy Meal
figures, 1997, 2¾in (7cm) high.
40–60p each   *PC*
*These are already being collected by adult
Disney enthusiasts, trying to build up the
complete set of figures.*

Fishing

A pair of Christopher Johnson & Co folding fishing scissors, in leather case, Sheffield, 1865–1920, 4½in (11.5cm) long.
£8–10 *AnS*

A mid-Victorian brass tackle clearing ring, with walnut retrieving line bobbin, c1870, 2½in (6.5cm) diam.
£120–150 *OTB*

r. A W. B. Gowland and Co greenheart boat rod, with brass furnishings, c1870, 84in (214cm) long.
£50–70 *OTB*

A stuffed and mounted porbeagle, by W. H. Rowe, from the St Michaels Mount Collection, Penzance, c1896, 40¼in (102cm) wide.
£150–200 *AXT*

An Allcock's patent nickel-silver and plated-brass scissor-style pike gag, c1900, 7½in (19cm) long.
£90–120 *OTB*

A set of 'sensitive' scales, by C. W. Brecknell Ltd, engraved 'Princess Royal Angling Society, Victoria Road, Aston', balance scale measuring 0–4lb, ounces and grams, complete with metal dish, in original box, early 20thC, 14in (35.5cm) wide.
£175–200 *MUL*

A J. Bernard and Son japanned metal cast box, with flies and casts, early 1900s, 5in (12.5cm) diam.
£150–170 *RTh*

A Hardy brass gaff, with spring balance scale, c1910, 15in (38cm) long.
£525–575 *RTh*

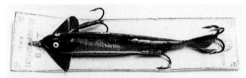

An Excelsior Phantom lure, with leather body, unused, 1920, 4in (10cm) long, on original card.
£40–45 *RTh*

A Hardy Bethune line dryer, c1900, 13in (33cm) long.
£700–800 *RTh*

This piece is rare and in excellent condition, hence its high price.

r. A collection of 27 baits and lures, including Percy Wadham, Land Em, Loach, Nature Baits and others, c1900.
£1,000–1,200 *ND*

A wicker fishing creel, c1920, 12in (30.5cm) wide.
£40–50 *JUN*

A Hardy Drifly Dresser, c1929, 3¼in (8.5cm) long.
£50–60 *PC*

l. An ash hooped landing net, with bamboo-handle, 1930s, 17½in (44.5cm) long.
£30–35 *WAB*

Two Hardy Neroda fly boxes, with chenille bar linings, c1940, 6½in (16.5cm) long.
£50–70 each *OTB*

Reels

A Hardy 2⅛in Transitional Perfect reel, with ventilated drum and ivory handle, 1892–93.
£4,000–5,000 *PC*

A 4in rosewood and brass Perth-style salmon reel, by Crockart of Blairgowrie, c1860.
£400–450 *OTB*

A Farlow 2⅛in brass crankwind trout reel, with raised rear check housing, and turned ivory handle, c1870.
£300–350 *OTB*

A 4in walnut, alloy and brass trotting reel, by Slater of Newark, c1895.
£400–450 *OTB*

A Hardy Perfect 2⅛in wide-drum reel, c1896.
£1,200–1,400 *PC*

A Hardy Perfect 3⅜in brass-faced reel, with ivory handle, c1900.
£450–500 *MUL*

A Hardy Perfect 3in wide drum alloy trout reel, c1906.
£550–600 *RTh*

An Edward Vom Hofe multiplying reel, American, 1910.
£500–550 *RTh*

A Hardy Super Silex 3⅜in casting reel, with black leaded alloy cage and bright alloy drum, c1935.
£300–350 *OTB*

A Hardy 5in Sea Silex reel, c1930s.
£300–350 *PC*

A Hardy Silex Major 4⅛in extra wide alloy casting reel, for mahseer fishing, with ribbed brass foot, c1930.
£120–150 *OTB*

An Illingworth No. 5 trout reel, with finger pickup, foot stamped No. 1269, in original leatherette box, c1937.
£130–150 *MUL*

Football

A French football programme, London v. Paris, 25 December, 1907, 8½in (21.5cm) high.
£130–150 *MUL*

A wooden football rattle, 1930s, 11in (28cm) long.
£25–35 *CPA*

A Northampton Town v. Cardiff City football programme, 20 March, 1937, 8½in (21.5cm) high.
£70–80 *P(C)*

A full-sized leather football, c1950.
£25–30 *SSW*

A framed and glazed signed photograph of Sir Stanley Matthews, with 1954 Cup Final programme signed by Tom Finney, programme 9in (23cm) high.
£45–55 *SAF*

A Manchester United F.C. postcard, signed in ink by 14 United players, with 3 other postcards, c1958, 5in (12.5cm) wide.
£210–230 *P(C)*

Signatures include Busby, Curry, Taylor, Edwards, Jones, Byrne, Colman, Whelan and Pegg, most of whom lost their lives in the Munich Air Disaster in 1958.

A souvenir programme, signed by Nat Lofthouse, Stanley Matthews (twice), Tom Finney (twice), Matt Busby, Alf Ramsey, Tommy Lawton, with signed 'Lion of Vienna' record, c1989, programme 8¼in (21cm) long.
£30–35 *SAF*

An English International long-sleeved round necked jersey, with No. 6 to back and embroidered badge, c1966.
£1,600–1,800 *P(C)*

This Jersey was worn by Bobby Moore, West Ham United and England, post-1966, and was presented to the surgeon, who delivered the first child of Moore and his wife Tina. It is accompanied by a black and white photograph of Moore, his wife and the child – signed by Moore 'Best wishes and thank you for all your help'.

Golf

A gutty golf ball mould, stamped Morris, with leather cushion pad and press, 1850, 15in (38cm) high.
£6,700–7,500 *MUL*

Gutty balls made from gutta percha, a rubber-like substance, were first introduced in 1848. One of the advantages was that they could be melted down and remoulded when they had been knocked out of shape. The original moulds are extremely rare and this example fetched a world record price when sold at auction.

r. A silver-headed golf club, inscribed 'Captain's Putter', c1930.
£1,000–1,200 *MUL*

Mecca cigarette cards, Champions Golf, set of 6, 1911.
£350–375 *HALL*

A bronze plaque, depicting the golfer Harry Vardon, by Markes, c1900, 17½in (44.5cm) high.
£700–800 *MSh*

A poker in the form of a golf club and ball, with cast iron enamelled base, 1930s, 15in (38cm) high.
£30–40 *TAC*

A plastic Roger de Courcey trophy, for the Benson & Hedges Golf Invitational, 1994, 5½in (14cm) high.
£1–2 *TRE*

Four gutty golf balls: *l.* 2 Colonel Bramble, *c.* Silver Town golf ball, *r.* Agrippa Bramble ball, and one other, c1910.
£60–80 each *MUL*

Horses & Hunting

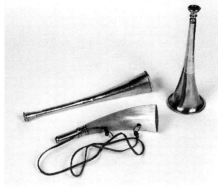

Two printed silk scarves, entitled 'The Derby 1875', and 'The Derby 1876', decorated with horses, 32in (81.5cm) wide, framed and glazed.
£200–220 *Bon(W)*

Three hunting horns, in copper, copper and brass and horn with silver mounts, 1890–1930, largest 7¾in (19.5cm) long.
£30–40 each *WAB*

l. A Irish silver hunting horn, c1900, 8¾in (22cm) long.
£450–500 *RTh*

A Victorian silver-mounted conical glass spirit flask, with leather carrying case and straps, Birmingham 1894, 10in (25.5cm) long.
£160–180 *AAV*

Rugby

A Cardiff Rugby Football Club sepia team photograph, captioned with playing record and players' names, 1885–6, 19¾in (50cm) wide.
£30–35 *P(C)*

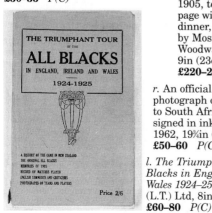

An album page, signed by 16 members of the Rugby Union All Blacks on 2nd December, 1905, together with a similar page with an invitation for the dinner, laid down and signed by Mosfan-Owen and Vivian Woodward, album page 9in (23cm) long.
£220–250 *VS*

r. An official black and white team photograph of the British Lions tour to South Africa, captioned to mount, signed in ink by 32 of the tour party, 1962, 19¾in (50cm) wide.
£50–60 *P(C)*

l. The Triumphant Tour of the All Blacks in England, Ireland and Wales 1924–25, published by Watkins (L.T.) Ltd, 8in (20.5cm) high.
£60–80 *P(C)*

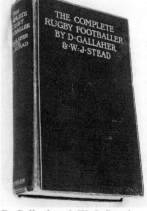

D. Gallagher & W. J. Stead *The Complete Rugby Footballer*, with cloth cover plates, signed by J. B. G. Thomas, 1906, 10in (25.5cm) high.
£100–120 *P(C)*

Shooting

A Scottish wooden decoy duck, c1880, 11in (28cm) long.
£200–225 *RTh*

A canvas and leather cartridge bag, 1930s, 6½in (16.5cm) long.
£25–30 *WAB*

An American decoy wading bird, with metal beak and pole, c1900, 8in (20.5cm) wide.
£130–150 *RTh*

A Cogswell & Harrison leather and oak magazine case, to take 600 cartridges, 1910, 16in (40.5cm) long.
£550–650 *RTh*

A bamboo shooting stick, with rattan seat and brass fittings, c1900, 30in (76cm) long.
£250–300 *RTh*

Tennis

A collection of 15 *Lawn Tennis and Badminton* magazines, c1912, 12in (30.5cm) high.
£200–250 *MUL*

A ceramic figure, depicting a lady playing tennis, c1920, 6in (15cm) high.
£65–85 *WaR*

r. A box of Slazenger Demon tennis balls, with box, 1950s, 10in (25.5cm) long.
£20–30 *WaR*

A Hazel Streamline Blue Star tennis racket, 1930s, 27in (68.5cm) long.
£180–220 *WaR*

SUFFRAGETTES

Suffragette was a name coined by *The Daily Mail* newspaper to describe the British women who fought for the vote, especially in the years 1903–14. They sought votes for women on the same property qualifications that applied to men and also universal suffrage.

Leading figures in the struggle included Mrs Emmeline Pankhurst (1858–1928), founder member of the Women's Social and Political Union, and her three daughters Christabel (1880–1958), Sylvia (1882–1960) and Adele (1885–1961). The militant members of the WSPU demonstrated in public, refused to pay taxes, damaged property and, famously, chained themselves to railings. 'We are not ashamed of what we have done,' claimed Christabel Pankhurst in a speech in 1908, 'because, when you have a great cause to fight for, the moment of greatest humiliation is the moment when the spirit is proudest.' The Suffragettes were repeatedly imprisoned, and when they went on hunger strike were brutally force fed. The Establishment treated them harshly and they were much mocked, hence the creation of ceramics which caricatured the so-called 'Shrieking Sisterhood'.

It wasn't until after WWI that Lloyd George in 1918 awarded women over 30 the vote (subject to property qualifications) in recognition of their war efforts. In 1928 these qualifications were removed, and women became, politically at least, the equals of men. Suffragette memorabilia is very sought after today and represents a fascinating period in our social history.

A German ceramic biscuit barrel, in the form of the head of a Suffragette, inscribed 'I say Down with the Trousers', c1912, 5½in (14cm) high.
£500–600 *TVM*

A Doulton inkwell, inscribed 'Votes for Women', c1912, 3¼in (8.5cm) high.
£400–450 *TVM*

A Swan crested china bell, in the form of a Suffragette on one side, inscribed 'She shall have votes', the reverse showing Mrs Gamp and the crest of Clacton-on-Sea, c1913, 3½in (9cm) high.
£75–85 *W&S*

Two Arcadian crested china bells, in the form of Suffragettes, decorated with Dovercourt and Hastings crests, 1907–14, 2¾in (7cm) high.
£130–150 *TVM*

Two Arcadian bells, in the form of Suffragettes, 1907–14, 2¾in (7cm) high.
£130–150 *TVM*

Oz underground magazine, issue No. 29, with back cover photograph showing a Suffragette being arrested, c1978, 11½in (29cm) high.
£10–12 *CTO*

TEDDY BEARS & SOFT TOYS
Teddy Bears

A German teddy bear, with original clothes, c1914, 18in (45.5cm) high.
£350–400 *CMF*

This bear is named William Pitt and was given to his owner in 1914 when she was 3 years old. He remained there until 1994 when his owner died, aged 83.

A straw-filled teddy bear, distressed condition, possibly English, c1910, 18in (45.5cm) high.
£200–250 *BaN*

A German teddy bear, with blonde plush fur, black boot button eyes, nose, mouth and claw stitching, replaced pads, c1906, 15in (38cm) high.
£750–850 *BaN*

A Steiff dancing bear skittle, c1890, 9½in (24cm) high.
£400–500 *TED*

A pink and blue coloured teddy bear, with black boot button eyes, replaced pads, distressed condition and colour faded, possibly English, c1915, 16in (40.5cm) high.
£200–250 *BaN*

An English mohair teddy bear, with elongated arms, glass eyes, stitched nose and mouth, 1920s, 17in (43cm) high.
£250–300 *CMF*

A miniature mascot teddy bear, with black glass bead eyes, nose missing, well worn condition, c1920, 5⅝in (14.5cm) high.
£150–175 *BaN*

A Schuco scent bottle mohair teddy bear, fully jointed, 1930s, 3in (7.5cm) high.
£250–275 *CMF*

Novelty teddy bears were very popular in the 1920s and '30s. The German company, Schuco, specialised in miniature bears, which came in various colours and styles. Bears concealed powder compacts or scent bottles, came with 2 faces – one happy and one sad – nodded and twisted their heads and were portrayed in many different guises. Today Schuco bears are very collectable and this example would appeal to scent bottle enthusiasts as well as arctophiles (bear collectors).

A German mohair teddy bear, with black boot button eyes, stitched nose and mouth, replacement pads and paws, 1920s, 13in (33cm) high.
£250–275 *CMF*

l. A ginger mohair teddy bear, maker unknown, 1930s, 9in (23cm) high.
£80–100 *TED*

A Schuco blonde mohair miniature teddy bear, fully-jointed, c1925, 3in (7.5cm) high.
£225–250 *CMF*

A Peacock gold mohair plush teddy bear, with amber glass eyes, protruding stitched snout and stitched claws, kapok filled swivel-jointed body, large felt pads and growler, wear to pads, 1930s, 27in (69cm) high.
£475–525 *P(Ba)*

A Knickerbocker teddy bear, with brown mohair fur, original label on chest, American, 1930s, 19¾in (50cm) high.
£200–250 *TED*

A pale gold mohair plush teddy bear, with large ears, amber plastic eyes, rounded stitched snout, excelsior filled body with swivel joints and felt pads, ears restitched, growler inoperative, late 1930s, 19¼in (49cm) high.
£90–120 *P(Ba)*

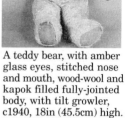

A teddy bear, with amber glass eyes, stitched nose and mouth, wood-wool and kapok filled fully-jointed body, with tilt growler, c1940, 18in (45.5cm) high.
£90–120 *BaN*

A Steiff caramel mohair fully-jointed miniature teddy bear, with button in ear and chest tag, 1950s, 4in (10cm) high.
£150–200 *TED*

r. A Chiltern long mohair teddy bear, with glass eyes, stitched snout, mouth and claws, label on foot, 1940s, 9in (23cm) high.
£150–175 *CMF*

A Chiltern mohair fully-jointed teddy bear, with glass eyes, stitched snout and mouth, 1940s, 15in (38cm) high.
£175–195 *CMF*

A Pedigree mohair teddy bear, with glass eyes, stitched nose and mouth, bells in ears, 1950s, 13in (33cm) high.
£100–125 *CMF*

A pale gold mohair plush teddy bear, with small ears, glass eyes, rounded stitched snout, excelsior filled swivel-jointed body, odd coloured eyes, squeaker inoperative, 1950, 8in (20.5cm) high.
£130–150 *P(Ba)*

A Wendy Boston
teddy bear, 1950s,
14in (35.5cm) high.
£30–40 *CMF*
*This bear was the
first fully washable
bear produced.*

A Schuco mohair fully
jointed teddy bear, with
glass eyes, stitched
snout and mouth,
and felt pads, 1960s,
23in (58.5cm) high.
£175–225 *CMF*

A teddy bear, with
nylon gold-coloured fur,
glass eyes, stitched
snout and mouth,
1970s, 20in (51cm) high.
£35–45 *HEI*

A Rupert Bear, with
glass eyes, white
nylon fur fabric head,
feet and paws, fitted
red nylon sweater,
yellow checked scarf
and trousers, 1970s,
24in (61cm) high.
£15–18 *CMF*

Soft Toys

A hide-covered cow, with repaired
leg, c1890, 4in (10cm) long.
£30–35 *PSA*

A Steiff white toy monkey,
with black boot button eyes,
and jointed limbs, underscored
'F' button in ear, c1910,
18in (45.5cm) high.
£700–800 *BaN*

A Schuco clockwork pig, with
glass bead eyes, felt-covered
metal body, dressed in green
trousers with red braces, key
missing, impressed 'Schuco
Patent Made in Germany',
1930–40s, 4½in (11cm) high.
£170–200 *P(Ba)*

A velveteen piglet,
excellent condition,
1920s, 4¼in (11cm) high.
£100–120 *TED*

*This piglet is similiar to the
original piglet in Christopher
Robin's* Winnie-the-Pooh.

A Steiff Niki rabbit, with
fully-jointed body, glass eyes,
felt open mouth, 'US Zone'
tag on left arm, c1950,
11¾in (30cm) high.
£140–160 *TED*

A Steiff stuffed toy dog, with
light and dark brown fur, glass
eyes, stitched snout, mouth
and claws, protruding tongue,
1950s, 6¼in (16cm) high.
£90–110 *MSB*

TELEPHONES

A Peel Conner telephone exchange, comprising 3-line 10-extension mahogany cased exchange with 6 jacks and wall bracket, 4 Beaven & Sons Ltd wooden/metal wall telephone boxes, fitted push-control handset with tortoiseshell-effect mouthpieces, side-winding handles activating twin bells, fuse boxes and wall panels with fitted bells, c1900, exchange 16in (40.5cm) wide.
£700–800 *GH*

A black Bakelite No. 11 wall telephone, with mahogany backboard and shelf, and 2 brass bells, c1910, 19in (48.5cm) high.
£300–350 *OTC*

r. A brass and Bakelite No. 150 candlestick telephone, with Type 25 bellset, c1920, 12in (30.5cm) high.
£350–400 *OTC*

A chrome and metal telephone, probably Danish or Swedish, c1900–1915, 10in (25.5cm) long.
£65–85 *MAC*

l. An American black Bakelite monophone, c1930, 9in (23cm) high.
£150–175 *CAB*

A wall-mounted telephone, with mahogany backboard and brass fittings, magneto boxcover missing, c1910, 17in (43.5cm) high.
£350–400 *JUN*

A Type 232 black Bakelite telephone, in working order, 1930s, 8in (20.5cm) high.
£140–160 *MAC*

An Ericsson brass and Bakelite house telephone, with mahogany base, 1920s, 5in (12.5cm) high.
£100–120 *OTC*

A Danish black Bakelite desk telephone, c1930, 7in (18cm) high.
£230–270 *OTC*

A Scrambler telephone, with jade green handset, 1940s, 9in (23cm) high.
£400–450 *CAB*

A Type 232 red Bakelite telephone, with matching bellset, c1938, 9in (23cm) wide.
£650–750 *CAB*

A Type 332 ivory Bakelite telephone, with bell on/off switch, 1938, 9in (23cm) high.
£200–235 *CAB*

Scrambler telephones were used during WWII. When the scramble button was pressed, voices would be distorted, thus preventing any unwanted or casual listeners from identifying the speakers. These black-bodied telephones came with a jade green handset in order to distinguish them from normal models. Period photographs of Sir Winston Churchill in the War Office, show a similar phone on his desk.

An AEI white acrylic telephone, with red handset, late 1950s, 9½in (24cm) high.
£30–35 *CAB*

A GEC sound-powered naval black telephone, with plated handset clamp, 1940s, 8in (20.5cm) high.
£120–150 *OTC*

A Type 300 clear plastic telephone, c1952, 9in (23cm) high.
£1,500–2,000 *CAB*

Plastic technology developed during WWII resulting in a wealth of plastic objects in the 1950s. Clear plastic, also known as Perspex or Lucite, was used for everything from handbags to stiletto shoes. Here, most unusually, it is applied to a telephone. This model was made for exhibition purposes. It is not only decorative, but extremely rare, hence its high value.

A Type 328 ivory Bakelite telephone, in working order, 1950s, 6in (15cm) high.
£160–200 *MAC*

A Type 232 green telephone, 1950s, 9in (23cm) wide.
£400–450 *CAB*

A Belgian black Bakelite telephone, 1950–60s, 4in (10cm) high.
£85–100 *CPA*

An Ericsson black wall phone, 1950s, 9½in (24cm) high.
£75–85 *CAB*

A Belgian blue and black desk telephone, 1950–60s, 5½in (14cm) high.
£110–130 *OTC*

A French black telephone, with additional receiver, 1950s, 6in (15cm) high.
£65–75 *CAB*

A cream Trimphone, 1970s, 7½in (19cm) long.
£15–18 *GIN*

A chrome finish Trimphone, with multi-coloured cable, c1965, 8in (20.5cm) long.
£100–125 *CAB*

Cross Reference
Fifties Style

---

r. A telephone coin box, with 'A' and 'B' buttons, 1950–65, 18in (45.5cm) high.
£145–155 *GIN*

A K2 red telephone kiosk, complete with interior, c1930.
Without interior
£7,500–8,000
With interior
£9,500–10,000 *CAB*

A British Telecom brown dial phone, c1981, 8in (20.5cm) long.
£20–25 *CAB*
This model was British Telecom's last dial phone.

TEXTILES

An embroidered panel, sewn into a cushion, depicting 2 parrots holding seed pods, finished with gold braid and damask, early 18thC, 13 x 19in (33 x 48.5cm).
£350–420 *JPr*

A Victorian Berlin woolwork picture, depicting an Italianate girl at a vine framed window, now mounted as a firescreen, 20½in (52cm) high.
£80–100 *DN*

l. A velvet dressing table set, decorated with a butterfly pattern, comprising a runner and 2 mats, 1920s, runner 24in (61cm) long.
£8–10 *Ech*

r. A pair of green suede gloves, with keyhole opening, 1960s, 8¼in (21cm) long.
£5–6 *BOH*

Gloves

A pair of brown leather motoring gauntlets, 1930s, 13in (33cm) long.
£10–15 *PC*

Hats

A Victorian child's burgundy velvet bonnet, complete with silk ribbon trim.
£90–100 *CCO*

An Edwardian brown velvet and plaited wool hat, with ostrich feather.
£125–145 *Ech*

> **FURTHER READING**
> Fiona Clark,
> *Hats,* published by
> B. T. Batsford, 1982

A straw cloche hat, trimmed with floral decorated ribbon and velvet flowers, 1920s.
£75–85 *Ech*

A green tweed cap, unworn condition, with label 'J. Birkett, Hatter & Hosier, 53 King Street, Whitehaven', 1930s.
£10–15 *CCO*

Ladies Fashions

A Victorian black lace
jacket, c1880.
£140–160 *TT*

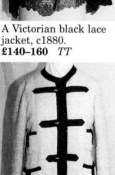

l. A Chanel black and
white woven wool
jacket, c1959.
£200–250 *TT*

A French black silk
dress, with jet bead
decoration, 1920s.
£200–250 *TCF*

A late Victorian two-
piece dress, of petrol
blue grosgrain silk,
decorated with lace
and velvet ribbon.
£150–180 *AAV*

A French chiffon dress,
with beaded flower
and gold ribbon
decoration, c1925.
£300–350 *TT*

Linen & Lace

A Brussels *point de gaz* needlelace fan leaf,
designed with a central bouquet surrounded by
palm leaves, blossom and scrolls, late 19thC,
28¼in (72cm) wide.
£300–350 *P*

An Edwardian
lawn and lace
handkerchief, c1910,
8in (20.5cm) square.
£10–12 *LB*

A silver lace shawl,
c1920, 51 x 44in
(130 x 112cms).
£100–150 *TT*

Samplers

A sampler, worked in green and black, the verse surrounded by stylised trees and birds, with an architectural view, by Elizabeth Mills, aged 11, 18thC, 17 x 18in (43 x 45.5cm).
£200–250 *LAY*

A cream linen map of England and Wales sampler, worked in coloured silks and black thread, by Eliza Kimber, 1809, 20 x 17in (51 x 43cm), gilt framed.
£300–350 *BIG*

A Georgian sampler, worked in coloured silks, with verse within a floral border, and signed 'Sarah Wheatley, May 1812', 14½ x 12¼in (37 x 31cm), in mahogany frame.
£440–480 *AH*

Condition

Condition is very important with samplers. Faded colours, moth holes and other damage will considerably reduce the value of a piece. Like any other textiles, they should be kept out of strong light and away from damp or extremes of temperature. For framing and restoration it is best to seek specialist advice.

Ties

A lady's silk velvet neck tie, with red, blue, yellow and green abstract pattern and mauve silk lining, 1930s, 36in (91.5cm) long.
£3–5 *Ech*

A gentleman's tie, depicting horse and hounds, 1940s, 50in (127cm) long.
£20–25 *RAD*

Shoes

A pair of green suede platform shoes, 1940s, 9⅞in (25cm) long.
£55–65 *PC*

A pair of Victorian lady's brown leather boots, lining printed with 'Royal Gay Boots'.
£1,150–1,250 *MUL*

TOYS

A brown painted wooden Noah's ark, on wheels with sliding door and window and a variety of carved wooden painted animals in pairs, including Noah and his wife, elephants, camels, giraffes, bears, leopards, kangaroos, birds and others, 19thC.
£500–550 *P*

A pair of Victorian wooden spinning tops, largest 2⅜in (6cm) high.
£5–8 each *OBS*

A selection of mid-Victorian marbles, largest 1in (25mm) diam.
50p–£20 each *MRW*

Values depend on the age of the marble and the quality and technique of the glass or china.

A collection of Schöenhut Humpty Dumpty circus toys, 1920s, Ringmaster 8¾in (22cm) high.
£1,000–1,200 *P*

A cast iron mangle, c1880, 10in (25.5cm) high.
£80–100 *SMI*

An American pine child's sleigh, with straw stuffed seat, late 19thC, 34½in (87.5cm) high.
£250–280 *MSB*

A set of Kew Tiger Tims' family, as new, in original box, c1932, 12in (30.5cm) long.
£400–450 *WAL*

This is a rare set.

A stacking snoopy, with green hat and red bow tie, 1980, 9¼in (23.5cm) high.
£15–20 *PC*

A Meccano Electron No. 1 outfit, some parts missing, boxed with instruction leaflet, c1933, 12in (30.5cm) wide.
£220–240 *CDC*

l. A Triang Minic balloon barrage wagon and trailer, and buckram and hessian type material balloon, c1940s, 18in (45.5cm), with original box.
£2,500–3,000 *WAL*

Corgi

A Corgi Toys gift set No. 1100 Bedford S-type articulated tanker, inscribed 'Shell, Benzeen, Tolueen, Xyleen', Dutch issue, 1961–62, 7½in (19cm) long.
£140–160 *P(Ba)*

A Corgi Toys No. 1104 machinery carrier, 1957, 9¼in (23.5cm) long, with original box.
£50–60 *AAC*

A Corgi Toys No. 419 police Ford Zephyr, white with red interior, 1960, 3¾in (9.5cm) long, with original box.
£35–40 *AAC*

A Corgi Toys gift set No. 41 car transporter and 6 cars, minor wear, boxed, 1960s, 10in (25.5cm) long.
£200–220 *WAL*

A Corgi Toys gift set No. 23 Circus Models, comprising 6 Chipperfields Circus vehicles/trailers and booking office, good condition, boxed, 1960s, 18in (45.5cm) long.
£300–350 *WAL*

r. A Corgi Toys No. 228 Volvo P180, boxed, c1962, 3¾in (9.5cm) long.
£40–45 *OTS*

A Corgi Toys Monkeemobile, 1960s, 5in (12.5cm) long.
£45–55 *SAF*

One of Corgi's best selling lines was film and TV related vehicles, most notably James Bond's Aston Martin. This car comes from The Monkees TV series, created in 1966. The Monkees were America's answer to the Beatles and effectively the grandaddy of bands such as the Spice Girls and Take That, since they were a manufactured group, designed and packaged for the TV generation, and not allowed to play instruments on their own records. The TV series was a big hit on both sides of the Atlantic inspiring spin-offs such as this Monkeemobile.

Dinky Toys

A Dinky Toys No. 62G Boeing 'Flying Fortress' monoplane, with gliding hole in top of fuselage, boxed, 1939, 3¾in (9.5cm) long.
£90–120 *AAC*

Did You Know?
The world record price for a Dinky Toy is £12,650 paid by a collector at auction for a 1937 Dinky Bentalls store delivery van.

A Dinky Supertoys No. 521 Bedford articulated lorry, slightly worn, boxed, 1948, 5¾in (14.5cm) long.
£35–40 *OTS*

A Dinky Toys No. 581 Horse Box, US issue, boxed, c1953, 8in (20.5cm) long.
£350–400 *RAR*

A Dinky Toys No. 38B Sunbeam Talbot sports car, c1949, 3½in (9cm) long.
£240–260 *RAR*

A Dinky Supertoys No. 514 Guy Slumberland van, 1st type cab, finished in red, boxed, 1950–52, 5½in (13.5cm) long.
£200–240 *Bon(C)*

Two Dinky Toys gift sets: *l.* No. 2 Commercial Vehicles, boxed, 1957–9, 10in (25.5cm) long.
£650–700
r. No. 149 Sports Cars, boxed, c1952, 12in (30.5cm) long.
£1,600–1,800 *TMA*

l. A Dinky Toys No. 504 Foden 14-ton tanker, inscribed 'Mobilgas', mint and boxed, 1950s, 7½in (19cm) long.
£250–300 *NTM*

r. A Dinky Toys No. 982 Pullmore car transporter, boxed, c1954, 9¾in (25cm) long.
£50–60 *OTS*

A Dinky Toys No. 34B Berliet container truck, French, boxed, 1950s, 5in (13cm) long.
£65–75 *NTM*

A Dinky Supertoys No. 512 Guy flat truck, with brown cab and green flat bed, boxed, 1950s, 5½in (14cm) long.
£110–130 *NTM*

A Dinky Toys No. 167 AC Aceca coupé, boxed, 1958, 3½in (9cm) long.
£130–150 *OTS*

A Dinky Supertoys No. 666 missile erector vehicle, with corporal missile and launching platform, mint and boxed, 1950–60s, 12in (30.5cm) long.
£180–200 *WAL*

A Dinky Supertoys No. 899 fire engine, French, boxed, c1960s, 6in (15cm) long.
£150–170 *RAR*

A Dinky Toys No. 702 DH Comet airliner, in white, silver and blue BOAC livery, with G-ALYV registration to right wing and rear tail fin, boxed, 1950–60s, 6in (15cm) wide.
£60–80 *WAL*

A Dinky Toys No. 883 AMX bridge laying tank, boxed, French, 1960s, 6in (15cm) long.
£100–125 *NTM*

l. A Dinky Toys No. 295 Atlas bus, boxed, 1963, 3¾in (9.5cm) long.
£25–30 *AAC*

r. A Dinky Toys No. 223 McLaren M8A Can Am, mint and boxed, 1971, 3¾in (9.5cm) long.
£30–35 *OTS*

Matchbox

The Lesney company was founded in 1947 by two ex-servicemen. In 1953, inspired by an employee's child who was only allowed to take playthings to school that were small enough to fit into a matchbox, they launched their most famous line. Matchbox toys were small, cheap enough for children to buy with their own pocket money, and were a huge success.

In 1956 the company introduced Models of Yesteryear, a series that is still in production today. These soon began to be collected by adults, which means that they are more likely to be found boxed and in good condition than the Matchbox miniatures aimed at children and known as the 1-75 series after the numbers applied to each model and which appear on the box. The most prized Matchbox models often date from the 1950s and early 1960s when the quality of manufacture was extremely high.

A Matchbox Series No. 31 Ford station wagon, boxed, 1957, 2¾in (7cm) long.
£20–30 *AAC*

A Matchbox Series No. 35 Marshall horse box MK7, with metal wheels, boxed, 1957, 2in (5cm) long.
£20–30 *AAC*

A Matchbox Series No. 38 Honda motorcycle and trailer, boxed, 1969, 3in (7.5cm) long.
£15–20 *AAC*

Model Soldiers

A Britains set No. 11 Highlanders Black Watch, first version, with officer, 1897, figures 2¼in (5.5cm), in original unnumbered box.
£200–220 *P(Ba)*

Three Britains figures from set No. 193 Arabs of the Desert, mint, 1920s, 4¼in (11cm) high.
£40–50 each *OTS*

A Märklin tinplate field gun, with tractor plates and kneeling artillery figure, pile of shells and Linoel 70mm tinplate rangefinder, 1937, rangefinder 2¾in (7cm) long.
£170–190 *P(Ba)*

A Britains British Infantry Soldiers of the British Empire Series, comprising officer and 7 men, 1948, figures 2¼in (5.5cm) high, in original box.
£750–800 *P(Ba)*

Paint style is c1948, and this is possibly a prototype sample of a set never issued under a regular set number.

A Britains Knights of Agincourt Series, boxed, 1954, figures 2¼in (5.5cm) high.
£220–250 *OTS*

Rocking Horses

A rocking horse, on bow rocker, possibly William Kain, c1820, 84in (213.5cm) wide.
£3,000–3,500 *STE*

A wooden rocking horse, with glass eyes, on twin pillar supports and platform base, 19thC, 44in (112cm) high.
£650–700 *DA*

A wooden horse tricycle, with horse hair mane and cast iron head, c1870, 26in (66cm) long.
£2,000–2,500 *AWT*

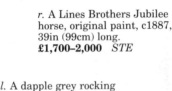

r. A Lines Brothers Jubilee horse, original paint, c1887, 39in (99cm) long.
£1,700–2,000 *STE*

l. A dapple grey rocking horse, with glass eyes, c1880, 51in (129.5cm) long.
£800–1,000 *AWT*

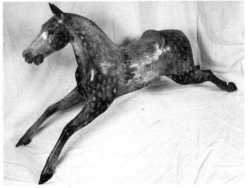

A wooden rocking horse body, requires restoration, c1880, 70in (178cm) long.
£3,000–3,500 *STE*

r. A Victorian child's painted toy horse, with pull-along wooden wheels and leather saddle, 33in (84cm) wide.
£550–600 *ANV*

A French wood and cast iron baby carriage, pulled by a horse, c1890, 60in (152.5cm) long.
£1,000–1,200 *STE*

A rocking horse, by F. H. Ayres, No. R1221, c1900, 61in (162.5cm) wide.
£1,500–1,600 *STE*

FURTHER READING

Hugo Marsh, *Miller's Toys & Games Antiques Checklist*, Miller's Publications, 1995

l. An Edwardian pull-along horse, on a four-wheeled cast-iron platform with pulling handle, metal eyes, grey Rexine saddle with satin braid harness, real horsehair mane and tail, distressed, 21in (53.5cm) high.
£160–180 *CDC*

A rocking horse, by F. H. Ayres, patent No. 5, inscribed to base 'Harrods Knightsbridge', c1900, 49in (124.5cm) long.
£1,800–2,000 *STE*

A dapple grey rocking horse, by F. H. Ayres, restored, original paint, new hair and leather, c1910, 50in (127cm) long.
£1,400–1,600 *STE*

Trestles gradually became preferred to bow rockers since they were both safer and took up less space in the nursery.

A push-along horse, made from wood off-cuts, c1910, 14in (35.5cm) long.
£80–100 *STE*

A Triang rocking horse, on trestle base, c1930, 32in (81.5cm) long.
£900–1,000 *STE*

Cross Reference
Colour Review

r. A pine rocking horse, c1930s, 29⅓in (74.5cm) long.
£75–95 *MSB*

A wooden hobby horse, with braid halter, 1950s, 48in (122cm) long.
£18–22 *WAB*

Science Fiction, Film & TV Toys

The popularity of science fiction, film and TV toys continues to grow. The fact that films and TV shows are released internationally means that there is a global market for related toys and accessories. Thanks to the Internet, enthusiasts in different countries can access each other and find out about old toys, new releases, fan clubs and events. Many collectors in this field have grown up with computers, and an increasing number of dealers now ply their trade on the worldwide web.

The most collectable subjects remain *Star Trek* and *Star Wars*. The *Star Wars* trilogy was responsible for launching the space race in terms of mass-merchandise. When the first *Star Wars* film opened in 1977 there was an unprecedented demand for toys, and by 1984, manufacturers Kenner and MPC had sold an astonishing 300 million *Star Wars* toys across the world. Many of those who became interested as children now collect *Star Wars* material as adults. Prices have risen sharply in recent years and this section includes a large selection of *Star Wars* toys. It is not just major films that attract a devoted following. Many TV series have their fans, who also seek out period

merchandise, 1960s and '70s material being particularly popular at the moment. Videos and repeats on television not only serve to keep the memories of favourite programmes alive, but are also attracting a new generation of children and potential collectors to cult shows ranging from *Thunderbirds* to *Doctor Who* to *Buck Rogers*.

Highest prices are reserved for rare toys – those produced only for a short run or perhaps only in one country, or for a specific range of shops. Condition is crucial and ideally toys should be mint, complete with packaging and all accessories. Toys and ephemera can very quickly become collectable, even if they cost nothing in the first place. In 1997, the Taco Bell fast food chain in the USA produced a series of four *Star Wars* toys to be given out free with kids meals. In Britain, where they were not available, a full set can retail for £20–30. Similarly *Star Wars* Tazos, which came free with Walker's crisps (*see Collectables of the Future, page 432*) were only distributed in the UK, and in consequence are now sought after by American collectors, as well as British enthusiasts, who failed to eat enough potato snacks to complete their sets.

A *Battlestar Galactica* Viper Launch Station, mint and boxed, c1978, 24in (61cm) long.
£40–50 *OW*

Two *Dr Who* Daleks, battery-operated, mint and boxed, 1964, 6in (15cm) high.
£100–150 *MRW*

A set of 5 *Planet of the Apes* bend and flex figures, mint and carded, 1967, card 8½in (21.5cm) high.
£100–140 set *TBoy*

A *Buck Rogers* Draconian Guard figure, mint and boxed, 1979, 12in (30.5cm) high.
£75–85 *OW*

A *Star Trek* Inter-Space Communicator, with plastic phones, boxed, 1974, 10in (25.5cm) wide.
£60–70 *CBP*

A Dinky Toys Thunderbird 2, boxed, 1978, 7in (18cm) long.
£80–100 *OW*

Star Wars

A *Star Wars* Rancorn, c1980, 12in (30.5cm) high. **£25–30** *CMF*

A *Star Wars* Jawa figure, with cape and gun, c1980, 2in (5cm) high. **£10–12** *TBoy*

A *Star Wars* R2D2 figure, with pop-up light sabre, c1984, 2¼in (5.7cm) high. **£60–70** *TBoy*

The value of this figure lies in the fact that it still retains its light sabre, which was very easily lost.

A *Star Wars* Stormtrooper, c1978, 12in (30.5cm) high. **£65–85** *TBoy*

The price of this toy depends on its condition, the white plastic can yellow with age thus lowering its value.

A *Star Wars* Tie Interceptor, c1980, 15in (38cm) wide. **£40–50** *CMF*

A *Star Wars* Luke Skywalker figure, in a stormtrooper's uniform, c1984, 3¾in (9.5cm) high. **£70–80** *TBoy*

It is rare to find this figure complete with helmet, hence its value.

A *Star Wars* Yak Face figure, c1985, 4in (10cm) high. **£80–100** *TBoy*

Yak Face was one of the series of action figures known as 'The Last 15', issued in the mid-1980s once Star Wars toys had begun to wane in popularity. It was never released in the US, only in Britain and Europe. As such, numbers were comparatively limited and in spite of its less than attractive features, it is a very desirable figure today.

l. A *Return of the Jedi* Battle at Sarlacc's Pit Game, with 3 dimensional board, 1980s, 14in (35.5cm) square. **£30–40** *Ada*

Star Wars Ephemera

A collection of *Star Wars* comics, Nos. 1–40, 1977–80.
£140–160 *CBP*

A *The Empire Strikes Back* story tape and book, c1980, 8in (20.5cm) wide.
£8–9 *CMF*

Six *Return of the Jedi* card backs, c1983, 8in (20.5cm) high.
£1–2 each *Ada*

In the toy world even packaging has a value. A resealed figure (ie replaced on a matching card) is worth considerably more than a loose toy.

Tinplate

A French tinplate woman pulling a cart, marked RF, c1910, 5in (12.5cm) long.
£140–170 *JUN*

A Lineol clockwork tinplate Mk II Panzer, with camouflage finish, slight damage, c1938, 7½in (19cm) long.
£350–400 *P(Ba)*

A tinplate aeroplane, fair condition, 1920s, 13in (33cm) long.
£50–60 *JUN*

Two clockwork tinplate birds, c1920, 10in (25.5cm) long.
£100–130 *JUN*

A Günthermann tinplate open-back truck and trailer, painted in green and orange, tipping loadbed with opening tailgate, minor wear, c1920, 17in (43cm) long.
£200–220 *WAL*

l. A Distler clockwork tinplate saloon car, painted in yellow and black, with battery-operated headlights, complete with driver, c1920, 10in (25.5cm) long.
£300–350 *WAL*

A Wells & Co tinplate
ambulance, with twin opening
rear doors and single piece
wheels, painted in cream
with black chassis, c1928,
6½in (16.5cm) long.
£200–250 *WAL*

A Meccano No. 1 constructor car, in
the form of a 4 seater open sports
tourer, with green body and tinplate wheels, yellow mudguards,
tonneau trim and red pressed
tinplate seats, some chipping,
c1930s, 10in (25.5cm) long.
£200–250 *WAL*

A tinplate Alfa Romeo P2
racing car, by CIJ of France,
painted in silver, with racing
No. 2 to bodywork and mesh
radiator grille, Alfa Romeo
Milano badge and radiator
cap to top of radiator,
good condition, c1930s,
18in (45.5cm) long.
£800–1,000 *WAL*

A tinplate circus horse musical box, 1950s,
12in (30.5cm) long.
£40–50 *RAC*

A Japanese tinplate Model 'T' Ford, battery-
operated, 1950s, 9½in (24cm) long.
£80–90 *OTS*

An American tinplate car, 1950s,
10½in (26.5cm) long.
£40–50 *SAF*

A tinplate clockwork cruiser, named *Diana*,
by Sutcliffe, c1980, 10in (25.5cm) long.
£70–80 *RAR*

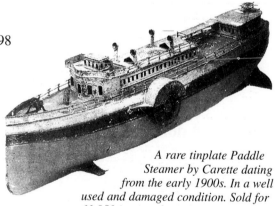

Trains & Railway Toys

r. A Hornby
O gauge LMS
623 tank engine,
1929, 7¼in
(18.5cm) long.
£80–100 *AAC*

A Hess lithographed tinplate
carpet train 0-4-0 locomotive,
with clockwork motor, tender,
wagon and carriage, c1900,
12in (30.5cm) long.
£100–120 *CDC*

Two Bassett-Lowke station
signs, c1935, 3¼in (8.5cm) high.
£12–15 each *HOB*

A Bowman O gauge live
steam locomotive, boxed,
c1930, 12in (30.5cm) long.
£230–250 *JUN*

A Hornby gun powder van,
1st series, mint and boxed,
1923, 12in (30.5cm) long.
£700–800 *HOB*

r. Two Bing O gauge tinplate
stations and a signal box, 1920s,
largest 16in (40.5cm) wide.
£35–45 *HAX*

A Hornby 'Mitropa' red carriage, mint condition,
c1937, 9½in (24cm) long.
£1,300–1,500 *HOB*

A Bassett-Lowke LNER 4472 'Flying Scotsman'
locomotive, with green livery and 20v electricity,
c1938, 5in (12.5cm) long.
£750–800 *HOB*

An Exley 'Golden Arrow' locomotive,
mint condition, c1938, 18in (47cm) long.
£4,500–4,700 *HOB*
This train is extremely rare.

A Märklin SK800 locomotive, 1951,
11¼in (28.5cm) long.
£500–600 *OTS*

A Hornby Dublo No. 3233 Co-Bo diesel electric
locomotive, boxed and with instructions, 1950s,
9in (23cm) long.
£110–130 *HCC*

A Budgie metal Noddy and Big Ears train,
1960s, 4½in (11.5cm) long.
£25–30 *CMF*

An Aster Fulgurex gauge 1 live steam 'DB Baureite
78' 4-6-4T locomotive, c1980, 18in (45.5cm) long.
£1,000–1,200 *RAR*

An Aster LNER 0 gauge live steam 'Silver Link',
c1980, 27½in (70cm) long.
£2,500–3,000 *RAR*

A Trix Twin 00 gauge mainline railway set, with
4-4-0 locomotive and six-wheel tender, green body
and tender, together with 2 bogie coaches 1st class
and 2nd brake end in maroon with pierced acetate
glazed windows, mint, with original box, 1950s,
30in (76cm) long.
£100–150 *WAL*

Aster

Aster locos are exact detailed models of real
trains. The Silver Link for example, ran
between London's King's Cross station and
Edinburgh in the 1930s, and was celebrated
for its silver-coloured carriages. These models
are live steam engines, with proper working
boilers etc, and very expensive to produce.
The average cost today is £2,000–3,000.
  Trains are produced in limited runs and as
can be seen from these examples their
collectable value is high.

TREEN & WOODEN COLLECTABLES

A beech nut cracker, 17thC,
5½in (14cm) long.
£600–700 *AEF*

A lignum vitae pounce pot,
18thC, 3½in (9cm) high.
£320–360 *AEF*

A large hollowed-out wooden
bowl, with iron handles, late
18thC, 27in (68.5cm) diam.
£500–600 *CoA*

l. A burr walnut snuff box,
c1800, 3½in (9cm) diam.
£450–500 *AEF*

A wooden paper knife, the handle carved in the form of a
mythical beast, mid-European, c1870, 9½in (24cm) long.
£35–40 *BIL*

A boxwood snuff box, commemorating George III's 80th birthday,
c1818, 2½in (6.5cm) diam.
£450–500 *AEF*

A Welsh carved sycamore love spoon, 19thC,
12in (30.5cm) long.
£700–800 *CoA*

A carved wood knitting needle sheath, inscribed
'Nitaway – WPM', dated '1826', 7in (18cm) long.
£450–500 *AEF*

A walking stick, the
carved wooden handle
in the form of a dog's
head, c1920–30,
35in (90cm) long.
£80–100 *CHe*

A carved oak clothes
brush holder, in the
form of an owl, with
2 brushes, 1900s,
5¾in (14.5cm) high.
£25–30 *SPU*

Tunbridge Ware

A Tunbridge ware letter rack, c1840, 8in (20cm) long.
£675–700 *AMH*

A Tunbridge ware glove box, inlaid with the Prince of Wales' feathers, the border of composite veneer resembling marbling, c1840, 10in (25.5cm) wide.
£500–600 *BAD*

A Tunbridge ware nutmeg grater, c1845, 2in (5cm) high.
£160–180 *AMH*

Two Tunbridge ware needle cases, *l.* depicting a castle, *r.* a windmill scene, c1850, 3in (7.5cm) high.
£280–300 each *AMH*

A Tunbridge ware handkerchief box, with satinwood background, depicting a half-timbered cottage, c1860, 6in (15.5cm) square.
£300–400 *BAD*

A pair of Tunbridge ware pictures, depicting Tonbridge Castle and Glena Cottage, Killarney, in rosewood frames, c1860, 12½ x 9¼in (31.5 x 23.5cm).
£600–700 *BAD*

A Tunbridge ware caddy spoon, c1850, 3½in (9cm) long.
£350–375 *AMH*

A Tunbridge ware book mark, with floral decoration, c1870, 3in (8cm) long.
£130–140 *AMH*

UNDERWEAR

Knickers and bras, the very foundations of our wardrobe, are both comparatively recent additions to feminine fashion. Knickers were not generally worn until the turn of the 18th century. The new high-waisted, neo-classical style in which dresses made of daringly transparent material hugged the body made some form of underclothing essential if a lady was to preserve her modesty: hence the invention of the pantaloon, the long-legged knicker. During the prim and proper Victorian age, bloomers, pantaloons (or 'unmentionables' as they were sometimes termed) became truly established. Even before they put on their outer dresses, women were literally laden down with garments: chemise, corset, several petticoats, crinoline cage and at the bottom of all these layers, a pair of divided drawers. The split was necessary so that women could relieve themselves as easily as possible given the constriction of so many clothes.

It wasn't until after WWI that women were liberated from this huge weight of underwear, abandoning the corset as they received the vote and, in ever-growing numbers, entered the work place. The bright young things of the 1920s shingled their hair, shortened their skirts and wore delicate camiknickers (camisole and knickers combined) that did not seek to mould the body into feminine curves. Another new item of clothing that became popular was the bra. Though the Victorians had worn short bust bodices over their corsets, the bra as we know it was devised in 1913. As underwear

expert Rosemary Hawthorne explains – Mary Jacobs, a New York debutante, was going to a ball and, sick of corsets, created a bust covering from two handkerchiefs and some pink silk ribbon. In 1914 she patented her 'backless brassiere', subsequently selling the rights to the Warner Brothers Corset Company for just $1,500, a small sum for an object that has literally shaped the lives of women ever since.

It is not only changes in fashions and social mores that have affected the form of underwear in the 20th century, but also advances in technology. The development of manmade fibres was crucial to the lingerie industry. 'You have been spared yesterday's agonies of whalebones and tight lacing,' boasted a 1950s manufacturer of nylon roll-on girdles. Invented just before WWII, nylon revolutionised all forms of underwear, in particular the stocking. Nylons were first manufactured in the USA in 1940 and, like chewing gum and denim jeans, were introduced to Europe by American GIs. In the late 1950s seamed stockings gradually gave way to the seamless bare-legged look, while in the 1960s, the development of tights or 'pantie-hose', was in part stimulated by the fashion for the mini skirt, which was simply too short and swinging for suspenders.

Many of those who collect vintage underwear also collect clothes from the same period, and experts maintain that the only way to truly understand a dress is to take a look at what was worn beneath it.

A pair of cotton bloomers, with lace frills, 19thC, 24in (61cm) long.
£10–12 *MAC*

A pair of Victorian cotton bloomers, with drawstring waist, and frilled bottoms, 27in (68.5cm) long.
£20–25 *PER*

r. A beige hand-made lace and silk camisole slip, 1920s, 36in (91.5cm) long.
£175–200 *PC*

A Victorian bustle-
back petticoat,
42in (106.5cm) long.
£50–60 *PER*

*Bustles became fashionable
from the 1870s. The ties
on this petticoat were
designed to be attached on
to the bustle itself, which
resembled a curved cage
sweeping over the posterior.*

A pair of lady's
Lena-Lastik
open-legged wool
combinations,
c1920, 34in
(86.5cm) long.
£40–50 *PC*

A black chiffon and
lace camisole, 1930s,
33in (84cm) long.
£40–45 *PC*

A black artificial silk
camisole slip, with beige
lace trim, straps repaired,
1920s, 26in (66cm) long.
£20–25 *PC*

A leather and cloth
silk stockings bag,
1930s, 9½ x 7½in
(24 x 19cm).
£25–30 *PC*

*Made from wool,
cotton and silk, and
sometimes beautifully
embroidered,
stockings were prized
and often very costly
garments. To protect
them they were kept
in specially designed
bags, in which the
stockings were folded
rather than rolled.*

Woman's Weekly
magazine, April 4, 1925,
11 x 7½in (28 x 19cm).
£10–12 *RAD*

A pair of pink wool
camiknickers, c1940,
31in (79cm) long.
£34–38 *PC*

A pair of yellow satin
garters, decorated with
purple sequins, 1920s,
5½in (14cm) wide.
£16–18 *PC*

r. A pair of purple
artificial silk stockings,
embroidered with an
arrow and dot design,
1920s, 33in (84cm) long.
£30–35 *PC*

A pair of green
Marshella Resolute
stockings, 1920s,
32in (81.5cm) long.
£6–8 *PC*

A pair of beige silk and
lace French knickers,
1930s, 19in (48.5cm) long.
£15–20 *PC*

A pink silk bra, by Valor, 1930s, size 36c.
£16–18 *PER*

A pink satin suspender belt, 1940s, 23in (58.5cm) long.
£10–12 *PC*

A pair of pink artificial silk French knickers, c1940, 14½in (37cm) long.
£6–8 *PC*

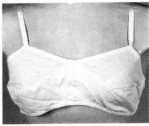

A pink cotton bra, c1940, size 36b.
£5–6 *PC*

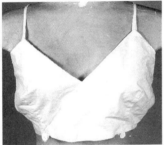

A Kestos utility nursing bra, ID No. 15, 1940s, size 38b.
£5–7 *PC*

A pair of blue silk French knickers, 1940s, 19in (48.5cm) long.
£8–10 *RAD*

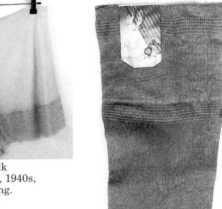

A pair of Paradise wool stockings, 1940s, 36in (91.5cm) long.
£4–5 *HUX*

A Curtis-Eddyform peach rayon and rubber girdle, with satin front panel, American, 1950s, 18in (45.5cm) long.
£10–15 *RMA*

A British Army man's woollen vest, 1944.
£5–6 *FAM*

A black circle stitched bra, 1950s, size 36c.
£10–12 *PER*

The 'Sweater Girl' fashion started by Lana Turner in the 1940s, continued into the 1950s, when Hollywood stars from Jane Russell to Marilyn Munroe popularised the big-busted look. Circle stitched bras were designed to make the breasts point and look suitably prominent under a close-fitting top.

A pair of British Army wool mixture underpants, 1944.
£5–6 *FAM*

An American yellow nylon and lace bouffant petticoat, by Fender, 1950s, 22in (56cm) long.
£15–20 *RMA*

FURTHER READING

Rosemary Hawthorne,
Bras, first published 1992
Knickers, first published 1985
Stockings & Suspenders, 1993
all Souvenir Press

A black nylon bum enhancer, with rounded foam rubber pads fitted into the lining, 1950s.
£20–25 *SPS*

Feminine curves were an essential part of fifties fashion. Familiarly known as a 'bum enhancer' this is a pair of nylon knickers fitted with shaped foam rubber pads. The manufacturers claimed that it would give a lady 'perfect uplift', 'unrivalled curves' and a natural look. 'Feels real!' promised the advertisements for this curious garment.

A pair of Textron white nylon tap dancing pants, American, 1950s, 17in (42cm) long.
£2–4 *RMA*

A pair of Heel Apeel nylons, with embroidered heels, c1950, 38in (96.5cm) long.
£10–12 *PC*

A pair of Fruits of the Loom white cotton man's shorts, American, 1950s, 16in (40.5cm) long.
£4–5 *RMA*

A pair of Charnos patterned stockings, designed by Ossie Clark, 1960s, 9 x 6½in (23 x 16.5cm).
£5–10 *BOH*

A pair of Bear Brand Fair Lady nylon stockings, 1960s, 9 x 7in (23 x 18cm).
£6–7 *RAD*

This pair of nylons is particularly desirable because the photograph on the front shows 1960s supermodel Jean Shrimpton.

r. A pair of Bond Street seamfree micromesh nylon stockings, in original packaging, 1960s, 7½ x 6¾in (19 x 17cm).
£3–4 *RAD*

A pair of Penny Farthing sheer micromesh crepe stockings, in original packaging, 1960s, 9in (23cm) high.
£4–5 *HUX*

A Breefer-Youth Forms Banlon black lace teddy, with padded bra section, American, 1960s, 25⅓in (65cm) long.
£8–10 *RMA*

WATCHES

An 18ct gold fob watch, with gold dial, c1840, 1½in (38mm) diam.
£300–350 *BWC*

A white metal No-Mag Swiss pocket watch, 15 jewels, with arabic numerals, 1910, 2in (5cm) diam.
£150–175 *TIH*

A Garrard lady's 9ct gold wristwatch, 1930–40s, 1¼in (32mm) diam.
£175–185 *HEI*

l. A Smiths magnetic motor watch, 1950s, 2in (5cm) diam.
£45–55 *TIH*

A Vertex Revue 9ct gold manual wristwatch, 1950s.
£130–150 *BWC*

A Verity silver automatic watch, with 25-jewel Swiss movement, machined dial, with date aperture, restored, 1960.
£125–150 *TIH*

A lady's 9ct white gold dress watch, with 17-jewel movement and second dial, c1973.
£170–200 *BWC*

An Omega Constellation gold capped automatic wristwatch, with date aperture, 1965.
£240–270 *BWC*

FAKES

The final section of the guide is devoted to fakes (*see also colour page 430*). Though a small number of other subjects are included, the majority of objects illustrated this year are fake Carlton Ware, a considerable amount of which has appeared on the market in the 1990s, in particular Guinness-related material. According to Helen Martin of the Carlton Ware Collectors Club, the problem really started in 1989 when the Carlton Factory sold their premises. The building was stripped of fixtures and fittings and some original moulds appear to have fallen into the wrong hands. Fakes began to surface, their production stimulated by the fact that Guinness pieces, as well as other novelty Carlton Ware items, have been fetching increasingly high prices. Though to the trained eye these ceramics are obviously counterfeit, they can easily trap the non-specialist purchaser. The following pictures provide a guideline to some fake items, but what is the best way to avoid being duped? 'Learn as much about your subject as possible and buy from a reputable dealer,' advises Helen Martin. 'Always make sure that you get a full receipt, including a complete description of the item and address and details of the vendor. Then you can regain your money legally if any problem emerges.'

The same advice also applies to any other item, and specialists also recommend that if, for example, you are knowingly sold a fake at an antiques fair it is important to let the fair organiser know. 'The only way we can stamp out these problems is by vigilance and exposure,' concludes Martin. If readers come across any other fakes, please let us know so we can include details in future editions of the *Miller's Collectables Price Guide*.

Carlton Ware

A fake Carlton Ware hangman's tankard, with devil on handle, black crown mark, c1994, 5¼in (13.5cm) high.
Fake, no commerical value
If original, with musical movement £250–300
If original, without musical movement £190–200 *CCI*

The original mug came in a matt rather than a shiny glaze as here, and had no gilding on the red devil handle. This piece has the wrong date stamp and the wording on the back is lithographed rather than transfer-printed with the initial letters hand-coloured as on the period example.

A fake Carlton Ware Schweppes Babycham deer, yellow with blue bow around neck, 1990s, 5in (12.5cm) high.
Fake, no commercial value
If original £90–100 *CCI*

The original figure came on a plinth and the mark underneath is incorrect.

l. A fake Carlton Ware Liquorice Allsorts mug, black script mark, 4in (10cm) high.
Fake, no commercial value *CCI*

As far as is known, this Liquorice Allsorts mug was never produced by Carlton Ware.

A fake Carlton Ware cruet set, in the form of 3 monks, Cooper black mark, tallest 4½in (11.5cm) high.
Fake, no commercial value
If original £25–35 *CCI*

The original monks came complete with a tray, and these examples are very poorly painted and have no depth of colour.

A fake Carlton Ware tortoise cruet, c1996, 3¾in (9.5cm) high.
Fake, no commercial value *CCI*

The shape of these tortoises is correct, but this incised mark was not used by Carlton Ware.

A fake Carlton Ware toucan bar decoration, with black script mark, 1993–97, 7in (18cm) high.
Fake, no commercial value
If original £200–250 *CCI*

The colours are incorrect, harsher than the original and the beer glass would have had a larger head on the Guinness. The bands of colour across the chest are also too clearly divided, on the original the colours bleed into each other.

A fake Carlton Ware penguin lamp base, with red script mark, 1993–97, 7in (18cm) high.
Fake, no commercial value
If original £250–300 *CCI*

The penguin on the original model holds a dark blue plaque, inscribed 'Draught Guinness'. The original lamp also came with a blue paper lampshade.

Susie Cooper

A reproduction Susie Cooper miniature teaset, decorated with the Tiger Lily pattern, 1990s, box 15in (38cm) wide.
£70–80 *TAC*

A series of 'Susie Cooper Production Limited Edition reproduction miniatures' has recently been manufactured without permission or copyright from the Wedgwood group, owners of the Susie Cooper trade name. Pieces include miniature teasets and this example is also stamped with Susie Cooper's famous leaping deer trademark. Susie Cooper did not design miniatures, but already unwary purchasers have been deceived into thinking that these are original travelling salesman's samples from the 1950s. Buyer beware!

Glass

These glasses are not fakes, but, with one exception, reproductions made in the late 19thC and early 20thC, when copying period styles was fashionable in glass as in other media. Though they were made in all honesty, they could be passed off to the unwary today as 18thC originals.

A genuine Beilby glass and a glass with fake decoration, c1770, tallest 6in (15cm) high.
l. **£1,200–1,500** *r.* **£80–100** *JHa*

*Both of these glasses are c1770, but the enamelled scene (*right*) is a fake probably executed in the 1920s.*

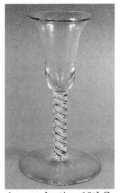

A reproduction 18thC drinking glass, with white opaque and red colour twist stem, late 19thC, 6in (15cm) high.
Fake £30–50
If Original
£1,800–2,000 *JHa*

On original 18thC glasses the twist runs from right to left down the stem whereas this one runs from left to right. The glass is soda glass and has no ring to it, instead of crystal, and the foot is flat instead of the thicker conical shape as on an original.

l. A reproduction Jacobite glass, with decorated bowl and twist stem, c1900.
Fake £80–100
If Original
£800–1,200 *JHa*

This piece has too many symbols to the decoration, a poor quality twist stem and a flat foot.

DIRECTORY OF SPECIALISTS

If you require a valuation for an item, it is advisable to check whether the dealer or specialist will carry out this service and if there is a charge. Please mention Miller's when making an enquiry. Having found a specialist who will carry out your valuation it is best to send a description and photograph of the item to the specialist together with a stamped addressed envelope for the reply. A valuation by telephone is not possible. Most dealers are only too happy to help you with your enquiry, however, they are very busy people and consideration of the above points would be welcomed.

Bedfordshire

Christopher Sykes,
The Old Parsonage,
Woburn, Milton Keynes,
MK17 9QL
Tel: 01525 290259
Corkscrews and wine-related items.

Berkshire

Below Stairs,
103 High Street,
Hungerford, RG17 0NB
Tel: 01488 682317
Collectables including kitchenware, taxidermy and lighting.

Collect It!
PO Box 3658,
Bracknell, RG12 7XZ
Tel: 01344 868280
Magazine for collectors.

Mostly Boxes,
93 High Street, Eton,
SL4 6AF
Tel: 01753 858470
Antique wooden boxes.

Special Auction Services,
The Coach House,
Midgham Park, Reading,
RG7 5UG
Tel: 0118 971 2949
Commemorative auctions.

Buckinghamshire

Gillian Neale Antiques,
PO Box 247, Aylesbury,
HP20 1JZ
Tel: 01296 423754
Blue & white transfer ware.

Cambridgeshire

Antique Amusement Co,
Mill Lane, Swaffham,
Bulbeck, CB5 0NF
Tel: 01223 813041
Mobile 0802 666755
Vintage amusement machines, also auctions of amusement machines, fairground art and other related collectables.

James Fuller & Son,
51 Huntingdon Road,
Chatteris, P16 6JE
Tel: 01354 692740
Architectural antiques, post boxes and telephone boxes.

Warboys Antiques,
Old Church School,
High Street, Warboys,
PE17 2SX
Tel: 01487 823686
Sporting antiques and tins.

Cheshire

Collectors' Corner,
PO Box 8, Congleton,
CW12 4GD
Tel: 01260 270429
Rock & pop collectables, sci-fi, TV and Beatles memorabilia.

Dollectable,
53 Lower Bridge Street,
Chester, CH1 1RS
Tel: 01244 344888/679195
Antique dolls.

Clifford Elmer Books,
8 Balmoral Avenue,
Cheadle Hulme, Cheadle,
SK8 5EQ
Tel: 0161 485 7064
Crime books. E-mail: CliffBooks@aol.com or TrueCrime@compuserve.com

Glass Collectors' Fair,
c/o 155 St John's Road,
Congleton, CW12 2EH
Tel: 01260 271975
Glass collectors' fairs.

Legend Lane,
Albion Mill,
London Road,
Macclesfield, SK11 7SQ
Tel: 01625 424661
Cottages and sculptures in miniature.

Nantwich Art Deco,
87 Welsh Row,
Nantwich, CW5 5ET
Tel: 01270 624876 or
01270 811541
Open Thursday–Saturday 10.00am–5.00pm.

On The Air,
42 Bridge Street Row,
Chester, CH1 1NN
Tel: 01244 348468
Vintage radios.

Sweetbriar Gallery,
Robin Hood Lane,
Helsby, WA6 9NH
Tel: 01928 723851
Paperweights.

Cornwall

Martyn Rowe,
Truro Auction Centre,
Calenick Street,
Truro, TR1 2SG
Tel: 01872 260020
Auctioneers.

Dorset

Ancient & Gothic,
PO Box 356,
Christchurch, BH23 1XQ
Tel: 01202 478592
Antiquities.

Books Afloat,
66 Park Street,
Weymouth, DT4 7DE
Tel: 01305 779774
Books, shipping.

Button Shop Antiques,
Old Button Shop, Lytchett
Minster, Poole, BH16 6JF
Tel: 01202 622169
Buttons and collectables.

Dalkeith Auctions,
Dalkeith Hall,
Dalkeith Steps, Rear of
81 Old Christchurch Rd,
Bournemouth, BH1 1YL
Tel: 01202 292905
Auctions of postcards, cigarette cards, ephemera and collectors' items.

Hardy's Collectables,
862 Christchurch Road,
Boscombe, Bournemouth,
BH7 6DQ
Tel: 01202 422407/303030
Poole Pottery and textiles.

The Nautical Centre,
Harbour Passage,
Hope Square, Weymouth,
DT4 8TR
Tel: 01305 777838
Open Tuesday–Friday. Thousands of nautical souvenirs and memorabilia. Sextants, logs, flags, clocks, telescopes, badges, blocks, compasses, bells, lights. Also maritime items wanted.

Poole Pottery,
The Quay,
Poole, BH15 1RF
Tel: 01202 666200
Poole Pottery.

Essex

GKR Bonds Ltd,
PO Box 1, Kelvedon,
CO5 9EH
Tel: 01376 571711
Old bonds and share certificates.

Haddon Rocking
Horses Ltd,
5 Telford Road,
Clacton-on-Sea,
CO15 4LP
Tel: 01255 424745
Rocking horses.

Megarry's and Forever
Summer,
Jericho Cottage,
The Green, Blackmore,
CM4 0RR
Tel: 01277 821031 and
01277 822170
Antiques, arts & crafts. Summer opening hours: 10am–6pm every day except Wednesday. Winter opening hours: 11am–5pm, Sunday, Monday, Tuesday, Thursday. Closed Wednesday. Open 11am–5.30pm Friday, Saturday. Member Essex Antiques Dealers Association.

Off World,
Unit 20, Romford
Shopping Halls,
Market Place, Romford,
RM1 3AT
Tel: 01708 765633
Sci-fi toys.

Old Telephone Company,
The Old Granary,
Battlesbridge Antiques
Centre, Nr Wickford,
SS11 7RF
Tel: 01245 400601
Period telephones.

Saffron Walden Saleroom,
1 Market Street, Saffron
Walden, CB10 1JB
Tel: 01799 513281
Auctioneers.

Tiger Collectibles,
104 Victoria Avenue,
Swanage, BH19 1AS
Tel: 01929 423411
*WWI & WWII Militaria.
Email: tigercoll@aol.com*

Gloucestershire

Oriental Gallery,
Tel: 01451 830944
*Oriental ceramics and
works of art.*

David Partridge,
Gable End House,
Pitchcombe, Stroud,
GL6 6LN
Tel: 01452 812166
Militaria.

Alan Sedgwick.
*E-mail: Alan.Sedgwick
@BTInternet.com
Carnival glass.*

Q&C Militaria,
22 Suffolk Road,
Cheltenham, GL50 2AQ
Tel & Fax: 01242 519815/
Mobile 0378 613977
*Militaria, uniforms,
medals, trench art.*

Samarkand Galleries,
8 Brewery Yard, Sheep
Street, Stow-on-the-Wold,
GL54 1AA
Tel: 01451 832322
Rugs and carpets.

Specialised Postcard
Auctions,
25 Gloucester Street,
Cirencester, GL7 2DJ
Tel: 01285 659057
Postcard auctions.

Elaine Whobrey,
Tel: 01451 821670
Dolls.

Pat Woodward and
Alma Shaw,
Unit G43, Ground Floor,
Gloucester Antiques
Centre, In The Historic
Docks, Severn Road,
Gloucester, GL1 2LE
*Specialising in British
commemorative china
and memorabilia 1837
onwards. Exhibiting at
Alexandra Palace and
Wembley Antique Fairs.*

Greater Manchester

Acorn Auctions,
P O Box 152, Salford,
M17 1BP
Tel: 0161 877 8818
*Postcard and ephemera
auctions.*

Gwynedd

A.P.E.S. Rocking Horses,
20 Tan-y-Bwlch,
Llandygai, Bangor
Gwynedd LL57 4DX
Tel: 01745 540365
Rocking horses.

Teapot Museum & Shop,
25 Castle Street,
Conway, LL32 8AY
Tel: 01493 593429
Teapots and related items.

Hampshire

Bona Arts
Decorative Ltd,
The Hart Shopping
Centre, Fleet, GU13 8AZ
Tel: 01252 616666
*Art Deco glass, china,
lighting.*

Cobwebs,
78 Northam Road,
Southampton, SO14 0PB
Tel: 01703 227458
*Ocean liner memorabilia,
naval and aviation items.*

Gasson Antiques,
PO Box 7225, Tadley,
RG26 5YB
Tel: 0118 981 3636
Decorative collectables.

Glitter & Dazzle,
Pat & Ken Thompson
Tel: 01329 288678
*Full range of American
designer jewellery.*

Goss & Crested China Co,
62 Murray Road,
Horndean, PO8 9JL
Tel: 01705 597440
Goss crested china.

The Old Toy Shop,
7 Monmouth Court,
Southampton Road,
Ringwood, BH24 1HE
Tel: 01425 476899
*Clockwork, steam &
electric vintage toys,
transport memorabilia
and military figures.*

Romsey Medals,
5 Bell Street, Romsey,
SO51 8GY
Tel: 01794 512069
*Orders, decorations
and medals.*

Solent Railwayana,
31 Newtown Road,
Warsash, SO31 9FY
Tel: 01489 578093/584633
*Railway relics and model
railway items. Also
Railwayana auctions.*

Herefordshire

Unicorn Fairs,
P O Box 30, Hereford,
HR2 8SW
Tel: 0161 773 7001
*Antiques and collectors'
fairs.*

Hertfordshire

Forget Me Knot Antiques,
Over the Moon, 27 High
Street, St Albans, AL3 4EH
Tel: 01727 848907
Jewellery, name brooches.

Magic Lanterns at By
George, 23 George Street,
St Albans, AL3 4ES
Tel: 01727 865680/853032
Lighting.

Ireland

Michelina & George
Stacpoole, Main Street,
Adare, Co Limerick.
Tel: 00 353 6139 6409
Pottery, ceramics & silver.

Isle of Wight

Nostalgia Toy Museum,
High Street, Godshill,
PO38 3HZ
Tel: 01938 526254
Diecast toys.

Kent

Amherst Antiques,
23 London Road,
Riverhead, Sevenoaks,
TN13 2BU
Tel: 01732 455047
Tunbridge ware, silver.

Bears Galore,
8 The Fairings, High St,
Tenterden, TN30 6QX
Tel: 01580 765233
*Specialist teddy shop.
Closed Wed and Sun.*

Beatcity, PO Box 229,
Chatham, ME5 0PW
Tel: 01634 305383/
0370 650890
*Beatles and rock & roll
memorabilia.*

Candlestick & Bakelite,
PO Box 308, Orpington,
BR5 1TB
Tel: 0181 467 3743/3799
Telephones.

Dragons Lee Collectables.
Tel: 01622 729502
*Specialising in Noritake
and Art Deco.*

Paul Haskell
Tel: 01634 669362
*Old mechanical slot
machines, Allwins,
bandits, fortune tellers,
mutoscopes etc.*

Stuart Heggie,
14 The Borough, Northgate,
Canterbury, CT1 2DR
Tel: 01227 470422
*Vintage cameras, optical
toys & photographic
images.*

J & M Collectables.
Tel: 01580 891657
*Postcards, crested china,
Osborne plaques, ivory eggs.*

Barbara Ann Newman,
London House Antiques,
4 Market Square,
Westerham, TN16 1AW
Tel: 01959 564479
Mobile 0850 016729
*Antique dolls, teddy bears
and collectables.*

Old Tackle Box,
PO Box 55, Cranbrook,
TN17 3ZU
Tel & Fax: 01580 713979
Old fishing tackle.

Posh Tubs,
Moriati's Workshop,
High Halden, Ashford,
TN26 3LZ
Tel: 01233 850155
Antique bathroom ware.

Neville Pundole,
8A & 9 The Friars,
Canterbury, CT1 2AS
Tel: 01227 453471
*Moorcroft and
contemporary pottery.*

Serendipity,
168 High Street, Deal,
CT14 6BQ
Tel: 01304 369165
Staffordshire pottery.

St Clere Antiques,
PO Box 161,
Sevenoaks, TN15 6GA
Tel: 01474 853630
*The UK's leading specialists
in Carlton Ware. Selling
and buying Carlton Ware
1890–1992. Mail orders
taken. Visa & Mastercard
accepted. Contact Helen
and Keith Martin.*

Stevenson Brothers,
The Workshop,
Ashford Road,
Bethersden,
Ashford, TN26 3AP
Tel: 01233 820363
Rocking horses.

Variety Box,
16 Chapel Place,
Tunbridge Wells,
TN1 1YQ
Tel: 01892 531868
*Tunbridge ware, silver
ware, glass, fans, hat
pins, writing, sewing and
other collectors' items.*

The Warehouse,
29-30 Queens Gardens,
Worthington Street,
Dover, CT17 9AH
Tel: 01304 242006
Toys and models.

Wenderton Antiques.
Tel: 01227 720295
(by appointment only)
Kitchenware.

Woodville Antiques,
The Street, Hamstreet,
Ashford, TN26 2HG
Tel: 01233 732981
Tools.

Lancashire

Farmhouse Antiques,
Corner Shop, 23 Main
Street, Bolton-by-Bowland,
Clitheroe, BB7 4NW
Tel: 01200 447294/441457
*Probably the largest stock
of antique textiles in
Lancashire. Open
Saturday, Sunday & Bank
Holidays all year round.
12noon–4.30pm or ring for
appointment 01200 441457.
Trade enquiries welcome.*

Glasform Ltd,
123 Talbot Road,
Blackpool, FY1 3QY
Tel: 01253 695849
Glass.

Tracks,
PO Box 117, Chorley,
PR7 2QZ
Tel: 01257 269726
*Beatles and rare pop
memorabilia.*

Leicestershire

Pooks Motor Bookshop,
Fowke Street, Rothley,
LE7 7PJ
Tel: 0116 237 6222
Books and automobilia.

Lincolnshire

20th Century Frocks,
65 Steep Hill, Lincoln,
N1 1YN Tel: 01522 545916
(after 6pm 01507 533638)
*Vintage clothing and
accessories bought and
sold. Open 11am–5pm,
Tuesday, Thursday, Friday
and Saturday.*

Anthony Jackson,
Rocking Horse Maker &
Restorer, 20 Westry
Corner, Barrowby,
Grantham, NG32 1DF
Tel: 01476 567477
Rocking horses.

Junktion,
The Old Railway Station,
New Bolingbroke,
Boston, PE22 7LB
Tel: 01205 480068
*Advertising and
packaging, amusement
machines, automobilia.*

Janie Smithson Antiques.
Tel: 01754 810265
Mobile 0831 399180
Kitchenware.

London

Angling Auctions,
P O Box 2095, W12 8RU
Tel: 0181 749 4175
Angling auctions.

The Antique Clothing Shop,
282 Portobello Road, W10
Tel: 0181 964 4830
Textiles and costume.

A. H. Baldwin & Sons Ltd,
Numismatists,
11 Adelphi Terrace,
WC2N 6BJ
Tel: 0171 930 6879
*Coins and
commemorative medals.*

Linda Bee,
Art Deco Stand J20-21,
Grays Antique Market,
1–7 Davies Mews,
W1Y 1AR
Tel: 0171 629 5921
Costume and perfume bottles.

Beverley,
30 Church Street,
Marylebone, NW8 8EP
Tel: 0171 262 1576
*Art Deco furniture, glass,
figures, metalware and
pottery.*

Daniel Bexfield Antiques,
The Bond Street Antiques
Centre, 124 New Bond
Street, W1Y 9AE
Tel: 0171 491 1720
Silver.

Christina Bishop
Kitchenware
Tel: 0171 221 4688
Kitchenware 1890s–1960s.

Bloomsbury Book Auctions,
3/4 Hardwick Street,
Off Rosebery Avenue,
EC1R 4RY
Tel: 0171 833 2636
Book auctions.

Button Queen,
19 Marylebone Lane,
W1M 5FF
Tel: 0171 935 1505
Buttons.

Jasmin Cameron,
Antiquarius,
131–141 King's Road,
SW3 5ST
Tel/Fax: 0171 351 4154
Mobile: 0374 871257
Home: 01494 774276
*Drinking glasses & decanters
1750–1910. Vintage fountain
pens, writing materials.*

Jack Casimir Ltd,
The Brass Shop,
23 Pembridge Road,
W11 3HG
Tel: 0171 727 8643
Metalware.

Cekay Antiques,
Gray's Antique Market,
58 Davies Street,
W1Y 1LB
Tel: 0171 629 5130
Walking sticks.

Chelsea Clocks &
Antiques, Antiquarius,
Stand H3–4,
135 Kings Road,
SW3 4PW
Tel: 0171 352 8646
*Clocks and antiques.
Also brass, oak,
deskware, barometers
and collectables.*

Christie's South
Kensington Ltd,
85 Old Brompton Road,
SW7 3LD
Tel: 0171 581 7611
Auctioneers.

Classic Collection,
Pied Bull Yard, Bury
Place, WC1A 2JR
Tel: 0171 831 6000
Collectable cameras.

The Collector,
Tom Power,
9 Church Street,
Marylebone, NW8 8EE
Tel: 0171 706 4586
*Royal Doulton, Beswick,
Pendelfin, Worcester,
Lladro, Border Fine Art,
Wade, Wedgwood,
Coalport, Bossons, Lilliput
Lane, David Winter, etc.*

Comic Book Postal
Auctions Ltd,
40-42 Osnaburgh Street,
NW1 3ND
Tel: 0171 424 0007
Comic book auctions.

Christopher Eimer,
PO Box 352, NW11 7RF
Tel: 0181 458 9933
Commemorative medals.

Liz Farrow t/a Dodo,
Admiral Vernon Market,
Portobello Road, W11
*Posters. Saturdays only
9am–4pm.*

Liz Farrow t/a Dodo,
Stand F073/83, Alfie's
Antique Market, 13–25
Church Street, NW8 8DT
Tel: 0171 724 0999
*Tuesdays–Saturdays
10.30am–5.30pm.*

Francis Joseph
Publications,
15 St Swithuns Road,
SE13 6RW
Tel: 0181 318 9580
Publishers.

Michael C. German,
38B Kensington Church
Street, W8 4BX
Tel: 0171 937 2771
Walking canes.

Richard Gibbon
(Costume Jewellery),
G067 Alfies Antique
Market, 13–25 Church
Street, NW8 8DT
Tel: 0171 723 0449
Costume jewellery.

Goldsmith & Perris,
Stand 327 Alfies Antique
Market, 13–25 Church
Street, NW8 8DT
Tel: 0171 724 7051
Silver.

Adrian Harrington,
64a Kensington High
Street, W8 4DB
Tel: 0171 937 1465
Fax: 0171 368 0912
*Antiquarian books, prints
and maps. E-mail:
adrianharrington@compu
serve.com*

Peter Harrington,
100 Fulham Road,
SW3 6HS
Tel: 0171 591 0220/0330
Antiquarian books.

Herzog, Hollender
Phillips & Company,
The Scripophily Shop,
PO Box 14376, NW6 1ZD
Tel & Fax: 0171 433 3577
*Scripophily. E-mail:
hollender@dial.pipex.com
http:/Currency.dealers-on-
line.com/ScripophilyShop*

Noel Hickey,
Stand F054, Alfies
Antique Market,
13–25 Church Street,
Marylebone, NW8 8DT
Tel: 0171 723 0678
Decorative collectables.

David Huxtable,
Alfies Antique Market,
Stand S03/05 (Top Floor),
13–25 Church Street,
Marylebone, NW8 8DT
Tel: 0171 724 2200
Old advertising collectables.

Enid Lawson Gallery,
36a Kensington Church
Street, W8 4DB
Tel: 0171 937 8444
*Studio ceramics, paintings
and original prints.*

Murray Cards
(International) Ltd,
51 Watford Way,
Hendon Central,
NW4 3JH
Tel: 0181 202 5688
Cigarette and trade cards.

Stevie Pearce,
G144, Ground Floor,
Alfies Antique Market,
13–25 Church Street,
NW8 8DT
Tel: 0171 723 1513/
0171 723 5754
*Costume jewellery and
fashion accessories
1900–70.*

Phillips,
Blenstock House,
101 New Bond Street,
W1Y 0AS
Tel: 0171 629 6602
Auctioneer.

Puppets & Masks,
3 Kensington Mall,
W8 4EB
Tel: 0171 221 8629
Puppets.

Radio Days,
87 Lower Marsh,
Waterloo, SE1 7AB
Tel: 0171 928 0800
*Costume, textiles and
collectables.*

John Rastall,
Stall GO47/8
Alfies Antique Market,
13–25 Church Street,
NW8 8DT
Tel: 0171 723 0449
The Reel Thing,
17 Royal Opera Arcade,
Pall Mall,
SW1Y 4UY
Tel: 0171 976 1830
*Vintage sporting
memorabilia.*

Geoffrey Robinson,
GO77-78 (Ground floor),
Alfies Antique Market,
13–25 Church Street,
NW8 8DT
Tel: 0171 723 0449
*Art Deco lighting, glass &
chrome etc.*

Rumours,
10 The Mall, Upper
Street, Camden Passage,
Islington, N1 0PD
Tel: 01582 873561
Moorcroft pottery.

Totem,
168 Stoke Newington,
Church Street, N16 0JL
Tel: 0171 275 0234
*LPs, MCs, CDs bought,
sold and exchanged.*

Trio (Theresa Clayton),
Gray's Mews, 1–7 Davies
Mews, W1Y 1AR
Tel: 0171 629 1184
Perfume bottles.

Vintage Cameras Ltd,
256 Kirkdale, Sydenham,
SE26 4NL
Tel: 0181 778 5416
*Antique and classic
cameras.*

Nigel Williams Rare
Books,
22 & 25 Cecil Court,
WC2N 4HE
Tel: 0171 836 7757
Books.

Wimpole Antiques,
Stand 349, Grays
Antique Market,
58 Davies Street,
W1Y 1AR
Tel: 0171 499 2889/
0171 624 7628
Jewellery.

Wonderful World of
Animation,
30 Bramham Gardens,
SW5 0HF
Tel: 0171 370 4859
*Animated art. E-mail http:/
www.animationartgallery
.com*

Yesterday Child,
Angel Arcade,
118 Islington High St,
N1 8EG
Tel: 0171 354 1601
*Antique dolls and dolls'
house miniatures.*

Merseyside

Treasures in Textiles,
53 Russian Drive,
Liverpool, L13 7BS
Tel: 0151 281 6025
*Antique textile and
vintage clothing.*

Middlesex

Albert's Cigarette Card
Specialists,
113 London Road,
Twickenham,
TW1 1EE
Tel: 0181 891 3067
Cigarette cards.

Joan & Bob Anderson,
Tel: 0181 572 4328
Midwinter ceramics.

Hobday Toys,
44 High Street,
Northwood,
HA6 2XY
Tel: 01923 820115
*Tinplate toys, trains and
doll's houses.*

John Ives,
5 Normanhurst Drive,
Twickenham, TW1 1NA
Tel: 0181 892 6265
*Reference books on
antiques and collecting.*

Vintage Pencils,
11–13 High Street,
Harefield, UB9 6BX
Tel: 01895 824920
*Restoration of fountain
pens and mechanical
pencils.*

When We Were Young,
The Old Forge, High
Street, Harmondsworth
Village, UB7 0AQ
Tel: 0181 897 3583
*Collectable items related
to British childhood
characters and
illustrators.*

Norfolk

Roger Bradbury Antiques,
Church Street,
Coltishall, NR12 7DJ
Tel: 01603 737444
*Nanking, Vung Tau and
Diana Cargo.*

Cat Pottery,
1 Grammar School Road,
North Walsham,
NR28 9JH
Tel: 01692 402962
Animal pottery.

Church Street Antiques,
2 Church Street,
Wells-next-the-Sea,
NR23 1JA
Tel: 01328 711698
*Linen, lace, textiles,
jewellery, hatpins,
kitchenalia.*

Northamptonshire

The Old Brigade,
10A Harborough Road,
Kingsthorpe, NN2 7AZ
Tel: 01604 719389
*Third Reich collectors'
items.*

Nottinghamshire

T. Vennett-Smith,
11 Nottingham Road,
Gotham, NG11 0HE
Tel: 0115 983 0541
*Ephemera and sporting
auctions.*

Vintage Wireless Shop,
The Hewarths,
Sandiacre,
Nottingham,
NG10 5NQ
Tel: 0115 939 3139
*Early wireless &
television sets.*

Oxfordshire

**Dauphin Display
Cabinet Co**, PO Box 602,
Oxford, OX44 9LU
Tel: 01865 343542
Display stands.

Stone Gallery,
93 The High Street,
Burford, OX18 4QA
Tel/Fax: 01993 823302
*Specialist dealer in
antique and modern
paperweights, gold and
silver designer jewellery
and enamel boxes.*

Teddy Bears,
99 High Street, Witney,
OX8 6LY
Tel: 01993 702616
Teddy bears.

Scotland

Bow-Well Antiques,
103 West Bow,
Edinburgh, EH1 2JP
Tel: 0131 225 3335
*Scottish collectables,
pottery, silver.*

Caithness Glass Ltd,
Inveralmond, Perth,
PH1 3TZ
Tel: 01738 637373
Glass/paperweights.

Edinburgh Coin Shop,
11 West Crosscauseway,
Edinburgh, EH8 9JW
Tel: 0131 668 2928/
0131 667 9095
*Coins, medals, militaria
and stamps.*

Henderson,
5 North Methven Street,
Perth, PH1 5PN
Tel: 01738 624836
Porcelain, glass, silver, etc.

Rhod McEwan–Golf Books,
Glengarden, Ballater,
Aberdeenshire, AB35 5UB
Tel: 013397 55429
*Rare and out-of-print
golfing books.*

Timeless Tackle,
Tullymoran Farmhouse,
Logiealmond, Perth,
PH1 3TE
Tel: 0131 667 1407
Fax: 01738 880310
Old fishing tackle.

Shropshire

Janet Beaumont,
Chapel House,
Aldenham Park, Morville,
Bridgnorth, WV16 4RN
Tel: 01746 714030
*Hummel figures and
collectables.*

Mullock & Madeley,
The Old Shippon,
Wall-under-Heywood,
Church Stretton,
SY6 7DS
Tel: 01694 771771
Sporting auctions.

Somerset

Bath Dolls' Hospital,
2 Grosvenor Place,
London Road, Bath,
BA1 6PT
Tel: 01225 319668
Doll restoration.

Box in the Lanes,
Cabinet 112 (Basement),
Bartlett Street Antiques
Centre, Bath, BA1 2QZ
Tel: 0468 720338
Boxes.

Lynda Brine,
Assembly Antique
Centre, 5–8 Saville Row,
Bath, BA1 2QP
Tel: 01225 448488
Perfume bottles.

Glenville Antiques,
120 High Street,
Yatton, BS19 4DH
Tel: 01934 832284
Collectables.

Jessie's Button Box,
Fountain Antique Centre,
3 Lansdown Road, Bath,
BA1 5DY
Tel: 0117 929 9065
Buttons.

Philip Knighton,
11 North Street,
Wellington, TA21 8LX
Tel: 01823 661618
*Wireless, gramophones
and all valve equipment.*

**London Cigarette Card
Co Ltd**,
Sutton Road, Somerton,
TA11 6QP
Tel: 01458 273452
Cigarette and trade cards.

Tim Millard Antiques,
Stand 31–32 Bartlett
Street Antique Centre,
Bartlett Street, Bath,
BA1 2QZ
Tel: 01225 469785
Boxes.

Joanna Proops,
Antiques/Textiles,
34 Belvedere,
Bath, BA1 5HR
Tel: 01225 310795
Textiles.

Richard Twort,
Tel: 01934 641900
Scientific instruments.

Staffordshire

Brian Bates
Tel: 01782 680667
*Old mechanical slot
machines, Allwins,
bandits, fortune tellers,
mutoscopes, etc.*

Keystones,
PO Box 387,
Stafford,
ST16 3FG
Tel: 01785 256648
Denby pottery.

Gordon Litherland,
25 Stapenhill Road,
Burton-on-Trent,
DE15 9AE
Tel: 01283 567213
*Bottles, breweriana, pub
jugs, commemoratives.*

Peggy Davies Ceramics,
28 Liverpool Road,
Stoke-on-Trent,
ST4 1VJ
Tel: 01782 848002
*Ceramics, limited edition
Toby jugs and figures.*

Trevor Russell.
Tel: 01889 562009
*Fountain pens and
repairs.*

The Tackle Exchange,
95B Trentham Road,
Dresden,
Stoke-on-Trent,
ST3 4EG
Tel: 01782 599858
Old fishing tackle.

Suffolk

Jamie Cross,
PO Box 73,
Newmarket, CB8 8RY
Tel: 01638 750132
Mobile: 0802 366631
*We buy and sell
German, Italian and
British WWI & WWII
medals, badges and
decorations.*

W. L. Hoad,
9 St Peter's Road,
Kirkley,
Lowestoft,
NR33 0LH
Tel: 01502 587758
Cigarette cards.

Surrey

David Aldous-Cook,
PO Box 413,
Sutton,
SM3 8SZ
Tel: 0181 642 4842
*Reference books
on antiques and
collectables.*

Childhood Memories,
Farnham Antique
Centre, 27 South Street,
Farnham,
GU9 7QU
Tel: 01252 724475/793704
*Antique teddies, dolls
and miniatures.*

Church Street Antiques,
10 Church Street,
Godalming,
GU7 1EH
Tel: 01483 860894
*Art Deco ceramics,
traditional antique
silverware, glass and
ceramics.*

Gooday Gallery,
20 Richmond Hill,
Richmond,
TW10 6QX
Tel: 0181 940 8652
*Art Deco, Art Nouveau,
tribal art.*

Doug Poultney,
219 Lynmouth Ave,
Morden, SM4 4RX
Tel: 0181 330 3472
Comics.

**Richard Joseph
Publishers Ltd**,
Unit 2, Monk's Walk,
Farnham, GU9 8HT
Tel: 01252 734347
Publishers.

West Promotions,
PO Box 257, Sutton,
SM3 9WW
Tel: 0181 641 3224
Banking collectables.

Sussex

Art Deco Etc,
73 Upper Gloucester
Road,
Brighton, BN1 3LQ
Tel: 01273 329268
Poole Pottery.

**John & Mary
Bartholomew**,
Mint Arcade,
71 The Mint,
Rye, TN31 7EW
Tel: 01797 225952
*Postcards and cigarette
cards.*

Bears Galore,
27 High Street, Rye.
Tel: 01797 223676
*Rye's specialist teddy
shop. Open 7 days
a week.*

Tony Horsley.
Tel: 01273 550770
*Candle extinguishers,
Royal Worcester and
other porcelain.*

Libra Antiques,
81 London Road,
Hurst Green,
Etchingham, TN19 7PN
Tel: 01580 860569
Lighting.

Limited Editions,
10 Old Printing House,
Tarrant Street, Arundel,
BN18 9DG
Tel: 01903 883950
*Ceramics – Kevin Francis,
David Winter, Lilliput Lane,
J. P. Editions, Moorcroft,
Royal Doulton, Pendelfin,
Belleek, Lladro, etc.*

Sue Pearson,
13½ Prince Albert Street,
Brighton, BN1 1HE
Tel: 01273 329247
Dolls and teddy bears.

Wallis & Wallis,
West Street Auction
Galleries, Lewes, BN7 2NJ
Tel: 01273 480208
*Specialist auctioneers of
militaria, arms, armour,
coins and medals, die-cast
and tinplate toys, teddy
bears, dolls, model railways,
toy soldiers and models.*

Witney and Airault,
The Lanes Gallery,
32 Meeting House Lane,
Brighton, BN1 1HB
Tel: 01273 735479
20thC decorative arts.

Tyne & Wear

Antiques at H & S
Collectables,
No1 Ashburton Road,
Corner Salters Road,
Gosforth, NE3 4XN
Tel: 0191 284 6626
Curios, Victoriana.

Wales

The Emporium,
112 St Teilo Street,
Pontarddulais,
Nr Swansea, SA4 1QH
Tel: 01792 885185
Brass and cast iron.

Paul Gibbs Antiques,
25 Castle Street, Conway,
Gwynedd, LL32 8AY
Tel: 01492 593429
Art Deco pottery.

Islwyn Watkins,
1 High Street, Knighton,
Powys, LD7 1AT
Tel: 01547 520145
*18th and 19thC pottery,
20thC country and studio
pottery, small country
furniture, treen and
bygones.*

Warwickshire

Antique Militaria &
Sporting Exhibitions
(Organisers), PO Box
104, Warwick, CV34 5ZG
Tel: 0115 947 4137 or
01926 497340
*'The International',
Birmingham. The UK's
largest one day fair for
antique arms, medals
and militaria.*

The Antique Shop,
30 Henley Street,
Stratford-upon-Avon,
CV37 6QW
Tel: 01789 292485
*Dolls, teddy bears, fishing
tackle, glass, porcelain,
jewellery, Oriental, silver
and collectables.*

Chris James Medals
& Militaria,
Warwick Antiques Centre,
22–24 High Street,
Warwick, CV34 4AP
Tel: 01926 495704
*Antique guns, edged
weapons, helmets, badges,
medals, war souvenirs,
aviation collectables,
historical documents and
militaria bought, sold and
exchanged. Commission
sales service available.*

Midlands Goss &
Commemoratives,
The Old Cornmarket
Antiques Centre,
70 Market Place,
Warwick, CV34 4SO
Tel: 01926 419119
*Goss and commemorative
china.*

Malcolm Russ-Welch,
PO Box 1122, Rugby,
CV23 9YD
Tel: 01788 810 616
*Buttons and buckles,
advertising items, paper
items including postcards.*

West Midlands

Birmingham Railway
Auctions & Publications,
7 Ascot Road, Moseley,
Birmingham, B13 9EN
Tel: 0121 449 9707
*Railway auctions and
publications.*

Mr P. Cane,
59 Vicarage Road,
Harborne,
Birmingham, B17 0SR
Tel: 0121 427 5991
*Toy cowboy cap guns, hats,
holsters, rifles and playsuits
from 1950s, 60s & early '70s.*

Tango Art Deco
22 Kenilworth Road,
Knowle, Solihull,
B93 0JA
*Tel: 01564 776679 /
0121 7044969
Open Friday and Saturday.
9am–6pm.*

Wiltshire

Bona Arts Decorative Ltd,
Bizarre House,
124 High Street,
Marlborough, SN8
Tel: 01252 514100
*Art Deco ceramics, glass,
furniture and lighting.*

Dominic Winter Book
Auctions,
The Old School, Maxwell
St, Swindon, SN1 5DR
Tel: 01793 611340
*Auctions of antiquarian and
general printed books &
maps, sports books and
memorabilia, art reference
and pictures, photography &
ephemera (including toys,
games and other collectables).*

Worcestershire

BBM Jewellery & Coins
(W. V. Crook),
8–9 Lion Street,
Kidderminster, DY10 1PT
Tel: 01562 744118
Inkwells, jewellery, coins.

Platform 6,
11A Davenport Drive,
The Willows,
Bromsgrove, B60 2DW
Tel: 01527 871000
*Vintage train and toy
auctions.*

Yorkshire

BBR,
Elsecar Heritage Centre,
Wath Road, Elsecar,
Barnsley, S74 8HJ
Tel: 01226 745156
*Advertising, breweriana,
pot lids, bottles, Doulton
and Beswick.*

The Camera House,
Oakworth Hall, Colne
Road (B6143), Oakworth,
Keighley, BD22 7HZ
Tel: /Fax01535 642333
*Cameras and photographic
equipment from 1850.
Purchases, sales, part ex-
changes, repairs, cine, slide
video transfers. Valuations
for probate and insurance.
Open Wednesday–Friday
10am–5pm, Saturday
10am–3pm, or by
appointment. Prop. C. Cox.*

Cottage Antiques,
5 Ropergate End,
Pontefract
Tel: 01977 611146
Pine, kitchenalia.

Country Collector,
11–12 Birdgate,
Pickering,
YO18 7AL
Tel: 01751 477481
*Art Deco ceramics,
pottery and porcelain.*

Crested China Co,
The Station House,
Driffield,
YO25 7PY
Tel: 01377 257042
Goss and crested china.

Echoes,
650a Halifax Road,
Eastwood,
Todmorden,
OL14 6DW
Tel: 01706 817505
*Antique costume, textiles
including linen & lace,
and jewellery.*

John & Simon Haley,
89 Northgate,
Halifax,
HX6 4NG
Tel: 01422 822148
*Old toys and money
boxes.*

Linen & Lace,
Shirley Tomlinson,
Halifax Antiques Centre,
Queens Road/Gibbet
Street, Halifax,
HX1 4LR
Tel: 01422 366657
*Antique linen, textiles,
period costume and
accessories.*

Marine Art Posters,
71 Harbour Way,
Merchants Landing,
Victoria Dock,
Port of Hull, HU9 1PL
Tel: 01482 321173
*Cunard memorabilia
including posters, postcards,
badges & first day covers.*

Old Copper Shop and
Posthouse Antiques,
69 & 75 Market Place,
South Cave,
HU15 2AS
Tel: 01430 423988
General stock.

Sheffield Railwayana
Auctions,
43 Little Norton Lane,
Sheffield, S8 8GA
Tel: 0114 274 5085
*Railwayana, posters and
models auctions.*

DIRECTORY OF MARKETS & CENTRES

Berkshire

Stables Antiques Centre,
1a Merchant Place,
(off Friar Street),
Reading, RG1 1DT
Tel: 0118 959 0290

Buckinghamshire

Antiques at Wendover,
The Old Post Office,
25 High Street,
Wendover, HP22 6DU
Tel: 01296 625335

Marlow Antique Centre,
35 Station Road, Marlow,
SL7 1NW
Tel: 01628 473223

*Wide range of antique and
collectable items from over
30 dealers. Georgian,
Victorian and Edwardian
furniture, country pine,
decorative furniture, silver
ware, glass, china, Art Deco,
bedsteads, cameras, old
tools, garden items, jewellery,
pens, cufflinks, vintage
toys. Also a secondhand
book section. Open 7 days,
Mon–Sat 10am–5.30pm,
Sun 11am–4.30pm.*

Cambridgeshire

Fitzwilliam Antiques Centre,
Fitzwilliam Street,
Peterborough, PE1 2RX
Tel: 01733 565415

Cheshire

Davenham Antique Centre,
461 London Road,
Davenham,
Northwick, CW9 8NA
Tel: 01606 44350

Alfreton Antique Centre,
11 King Street, Alfreton,
DE55 7AF
Tel: 01773 520781

*40 dealers on two floors.
Antiques, collectables,
furniture, books, postcards,
etc. Open 7 days Mon–Sat
10am–4.30pm, Sundays,
Bank Holidays 11am–3pm.*

Derbyshire

Bakewell Antiques &
Collectors' Centre, King
Street, Bakewell, DE45 1DZ
Tel: 01629 812496

*30 established dealers of
quality antiques and
collectables. Tea and coffee
house. Open Mon–Sat
10am–5pm. Sun 11am–5pm.
Closed Christmas, Boxing
Day and New Year's Day.*

Gloucestershire

Antiques Emporium,
The Old Chapel, Long
Street, Tetbury, GL8 8AA
Tel: 01666 505281

Cirencester Arcade & Ann's
Pantry, 25 Market Place,
Cirencester, GL7 2PY
Tel: 01285 644214

*Antiques, gifts, furnishings,
etc. Restaurant/tea rooms.
Private room for hire.*

Dale House Antiques,
High Street,
Moreton-in-Marsh,
GL56 0AD
Tel: 01608 650763

Durham House Antiques
Centre, Sheep Street,
Stow-on-the-Wold,
GL54 1AA
Tel: 01451 870404

*30+ dealers. An extensive
range of town and country
furniture, metalware, books,
pottery, porcelain, kitchenalia,
silver, jewellery and art.
Mon–Sat 10am–5pm,
Sunday 11am–5pm.*

Gloucester Antique Centre,
The Historic Docks,
1 Severn Road, Gloucester,
GL1 2LE
Tel: 01452 529716

Hampshire

Dolphin Quay Antique
Centre, Queen Street,
Emsworth, PO10 7BU
Tel: 01243 379994

*Open 7 days (and Bank
Holidays). Mon–Sat
10am–5pm, Sun 10am–4pm.
Marine, naval antiques,
paintings, watercolours,
prints, antique clocks,
decorative arts, furniture,
sporting apparel, luggage,
specialist period lighting,
conservatory, garden
antiques, antique pine
furniture.*

Lymington Antiques Centre,
76 High Street, Lymington,
SO41 9AL
Tel: 01590 670934

Squirrel Collectors' Centre,
9 New Street, Basingstoke,
RG21 1DE
Tel: 01256 464885

Herefordshire

Antique Market,
6 Market Street,
Hay-on-Wye, HR3 5AF
Tel: 01497 820175

Mulberry's Antiques
& Collectables,
30/32 St Owen St,
Hereford, HR1 2PR
Tel: 01432 269925

*Furniture, fine china,
porcelain, silver, jewellery,
textiles, pre-1930s clothing
and accessories, objets
d'art, prints, oils and
watercolours.
Trade welcome.*

Hertfordshire

Herts & Essex Antiques
Centre, The Maltings,
Station Road,
Sawbridgeworth,
CM21 9JX
Tel: 01279 722044

*Open every day (except
Mon). Tues–Fri 10am–5pm.
Sat–Sun 10.30am–6pm.
(Including most Bank
Holidays). Over 10,000
items of antiques, furniture,
jewellery, porcelain,
collectables, stamps, coins,
postcards, costume,
paintings, glass, ceramics
and ephemera.
All in pleasant, well-lit
showrooms serviced by
friendly staff.*

Humberside

Mall Antique Centre,
400 Wincolmlee,
Hull, HU2 0QL
Tel: 01482 327858

*60 local antique dealers.
12,500 sq ft of Georgian,
Victorian, Edwardian,
reproduction and 1930s
furniture, silver, china,
clocks, hardware, etc.
Open Mon–Fri 9am–5pm,
10am–4pm Sat/Sun.*

Kent

Copperfields Antique
& Craft Centre,
3c/4 Copperfields,
Spital Street,
Dartford, DA9 2DE
Tel: 01322 281445

*Open 10am–5pm Mon–Sat.
Antiques, bygones,
collectables, stamps,
Wade, SylvaC, Beswick,
Royal Doulton, clocks,
Victoriana, 1930s–60s,
Art Deco, craft, handmade
toys, dolls' houses &
miniatures, jewellery,
glass, china, furniture,
Kevin Francis character
jugs, silk and lace and
lots more.*

Malthouse Arcade,
Malthouse Hill,
Hythe,
CT21 5BW
Tel: 01303 260103

Noah's Ark Antiques Centre,
5 King Street,
Sandwich, CT13 9BT
Tel: 01304 611144

Sidcup Antique & Craft
Centre, Elm Parade,
Main Road, Sidcup,
DA4 9DR
Tel: 0181 300 7387

*Over 100 dealers and crafts
people in one unique
setting. Coffee shop.
Open 7 days 10am–5pm.
Easy parking nearby.*

Lancashire

GB Antiques Centre,
Lancaster Leisure Park,
(the former Hornsea
Pottery), Wyresdale Road,
Lancaster LA1 3LA
Tel: 01524 844734

*Over 140 dealers in 40,000
sq ft of space. Showing
porcelain, pottery, Art Deco,
glass, books and linen.
Also a large selection of
mahogany, oak and pine
furniture. Open 7 days
10am–5pm.*

Kingsmill Antique Centre,
Queen Street,
Harle Syke,
Burnley
Tel: 01282 431953

Pendle Antique Centre,
Union Mill, Watt Street,
Sabden, BB7 9ED
Tel: 01282 776311

Leicestershire

Oxford Street Antiques
Centre Ltd,
16-26 Oxford Street,
Leicester, LE1 5XU
Tel: 0116 255 3006

Lincolnshire

Sue's Collectables,
61 Victoria Road,
Mabelthorpe, LN12 2AF
Tel: 01507 472406

*Open daily 10am–5pm.
20,000 collectable items
including old glass
lampshades, gas &
electrical fittings.
Breweriana, kitchenalia,
Bakelite, chalk figures,
Xmas lights & decorations.
Pendelfins bought and sold.*

Enjoy a little piece of Heaven in Piccadilly

St. James's ANTIQUES MARKET

OPEN

TUESDAYS 8 a.m.~6 p.m.

Tube: Piccadilly Circus or Green Park
Omnibus: 3, 6, 9, 12, 14, 15, 19, 22, 38
Rail: Victoria/Charing Cross
197 PICCADILLY LONDON W1V OLL
Tel: 0171 ~ 734 4511
Fax: 0171 ~ 734 7449

SJAMES'S PICCADILLY

London

Alfies Antique Market,
13–25 Church Street,
NW8 8DT
Tel: 0171 723 6066

Antiquarius Antique Market,
131/141 King's Road, Chelsea,
SW3 5ST
Tel: 0171 351 5353

Bond Street Antiques Centre,
124 New Bond Street,
W1Y 9AE
Tel: 0171 351 5353

Bourbon-Hanby Antique Centre,
151 Sydney Street,
Chelsea, SW3 6NT
Tel: 0171 352 2106

Gray's Antique Market,
South Molton Lane,
W1Y 2LP
Tel: 0171 629 7034

Mall Antiques Arcade,
Camden Passage, N1
Tel: 0171 351 5353

Northcote Road Antique
Market, 155a Northcote Road,
Battersea, SW11 6QB
Tel: 0171 228 6850

St James's Antiques Market,
197 Piccadilly, W1V 0LL
Tel: 0171 734 4511
Open Tuesdays 8am–6pm.

Middlesex

Jay's Antique Centre,
25/29 High Street,
Harefield, UB9 6BX
Tel: 01895 824738

Nottinghamshire

Newark Antiques Centre,
Regent House,
Lombard Street,
Newark, NG24 1XP
Tel: 01636 605504

Top Hat Antiques Centre,
66-72 Derby Road,
Nottingham, NG1 5FD
Tel: 0115 941 9143

Oxfordshire

Lamb Arcade,
83 High Street, Wallingford,
OX10 0BS
Tel: 01491 835166
*Open 10am–5pm daily, Sat until
5.30pm. Bank Hols 11am–5pm.
Furniture, silver, porcelain,
glass, books, boxes, crafts, rugs,
jewellery, brass bedsteads and
linens, pictures, antique stringed
instruments, sports and fishing
items, decorative and
ornamental items.
Coffee shop and wine bar.*

Shropshire

Princess Antique Centre,
14a The Square,
Shrewsbury
Tel: 01743 343701

Shrewsbury Antique
Centre,
15 Princess House,
The Square,
Shrewsbury, SY1 1JZ
Tel: 01743 247704

Shrewsbury Antique
Market,
Frankwell Quay Warehouse,
Shrewsbury, SY3 8LG
Tel: 01743 350916

Stretton Antiques Market,
Sandford Avenue,
Church Stretton, SY6 6BH
Tel: 01694 723718

Somerset

Assembly Antique Centre,
5-8 Saville Row,
Bath, BA1 2QP
Tel: 01225 333294

Open Mon–Sat
10am–5pm

Bath Antiques Market,
Guinea Lane,
(off Landsdown Rd),
Bath, BA1 5NB
Tel: 01225 337638

County Antiques Centre,
17 Court Barton,
Ilminster, TA19 0DU
Tel: 01460 54151

Fountain Antiques Centre,
3 Fountain Buildings
Lansdown Road,
Bath, BA1 5DU
Tel: 01225 428731/471133

Staffordshire

Tudor of Lichfield Antique
Centre,
Lichfield House,
Bore Street,
Lichfield, WS13 6LL
Tel: 01543 263951

Tutbury Mill Antiques
Centre,
Tutbury Mill Mews,
Tutbury, DE13 9LU
Tel: 01283 520074

Mon–Sat 10.30am–5.30pm
Sun 12 noon–5.00pm.

Surrey

Antiques Arcade,
77 Bridge Road,
East Molesey, KT8 9HH
Tel: 0181 979 7954

Antiques Centre,
22 Haydon Place,
Corner of Martyr Road,
Guildford, GU1 4LL
Tel: 01483 567817

Fern Cottage Antique
Centre,
28/30 High Street,
Thames Ditton,
KT7 0RY
Tel: 0181 398 2281

Maltings Monthly Market,
Bridge Square,
Farnham, Surrey,
GU9 7QR
Tel: 01252 726234

Serendipity Antique
Centre,
7 Petworth Road,
Haslemere, GU27 2JB
Tel: 01428 642682

Sussex

Antiques & Collectors
Market,
Old Orchard Building,
Old House,
Adversane,
Nr Billingshurst,
RH14 9JJ
Tel: 01403 783594

Churchill Antiques Centre,
6 Station Street,
Lewes, BN7 2DA
Tel: 01273 474842

Horsebridge Antiques
Centre,
1 North Street,
Lower Horsebridge,
Nr Hailsham, BN27 1DQ
Tel: 01323 844414

Email: leung@enterprise.net

Seaford's Barn Collectors
Market & Studio
Book Shop,
The Barn,
Church Lane,
Seaford, BN25 1HJ
Tel: 01323 890010

Tyne & Wear

The Antique Centre,
2nd floor,
142 Northumberland St,
Newcastle-upon-Tyne,
NE1 7DQ
Tel: 0191 232 9832

Open Mon–Sat 10am–5pm

Wales

Offa's Dyke Antique
Centre,
4 High Street,
Knighton,
Powys, LD7 1AT
Tel: 01547 528635

Second Chance Antiques
& Collectables Centre,
Ala Road,
Pwllheli, Gwynedd,
LL53 5BL
Tel: 01758 612210

Warwickshire

Barn Antiques Centre,
Station Road,
Long Marston,
Nr Stratford-upon-Avon,
CV37 8RB
Tel: 01789 721399

Open 7 days 10am–5pm.
Large selection of antique
furniture, antique pine,
linen and lace, old fireplaces
and surrounds, collectables,
pictures and prints, silver,
china, ceramics, objets
d'art, antique style
reproduction furniture,
clocks including longcase
clocks, country kitchens.

Malthouse Antiques Centre,
4 Market Place,
Alcester, B49 5AE
Tel: 01789 764032

Stratford Antiques Centre,
59–60 Ely Street, Stratford-
upon-Avon, CV37 6LN
Tel: 01789 204180

West Midlands

Birmingham Antique Centre,
1407 Pershore Road,
Stirchley, Birmingham,
B30 2JR
Tel: 0121 459 4587

Worcestershire

Worcester Antiques Centre,
Reindeer Court,
Mealcheapen Street,
Worcester, WR1 4DF
Tel: 01905 610680

Yorkshire

Halifax Antiques Centre,
Queens Road/Gibbet Street,
Halifax, HX1 4LR
Tel: 01422 366657

Sheffield Antiques
Emporium & The Chapel,
15–19 Clyde Road,
off Broadfield Road,
Sheffield, S8 0YD
Tel: 0114 258 4863

Over 70 dealers displaying
a wide range of antiques
and collectables, including
specialists in clocks,
Art Deco, French furniture,
books, pine, fabrics,
porcelain and much more.
Services include upholstery,
furniture restoration, re-
caning, pottery restoration,
French polishing, delivery,
refreshments.
Suitable for trade and retail.
Open 7 days.

DIRECTORY OF COLLECTORS' CLUBS

This directory is in no way complete. If you wish to be included in next year's directory or if you have a change of address or telephone number, please inform us by November 1st 1998. Entries will be repeated in subsequent editions unless we are requested otherwise.

Antiquarian Horological Society
New House, High Street, Ticehurst, E. Sussex
TN5 7AL Tel: 01580 200155
Antique Collectors' Club
5 Church Street, Woodbridge, Suffolk IP12 1DS
Arms and Armour Society
Hon Sec Anthony Dove, PO Box 10232,
London SW19 9ZD
Association of Bottled Beer Collectors
Thurwood, 5 Springfield Close, Woodsetts,
Worksop, Nottinghamshire S81 8QD
Tel: 01909 562603
Association of Comic Enthusiasts: ACE!
8 Silverdale, Sydenham, London SE26 4SJJ
Avon Magpies Club
36 Castle View Road, Portchester, Fareham,
Hampshire PO16 9LA Tel: 01705 642393
Badge Collectors' Circle
3 Ellis Close, Quorn, Nr Loughborough,
Leicestershire LE12 8SH Tel: 01509 412094
BBR Bottle Collectors
Elsecar Heritage Centre, Wath Road, Elsecar,
Barnsley, Yorkshire S74 8HJ Tel: 01226 745156
British Art Medal Society c/o Dept of Coins
and Medals, The British Museum, London
WC1B 3DG Tel: 0171 323 8170 Extn 8227
British Association of Sound Collections
National Sound Archive, 29 Exhibition Road,
London SW7 2AS Tel: 0171 589 6603
British Beermat Collectors' Society
30 Carters Orchard, Quedgeley,
Gloucestershire GL2 6WB Tel: 01452 721643
British Button Society
The Old Dairy, Newton Kettering,
Northamptonshire NN14 1BW
British Compact Collectors' Society
PO Box 131, Woking, Surrey GU24 9YR
British Iron Collectors
87 Wellsway, Bath, Avon BA2 4RU
Tel: 01225 428068
British Matchbox Label and Booklet Soc
Arthur Alderton (Hon Sec) 122 High Street,
Melbourn, Cambridgeshire SG8 6AL
British Model Soldier Society
22 Lynwood Road, Ealing, London W5 1JJ
British Numismatic Society
Hunterian Museum, Glasgow University,
University Avenue, Glasgow G12 8QQ
British Stickmakers' Guild
44a Eccles Road, Chapel-en-le-Frith,
Derbyshire SK12 6RG Tel: 01298 815291
British Teddy Bear Association
PO Box 290, Brighton, Sussex BN2 1DR

British Telecom Heritage Group
Tamarisk, 2 Gig lane, Heathand Reach,
Leighton Buzzard, Bedfordshire LU7 0BQ
Tel: 01525 237676
British Telecom Phonecard Collectors' Club
Camelford House, 87 Albert Embankment,
London SE1 7TS
British Watch & Clock Collectors' Assoc
5 Cathedral Lane, Truro, Cornwall TR1 2QS
Tel: 01872 241953
Buttonhook Society
2 Romney Place, Maidstone, Kent ME15 6LE
Byngo Collectors' Club
23 Longhedge, Caldecotte, Bucks MK7 8LA
Calculator Collectors' Club
77 Welland Road, Tonbridge, Kent TN10 3TA
Cambridge Paperweight Circle,
34 Huxley Road, Welling, Kent DA16 2EW
Tel: 0181 303 4663
Carlton Ware Collectors' International
PO Box 161, Sevenoaks, Kent TN15 6GA
Tel: 01474 853630
Carnival Glass Society (UK) Ltd
PO Box 14, Hayes, Middlesex UBC 5NU
Cartophilic Society of Great Britain
116 Hillview Road, Ensbury Park,
Bournemouth, Dorset BH10 5BJ
Charlotte Rhead (Newsletter)
c/o 49 Honeybourne Road, Halesowen,
West Midlands B63 3ET
Chintz Club of America The Chintz
Collector, PO Box 6126, Folsom, CA 95763,
USA Tel: 001 (916) 985 6762 (& fax)
**Cigarette Packet Collectors' Club of
Great Britain** Nathan's Pipe Shop,
60 Hill Rise, Richmond, Surrey TW10 6UA
Tel: 0181 940 2404
**City of London Photograph
& Gramophone Society** 63 Vicarage Way,
Colnbrook, Buckinghamshire S13 0JY
Clarice Cliff Collectors' Club
Fantasque House, Tennis Drive, The Park,
Nottingham, Nottinghamshire NG7 1AE
Comic Enthusiasts' Society
80 Silverdale, Sydenham, London SE26 4SJ
Comics Journal 17 Hill Street, Colne,
Lancashire BB8 0DH Tel: 01282 865468
Commemorative Collectors' Society
Lumless House, Gainsborough Road,
Winthorpe, Nr Newark, Nottinghamshire
NG24 2NR Tel: 01636 71377
Corgi Collector Club PO Box 323, Swansea,
Wales SA1 1BJ Tel: 01792 476902

Costume Society
c/o The State Apartments, Kensington Palace, London W8 4PX Tel: 0171 937 9561
Crested Circle 42 Douglas Road, Tolworth, Surbiton, Surrey KT6 7SA
Cricket Memorabilia Society
29 Highclere Road, Higher Crumpsall, Greater Manchester M8 4WH Tel: 0161 740 3714
Crunch Club (Breakfast Cereal Collectables)
15 Hermitage Road, Parkstone, Poole, Dorset BH14 0QG Tel: 01202 715854
Disney Enthusiasts Club, Magical Moments & Memories
31 Rowan Way, Exwick, Exeter, Devon EX4 2DT Tel & Fax: 01392 431653
Doll Club of Great Britain
16E Chalwyn Industrial Estate, St Clements Road, Parkstone, Poole, Dorset BH15 3PE
Embroiderers' Guild
Apartment 41, Hampton Court Palace, East Molesey, Surrey KT8 9AU Tel: 0181 943 1229
English Playing Card Society
11 Pierrepont Street, Bath, Avon BA1 1LA Tel: 01225 465218
Fan Circle International
Sec: Mrs Joan Milligan, Cronk-y-Voddy, Rectory Road, Coltishall, Norwich, Norfolk NR12 7HF
Festival of Britain Society
c/o 124 Havant Road, North End, Portsmouth, Hampshire PO2 0BP
Tel: 01705 665630/0181 471 2165
Flag Institute 10 Vicarage Road, Chester, Cheshire CH2 3HZ Tel: 01244 351335
Friends of Blue 10 Sea View Road, Herne Bay, Kent CT6 6JQ
Friends of Broadfield House Glass Museum Compton Drive, Kingswinford, West Midlands DY6 9NS Tel: 01384 273011
Furniture History Society
c/o Dr. Brian Austen, 1 Mercedes Cottages, St John's Road, Haywards Heath, Sussex RH16 4EH Tel: 01444 413845
Goss Collectors' Club
31a The Crescent, Stanley Common, Derbyshire DE7 6GL Tel: 0115 930 0441
Goss & Crested China Club
62 Murray Road, Horndean, Hampshire PO8 9JL Tel: 01705 597440
Hat Pin Society of Great Britain
PO Box No 74, Bozeat, Northamptonshire NN29 7JH
Historical Model Railway Society
59 Woodberry Way, London E4 7DY
Honiton Pottery Collectors' Society (Honiton & Crown Dorset Pottery)
c/o Robin Tinkler, 12 Beehive Lane, Great Baddow, Chelmsford, Essex CM2 9SX Tel: 01245 353477

Hornby Railway Collectors' Association
2 Ravensmore Road, Sherwood, Nottingham, Nottinghamshire NG5 2AH
Hurdy-Gurdy Society The Old Mill, Duntish, Dorchester, Dorset DT2 7DR
International Bank Note Society
36B Dartmouth Park Hill, London NW5 1HN
International Bond and Share Society
Hobsley House, Frodesley, Shrewsbury, Shropshire SY5 7HD
International Collectors' of Time Association 173 Coleherne Court, Redcliffe Gardens, London SW5 0DX
International Correspondence of Corkscrew Addicts
4201 Sunflower Drive, Mississauga, Ontario L5L 2L4, Canada
King George VI Collectors' Society (Affiliated to the Association of British Philatelic Societies)
98 Albany, Manor Road, Bournemouth, Dorset BH1 3EW Tel: 01202 551515
Knife Rest Collectors' Club Braughingbury, Braughing, Hertfordshire SG11 2RD Tel: 01920 822654
Eric Knowles Collectors' Club PO Box 14388, London NW11 7ZE Tel: 0181 458 4500
Lace Guild The Hollies, 53 Audnam, Stourbridge, West Midlands DY8 4AE
Legend Lane Collectors' Club
Albion Mill, London Road, Macclesfield, Cheshire SK11 7SQ Tel: 01625 665010
Matchbox International Collectors' Assoc The Toy Museum, 13a Lower Bridge Street, Chester, Cheshire CH1 1RS Tel: 01244 345297
Mauchline Ware Collectors' Club
Unit 37 Romsey Industrial Estate, Greatbridge Road, Romsey, Hampshire SO51 0HR
Memories UK, Mabel Lucie Attwell Collectors' Club
63 Great Whyte, Ramsey, Nr Huntingdon, Cambridgeshire PE17 1HL Tel: 01487 814753
Merrythought International Collectors' Club Ironbridge, Telford, Salop TF8 7NJ Tel: 01952 433116
Model Railway Club Keen House, 4 Calshot Street, London N1 9DA
Musical Box Society of Great Britain PO Box 299, Waterbeach, Cambs CB4 4PJ
National Horse Brass Society
12 Severndale, Droitwich Spa, Worcester WR9 8PD
New Baxter Society c/o Museum of Reading, Blagrave Street, Reading, Berkshire RG1 1QH
Ophthalmic Antiques International Collectors' Club 3 Moor Park Road, Northwood, Middlesex HA6 2DL

Orders and Medals Research Society
123 Turnpike Link, Croydon, Surrey CR0 5NU
Oriental Ceramic Society
30b Torrington Square, London WC1E 7JL
Tel: 0171 636 7985
Pen Delfin Family Circle
Cameron Mill, Howsin Street, Burnley,
Lancashire BB10 1PP Tel: 01282 32301
Pen Delfin Family Circle
Shop 28, Grove Plaza, Stirling Highway,
Peppermint Grove, 6011, Australia
Tel: 09 384 9999
Pen Delfin Family Circle Fazantenlaan 29,
2610 Antwerp, Belgium Tel: 03 440 5668
Pen Delfin Family Circle 1250 Terwillegar
Avenue, Oshawa, Ontario, L1J 7A5, Canada
Tel: 0101 416 723 9940
Pen Delfin Family Circle Svebi AB, Box
143, S-562 02 Taberg, Sweden Tel: 036 656 90
Pen Delfin, Family Circle 230 Spring Street
N.W., Suite 1238, Atlanta, Georgia, 30303, USA
Tel: Freephone US only 1-800 872 4876
Pewter Society Hunters Lodge, Paddock
Close, St Mary's Platt, Sevenoaks, Kent
TN15 8NN Tel: 01732 883314
**Photographic Collectors' Club of Great
Britain** 5 Station Industrial Estate, Prudhoe,
Northumberland NE42 6NP
Poole Pottery Collectors' Club
Poole Pottery Ltd, The Quay, Poole, Dorset
BH15 1RF Tel: 01202 666200
Postcard Club of Great Britain
34 Harper House, St James's Crescent,
London SW9 7LW Tel: 0171 771 9404
Pot Lid Circle
Buckinghamshire Tel: 01753 886751
Quimper Association Odin, Benbow Way,
Cowley, Uxbridge, Middlesex UB8 2HD
Railwayana Collectors' Journal
7 Ascot Road, Moseley, Birmingham,
West Midlands B13 9EN
Robert Harrop Designs Collectors' Club
Coalport House, Lamledge Lane, Shifnal,
Shropshire TF11 8SD Tel: 01952 462721
Royal Doulton International Collectors' Club
Minton House, London Road, Stoke-on-Trent,
Staffordshire ST4 7QD
Royal Numismatic Society
c/o Department of Coins and Medals,
The British Museum, London WC1B 3DG
Tel: 0171 636 1555 extn 404
Royal Winton International Collectors' Club
Dancers End, Northall, Bedfordshire
LU6 2EU Tel: 01525 220272
Scientific Instrument Society
31 High St, Stanford in the Vale, Faringdon,
Oxfordshire, SN7 8LH Tel: 01367 710223
Shelley Group 4 Fawley Road, Regents
Park, Southampton, Hampshire SO2 1LL

Silhouette Collectors' Club
Flat 5, 13 Brunswick Square, Hove, Sussex
BN3 1EH Tel: 01273 735760
Silver Spoon Club Glenleigh Park, Sticker,
St Austell, Cornwall PL26 7JD
Tel/Fax 01726 65269
Silver Study Group The Secretary,
London Tel: 0181 202 0269
Studio Szeiler Collectors' Circle
Gwent, Wales Tel: 01291 620715
Susie Cooper Collectors' Group
PO Box 7436, London N12 7QF
Sylvac Collectors' Circle
174 Portsmouth Road, Horndean,
Hampshire PO8 9HP Tel: 01705 591725
Thimble Society of London
Shop 134, Grays Antique Market, 58 Davies
Street, London W1Y 2LP Tel: 0171 493 0560
Tool and Trades History Society
60 Swanley Lane, Swanley, Kent BR8 7JG
Tel: 01322 662271
Torquay Pottery Collectors' Society
Torre Abbey, Avenue Road, Torquay,
Devon TQ2 5JX
Train Collectors' Society
Lock Cottage, Station Foot Path,
Kings Langley, Hertfordshire WD4 8DZ
Transport Ticket Society
4 Gladridge Close, Earley, Reading,
Berkshire RG6 7DL Tel: 01734 579373
Trix Twin Railway Collectors' Association
6 Ribble Avenue, Oadby, Leicester LE2 4NZ
UK Perfume Bottles Collectors' Club
Assembly Antique Centre, 5-8 Saville Row,
Bath, Avon BA1 2QP Tel: 01225 448488
Unofficial McDonalds Collectors' Newsletter
c/o Ian Smith, 14 Elkstone Road, Chesterfield,
Derbyshire S40 4UT
USSR Collectors Club
Bob & June Moore, PO Box 6, Virginia Water,
Surrey GU25 4YU Tel: 01344 843091
Victorian Military Society
Moore-Morris, 3 Franks Road, Guildford,
Surrey GU2 6NT Tel: 01483 60931
Vintage Model Yacht Group 8 Sherard Rd,
London SE9 6EP Tel: 0181 850 6805
Wade Collectors' Club 14 Windsor Road,
Selston, Nottinghamshire NG16 6JJ
Tel: 01773 860933/0374 209963
Wedgwood Society of Great Britain
89 Andrewes House, The Barbican,
London EC2Y 8AY
**Wireless Preservation Society & CEM
National Wireless Museum**
52 West Hill Road, Ryde, Isle of Wight
PO33 1LN Tel: 01983 567665
Writing Equipment Society
Cartledge Cottage, Cartledge Lane,
Holmesfield, Derbyshire S18 5SB

INDEX TO ADVERTISERS

INDEX

Italic page numbers denote colour pages; **bold** numbers refer to information and pointer boxes.

MYSTERY OBJECTS

A boxwood clacker, 19thC, 8in (20.5cm) long.
£16–20 *MRT*

A clacker was used by a school mistress to keep order or to beat time.

A car radio, 1920s, 5in (12.5cm) wide.
£45–55 *GIN*

A blue and white transfer printed pipe rack, 1830, 5in (12.5cm) wide.
£65–85 *CaC*

A Wm Penn 'Eezit' shoe stretcher, 1920–30s, 4in (10cm) long.
£2–3 *TRE*

A mahogany folding gout stool, early 19thC, 18in (45.5cm) wide.
£80–100 *AAN*

Key to Front Cover Illustrations

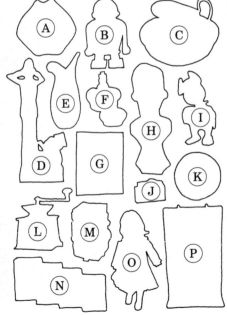

A. A Poole Pottery vase, 1960s. **£80–120** *Har*
B. A Steepletone radio, 1970s. **£20–25** *GIN*
C. A Wedgwood blue and white transfer printed jug and bowl, 19thC. **£230–280** *MEG*
D. A ceramic suffragette 'Votes For Women' model, c1910, 6½in (16.5cm) high. **£800–900** *TVM*
E. A Murano glass vase, c1950, 9½in (24.5cm) high. **£120–150** *Bon*
F. Two Princess Matchabelli glass perfume bottles, 1940s. Large **£100–125**, small **£85–95** *LBe*
H. A plaster model head, 1920s, 22½in (57cm) high. **£130–150** *SUS*
I. A Gund Lulu-Belle felt toy, American, c1960, 14¼in (36cm) high. **£60–80** *TED*
G. *Picture Post* magazine, 4 June 1949. **£3–5** *RAD*
J. A Matchbox 75 Ferrari Berlinetta, c1965. **£100–125** *AAC*
K. A Clichy glass paperweight, 19thC. **£2,800–3,200** *SWB*
L. A Kenrick coffee grinder, c1860. **£90–120** *CPA*
M. A Rolleiflex camera. **£450–600** *ARP*
N. A set of French storage jars, c1930. **£75–85** *CPA*
O. A French SFBJ bisque-headed doll, c1914. **£350–400** *YC*
P. A wall-mounted 'penny-in-the-slot' amusement machine, by Oliver Whales, 1950s. **£400–450** *JUN*

GRAYS
ANTIQVE   MARKET

With the fast moving stock of more than 200 professional dealers Grays
has been described as *"the best antique market in the world"*. Grays occupies
two air conditioned and splendid Edwardian buildings sitting
back to back BY BOND STREET TUBE

SOUTH MOLTON LANE LONDON W1Y 2LP

Tel 0171 629 7034   Fax 0171 493 9344   Mon-Fri 10-6